W9-BZV-169

MCSE Guide to

Microsoft® Windows® XP Professional

Ed Tittel
James Michael Stewart

COURSE
TECHNOLOGY
™
THOMSON LEARNING

Australia • Canada • Mexico • Singapore • Spain • United Kingdom • United States

**COURSE
TECHNOLOGY**
™
THOMSON LEARNING

MCSE Guide to Windows XP Professional

by Ed Tittel and James Michael Stewart

Managing Editor:
Stephen Solomon

Product Manager:
Charles Blum

Technical Editors:
Tom Lancaster
Warren Wyrostek

Quality Assurance Manager:
John Bosco

Associate Product Manager:
Tim Gleeson

Editorial Assistant:
Nick Lombardi

Marketing Manager:
Toby Shelton

Text Designer:
GEX Publishing Services

Compositor:
GEX Publishing Services

Cover Design:
Efrat Reis

COPYRIGHT © 2001 Course Technology, a division of Thomson Learning, Inc. Thomson Learning™ is a trademark used herein under license.

Printed in Canada

1 2 3 4 5 6 7 8 9 WC 04 03 02 01

For more information, contact Course Technology, 25 Thomson Place, Boston, Massachusetts, 02210.

Or find us on the World Wide Web at: www.course.com

ALL RIGHTS RESERVED. No part of this work covered by the copyright hereon may be reproduced or used in any form or by any means—graphic, electronic, or mechanical, including photocopying, recording, taping, Web distribution, or information storage and retrieval systems—without the written permission of the publisher.

For permission to use material from this text or product, contact us by
Tel (800) 730-2214
Fax (800) 730-2215
www.thomsonrights.com

Disclaimer
Course Technology reserves the right to revise this publication and make changes from time to time in its content without notice.

ISBN 0-619-12031-2

BRIEF
Contents

PREFACE   xv

CHAPTER ONE
Introduction to Windows XP Professional   1

CHAPTER TWO
Installing Windows XP Professional   33

CHAPTER THREE
Using the System Utilities   73

CHAPTER FOUR
Managing Windows XP File Systems and Storage   113

CHAPTER FIVE
Users, Groups, Profiles, and Policies   175

CHAPTER SIX
Windows XP Security and Access Controls   215

CHAPTER SEVEN
Network Protocols   251

CHAPTER EIGHT
Internetworking with Remote Access   313

CHAPTER NINE
Printing and Faxing   361

CHAPTER TEN
Performance Tuning   401

CHAPTER ELEVEN
Windows XP Professional Application Support   447

CHAPTER TWELVE
Working with the Windows XP Registry   487

CHAPTER THIRTEEN
Booting Windows XP   515

CHAPTER FOURTEEN
Windows XP Professional Fault Tolerance   543

CHAPTER FIFTEEN
Troubleshooting Windows XP   567

APPENDIX A
Exam Objectives Tracking for MCSE Certification
Exam # 70-270: Installing, Configuring, and Administering
Microsoft Windows XP Professional   603

GLOSSARY   615

TABLE OF
Contents

PREFACE   XV

CHAPTER ONE
Introduction to Windows XP Professional   1
    The Microsoft Networking Family   2
        Windows XP Family   2
        Other Client Operating Systems 3
    The Windows XP Environment   3
        Multiple Processors   3
        Multitasking   4
        Multithreading   4
        File Systems   5
        Active Directory   6
        Security   6
        Compatibility   6
        Storage   7
        Connectivity   7
        System Recovery   7
        Remote Capabilities   8
        Help and Support Services   8
    Intelligent User Interface   8
    Windows XP Professional Hardware Requirements   10
        Hardware Compatibility List   11
        Finding the HCL   11
        Why the HCL Is So Important   11
        Preparing a Computer to Meet Upgrade Requirements   12
    Networking Models   13
        Workgroup Model   13
        Domain Model   13
    Windows XP Architecture   14
        User Mode   15
        Kernel Mode   16
        Memory Architecture   17
    Overview of New Features   20
    Chapter Summary   20
    Key Terms   21
    Review Questions   23
    Hands-on Projects   27
    Case Projects   30

CHAPTER TWO
Installing Windows XP Professional   33
    Upgrading versus Installing   34
    Booting Multiple Operating Systems   35

Planning the Installation   36
    Types of Installations   37
Important Setup Option Differences   39
Advanced Installation Options   40
    Automated Installations   41
    Remote Installation Service   44
    Using the SYSDIFF Utility   4
    Using SYSPREP   45
WINNT and WINNT32   47
    Partitioning the Hard Disk   51
Activating Windows XP   52
Windows XP Profesional Setup: Step-by-Step from Floppies   53
    Text-Only Portion of Setup   54
GUI Portion of Setup   56
Troubleshooting An Installation   59
Removing Windows XP Professional   59
    Destroying Partitions   60
    Removing Windows XP from FAT   6
Chapter Summary   60
Key Terms   61
Review Questions   62
Hands-on Projects   66
Case Projects   71

CHAPTER THREE
Using the System Utilities

                                                                              73
Control Panel Overview   74
    Accessibility Options   76
    Add Hardware   77
    Add or Remove Programs   78
    Administrative Tools   80
    Date and Time   80
    Display   8
    Folder Options   81
    Fonts   82
    Game Controllers   82
    Internet Options   82
    Keyboard and Mouse   82
    Network Connections   83
    Phone and Modem Options   83
    Power Options   83
    Printers and Faxes   84
    Regional and Language Options   84
    Scanners and Cameras   85
    Scheduled Tasks   85
    Sounds and Audio Devices   86
    Speech   86
    System   86
    Taskbar and Start Menu   94
    User Accounts   94

Microsoft Management Console Overview   95
     The MMC Console   95
     Snap-Ins   96
Using the MMC   97
Administrative Tools   97
PCMCIA or PC Cards   100
Chapter Summary   101
Key Terms   101
Review Questions   103
Hands-on Projects   106
Case Projects   111

CHAPTER FOUR
Managing Windows XP File Systems and Storage   113

File Storage Basics   114
     Basic Storage   114
     Dynamic Storage   115
     Removable Storage Devices   119
Drive Configurations   120
File Systems   120
     FAT and FAT32   121
     NTFS   122
     Converting File Systems   123
Disk Management Actions   124
     Drive Letters and Mount Points   132
     Disk Cleanup   132
     Check Disk   133
     Defragmentation   134
     FSUTIL   135
File System Object Level Properties   136
     NTFS Folder Object   136
     FAT/FAT32 Folder Object   138
     NTFS File Object   139
     FAT/FAT32 File Object   141
     NTFS Mounted Volume Object   142
     FAT/FAT32 Mounted Volume Object   143
Managing NTFS Permissions   144
     NTFS File and Folder Permissions   144
     NTFS Permission Basics   148
     Copying and Moving NTFS Objects   149
Managing Shared Folders   149
Media Folders and the Customize tab   152
Simple File Sharing   154
Zipping Files and Compressed Folders   154
CD Burning   155
Offline Files   155
Folder Redirection   157
Removable Media   158
Troubleshooting Access Problems   158
The Microsoft Distributed File System   159
Chapter Summary   160
Key Terms   160

Review Questions   162
Hands-on Projects   165
Case Projects   174

CHAPTER FIVE
Users, Groups, Profiles, and Policies   **175**
Windows XP Professional User Accounts   176
Logging Onto Windows XP   178
    Administrator   179
    Guest   179
Naming Conventions   180
Managing User Accounts   180
    User Accounts Applet   181
    Local Users and Groups   184
    Users   184
    Groups   187
    System Groups and Other Important Groups   190
User Profiles   191
    Local Profiles   192
    Roaming Profiles   193
Local Security Policy   193
    Password Policy   194
    Account Lockout Policy   195
    Audit Policy   196
    User Rights Policy   196
    Security Options   198
Troubleshooting Cached Credentials   201
File and Settings Transfer Wizard   202
Chapter Summary   202
Key Terms   203
Review Questions   204
Hands-on Projects   208
Case Projects   214

CHAPTER SIX
Windows XP Security and Access Controls   **215**
The Windows XP Security Model   216
    Logon Authentication   217
    Objects   218
    Access Control   219
Customizing the Logon Process   219
    Disabling the Default Username   221
    Adding a Security Warning Message   221
    Changing the Shell   221
    Disabling the Shutdown button   222
    Automating Logons   223
    Automatic Account Lockout   223
Domain Security Concepts and Systems   224
    Domain Security Overview   224
    Kerberos and Authentication Services   224

Local Computer Policy   226
    Computer Configuration   227
    User Configuration   230
    Secedit   231
Auditing   233
Encrypted File System   236
Internet Security   238
Chapter Summary   238
Key Terms   238
Review Questions   240
Hands-on Projects   243
Case Projects   250

CHAPTER SEVEN
Network Protocols   **251**

Windows XP Network Overview   252
Windows XP Network Components   252
Network Protocols   253
    TCP/IP   253
    NWLink (IPX/SPX)   257
    NetBEUI and DLC   258
Interprocess Communication   258
    IPC File System Mechanisms   259
    IPC Programming Interfaces   260
Redirectors   262
    Workstation Service   263
    Server Service   263
    Multiple Universal Naming Convention Provider   264
    Universal Naming Convention Names   264
    Multi-Provider Router   264
Networking Under Windows XP   265
Network Bridge   269
Networking Wizard   270
Managing Bindings   271
TCP/IP Architecture   272
    Internet Protocol   272
    Transmission Control Protocol   275
TCP/IP Configuration   282
IPv6: Looking to the Future   286
Windows XP Remote Tools   287
    Remote Assistance   287
    Remote Desktop   288
Windows XP and NetWare Networks   288
NetWare Compatibility Components   289
    NWLink   289
    Client Service for NetWare   292
    Bindery and NDS Support   293
    Installing and Configuring Client Service for NetWare   294
Connecting to NetWare Resources   297
    Choosing Appropriate NetWare Client Software   298

Chapter Summary   298
Key Terms   299
Review Questions   302
Hands-on Projects   306
Case Projects   312

CHAPTER EIGHT
Internetworking with Remote Access   **313**
Remote Access   314
Features of Remote Access in Windows XP   315
    PPP Multilink   315
    VPN Protocols   316
    Restartable File Copy   316
    Idle Disconnect   316
    Autodial and Log-on Dial   316
    Client and Server Enhancements   316
    Look and Feel   317
    Callback Security   317
    WAN Connectivity   317
Internet Network Access Protocols   317
    PPP   318
    PPTP   318
    PPP-MP   319
    SLIP   319
    Telephony Features   319
Remote Access Configuration   320
    Connecting to the Internet   321
    Connecting To The Network At My Workplace   331
    Setting Up An Advanced Connection   332
Installing Remote Access Hardware   334
Phone and Modem Options   334
Remote Access Security   336
Internet Options Applet   337
Internet Connection Sharing   339
Internet Connection Firewall   340
Windows XP and the Internet   342
    Internet Explorer   342
    Outlook Express   342
    FTP Client   343
    Telnet Client   343
    Internet Information Server   343
Order Prints Online   345
Clients vs. Server-Based Remote Access   345
Remote Access Troubleshooting   346
Chapter Summary   346
Key Terms   347
Review Questions   348
Hands-on Projects   351
Case Projects   360

CHAPTER NINE
Printing and Faxing   **361**
    Windows XP Printing Terminology   362
    Windows XP Print Subsystem Architecture   364
        Graphical Device Interface   364
        Printer Driver   365
        Print Spooler   365
    Printer Driver Software   369
    Printing Across the Network   370
    The Printing Process   370
    Installing and Managing Printers   371
        Managing Print Jobs   371
        Creating a Local Printer   373
        Connecting to a Remote Printer   374
    Configuring a Printer   374
        General Tab   374
        Sharing Tab   376
        Ports Tab   376
        Advanced Tab   377
        Color Management Tab   380
        Security Tab   380
        Device Settings Tab   382
    Printers and the Web   383
    Managing the Print Server   384
    Troubleshooting Printing Problems   385
        Troubleshooting Printing in General   385
        Troubleshooting Network Printing 386
        Stopping and Restarting the Print Spooler   386
    Fax Support   387
    Chapter Summary   389
    Key Terms   390
    Review Questions   393
    Hands-on Projects   396
    Case Projects   400

CHAPTER TEN
Performance Tuning   **401**
    Establishing a Baseline   402
    Monitoring and Performance Tuning   402
        Task Manager   403
        System Monitor   407
    Logging and Using Logged Activity   415
        Event Viewer   419
        Performance Options   421
        Setting Application Priority   422
    Performance Tuning in the System Applet   424
        The Visual Effects Tab   424
        The Advanced Tab   426
    Recognizing and Handling Bottlenecks   427
        Common Bottlenecks   429
        Network Bottlenecks   430

Eight Ways to Boost Windows XP Professional Performance 431
Optimizing Performance for Mobile Windows XP Users 433
Chapter Summary 434
Key Terms 435
Review Questions 436
Hands-on Projects 439
Case Projects 446

CHAPTER ELEVEN
Windows XP Professional Application Support **447**
Windows XP Professional System Architecture 448
    Kernel Mode Versus User Mode 449
    Processes and Threads 450
    Environment Subsystems 452
Win32 Applications 454
    The Environment Subsystem 454
    Multithreading 454
    Memory Space 455
    Input Message Queues 456
    Base Priorities 456
DOS and the Virtual DOS Machine 457
    VDM Components 458
    Virtual Device Drivers 458
    AUTOEXEC.BAT and Config.sys 458
    Custom DOS Environments 460
Win16 Concepts and Applications 463
    Win16-on-Win32 Components 464
    Memory Space 465
Other Windows Application Management Facilities 467
    Program Compatibility Wizard 467
    Assigning and Publishing Applications on Windows XP Professional 471
    Resolving DLL Conflicts in Windows XP 473
Chapter Summary 473
Key Terms 474
Review Questions 476
Hands-on Projects 479
Case Projects 485

CHAPTER TWELVE
Working with the Windows XP Registry **487**
Windows Registry Overview 490
Important Registry Structures and Keys 493
    HKEY_LOCAL_MACHINE 493
    HKEY_CLASSES_ROOT 496
    HKEY_CURRENT_CONFIG 497
    HKEY_CURRENT_USER 498
    HKEY_USERS 498
    HKEY_DYN_DATA 499
Registry Editors 499
Registry Size Limitations 501
Registry Storage Files 502

Registry Fault Tolerance   503
Restoring the Registry   506
Windows XP Professional Resource Kit Registry Tools   507
Chapter Summary   508
Key Terms   509
Review Questions   511
Hands-on Projects   514
Case Projects   517

CHAPTER THIRTEEN
Booting Windows XP   **515**
The Boot Process   516
Windows XP Boot Phase   516
    Power-On Self Test   516
    Initial Startup   518
    Boot Loader   519
    Detecting Hardware   522
Troubleshooting and Advanced Startup Options   522
Boot Configuration and Selecting an Operating System   524
    [boot loader]   524
    [operating systems]   525
    Advanced RISC Computing Pathnames   526
Editing Boot.ini   527
    Using the Control Panel   527
    Using a Text Editor   528
Windows XP Load Phase   528
    Loading the Kernel   529
    Initializing the Kernel   529
    Services Load   530
    Windows XP System Startup   531
    Logging On   531
Multiple-Boot Systems   531
    Multiple Windows Operating Systems   532
    Multiple Installation Order   532
Chapter Summary   532
Key Terms   533
Review Questions   534
Hands-on Projects   538
Case Projects   541

CHAPTER FOURTEEN
Windows XP Professional Fault Tolerance   **543**
Microsoft IntelliMirror   544
Data Backup   544
    PC Configuration Recovery   545
    Application Installation and Repair   545
Microsoft Backup Utility   546
Preventive Maintenance   549
    Device Driver Rollback   549
    Windows File Protection   550
    Automatic Updates - Windows Update   551
    Desktop Cleanup Wizard   551
    Hibernate vs. Standby   551

Repairing Windows XP Professional   552
    System Restore   552
    Recovery Console   554
    Emergency Repair Process   555
    Remote OS Installation   555
Chapter Summary   557
Key Terms   557
Review Questions   558
Hands-on Projects   561
Case Projects   566

CHAPTER FIFTEEN
Troubleshooting Windows XP   **567**
General Principles of Troubleshooting   568
    Collect Information   568
    Use Common-Sense Troubleshooting Guidelines   570
Troubleshooting Tools   572
    Event Viewer   572
    Computer Management Tool   573
    Troubleshooting Wizards and Widgets   575
Troubleshooting Installation Problems   577
Troubleshooting Printer Problems   578
Troubleshooting RAS Problems   581
Troubleshooting Network Problems   584
Troubleshooting Disk Problems   585
Miscellaneous Troubleshooting Issues   585
    Permissions Problems   586
    Master Boot Record Problems   586
    Using the Dr. Watson Debugger   587
Applying Service Packs and Hot Fixes   588
Microsoft Troubleshooting References   590
Chapter Summary   590
Key Terms   591
Review Questions   592
Hands-on Projects   595
Case Projects   601

APPENDIX A
Exam Objectives Tracking for MCSE Certification   **603**
Exam # 70-270: Installing, Configuring, and Administering
Microsoft Windows XP Professional
Installing Windows XP Professional   603
Implementing and Conducting Administration of Resources   604
Implementing, Managing, Monitoring, and Troubleshooting Hardware Devices and Drivers   605
Monitoring and Optimizing System Performance and Reliability   606
Configuring and Troubleshooting the Desktop Environment   607
Implementing, Managing, and Troubleshooting Network Protocols and Services   608
Configuring, Managing, and Troubleshooting Security   609

GLOSSARY   **615**

Preface

Welcome to the *MCSE Guide to Windows XP Professional*. This book offers you real-world examples, interactive activities, and hundreds of hands-on projects that reinforce key concepts and help you prepare for the Microsoft certification exam #70-270: Installing, Configuring, and Administering Microsoft Windows XP Professional. This book will also help prepare you for MCSA certification. This book also features troubleshooting tips for solutions to common problems that you will encounter in the realm of Windows XP Professional administration.

This book offers in-depth study of all the salient functions and features of installing, configuring, and maintaining Windows XP Professional as a client operating system. Throughout the book, we provide pointed review questions to reinforce the concepts introduced in each chapter and to help prepare you for the Microsoft certification exam. In addition to the review questions, we provide detailed hands-on projects that let you experience firsthand the processes involved in Windows XP Professional configuration and management. Finally, to put a real-world slant on the concepts introduced in each chapter, we provide case studies to prepare you for situations that must be managed in a live networking environment.

The Intended Audience

This book is intended to serve the needs of those individuals and information systems professionals who are interested in learning more about Microsoft Windows XP Professional, as well as individuals who are interested in obtaining Microsoft certification on this topic. These materials have been specifically designed to help individuals prepare for this certification exam.

Chapter 1, "Introduction to Windows XP Professional," introduces the latest Windows operating systems family—including Windows XP Professional and Windows .NET Server—and describes the major features of the Windows environment. In addition, it explores the architecture of Windows XP Professional and related operating systems. Finally, it defines the minimum system requirements for Windows XP Professional and introduces the two major networking models under which Windows XP can be used.

In **Chapter 2**, "Installing Windows XP Professional," we discuss how to decide whether to perform an upgrade or a fresh installation of Windows XP Professional. We also explore how to boot using multiple operating systems. In addition, we examine installation options such as unattended installations; whether to install using Windows XP setup disks, a CD-ROM, or the network; and, finally, we describe the various setup and advanced installation options.

Chapter 3, "Using the Systems Utilities," examines the tools used to manage Windows XP Professional, namely, the Microsoft Management Console (MMC), Administrative Tools, Task Scheduler, and Control Panel applets. These tools are used to install and configure new hardware, create hardware profiles for changing system configurations, as well as configure PC cards and multiple displays.

In **Chapter 4**, "Managing Windows XP File Systems and Storage," we explore the differences between basic and dynamic storage and discuss the drive configurations supported by Windows XP. This chapter also introduces file systems supported by Windows XP Professional: FAT, FAT32, and NTFS. Additionally, we describe permissions, sharing, and other security issues related to file systems. From an administrative standpoint, we also discuss drive, volume, and partition maintenance and administration under Windows XP Professional.

We introduce you to the concepts involved in working with users, groups, profiles, and policies in **Chapter 5**, "Users, Groups, Profiles, and Policies." This discussion includes setting up, naming, and managing local users and groups and default user and group accounts. From there, we examine the Windows XP Professional logon authentication process. This chapter concludes with in-depth coverage of the creation and management of user accounts, profiles, and local security policies.

Chapter 6, "Windows XP Security and Access Controls," teaches you about the Windows XP security model and the key role of logon authentication. We show you how to customize the logon process, discuss domain security concepts, and provide additional instructions for setting up the local computer policy. This chapter also shows you how to enable and use auditing. We conclude this discussion on security with details on encrypting NTFS files, folders, or drives using the Encrypting File System (EFS).

We cover the world of networking Windows XP in **Chapter 7**, "Network Protocols." Here, you'll explore the protocols supported by Windows XP Professional. In addition, we detail the intricacies of configuring and managing TCP/IP, and of configuring and managing NetWare access using the NWLink protocol and the Client Service for NetWare (CSNW).

We examine remote access to Windows XP Professional in **Chapter 8**, "Internetworking with Remote Access Service." You'll learn how to use remote access under Windows XP, configure various RAS connection types, work with telephony services and connections, manage RAS security, and troubleshoot RAS connection problems.

In **Chapter 9**, "Printing and Faxing," we discuss Windows XP print terminology and architecture, and examine the special features of the Windows XP print system. We provide hands-on instruction for creating and managing printers and printer permissions, and explain how to take advantage of XP's built-in fax and fax-sharing support. This chapter concludes with a discussion on troubleshooting printing and faxing problems.

Chapter 10, "Performance Tuning," gives you the information you need to understand the performance and monitoring tools found in Windows XP. You'll learn how to create a Counter log for historical analysis, configure Alert events to warn of performance problems, and establish a baseline of normal system operation against which to measure Windows XP Professional performance. Finally, we discuss how to detect and eliminate bottlenecks to keep your system running as efficiently as possible.

In **Chapter 11**, "Windows XP Professional Application Support," we discuss how to deploy applications that were created for use in other operating environments, such as DOS or older versions of Windows. Finally, we explore how to fine-tune the application environment for DOS and Win16.

Chapter 12, "Working with the Windows XP Registry," discusses the function and structure of the Registry, which is the underlying database that stores system configuration information in Windows XP. This chapter describes the purpose of each of the five Registry keys, how to use the Registry editing tools, defines the fault-tolerant mechanisms for the Registry, and provides information on how to back up and restore the Registry.

In **Chapter 13**, "Booting Windows XP," we explain the steps that Windows XP Professional goes through during the boot process. This discussion includes the operation of the key Windows XP startup files, the boot options offered via the Windows Advanced Options Menu, and how to troubleshoot system restoration by using Safe Mode. In addition, we explore how to edit the Boot.ini file to manipulate the boot process, and how multi-boot configurations are created and function.

We introduce you to disaster protection and recovery concepts in **Chapter 14**, "Windows XP Professional Fault Tolerance." Here, you'll learn how to back up data and settings on Windows XP Professional and recover a Windows XP Professional client's applications and data. Additionally, we introduce IntelliMirror technology and describe its key features, as well as remote operating system installation, and how it can be used with IntelliMirror to recover a PC remotely. Finally, we show you how to use the Recovery Console and the Safe Mode options for recovering or repairing damaged Windows XP Professional installations.

This book concludes with **Chapter 15**, "Troubleshooting Windows XP." Here, we examine how to collect documentation about your systems to aid in troubleshooting and preventing problems, and review common sense approaches to troubleshooting. In addition, we discuss how to troubleshoot general problems with Windows XP and use some of the troubleshooting tools found in Windows XP Professional.

Features

Many features in this book are designed to improve its pedagogical value and aid you in fully understanding Windows XP Professional concepts.

- **Chapter Objectives.** Each chapter begins with a detailed list of the concepts to be mastered within that chapter. This list provides you with a quick reference to the contents of the chapter as well as a useful study guide.

- **Illustrations and Tables.** Numerous illustrations of screens and components help you visualize common setups, theories, and architectures. In addition, tables provide details and comparisons of both practical and theoretical information.

- **Chapter Summaries.** The text of each chapter concludes with a summary of the concepts it has introduced. These summaries provide a helpful way to recap and revisit the ideas covered in each chapter.

- **Key Terms.** Following the Chapter Summary, a list of key Windows XP terms and their definitions encourages proper understanding of the chapter's key concepts and provides a useful reference.

- **Review Questions.** End-of-chapter assessments begin with a set of review questions that reinforce the ideas introduced in each chapter. These questions not only show you whether you have mastered the concepts, but also are written to help prepare you for the Microsoft certification exam.

- **Hands-on Projects.** Although it is important to understand the theory behind technology, nothing can improve upon real-world experience. Each chapter provides a series of exercises aimed at giving students hands-on implementation experience.

- **Case Projects.** Finally, each chapter closes with a section that proposes certain situations. You are asked to evaluate the situations and decide upon the course of action to be taken to remedy the problems described. This valuable tool will help you sharpen your decision-making and troubleshooting skills, which are important aspects of network administration.

Text and Graphic Conventions

Wherever appropriate, additional information has been added to this book to help you better understand what is being discussed in the chapter. Icons throughout the text alert you to additional materials. The icons used in this book are described here:

Tips give extra information on how to attack a problem, time-saving shortcuts, or what to do in certain real-world situations.

Important information about potential mistakes or hazards is highlighted with a Caution icon.

Each step-by-step Hands-on Project is marked by the Hands-on Project icon.

Case Project icons mark scenario-based assignments in which you are asked to implement independently the information you have learned.

Instructor's Materials

The following supplemental materials are available when this book is used in a classroom setting. All of the supplements available with this book are provided to the instructor on a single CD-ROM.

Electronic Instructor's Manual. The Instructor's Manual that accompanies this textbook includes:

- Additional instructional material to assist in class preparation, including suggestions for lecture topics, suggested lab activities, tips on setting up a lab for the hands-on assignments, and alternative lab setup ideas in situations where lab resources are limited.

- Solutions to all end-of-chapter materials, including the Review Questions, Hands-on Projects, and Case Projects.

ExamView® This textbook is accompanied by ExamView, a powerful testing software package that allows instructors to create and administer printed, computer (LAN-based), and Internet exams. ExamView includes hundreds of questions that correspond to the topics covered in this text, enabling students to generate detailed study guides that include page references for further review. The computer-based and Internet testing components allow students to take exams at their computers, and also save the instructor time by grading each exam automatically.

PowerPoint presentations. This book comes with Microsoft PowerPoint slides for each chapter. These are included as a teaching aid for classroom presentation, to make available to students on the network for chapter review, or to be printed for classroom distribution. Instructors, please feel at liberty to add your own slides for additional topics you introduce to the class.

MeasureUp® Test Prep Software Test preparation software for the Windows XP Professional exam is available at the Course Technology website. You can download copies of this software free of charge at: *www.course.com/networking*. Click the link for the Windows XP Professional Exam. The username and password is: xptestprep. The password is case sensitive and does not contain a space between the two words. Once the test prep software is available, it will be included on CD in future printings of this book.

Student's Materials

Student case assignment files. The instructor's CD-ROM comes with student case assignment files for each chapter. These files contain the end-of-chapter Case Project in electronic format so that students can enter their answers and submit them through e-mail, to a shared network folder, or print them for submission to the instructor.

Electronic glossary. An electronic glossary with hyperlinks is provided on the instructor's CD-ROM for distribution to each student, such as through a Web page or a shared network folder.

Where Should You Start?

This book is intended to be read in sequence, from beginning to end. Each chapter builds upon those that precede it, to provide a solid understanding of Windows XP Professional. After completing the chapters, you may find it useful to go back through the book and use the review questions and projects to prepare for the Microsoft certification test for Windows XP Professional. Readers are also encouraged to investigate the many pointers to online and printed sources of additional information that are cited throughout this book.

Acknowledgments

Ed Tittel: I would like to thank my co-author, James Michael Stewart, for shouldering the burden of this book, and for helping us to meet another aggressive schedule. I'd also like to thank Microsoft, for publishing the 70-270 objectives earlier than expected, thereby making our work on this project much more sane and manageable! I'd also like to thank Dawn Rader yet again for her magnificent efforts in coordinating this project on the LANWrights side. I'd also like to thank my family and friends for their continued support for my oh-so-interesting career, especially Leah and Chloe, Mom and Dad, Kat, Mike, Helen, and Colin, plus Wiggo and Blackie—my two best friends in the whole wide world.

Michael Stewart: Thanks to my boss and co-author, Ed Tittel, for including me in this book series. Thanks to my project manager/editor Dawn Rader who makes me sound coherent. To Mark: I don't think I want to visit anymore if you are gonna have me repaint your house again. And finally, as always, to Elvis—so long and thanks for all the fish. No wait, that's the wrong cool frood—we'll miss you Douglas Adams.

Collectively: Both of us would like to thank the crew at Course Technology for making this book possible, including Stephen Solomon and Will Pitkin, our acquisitions team; Charlie Blum, our project editor; Warren Wyrostek, our technical editor; and all the other people at Course Technology who helped with the book. We'd also like to thank Carole McClendon, our agent at Waterside Productions, for helping us to cement a business relationship that has proved so worthwhile to everyone. Thanks to one and all!

Microsoft Windows XP Professional Hardware Requirements

Following are the Microsoft defined minimum requirements to install and run Windows XP Professional:

- 233-MHz Pentium or higher microprocessor (P5 or equivalent compatible clone) or a Compaq Alpha processor with the latest firmware version installed (except for DECpc 150 AXP, DEC 2000-500, Multia, and AXPpci 33 processors)
- 128 MB of RAM for Intel (256 MB or more recommended; 4 GB maximum)
- 2 GB hard disk with a minimum of 1.5 GB of free space
- SVGA or higher resolution monitor
- Keyboard
- Microsoft Mouse or compatible pointing device
- A CD-ROM drive (12X or faster recommended) (or network access, for networked installations)
- A high-density 3.5-inch disk drive
- A Windows XP compatible network adapter card and related cable

1

INTRODUCTION TO WINDOWS XP PROFESSIONAL

After reading this chapter and completing the exercises, you will be able to:

♦ Describe the Windows XP product family

♦ Describe the major features of the Windows XP environment

♦ Understand the Windows XP intelligent user interface

♦ Define the minimum system requirements for Windows XP Professional

♦ Understand the two major networking models under which Windows XP can be used

♦ Understand the architecture of Windows XP

The pace of technological advances in the computing world is faster than ever before. Consumers can now purchase computer systems with power and capabilities that were mere fantasies just a few years ago, and do so at a lower cost. Microsoft has endeavored to remain competitive among these new powerful systems by continuing to improve its operating system (OS) products. The latest offering in the Microsoft OS product line is Windows XP, a network and desktop OS designed to take advantage of new hardware and the Internet to produce unsurpassed performance for network activities and application execution.

THE MICROSOFT NETWORKING FAMILY

The Microsoft networking family is a collection of **operating systems (OS)**, each of which offers the capability of participating in a network as either a **server** or **client**. This family includes operating systems currently in production as well as older products. Products in production include Windows XP, Windows 2000, and Windows Me; older family members include Windows NT, Windows 98, Windows 98 Second Edition (SE), Windows 95, and Windows for Workgroups.

Windows XP Family

The Windows XP product family builds upon the best features of Windows 2000 and Windows 98/SE/Me, and includes advanced Internet, security, and connectivity technologies. The result is a network and desktop operating system that offers unsurpassed functionality, security, resource management, and versatility. Windows XP currently consists of two products: Windows XP Professional and Windows XP Home. Microsoft has also released a 64-bit version of Windows XP Professional to operate on the new Iridium Intel 64-bit processor. Because 64-bit technology requires very expensive hardware, it most likely will not be widely deployed by home, business, or educational communities. Additionally, this technology is not mentioned on the 70-270 certification exam.

The Home version of Windows XP is designed for standalone home use. It is basically the same OS as Windows XP Professional, but does not support several of the business-level features, including Encrypting File System (EFS), **domain** client capability, offline files, Internet Protocol Security (IPSec), Automated System Recovery (ASR), Remote Desktop, and Internet Information Server (IIS). For a complete list of "missing" features, see the *Microsoft Windows XP Professional Resource Kit.*

Windows XP Professional can be used as a stand-alone system or can be a workgroup or domain network client. Designed for speed and reliability, Windows XP Professional brings a solid computing environment to desktop and mobile computers. Windows XP Professional is the ideal client operating system for connecting to and interacting with a Windows 2000 or .NET domain. The majority of this book focuses on this product.

The Windows XP family will be expanded by the Windows .NET product line. Windows XP and Windows .NET were originally combined under the project name "Whistler." However, Microsoft decided to develop the server products of Whistler much further than the client products. As a result, the client products (Windows XP Professional and Windows XP Home) were released in October of 2001. The Windows .NET server products will not be released until sometime in early 2002.

When Windows .NET is finally released, it will most likely consist of three products: Windows .NET Server, Windows .NET Advanced Server, and Windows .NET DataCenter Server. .NET Server has gone through several name changes: originally Whistler, then XP Server, 2002 Server, and .NET Server. It is possible that Microsoft will once again change the final product name and even alter the names of Advanced Server and DataCenter Server to meet new marketing demands.

Windows .NET builds on Windows 2000, borrows heavily from Windows XP, and includes numerous new advances as well. Windows .NET is a platform for Microsoft's XML Web services. Basically, a Web service consists of application logic that provides data and services to other applications. The Extensible Markup Language (XML) Web service technology allows applications to access Web services through Web protocols and formats such as Hypertext Markup Language (HTTP), XML, and Simple Object Access Protocol (SOAP), with no need to worry about how each Web service is implemented. This platform will revolutionize how applications and network services are distributed to network clients and even individuals. Microsoft is moving toward a subscription-based application service. Such a service would not offer boxed software products; you would lease usage time for applications over the Internet. As the .NET product line solidifies, keep an eye on the Microsoft .NET Web site for new and updated information: *www.microsoft.com/net/*.

Other Client Operating Systems

Microsoft's Windows product line includes several client operating systems in addition to Windows XP Professional, including Windows 2000 Professional, Windows NT 4.0 Workstation, Windows Me, Windows SE, Windows 98, Windows 95, and Windows for Workgroups. Any Microsoft Windows client system can be used on a Microsoft network. However, the old platforms typically support fewer network capabilities than the new platforms. Only Windows XP Professional, 2000, and NT clients can actually become domain members. All other client operating systems can access domain shared resources but are not true domain members. See the "Domain Model" section later in this chapter.

For more information on earlier Windows operating systems, see the Microsoft Web site: *www.microsoft.com/windows/*.

The Windows XP Environment

The Windows XP operating environment is a hybrid of Windows 2000 and Windows Me. The combination of the Windows 2000 core reliability and security with the Windows Me **Plug and Play** capability and connectivity has produced an operating system that is unsurpassed in function and features. The following sections highlight many of the characteristics of the Windows XP environment.

Multiple Processors

Windows XP Professional supports true **multiprocessing**; support for up to two CPUs is included in every standard version of Windows XP Professional. Windows XP Home can support only a single CPU. Windows .NET Server will most likely support four

CPUs, and the more advanced server versions will probably have even greater CPU capacity.

On multiple-CPU systems, as many processes or threads as there are CPUs can execute simultaneously; that is, if you are running Windows .NET Server on a system that has four CPUs, then four threads or processes can run at the same time. This means that multiple applications can execute simultaneously, each on a different processor. The network administrator can adjust the priority levels for different processors, to make sure that preferred applications get a bigger slice of the CPUs that are available.

Multitasking

One of the great features of Windows XP is **multitasking**, a mode of CPU operation in which a computer processes more than one task at a time. Windows XP supports two types of multitasking—preemptive and cooperative. **Preemptive multitasking** is a processor scheduling regime in which the OS maintains strict control over how long any execution thread (a single task within a multithreaded application, or an entire single-threaded application) may take possession of the CPU. This scheduling regime is called preemptive because the operating system can decide at any time to swap out the currently executing thread if a higher-priority thread makes a bid for execution; the termination of the lower-priority thread is called preemption. Windows XP supports multiple threads and allows duties to be spread among processors. Most native Windows XP applications are written to take advantage of threads, but older applications may not be as well equipped.

Cooperative multitasking describes a processor scheduling regime wherein individual applications take control over the CPU for as long as they like (because this means that applications must be well-behaved, this approach is sometimes called "good guy" scheduling). Unfortunately, this type of multitasking can lead to stalled or hung systems, should any application fail to release its control over the CPU. Windows 3.x is one of the most familiar examples of this type of environment; it runs on top of **MS-DOS**, a single-threaded operating system. In contrast, native 32-bit Windows XP applications have no such limitations. The default for Windows XP is that all 16-bit Windows applications run within a single virtual machine, which is granted only preemptive CPU access. This guarantees that other processes active on a Windows XP machine will not be stymied by an ill-behaved Windows 3.x application.

Multithreading

Multithreading refers to a code design in which individual tasks within a single process space can operate more or less independently as separate, lightweight execution modules called **threads**. Threads are called lightweight execution modules because switching among or between threads within the context of a single process involves very little overhead, and is therefore extremely quick. A thread is the minimal unit of code in an application or system that can be scheduled for execution.

Within a process, all threads share the same memory and system resources. A **process**, on the other hand, is a collection of one or more threads that share a common application or system activity focus. Processes are called heavyweight execution modules because switching among them involves a great deal of overhead, including copying large amounts of data from RAM to disk for outbound processes; that process must be repeated to copy large amounts of data from disk to RAM for inbound processes. Under Windows XP, it normally takes more than 100 times longer to switch among processes than it does to switch among threads.

Multithreading allows an operating system to execute multiple threads from a single application concurrently. If the computer on which such threads run includes multiple CPUs, threads can even execute simultaneously, each on a different CPU. Even on single-CPU computers, threaded implementations speed up applications and create an environment in which multiple tasks can be active between the foreground (what's showing on the screen) and the background (what's not on screen). Windows XP is extremely adept and efficient at multithreading.

File Systems

Windows XP supports three file systems that can be used to format volumes/partitions on hard drives:

- **FAT (File Allocation Table)**—The file system originally used by DOS (actually, the Windows XP implementation is an extension of Virtual FAT [VFAT], which includes support for long filenames and 4 GB files and volumes). Windows XP FAT is also known as FAT16.

- **FAT32**—An enhancement of the FAT16 file system developed for Windows 95 OSR2, and included in Windows 98. Windows XP includes support for FAT32 primarily to gain the 32 GB file and volume size improvement over FAT16. FAT32 volumes created by Windows 95 OSR2 or Windows 98 can be mounted under Windows XP.

- **New Technology File System (NTFS)**—A high-performance, secure, and object-oriented file system introduced in Windows NT. This is the preferred file system for Windows XP.

 Versions of Windows NT up through 3.51 (that is, not including NT 4.0 or Windows 2000) supported HPFS (High Performance File System), which was originally present in OS/2 and LAN Manager. Windows XP does not support HPFS.

Active Directory

Active Directory is the control and administration mechanism of Windows XP that is supported by Windows 2000 or Windows .NET Server to create, sustain, and administer a domain or group of related domains. Active Directory combines the various aspects of a network—users, groups, hosts, clients, security settings, resources, network links, and transactions—into a manageable hierarchical structure. Active Directory simplifies network administration by combining several previously distinct activities, including security, user account management, and resource access, into a single interface.

Windows XP Professional does not include support utilities for installing or managing Active Directory. However, by joining a domain, Windows XP Professional will interact with the Active Directory for all resource- and security-related communications.

Security

Windows XP incorporates a variety of security features with a common aim: to enable efficient, reliable control of access to all resources and assets on a network. Windows XP security features begin with a protected mandatory logon system, and includes memory protection, system auditing over all events and activities, precise controls on file and directory access, and all types of network access limitations.

Windows XP was developed to address the following business security needs:

- Enterprise isolation
- Multilevel security
- Auditing and resource tracking
- Isolation of hardware-dependent code

Also, numerous third-party companies offer security enhancements or extensions to Windows XP that cover everything from biometric authentication add-ons (allowing fingerprints or retinal scans to be used in controlling system access) to firewalls and proxy servers that isolate Windows XP-based networks from the Internet or other publicly accessible networks.

One of the more popular features of the Windows XP security system is the inclusion of the Kerberos v5 authentication protocol. Basically, Kerberos is used to authenticate a client to a server (that is, to ensure that they are both valid members of a domain) before communication between them is permitted.

Compatibility

Windows XP supports a wide range of applications through application subsystems that emulate the native environment of each application type. In other words, a virtual machine is created for each application, which is fooled into seeing itself as the sole inhabitant of a computer system that matches its execution needs. Windows XP supports the following application types:

- DOS 16-bit
- Native 32-bit (**Win32**)
- Windows 3.1 and Windows for Workgroups 16-bit (**Win16**)

 Windows XP Professional supports most Windows 95/98/2000-based programs, in particular Windows 32-bit business programs. It also supports MS-DOS-based programs, except for those that access the hardware directly.

Storage

Windows XP Professional supports huge amounts of hard disk and memory space:

- *RAM*—4 GB (gigabytes)
- *Hard disk space*—2 TB (terabytes) for NTFS volumes, 32 GB for FAT32 volumes, and 4 GB for FAT16 volumes

Connectivity

The Windows XP core OS supports a wide variety of networking protocols:

- **NWLink**—Microsoft's 32-bit implementation of Novell's NetWare native protocol stack, IPX/SPX (Internetwork Protocol Exchange/Sequenced Packet Exchange).
- **TCP/IP (Transmission Control Protocol/Internet Protocol)**—The set of protocols used on the Internet. This protocol suite has been embraced by Microsoft as a vital technology.

Windows XP is compatible with many existing network types and environments and has native support for the following:

- TCP/IP intranets/Internet
- Integrated remote access networks
- Macintosh networks
- Microsoft networks (MS-DOS, Windows for Workgroups, LAN Manager)
- Enhanced NetWare connectivity

System Recovery

Windows XP boasts the broadest system recovery mechanisms of any Windows OS to date. In addition to traditional backup capabilities and the automated self-protecting mechanisms of NTFS and the Registry, Windows XP includes System Restore, Automated System Recovery (ASR), Recovery Console, device driver rollback, and numerous alternate boot options.

Remote Capabilities

Windows XP builds on the networking capabilities of the Windows product line by introducing more options for remote connectivity. Two such features are Remote Desktop and Remote Assistance. Remote Desktop allows you to access your office computer's user environment from a remote system as you would through a Terminal Services connection. Remote Assistance is used to invite a remote user to view or control your desktop, often to help you perform some work or configuration task.

Help and Support Services

Windows XP boasts the most comprehensive help system ever included in a Windows OS. The Help and Support Center offers several means to access information, including many step-by-step guides, topical and index organizations, and online help for new items.

INTELLIGENT USER INTERFACE

Windows XP has a whole new desktop layout and look, which Microsoft has labeled the "user experience." The user experience is simply the task-based visual design of the operating system. The new user experience is fresh and easy to use, but not so different that you can't make use of existing Windows know-how. Over the course of writing this book, we were first a bit frustrated by the new layout and organization, but within a week we found that we preferred the XP user experience over those of Windows 2000 or Windows Me. It seems more straightforward, more intelligent, and focused on getting things done.

Windows XP comes with a new default color scheme based on greens and blues, though the color scheme can be fully customized. If you prefer the boxy gray interface of Windows 2000, you can always switch over to the Windows Classic visual style. Additionally, Windows XP includes new 3D graphical elements and smoothing of edges and corners. The new look and feel is known as a visual styling, and is nothing more than a "skin" for the entire OS.

One of the most obvious changes to the interface is the Start menu. It appears too bulky at first due to its double-column format (see Figure 1-1). The left column of icons includes a quick line to a Web browser and e-mail client. Under these you can "pin" your own selection of icons (we've pinned Windows Explorer). Pinning is accomplished by right-clicking over an item anywhere in the Start menu and clicking on the Pin to Start menu command in the pop-up menu. Below the pinned items is a list of the most recently accessed applications. By default, only the last six are displayed, this can be extended up to 30. At the bottom of the column is the All Programs item, which contains the rest of the Start menu subfolders and icons that were located within the Programs section of the Windows 2000 Start menu. The right column of the Windows XP Start menu includes quick links to My Documents, My Recent Documents, My Pictures, My Music, My Computer, My Network Places, Control Panel, Printers and Faxes, Help and Support, Search, and the Run command.

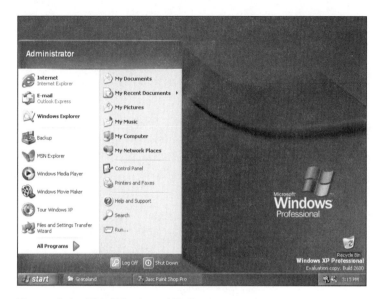

Figure 1-1   The Windows XP Start menu

As you explore the new Windows XP interface, you are bound to find many subtle changes and added features that make using the computer easier. Another interesting tweak is the improved taskbar. Within Windows XP, active application buttons on the taskbar are grouped by type. For example, if you have more than five or six applications running, two or three of which are Windows Explorer-type applications, they will be cascaded into a single taskbar button. This multi-application taskbar button will act like a pull-down list, enabling you to select the individual application with a single click. Windows XP offers a quick launch icon bar. It is disabled by default, but when enabled, it appears just to the right of the Start button. It's a great place to store often-accessed applications for quick one-click launching. Windows XP also has improved system tray icon management (note that Microsoft has altered this terminology—what was called the "system tray" in previous Windows versions is referred to as the "Notification Area" in Windows XP Professional). Instead of allowing icons to string out beside the clock taking up taskbar space, the inactive or rarely accessed icons are hidden. If you ever need access, just click the round arrow button to see them all. You can also custom-configure each icon as to whether it is always hidden, hidden when inactive, or always displayed.

For a hands-on tour of the new features of Windows XP's user interface, take the Windows XP tour offered to you during your first log on.

Overview of New Features

Windows XP includes a broad range of new features or improvements that add capabilities to the Windows product line. While most of these are not covered on the certification exams, you'll probably discover they are welcome additions to the previous versions of Windows.

Although IntelliMirror is not new, it has been fully integrated into Windows XP. IntelliMirror was first developed for Windows 2000. It offers a fault-tolerant system to protect system and data files from loss. It backs up user data, maintains user system configuration, automates application installation, and can even be used to deploy new clients. IntelliMirror is discussed in greater detail in Chapter 14, "Windows XP Professional Fault Tolerance."

Windows XP includes integrated video, voice, and text conferencing. As part of the Windows Messenger Service, Windows Messenger makes online collaboration easier and better than ever. With this tool you can trade contact lists, exchange files, share applications, and even write on a multi-user whiteboard. Communicating over an office LAN or the Internet has never been as elegant or as simple.

Windows XP sports the new Windows Media Player 8. The latest version of this Microsoft multi-media tool can be used to play CDs and DVDs, view recorded movies, play live or recorded music or local music files, search and organize digital media, copy music to portable devices, and even burn your own CDs.

Windows Movie Maker is a new application within the Windows environment. It enables you to transform your own camcorder recordings into amateur home movies. This multi-faceted application can combine video or audio from external analog and digital recording devices with downloaded content to produce a custom presentation. Just think, you can produce your own home movies if you can cut-and-paste, drag-and-drop, and point-and-click.

Windows XP has broader support for digital images than any previous version of Windows. This includes specialized media folders that operate like thumbnail depositories or slideshows right in Windows Explorer. Windows XP offers image manipulation and editing capabilities and quick access to online photo printing. You can submit your images to a print shop and have them shipped to you.

Autoplay is not a feature new to Windows, but Windows XP has taken Autoplay to a whole new level. Instead of automatically playing an audio CD or launching an application when a CD is inserted, you can custom-configure what the system does based on the type of CD. You can play the CD, open a slide show, print, and more.

WINDOWS XP PROFESSIONAL HARDWARE REQUIREMENTS

Windows XP Professional requires a minimum configuration of hardware to function. It is important that your system comply with these minimum requirements. However, in nearly all cases, you should attempt to purchase the fastest, largest, or best device you can afford. Compliance with the minimum hardware requirements only guarantees functionality; optimum performance requires exceeding these requirements. Here are the Microsoft-defined minimum requirements:

- 233 MHz CPU or higher microprocessor
- 64 MB of RAM (128 MB or more recommended; 4 GB maximum)
- 1.5 GB of free space
- SVGA (800 x 600) or higher resolution monitor
- Keyboard
- Microsoft Mouse or compatible pointing device (optional)

If you are installing from a CD-ROM drive, you'll need:

- A CD-ROM or DVD drive
- High-density 3.5-inch disk drive, unless you configured your PC to boot from the CD-ROM drive and can start the setup program from a CD, or if you have an existing OS that can access the CD-ROM drive

If you are installing over a network, you'll need:

- Windows XP-compatible network interface card (NIC) and related cable
- Access to the network share that contains the setup files

Hardware Compatibility List

When it comes to configuring a Windows XP machine, the Microsoft **Hardware Compatibility List (HCL)** is an essential piece of documentation. The HCL contains all known Windows XP-compatible hardware devices. The HCL also points to each device's driver, which may be native (included as part of the Windows XP installation program), on a subdirectory on the Windows XP CD, or available only from the device's vendor. Because Windows XP works properly only if a system's hardware is Windows XP-compatible, it's always a good idea to use the HCL as your primary reference when evaluating a prospective Windows XP system or when selecting components for such a system.

Finding the HCL

Finding the HCL is not always easy. The easiest place to look is on your Windows XP CD-ROM in the Support folder, where it exists as a text and a Help file. However, the HCL is not a static document; Microsoft's Quality Labs are constantly updating this file.

The version of the HCL on the Windows XP CD-ROM will quickly become outdated, because many new drivers and devices are introduced on a regular basis.

 It's a good idea to consult the most current version of the HCL, especially when you'll be working with brand-new hardware. The most recent version of the HCL is available for online viewing through the Help and Support Center's "Find compatible hardware and software for Windows XP" link or on Microsoft's Web site: *www.microsoft.com/hcl/default.asp*. On the other hand, if you have access to a copy of the TechNet CD, a new copy of the HCL is published on TechNet each time it changes.

Why the HCL Is So Important

Windows XP controls hardware directly; it does not require access to a PC's BIOS (basic input/output system), as is the case with Windows 95/98 and earlier versions of DOS and Windows. Although this gives Windows XP a much finer degree of control over hardware, it also means that Windows XP works only with devices with drivers written specifically for it. This is especially true for SCSI adapters, video cards, and network interface cards.

 Don't be misled into thinking that because a device works with previous versions of Windows, it will work as well (or at all) with Windows XP. There's no substitute for systematically checking every hardware device on a system against the HCL. Windows XP does support most hardware supported by Windows 2000 and Windows Me, but there may be exceptions.

In addition, it is important to note that Microsoft's technical support policy is that any hardware that is not on the HCL is not supported for Windows XP. If you ask Microsoft for support on a system that contains elements not listed in the HCL, they may blame all problems on the incompatible hardware and not provide any technical support at all. Instead, they may refer you back to the non-HCL device's manufacturer.

Fortunately, Windows XP automatically investigates your hardware and determines whether the minimum requirements are met and whether any known incompatibilities or possible device conflicts are present in the system. So, if you check out the major components manually on the HCL, you can probably get away with letting the installation routine check the rest of the system. If you *really* want to be sure, you can employ the Windows XP Hardware Compatibility Tool to detect your hardware and declare it compatible or not. This tool can be ordered online at: *www.microsoft.com/hwtest/default.asp*. Once this page loads, click the "System Testing Home" link, then click "System Test Kits and Procedures," click "Order," and finally, click "Order the Windows XP HCT 10.0." Additionally, you can run the WINNT 32 command with the /checkupgradeonly parameter to run the Upgrade Advisor. See Chapter 2, "Installing Windows XP Professional," for more information.

Preparing a Computer to Meet Upgrade Requirements

To upgrade a computer from a previous operating system to Windows XP, you must first verify that the components of that computer (CPU, memory, storage space, video, keyboard, mouse, etc.) match or exceed the minimum system requirements defined by Microsoft. To perform this activity, follow these steps:

1. Open the computer case.

2. Make a list of all present components, including model and manufacturer.

3. For each of the hardware requirements of Windows XP, verify that the component in your computer meets or exceeds the requirements.

4. For each additional component found in the computer, verify that it is listed on the HCL.

5. Remove any non-HCL compliant devices and replace them with HCL-compliant devices.

6. Proceed with your system installation.

NETWORKING MODELS

There are two networking models to which a Windows XP Professional computer can belong: a **workgroup** or a **domain**.

Workgroup Model

Microsoft's **workgroup model** for networking distributes resources, administration, and security throughout a network. Each computer in a workgroup may be a server, a client, or both. All computers in a workgroup are equal in stature and responsibility and are therefore called peers. That's why a workgroup model network is also known as a **peer-to-peer** network.

In a workgroup, each computer also maintains its own unique set of resources, accounts, and security information. Workgroups are quite useful for groups of less than 10 computers and may be used with groups as large as 25 to 50 machines (with increasing administration difficulty). Table 1-1 lists the pros and cons of workgroup networking.

Table 1-1   Pros and Cons of Workgroup Networks

Advantages	Disadvantages
Easy-to-share resources	No centralized control of resources
Resources are distributed across all machines	No centralized account management
Little administrative overhead	No centralized administration
Simple to design	No centralized security management
Easy to implement	Inefficient for more than 20 workstations
Convenient for small groups in close proximity	Security must be configured manually
Less expensive, does not require a central server	Increased training to operate as both client and server

Domain Model

By dedicating one or more servers to the job of controlling a domain, the **domain model** adds a layer of complexity to networking. But the domain model also centralizes all shared resources and creates a single point of administrative and security control. In a domain, it is recommended that any member act exclusively either as a client or as a server. In a domain environment, servers control and manage resources, whereas clients are user computers that can request access to the resources controlled by servers.

Centralized organization makes the domain model simpler to manage from an administrative and security standpoint, because any changes made to the domain accounts database will automatically proliferate across the entire network. According to Microsoft, domains are useful for groups of 10 or more computers. Microsoft estimates that the maximum practical size of a single domain is somewhere around 25,000 computers, but also describes other multidomain models that it claims have no upper limit on size. In real-world application, 3000 computers is believed to represent a reasonable upper boundary on the number of machines in a single domain.

No matter how many computers it contains, any Windows domain requires at least one **domain controller (DC)**. The domain controller maintains the domain's Active Directory, which stores all information and relationships about users, groups, policies, computers, and resources. More than one domain controller can exist in a domain; in fact, it is recommended that you deploy a domain controller for every 300 to 400 clients. Unlike domain controllers in a Windows NT 4.0 network, all Windows 2000 and Windows .NET domain controllers are peers. All other servers and clients on a domain-based network interact with a domain controller to handle resource requests. Table 1-2 summarizes the pros and cons of the domain model.

Table 1-2   Pros and Cons of Domain Networks

Advantages	Disadvantages
Centralized resource sharing	Significant administrative effort and overhead
Centralized resource controls	Complicated designs; requires advanced planning
Centralized account management	Requires one or more powerful, expensive servers
Centralized security management	Absolute security is hard to achieve
Efficient for virtually unlimited number of workstations	Expense for domain controllers and access lags increase with network size
Users need to be trained only to use clients	Some understanding of domain networks remains necessary
Not restricted to close proximity	Larger scope requires more user documentation and training

WINDOWS XP ARCHITECTURE

The Windows XP internal organization and **architecture** deeply influence its capabilities and behavior. The following sections explain the Windows XP operating system components and its two major operating modes in detail.

Windows XP is a modular operating system. In other words, Windows XP is not built as a single large program; instead, it is composed of numerous small software elements, or modules, that cooperate to provide the system's networking and computing capabilities. Each unique function, code segment, and system control resides in a distinct module, so that no two modules share any code. This method of construction allows Windows XP to be easily amended, expanded, or patched as needed. Furthermore, the Windows XP components communicate with one another through well-defined interfaces. Therefore, even if a module's internals change (or a new version replaces an old one), as long as the interface is not altered, other components need not be aware of any such changes (except perhaps to take advantage of new functionality that was previously unavailable).

All Windows XP processes operate in one of two modes: **user mode** or **kernel mode**. A **mode** represents a certain level of system and hardware access, and is distinguished by its programming, the kinds of services and functions it is permitted to request, and the controls that are applied to its requests for system resources. Each mode contains only those specific components and capabilities that might be needed to perform the set of operations that is legal within that mode. User mode and kernel mode are explained further in the following sections. The use of modes in Windows XP is very similar to their use in UNIX and VMS, and contributes to the modularity and built-in security mechanisms of Windows XP.

Windows XP is an object-oriented operating system; in user mode, any request for a system resource ultimately becomes a request for a particular **object**. An object is a collection of attributes with associated data values, plus a set of related services that can be performed on that object. Files, folders, printers, and processes are examples of objects. Because objects may be shared or referenced by one or more processes, they have an existence independent of any particular process in the Windows XP environment. Objects are identified by type (which defines what attributes and services they support) and by instance (which defines a particular entity of a certain type—for example, there may be many objects of type "file," but only one object can have a particular unique combination of directory specification and filename). Windows XP can control access to individual objects, and it can even control which users or groups are permitted to perform particular services related to such objects.

User Mode

All user interaction with a Windows XP system occurs through one user mode process. User mode is an isolated portion of the system environment in which user applications execute. User mode permits only mediated access to Windows XP system resources. In other words, any user mode requests for objects or services must pass through the Executive Services components in the kernel mode to obtain access. In addition to supporting native 32-bit Windows **APIs (application programming interfaces)**, a variety of user mode subsystems enable Windows XP to emulate Win16 and DOS environments.

Windows XP supports three core environment subsystems: Win32, Win16, and DOS. The Win32 subsystem supports Windows XP, Windows 2000, Windows NT, and Windows 9x 32-bit applications directly. Through the emulation of virtual DOS machines (VDMs) and Windows 3.x (WOWEXEC), Windows XP supports both DOS and Windows 16-bit applications.

Each subsystem is built around an API that enables suitable Win16 or DOS applications to run by emulating their native operating systems. However, even though other subsystems may be involved in some applications, the Win32 subsystem controls the Windows XP user interface and mediates all input/output requests for all other subsystems. In that sense, it is the core interface subsystem for applications in user mode.

As part of the Windows XP user mode, the security subsystem is solely responsible for the logon process. The security subsystem works directly with key elements in the kernel mode to verify the username and password for any logon attempt, and permits only valid combinations to obtain access to a system. Here's how: During a logon attempt, the security subsystem creates an authentication package that contains the username and password provided in the Windows XP Security logon window. This authentication package is then turned over to the kernel mode, where a module called the security reference monitor (SRM)—the portion of the security subsystem that verifies usernames and passwords against the security accounts database—examines the package and compares its contents to a security accounts database. If the logon request is invalid, an incorrect logon message is returned to the user mode. For valid requests, the SRM constructs an access token, which contains a summary of the logged-on user's security access rights. The token is then returned to the security subsystem used to launch the shell process in user mode.

 To gain access to the Windows XP logon interface (as a domain client or as a workgroup/standalone system in class logon mode), the user must enter a special key combination called the Windows XP attention sequence: Ctrl+Alt+Delete are pressed simultaneously. The attention sequence invokes the Windows XP logon process; because this key sequence cannot be faked remotely, it guarantees that this process (which also resides in a protected memory area) is not subject to manipulation by would-be crackers.

Kernel Mode

The kernel mode, which is a highly privileged processing mode, refers to the inner workings, or **kernel**, of Windows XP. All components in kernel mode take execution priority over user mode subsystems and processes. In fact, some key elements within the kernel mode remain resident in memory at all times, and cannot be swapped to disk by the Virtual Memory Manager. This is the part of the operating system that handles process priority and scheduling; it's what provides the ability to preempt executing processes and schedule new processes, which is at the heart of any preemptive multi-tasking operating system such as Windows XP.

The kernel insulates hardware and core system services from direct access by user applications. That's why user applications must request any accesses to hardware or low-level resources from the kernel mode. If the request is permitted to proceed—and this mediated approach always gives Windows XP a chance to check any request against the access permitted by the access token associated with the requester—the kernel handles the request and returns any related results to the requesting user mode process. This mediated approach also helps maintain reliable control over the entire computer and protects the system from ill-behaved applications. At a finer level of detail, the kernel mode may be divided into three primary subsystems—the Executive Services, the kernel, and the hardware abstraction layer (HAL)—each of which is discussed in the following subsections.

Executive Services

The **Executive Services** are the interfaces that permit kernel and user mode subsystems to communicate. The Windows XP Executive Services consist of several modules:

- I/O Manager
- Security Reference Monitor (SRM)
- Internal Procedure Call (IPC) Manager
- Virtual Memory Manager (VMM)

- Process Manager
- Plug and Play Manager
- Power Manager
- Windows Manager
- File Systems Manager
- Object Manager
- Graphics device drivers

The I/O Manager handles all operating system input and output, including receiving requests for I/O services from applications, determining what driver is needed, and requesting that driver for the application. The I/O Manager is composed of the following components:

- *Cache Manager*—Handles disk caching for all file systems. This service works with the Virtual Memory Manager to maintain performance. It also works with the file system drivers to maintain file integrity.
- *Network drivers*—Actually a subarchitecture in and of itself, network drivers are the software components that enable communication on the network.
- *Device drivers*—32-bit and multiprocessor-compatible minidrivers that enable communication with devices.

The Security Reference Monitor compares the access rights of a user (as encoded in an access token) with the access control list (ACL) associated with an individual object. If the user has sufficient rights to honor an access request after the access token and ACL are reconciled, the requested access will be granted. Whenever a user launches a process, that process runs within the user's security context and inherits a copy of the user's security token. This means that under most circumstances, any process launched by a Windows XP user cannot obtain broader access rights than those associated with the account that launched it.

The Internal Procedure Call (IPC) Manager controls application communication with server processes such as the Win32 subsystem—the set of application services provided by the 32-bit version of Microsoft Windows. This makes applications behave as if **dynamic link library (DLL)** calls were handled directly, and helps to explain the outstanding ability of Windows XP to emulate 16-bit DOS and Windows runtime environments.

The **Virtual Memory Manager (VMM)** keeps track of the addressable memory space in the Windows XP environment. This includes both physical RAM and one or more paging files on disk, which are called **virtual memory** when used in concert. The operation of the VMM will be discussed in more detail later in this chapter.

The Process Manager primarily tracks two kernel-dispatched objects: processes and threads. It is responsible for creating and tracking processes and threads and then for deleting them (and cleaning up) after they're no longer needed.

The Plug and Play Manager handles the loading, unloading, and configuration of device drivers for Plug and Play hardware. This manager allows the hot-swapping of devices and on-the-fly reconfiguration. Additionally, if a non-Plug-and-Play device uses a Plug-and-Play supporting device driver, it can be controlled through this manager.

The Power Manager is used to monitor and control the use of power. Typically, the services offered by the Power Manager are employed on notebook computers running on batteries or in other environments in which power is an issue. Some of the power-saving features offered include hard drive and CD-ROM drive power-down, video/monitor shutdown, and peripheral disconnection.

The Windows Manager introduces a method of network-based centralized control to Windows XP. It can be used to distribute software, manage systems remotely, and provide a programming interface for third-party management software.

The File System Manager is responsible for maintaining access and control over the file systems of the Windows XP environment. The File System Manager controls file I/O transfers for all the file systems.

The Object Manager maintains object naming and security functions for all system objects; it allocates system objects, monitors their use, and removes them when they are no longer needed. The Object Manager maintains the following system objects:

- Directory objects
- ObjectType objects
- Link objects
- Event objects
- Process and thread objects
- Port objects
- File objects

The Kernel

All processes in Windows XP consist of one or more threads coordinated and scheduled by the kernel. Executive Services use the kernel to communicate with each other concerning the processes they share. The kernel runs in privileged mode along with the HAL and the other Executive Services. This means that the kernel is allowed direct access to all system resources. It cannot be paged to disk, meaning that it must run in real memory. A misbehaving kernel process can stall or crash the operating system—a primary reason why direct access to this level of system operation is not available to user mode applications.

The Hardware Abstraction Layer

The goal of the **hardware abstraction layer (HAL)** is to isolate any hardware-dependent code in order to prevent direct access to hardware. This is the only module written entirely in low-level, hardware-dependent code. It is the HAL that helps to make Windows XP scalable across multiple processors.

Memory Architecture

The memory architecture of Windows XP helps make this operating system robust, reliable, and powerful. As noted earlier, Windows XP Professional can manage as much as 4 GB of RAM.

Windows XP uses a flat (non-multidimensional) 32-bit memory model. It is based on a virtual memory, **demand paging** method that is a flat, linear address space of up to 2 GB allocated to each 32-bit application. Non-32-bit Windows applications, such as Win16 and MS-DOS, are managed similarly, except that all subsystem components, including the actual application, run within a single 2 GB address space.

The unit of memory that the VMM manipulates is called a **page**, 4 KB in size. Pages are stored to and retrieved from disk-based files called page files or paging files. These files are also used for memory reindexing and mapping to avoid allocating memory between unused contiguous space or to prevent fragmentation of physical memory.

CHAPTER SUMMARY

- This chapter introduced you to the features and architecture of Windows XP. Windows XP Professional and Windows XP Home are both related to the up-and-coming Windows .NET Server product line. Windows XP offers a distinct operating environment that boasts portability, multitasking, multithreading, multiple file systems (FAT, FAT32, NTFS), Active Directory, robust security, multiple clients, multiple processors, wide application support, large RAM and storage capacity, and a wide range of network connectivity options. Windows XP is an inherently networkable operating system with built-in connectivity solutions for NetWare and TCP/IP, allowing easy implementation on multivendor networks.

- Windows XP has specific minimum hardware requirements; the Hardware Compatibility List (HCL) lists all devices known to be compatible with Windows XP.

- Windows XP can participate in either of two networking models—workgroup or domain.

- Windows XP is based on a modular programming technique. Its main processing mechanism is divided into two modes. User mode hosts all user processes and accesses resources through the Executive Services. The kernel mode hosts all system processes and mediates all resource access. The separation of modes provides for a more stable and secure computing environment. User mode supports the application subsystems that enable Windows XP to execute DOS, WIN16, and WIN32 software. Kernel mode's Executive Services manage all operations, including I/O, security, IPC, memory, processes, Plug and Play support, power, distributed control, file systems, objects, and graphical devices.

❑ The Windows XP virtual memory model combines the use of both physical RAM and paging files into a demand paging mechanism to maximize memory use and efficiency. Windows XP is easy to use, offers new storage capabilities, provides improved Internet access, and maintains strict security.

KEY TERMS

Active Directory — A centralized resource and security management, administration, and control mechanism used to support and maintain a Windows 2000 or .NET domain. The Active Directory is hosted by domain controllers.

application programming interface (API) — A set of software routines referenced by an application to access underlying application services.

architecture — The layout of operating system components and their relationships.

client — A computer used to access network resources.

cooperative multitasking — A computing environment in which the individual application maintains control over the duration that its threads use operating time on the CPU.

demand paging — The act of requesting free pages of memory from RAM for an active application.

domain — A centralized enterprise model used in Microsoft networks.

domain controller (DC) — A computer that maintains the domain's Active Directory, which stores all information and relationships about users, groups, policies, computers, and resources.

domain model — The networking setup in which there is centralized administrative and security control. One or more servers are dedicated to the task of controlling the domain by providing access and authentication for shared domain resources to member computers.

dynamic link library (DLL) — A Microsoft Windows executable code module that is loaded on demand. Each DLL performs a unique function or small set of functions requested by applications.

Executive Services — The collection of kernel mode components designed for operating system management.

FAT (file allocation table) or **FAT16** — The file system used in versions of MS-DOS. Supported in Windows XP in its VFAT form, which adds long filenames and 4 GB file and volume sizes.

FAT32 — The 32-bit enhanced version of FAT introduced by Windows 95 OSR2 that expands the file and volume size of FAT to 32 GB. FAT32 is supported by Windows XP.

hardware abstraction layer (HAL) — One of the few components of the Windows XP architecture that is written in hardware-dependent code. It is designed to protect hardware resources.

Hardware Compatibility List (HCL) — Microsoft's updated list of supported hardware for Windows XP.

kernel — The core of the Microsoft Windows XP operating system. It is designed to facilitate all activity within the Executive Services.

kernel mode — The level where objects can be manipulated only by threads directly from an application subsystem.

mode — A programming and operational separation of components, functions, and services.

MS-DOS — One of the most popular character-based operating systems for personal computers. Many DOS concepts are still in use by modern operating systems.

multiprocessing — The ability to distribute threads among multiple CPUs on the same system.

multitasking — The ability to run more than one program at the same time.

multithreading — The ability of an operating system and hardware to execute multiple pieces of code (or threads) from a single application simultaneously.

New Technology File System (NTFS) — The high-performance file system supported by Windows XP that offers file-level security, encryption, compression, auditing, and more. Supports volumes up to 16 exabytes theoretically, but Microsoft recommends volumes not exceed 2 terabytes.

NWLink — Microsoft's implementation of Novell's IPX/SPX protocol, used for Microsoft Networking or for facilitating connectivity with Novell networks.

object — A collection of data and/or abilities of a service that can be shared and used by one or more processes.

operating system (OS) — Software designed to work directly with hardware to provide a computing environment within which production and entertainment software can execute, and which creates a user interface.

page — An individual unit of memory that the Virtual Memory Manager manipulates (moves from RAM to paging file and vice versa).

peer-to-peer — A type of networking in which each computer can be a client to other computers and act as a server as well.

Plug and Play — The ability of Windows XP to recognize hardware, automatically install drivers, and perform configuration changes on the fly.

preemptive multitasking — A computing environment in which the operating system maintains control over the duration of operating time any thread (a single process of an application) is granted on the CPU.

process — A collection of one or more threads.

server — The networked computer that responds to client requests for network resources.

TCP/IP (Transmission Control Protocol/Internet Protocol) — A suite of protocols evolved from the Department of Defense's ARPANet. It is used for connectivity in LANs as well as the Internet.

thread — The most basic unit of programming code that can be scheduled for execution.

1

user mode — The area in which private user applications and their respective subsystems lie.

virtual memory — A Windows XP kernel service that stores memory pages that are not currently in use by the system in a paging file. This frees up memory for other uses. Virtual memory also hides the swapping of memory from applications and higher-level services.

Virtual Memory Manager (VMM) — The part of the operating system that handles process priority and scheduling, providing the ability to preempt executing processes and schedule new processes.

Win16 — The subsystem in Windows XP that allows for the support of 16-bit Windows applications.

Win32 — The main 32-bit subsystem used by Win32 applications and other application subsystems.

workgroup — A networking scheme in which resources, administration, and security are distributed throughout the network.

workgroup model — The networking setup in which users are managed jointly through the use of workgroups to which users are assigned.

REVIEW QUESTIONS

1. Which of the following application environments does Windows XP support as long as kernel mode/user mode restrictions are maintained?

   a. PICK

   b. SunOS

   c. OS/2

   d. X-Windows

   e. MS-DOS

2. Windows XP supports _____ of memory and _____ of disk space.

3. Which of the following are kernel mode components in Windows XP? (Choose all that apply.)

   a. Virtual DOS machines

   b. Security Reference Monitor

   c. hardware abstraction layer

   d. Win16 subsystem

4. Windows XP supports only cooperative multitasking. True or False?

5. Windows XP supports the HPFS file system. True or False?

6. Windows XP has inherent support for facilitating connectivity to which of the following? (Choose all that apply.)

   a. Novell NetWare

   b. Solaris printers

   c. Linux

   d. TCP/IP networks

7. Memory pages are stored in units of:

   a. 2 KB

   b. 4 KB

   c. 16 KB

   d. 64 KB

8. Windows XP Professional is the client product that came out of the Whistler development project. What is the server product that will come out of this development project?

   a. Windows XP Server

   b. Windows Advanced Server

   c. Windows 2000 Server

   d. Windows .NET Server

9. If you want users to share resources, but have no concern for local security on the system, which operating system would be your best choice?

   a. Windows 98

   b. Windows NT Workstation

   c. Windows XP Professional

   d. Windows 2000 Server

10. Which of these configuration specifications will allow for the installation of Windows XP Professional? (Choose all that apply.)

    a. Intel 233 MHz Pentium, 128 MB of RAM, 2 GB disk space

    b. Compaq Alpha, 48 MB of RAM, 2 GB disk space

    c. Intel 486DX/66, 16 MB of RAM, 800 MB disk space

    d. Intel 133 MHz Pentium, 24 MB of RAM, 2 GB disk space

11. A dual-boot computer hosts both Windows 98 and Windows XP Professional. You need to download an 8 GB datafile that will be used by both operating systems. What file system should you use to format the host volume?

    a. FAT

    b. FAT32

    c. NTFS

1

12. You are setting up a computer for the purpose of sharing files. Each user must have specific levels of access based on their identity. You also want the security system to employ encryption authentication to verify the identity of both the server and client before data transfer can occur. Which operating system would be the most effective solution?

   a. Windows 98

   b. Windows XP Professional

   c. Windows NT Workstation

   d. Windows XP Home

13. The two networking models supported in Windows XP are _____ and _____.

14. The three file systems supported in Windows XP are _____, _____, and _____.

15. When a user presses the Ctrl+Alt+Delete key combination in Windows XP after booting, what happens?

   a. The computer reboots.

   b. The logon screen appears.

   c. A "blue screen of death" occurs.

   d. A command prompt appears.

16. Windows XP runs on top of DOS. True or False?

17. Which of the following are required to install Windows XP on Intel-based computers?

   a. an SCSI CD-ROM drive

   b. a tape backup device

   c. a network interface card

   d. none of the above

18. Which of the following new features of Windows XP are system recovery mechanisms?

   a. ASR

   b. Autoplay

   c. System Restore

   d. Device driver rollback

19. Administrators desiring a centralized model of resource management should consider the _____ network model.

   a. workgroup

   b. domain

20. All direct access to hardware is mediated by which component?

    a. kernel

    b. Win32 subsystem

    c. hardware abstraction layer

    d. Executive Services

21. Windows XP Professional natively supports _____ processors.

    a. 1

    b. 2

    c. 4

    d. 32

22. Which of the following is a disadvantage of workgroup networking?

    a. Resources are distributed across all machines

    b. No centralized security management

    c. Efficient for virtually unlimited workstations

    d. Requires one or more powerful, expensive servers

23. Which of the following is an advantage of domain networking?

    a. Absolute security is hard to achieve

    b. Simple to design

    c. Centralized resource controls

    d. Inefficient for more than 20 workstations

24. When a DOS application that is used to manipulate files on a hard drive is launched on a Windows XP Professional system, in what mode does the process execute?

    a. user

    b. kernel

    c. protected

    d. IPC

25. Windows XP boasts which of the following abilities?

    a. burn CDs

    b. submit images for online printing

    c. video conference over the Internet

    d. create home movies

HANDS-ON PROJECTS

Project 1-1

To explore the desktop and Start menu:

1. Boot and log on to a Windows XP Professional system (which is a domain client or configured for Classic logon) by pressing **Ctrl+Alt+Delete**, then providing a valid username and password.

2. Notice the lack of icons on the desktop.

3. Double-click the **Recycle Bin**. This reveals all items that have been deleted but are still recoverable.

4. Select **File | Close**.

5. Click the **Start** button on the taskbar.

6. Notice the items that occur in the Start menu by default: Internet, E-mail, My Documents, My Recent Documents, My Pictures, My Music, My Computer, Control Panel, Printers and Faxes, Help and Support, Search, Run, Log Off, and Turn Off Computer.

7. Click **Turn Off Computer**. This reveals a dialog box where you can select to hibernate, turn off the computer, restart the computer, or cancel.

8. Click **Cancel**.

9. Select **Start | Run**. This reveals the Run dialog box, where you can enter or browse to a path and filename to launch.

10. Click **Cancel**.

11. Select **Start | Help and Support**. This opens the Help and Support Center interface. Explore this interface.

12. Close the Help system by clicking the **X** button in the upper-right corner of the dialog box.

13. Select **Start | Search**. This opens a menu with many selections: Each of these is an interface used to locate different types of objects, files, people, etc.

14. Select **File | Close**.

15. Select **Start | My Recent Documents**. This opens a menu that lists the most recently accessed documents or files.

16. Select **Start | All Programs**. This opens the first of several levels of menus in which all of the applications, tools, and utilities of the system are organized for easy access. Explore this multilevel menu.

17. Select **Start | My Documents**. This reveals the default storage location for your personal documents, faxes, and pictures.

18. Select **File | Close**.

19. Select **Start | My Computer**. This reveals a list of all drives present on the system, plus a link to the Control Panel.

20. Select **File | Close**.

Project 1-2

To view the Windows XP administration tools:

1. Select **Start | Control Panel**. This opens the Control Panel window.

2. If Control Panel is in category mode, click **Switch to Classic View**.

3. Double-click the **Date and Time** applet. This reveals the Date and Time interface, where the current time and date can be changed (see Chapter 3 for a complete explanation of this applet).

4. Click **Cancel**.

5. Double-click the **Fonts** applet. This reveals a list of all the fonts currently present on the system.

6. Click **Back** in the button bar to return to the Control Panel.

7. Double-click **Administrative Tools**. This reveals all of the administrative tools for Windows XP.

8. Double-click **Computer Management**. This opens an MMC console, where you can access information on a wide range of components. Explore this interface but be careful not to make any changes.

9. Close Computer Management by clicking the **X** in the upper-right corner of the window.

10. Close the Control Panel by selecting **File | Close**.

Project 1-3

To explore Task Manager:

1. Right-click over a blank area of the taskbar. This reveals a menu. Select **Task Manager** from the menu.

2. Take a look at the **Applications** tab of Task Manager. This lists all applications currently active in user mode.

1

3. Click the **Processes** tab of Task Manager. This lists all processes currently active. It also lists details about each process, such as its process ID, its CPU usage percentage per second, and its total CPU execution time.

4. Click the **Performance** tab of Task Manager. This tab shows graphs detailing the current and historical use of the CPU and memory. This tab also lists details about memory consumption, threads, and handles.

5. Click the **View** menu, then click **Show Kernel Times**. This alters the graphs so activities of the kernel mode are shown in red, and activities of the user mode are shown in green.

6. After watching this interface for a while, close it by selecting **File | Exit Task Manager** from the menu.

Project 1-4

To customize the desktop:

1. Right-click a blank area of the desktop.

2. Select **New | Shortcut** from the menu.

3. Click **Browse** in the window that appears.

4. Locate and select **Notepad.exe** in the main Windows XP directory (the default is WINDOWS). Click **OK**.

5. Click **Next**.

6. Click **Finish**. A shortcut to Notepad now appears on the desktop.

7. Right-click over a blank area of the desktop.

8. Select **Arrange Icons By**, then **Auto Arrange**.

9. Notice that the icons on the desktop have repositioned themselves in a uniform pattern.

10. **Right-click** over a blank area of the desktop.

11. Select **Properties**.

12. On the **Desktop** tab, take note of the current selection, then select an item from the list of background images.

13. Click **OK**.

14. To restore the desktop to its original settings, repeat steps 10 through 13 using the original setting. Delete the shortcut you created by selecting it and pressing the **Delete** key, then confirm the deletion.

CASE PROJECTS

1. You are planning a network in which users need to have a centralized location, where discretionary access control is a necessity. This will be an environment in which consistency is a must.

   Required Result:

   ❐ All users must be able to access the server from any computer within the network through a single logon.

   Optional Desired Results:

   ❐ Users must also be required to log on before accessing anything on their local machine.

   ❐ Users will have the exact same desktop GUI.

   Proposed Solution:

   ❐ Install Windows 2000 Server as the server platform. Establish a Windows domain. On half of the users' desktops install Windows 98, and on the other half install Windows XP Professional. Have all computers configured as part of the Windows domain.

   Which results does the proposed solution produce? Why?

   a. The proposed solution produces the required result and produces both of the optional desired results.

   b. The proposed solution produces the required result but only one of the optional desired results.

   c. The proposed solution produces the required result but neither of the optional desired results.

   d. The proposed solution does not produce the required result.

2. You have been instructed to evaluate the status of the network environment at Site A. Your goal is to evaluate the current network and determine, first of all, whether upgrading is necessary. If so, the next step is to determine which operating system will be the migration choice: Windows XP Professional or Windows 98. Finally, determine what steps are necessary before the migration can proceed.

Site A has 220 computers currently running Windows 3.1. They are running all 16-bit applications from the DOS and Windows environments. They plan on migrating to Microsoft Office 2000. Each computer has the following hardware configuration:

❑ Intel 486 DX4/100

❑ 8 MB of RAM

❑ 540 MB hard drive

❑ NIC (network interface card)

❑ VGA monitor

Users will not be allowed to share files at the desktop. They will not roam from computer to computer, so all of their files can be stored locally on their own computers.

Which migration path makes the most sense? Why?

a. No migration

b. Windows XP Professional

c. Windows 98

If migration to Windows XP Professional is necessary, what must be done to establish optimum but cost-effective performance?

2

INSTALLING WINDOWS XP PROFESSIONAL

After reading this chapter and completing the exercises, you will be able to:

♦ Understand how to install and upgrade Windows XP Professional

♦ Plan an installation or upgrade

♦ Install Windows XP using a CD-ROM or the network

♦ Understand the installation process

♦ Describe the advanced installation options

♦ Remove Windows XP Professional

A number of issues must be considered when installing any operating system (OS), and Windows XP Professional is no exception. This chapter details the various steps that must be taken to get Windows XP up and running. It also examines such issues as whether to perform a fresh installation or to upgrade from an earlier version. It covers the various methods used to install Windows XP (CD-ROM or network-based), as well as a few things to watch out for along the way.

Windows XP has broader hardware support than Windows 2000, but you must still verify that your hardware is included in the Hardware Compatibility List (HCL), which can be downloaded from Microsoft's Web site at *www.microsoft.com/hcl*. Before installing Windows XP Professional, you must first ensure that your computer meets the minimum requirements (and, preferably, the recommended requirements), as detailed in Chapter 1, "Introduction to Windows XP Professional," and that all hardware to be used with Windows XP is listed on the HCL.

UPGRADING VERSUS INSTALLING

When installing Windows XP Professional, you have a choice between upgrading an existing installation or performing a completely clean installation. Upgrading is an option when you have a version of Windows already installed and want to preserve some settings and other information from the previous installation, including password files, desktop settings, and general configuration. A **clean installation** installs a completely new version of Windows XP Professional without regard to any existing files or settings.

Windows XP Professional can be installed as an **upgrade** over an existing installation of the following operating systems:

- Windows 95 OSR2, Windows 98, Windows 98 SE, and Windows Me

- Windows NT 4.0 Workstation (with Service Pack 6 or later)

- Windows 2000 Professional (with any service packs)

- Windows XP Home

 You can upgrade from Windows 95. However, because Microsoft no longer supports Windows 95, it is effectively off their radar. The upgrade won't retain as much information as an upgrade from Windows 98, but it is possible.

To migrate from any other OS not included in this list requires a full or clean installation. This means that Windows NT Server, Windows 2000 Server, and Windows 3.1 are "upgraded" only by a clean installation that overwrites them instead of retaining data.

Typically, you'd select an upgrade installation when you want to retain your existing desktop, system settings, and network configuration. If you are having problems with your existing OS and the environmental settings are not that important, a clean installation is a better option. A clean or complete installation can be performed onto a system with a blank hard drive, over an existing OS, or in such a way as to create a multi-boot system. A **multi-boot system** is a computer that hosts two or more operating systems that can be booted to by selecting one from a boot menu or boot manager each time the computer is powered up.

The process of upgrading to Windows XP Professional from Windows 2000 Professional is fairly straightforward, having been designed to retain as many of the existing configuration and software settings as possible. The only items that will not be retained are system utilities or drivers specific to the existing OS that are updated or removed for Windows XP. To upgrade, launch **WINNT32** from the \I386 folder on the CD, then select the upgrade option from the pull-down list (see Figure 2-1). Try Hands-on Project 2-5 to practice upgrading.

Figure 2-1   Choosing the upgrade option from the Windows Setup Wizard

BOOTING MULTIPLE OPERATING SYSTEMS

It is possible to install more than one OS on the same computer, allowing you to choose the OS to be used at boot time. Unless you deliberately overwrite, or **format**, the **partition** or volume (a space set aside on a disk and assigned a drive letter that can occupy all or part of the disk) where another OS is located, installing Windows XP Professional will not affect the other OS.

Windows XP can be dual-booted with any Microsoft OS and even OS/2. You can create a **dual-boot system** with Windows XP and other operating systems, such as Linux. However, these operating systems require third-party boot and partition managers such as Partition Magic from PowerQuest (*www.powerquest.com*) or System Commander from V Communications (*www.v-com.com*).

In most cases (when third-party multi-boot software is not used), you'll want to install Windows XP on a system with an existing OS rather than installing Windows XP before another OS. This enables the Windows XP Setup routine to configure the boot loader properly. The **boot loader** is the software that shows all currently available operating systems and permits the user to choose which one should be booted through a menu. At boot time, you can choose the OS you want to run, as shown in Figure 2-2.

Startup and Recovery

The Startup and Recovery Options dialog box (see Figure 3-15) allows you to define system startup parameters and specify how STOP errors are handled. You access this dialog box by clicking the Settings button under the Startup and Recovery heading on the Advanced tab of the System applet. Startup controls are found the region of this window labeled System startup and are used to set the default operating system and selection timer for the boot menu. The default is 30 seconds, but is often reduced to 5 or 10 seconds to speed system startup (an alternative is to edit the boot.ini file's timeout= value to 5 or 10, which has the same effect).

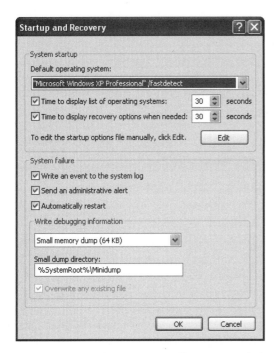

Figure 3-15   The Startup and Recovery dialog box

The options in the area labeled System failure in this window are a bit more esoteric. They provide special controls to deal with an outright Windows XP system crash. When the whole system halts due to a STOP error, the entire contents of the computer's virtual memory are dumped to a .DMP file (which resides in the *%systemroot%*\minidump or \windows\minidump folder, by default). Although this dump file is of little use to most users and can usually be discarded, the information it contains can be invaluable when debugging system or application problems. There are also options for writing an event to the system log, sending administrative alerts, and rebooting the system automatically.

Environmental Variables

The Environment Variables dialog box is accessed by clicking the Environment Variables button on the Advanced tab of the System applet. The top pane of the tab controls settings for system-wide environment variables; the bottom pane controls local user environment variables. Only a local user who is currently logged on can set variables on this tab. These variables are used to control how Windows XP operates, particularly how older 16-bit Windows or DOS programs behave within Virtual DOS Machines (VDMs), within which they must run in the Windows XP environment.

Error Reporting

Microsoft has provided Windows XP the ability to report errors regarding the OS and installed applications. Whenever a system or application error occurs and Internet access is available, an anonymous error report is sent to Microsoft. Error reporting is enabled by default. You can select to report OS and/or program errors. You can even select which programs to report. You reach this tool by clicking the Error Reporting button on the Advanced tab of the System applet.

 This feature has no immediate benefits or drawbacks for you, but it can help Microsoft develop fixes and patches for Windows XP and possibly improve its future OS products.

Taskbar and Start Menu

The Taskbar and Start Menu applet is the same properties dialog box accessed by right-clicking over the Start button and selecting the Properties command from the pop-up menu. The Taskbar tab controls taskbar appearance (lock, auto-hide, keep on top, group similar, and show quick launch) and notification area settings (show clock, hide inactive Notification Area icons). The Customize button allows you to define whether specific system tray icons disappear when inactive, remain hidden, or always display. The Start Menu tab is used to select from the Windows XP new stylized Start menu or the Classic Start menu (from Windows 2000). The Customize button for each of these options is used to configure additional settings, such as large/small icons, number of recently accessed programs to display, Internet and e-mail shortcuts, and Start menu items such as link, menu, or hidden.

User Accounts

The User Accounts applet is used to create and manage local user accounts, passwords, and .NET passports, to access the Local Users and Groups tool (part of Computer Management from Administrative Tools), and to specify whether Ctrl+Alt+Delete is required to log on. This tool is discussed in Chapter 5.

MICROSOFT MANAGEMENT CONSOLE OVERVIEW

The **Microsoft Management Console (MMC)** is a graphical interface shell. The MMC provides a structured environment for consoles, **snap-ins**, and extensions that offer controls over services and objects. A **console** is like a document window; one or more consoles can be loaded into the MMC. Each console can host one or more snap-ins. A snap-in is a component that adds control mechanisms to the MMC console for a specific service or object. Each snap-in can support one or more extensions (i.e., specialized tools). Each snap-in (and any of its related extensions) is designed to manipulate a specific service or type of object in the Windows XP local, remote, domain, or Active Directory environment. For example, the Users and Groups snap-in is used to manage local users and groups. The MMC does not provide any management capabilities itself; it merely provides the interface mechanism and environment for system and object controls.

The MMC architecture was created to simplify administration of the Windows networking environment. Versions of the MMC are included with IIS 4.0 and other products deployed on Windows 98 and Windows NT. However, MMC was not fully realized until the final release of Windows 2000 and has been included as a core element of Windows XP.

The most beneficial feature of the MMC is its flexibility. The MMC provides a general-purpose framework that Microsoft has used to consolidate systems management facilities of all kinds, and that third parties often use to incorporate snap-ins for managing their tools as well. It provides a consistent interface for all management tools, thereby enhancing usability and shortening the learning curve when new snap-ins are added. Additionally, multiple snap-ins can be combined in a custom administration layout to suit each administrator's particular needs or responsibilities. No other management tool offers such a wide range of customization.

MMC settings and layout can be stored as an .msc file, allowing your custom configurations of snap-ins and extensions to be re-used later on the same computer or transferred to other systems. The .msc file contains all of the windows currently open in the MMC. These files can be moved from system to system with ease. In addition, you can assign, grant, or restrict access to the .msc files (and the controls they offer) through system policies based on user, group, or computer. Thus, you can selectively and securely assign administrative tasks to non-administrative users.

The MMC Console

The MMC console itself is a fairly straightforward interface. To open the MMC without a snap-in, just execute MMC from the Start|Run command. There are really only two parts to the main MMC console: the main menu bar and the console window display area. The main menu bar contains the Console, Window, and Help drop-down menus and a movable mini-icon bar with one-click shortcuts to common activities

(New, Open, Save, and New Windows). The console display area functions just like any other Windows application that supports multiple document windows.

Consoles have three important parts (see Figure 3-16): console menu bar, console tree, and details pane. The console menu bar contains the Action and View menus, the contents of which change based on the snap-ins and extensions present and active in the console. The console menu bar also contains a mini-icon toolbar of one-click shortcuts to common functions found in the Action and View menus. The console tree is the left pane or division of the console display area, where the loaded snap-ins and extensions are listed, along with context selections (such as computers, domains, users, divisions, etc.). The details pane is the right pane or division of the console display area, where the details associated with the active item from the console tree are displayed.

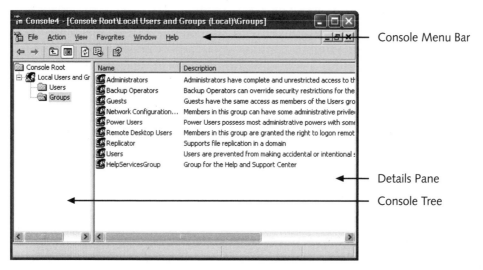

Figure 3-16   The parts of the Microsoft Management Console

Snap-Ins

Snap-ins are the components added into a console that actually perform the actions on services or objects. There are two types of snap-ins: stand-alone snap-ins and extension snap-ins. Stand-alone snap-ins are typically referred to simply as snap-ins. They provide the main functions for system administration and control; Windows XP Professional is equipped with a set of snap-ins. The extension snap-ins add functionality to a stand-alone snap-in. A single extension can be used on any snap-in with similar service/object context. Multiple extensions can be present for a single snap-in. For example, the Computer Management snap-in can be extended by the Event Viewer and Device Manager extensions.

Once you've added and configured a console's snap-ins (see later this chapter), you can save the console to an .msc file in one of four formats. The first and default format is

Author Mode, which allows users to add and remove snap-ins, create new windows, view the entire console tree, and save new versions of the console. The other three formats are all **User Mode**. Intended for end-users, these formats prevent adding or removing snap-ins or re-saving the console file. The three types of User Mode formats are: Full Access; Delegated Access, Multiple Windows; and Delegated Access, Single Window. Full Access allows users to create new windows and view the entire console tree. The Delegated Access formats prevent users from viewing portions of the console tree. The Multiple Windows version allow users to create new windows but not close existing windows, whereas the Single Window allows viewing of only one window. The format of the .msc file is changed through the Console | Options command.

Using the MMC

Windows XP is equipped with several preconfigured consoles designed to offer administrative control over your system. These tools are found mainly in Administrative Tools (see following section), a folder within the Control Panel, though it also can appear on the Start menu if configured through the Taskbar and Start Menu applet.

You can utilize all of the snap-ins used to create the Administrative Tools to create your own custom consoles. In addition to these predefined consoles, installing other services or applications can add other predefined consoles for custom or unique console controls.

Creating custom consoles is simple. Just launch the MMC through the Start | Run command. Then use the Add or Remove Snap-In command from the Console menu to open the Add or Remove Snap-in dialog box. Click on the Add button to view the Add Standalone Snap-in dialog box (refer to Figure 3-2 earlier in this chapter). Select the snap-in, and click Add. If the snap-in supports both local and remote operation, you'll be prompted to indicate whether to pull data locally or from a remote system.

Some snap-ins can serve as stand-alone snap-ins or as extensions to another snap-in. For example, Device Manager and Event Viewer can be configured to stand alone or as extensions of Computer Management. Once you've added one or more snap-ins (i.e., they appear in the list on the Add or Remove Snap-In dialog box), you can add or modify extensions by selecting the Extension tab.

Administrative Tools

The Administrative Tools are a collection of system configuration utilities that Microsoft deemed powerful and dangerous enough to separate from the Control Panel applets. You must have administrative privileges to use the seven Administrative Tools on Windows XP Professional: Component Services, Data Sources (ODBC), Event Viewer, Local Security Policy, Performance, Services, and Computer Management.

Component Services is a tool used mainly by application developers. However, this tool can also be used by system administrators who need to custom-configure a system for a specific application. This tool is used to administer COM and COM+ applications. If you want to explore the uses of this tool, consult the online Help material and the *Microsoft Windows .NET Server Resource Kit*.

Data Sources (ODBC) is a tool used configure the OS to interact with various database management systems, such as SQL Server or FoxPro. This tool is often used in applications designed for enterprise-wide or Web-based deployments; if your application can already access data from a SQL server, proper configuration of the ODBC Source Administrator will let it access data from a FoxPro database as well. To explore the uses of this tool, consult the online Help material and the *Microsoft Windows .NET Server Resource Kit*.

The Event Viewer is used to view system messages regarding the failure and/or success of various key occurrences within the Windows XP environment. Details of system errors, security issues, and application activities are recorded in the logs viewed through the Event Viewer. This tool is discussed in Chapter 10, "Performance Tuning."

Local Security Policy is used to configure local security settings for a system. It is similar to, but more specific than, a group policy for a domain, site, or OU. This tool is discussed on Chapter 6, "Windows XP Security and Access Controls."

The Performance item is used to access System Monitor and the Performance Logs and Alerts tool. This is discussed in Chapter 10, "Performance Tuning."

Services is used for stopping and starting services and configuring the startup parameters for services (such as whether or not to launch when the system starts, whether to employ a user account security context to launch the service, etc.). There is a Hands-on Project for using this tool in Chapter 15, "Troubleshooting Windows XP."

Computer Management (see Figure 3-17) is an MMC console that serves as a common troubleshooting and administration interface for several tools. The Computer Management console is divided into three sections: System Tools, Storage, and Services and Applications.

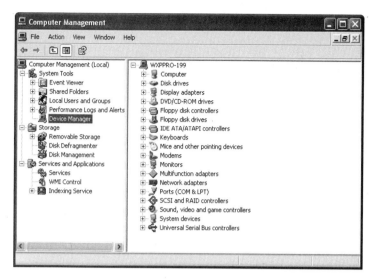

Figure 3-17   Computer Management, with Device Manager selected

The System Tools section contains five tools:

- *Event Viewer*—Described earlier in this chapter. This tool is discussed in Chapter 10 and Chapter 15.

- *Shared Folders*—Used to view the shared folders on the local system. This interface shows hidden shares, current sessions, and open files. This tool also allows you to view and alter the share configuration settings of user limit, caching, and permissions.

- *Local Users and Groups*—Used to create and manage local user accounts and groups. Details on use, examples, and Hands-on Projects for this tool are found in Chapter 5.

- *Performance Logs and Alerts*—Another means to access the Performance monitoring tool of Windows XP. The use of this tool in troubleshooting is rather tedious and complex (see Chapter 10 for examples and Hands-on Projects involving this tool).

- *Device Manager*—Used to view and alter current hardware configurations of all existing devices. See the description of the Device Manager earlier in this chapter.

The Storage section of Computer Management has three tools for storage device administration. Details on use, examples, and Hands-on Projects for these tools are found in Chapter 4.

- *Removable Storage*—Used to manage removable media such as floppy disks, tapes, and Zip drives.

- *Disk Defragmenter*—Used to improve the layout of stored data on drives by reassembling fragmented files and aggregating unused space.

- *Disk Management*—Used to view and alter the partitioning and volume configuration of hard drives.

The Services and Applications section contains management controls for various installed and active services and applications. The actual contents of this section depend on what is installed on your system. Some of the common controls on a Windows XP Professional system include:

- *Indexing Service*—Used to define the corpus (collection of documents indexed for searching) for Indexing Service. For information on using this tool, consult the *Microsoft Windows .NET Server Resource Kit.*

- *WMI Control*—Used to configure Windows Management Instrumentation (WMI).

- *Services*—See the description of Services earlier in this chapter. This tool is discussed in Chapter 15.

PCMCIA OR PC CARDS

As a fully Plug and Play-compatible operating system, Windows XP includes support for **PCMCIA** or **PC Cards**. These are credit card-sized devices that plug into a slit port found on most notebooks and some desktop computers. The plug-in operation is very similar to inserting a cartridge into a game. Most computers that support PC Cards have two slots, allowing up to two additional devices to be added to the system. PC Cards can be just about any device, including memory expansions, SCSI cards, NICs, modems, or proprietary peripheral interfaces.

Card services are installed automatically when Windows XP is installed onto a HAL-supported notebook or portable computer (or a desktop computer with a PC Card slot device). Once installed, most of the tasks and processes required to manage and enable PC Card support are handled automatically by Windows XP. Unlike Windows NT and Windows 95/98, Windows XP does not have a PC Card (or PCMCIA) applet. Your only real control is through the Unplug or Eject Hardware icon in the Notification Area. Double-click this icon to instruct the system to stop using and release control of the PC Card device so it can be removed. In most cases, it is a good idea to use this tool to stop the driver of a particular device before unplugging it from the system. This helps prevent system errors and data loss by allowing the system to finish using the device, clear all related buffers, and disable the drivers and dependent services. Once a new card is reinserted, the system detects and enables it automatically.

3

Chapter Summary

❏ In this chapter, you learned about the various applets and tools found in the Control Panel and Administrative Tools. The Accessibility Options applet is used to configure special interface enhancements for the visual-, audio-, or movement-impaired user. The Add Hardware applet is used to install and troubleshoot devices. The Add or Remove Programs applet is used to change or remove applications, install new applications, or change installed Windows components. The Administrative Tools applet is used to access the administrative tools. The Date and Time applet is used to set calendar date, clock time, and time zone. The Display applet is used to configure the display interface features. The Folder Options applet is used to configure folder features. The Fonts applet is used to manage fonts. The Game Controllers applet is used to install and configure gaming devices. The Internet Options applet is used to configure Internet access for Internet Explorer. The Keyboard and Mouse applets are used to configure these two device types. The Network Connections applet is a link to the configuration interface for all network connections. The Phone and Modem Options applet is used to configure RAS and TAPI devices. The Power Options applet is used to configure power saving features. The Printers and Faxes applet is used to install and configure printers and faxes. The Regional and Language Options applet is used to set location-specific language items. The Scanners and Cameras applet is used to configure imaging devices. The Scheduled Tasks applet is used to automate tasks. The Sounds and Audio Devices applet is used to configure audio schemes. The Speech applet configures text-to-speech functionality. The System applet is used to configure several aspects of the operating system, including virtual memory, environmental variables, and system startup parameters. The Taskbar and Start Menu applet is used to configure how the taskbar and Start menu operate. The User Accounts applet is used to manage local users and groups.

❏ This chapter also discussed the Microsoft Management Console and the Administrative Tools. The Component Services utility configures the system for COM usage. The Data Sources (ODBC) utility configures interaction with database management systems. The Local Security Policy controls local security settings. The Services utility manages services. The Event Viewer is used to view the system's log files. The Performance item accesses the System Monitor and Performance Logs and Alerts utilities. Computer Management is a collective interface for several tools used for system management and troubleshooting. This chapter also discussed the processes of installing hardware, using hardware profiles, and dealing with PC Cards.

Key Terms

applet — A tool or utility found in the Control Panel that typically has a single focused purpose or function.

Author Mode — The condition of a console that allows users to add and remove snap-ins, create new windows, view the entire console tree, and save new versions of the console.

console — The collection of snap-ins and extensions saved as an .msc file loaded into the MMC that offers administrative controls.

Control Panel — The collection of tools and utilities (called applets) within Windows, where most system- and hardware-level installation and configuration take place.

device — A physical component, either internal or external to the computer, that is used to perform a specific function. Devices include hard drives, video cards, network interface cards, printers, etc.

DMA (Direct Memory Access) — A channel used by a hardware device to access memory directly, i.e., bypassing the CPU. Windows XP supports eight DMA channels, numbered 0 to 7.

driver — A software element that is used by an operating system to control a device. Drivers are usually device-specific.

hardware profile — A collection of custom device settings used on computers with changing physical components.

input locale — A combination language and keyboard layout used to define how data is entered into a computer.

I/O port — The section of memory used by the hardware to communicate with the operating system. When an IRQ is used, the system checks the I/O port memory area for additional information about what function is needed by the device. The I/O port is represented by a hexadecimal number.

IRQ (interrupt request) — The interrupt request level that is used to halt CPU operation in favor of the device. Windows supports 16 interrupts, namely IRQ 0 to 15.

Microsoft Management Console (MMC) — The standardized interface into which consoles, snap-ins, and extensions are loaded to perform administrative tasks.

PC Cards — The modern name of the PCMCIA technology. PC Cards are credit card-sized devices typically used to expand the functionality of notebook or portable computers.

PCMCIA — The older name for the technology now called PC Cards. PCMCIA stands for Personal Computer Memory Card International Association.

Plug and Play (PnP) — A technology that allows an operating system to inspect and identify a device, install the correct driver, and enable the device, all without user interaction. Plug and Play simplifies the adding and removing of hardware and can often offer on-the-fly reconfiguration of devices without rebooting.

Scheduled Tasks — The component of Windows XP used to automate the execution or launch of programs and batch files based on time and system conditions.

service — A software element used by the operating system to perform a function. Services include offering resources over the network, accessing resources over the network, print spooling, etc.

snap-in — A component that adds control mechanisms to a console for a specific service or object, thereby extending the functionality of that console (as with snap-ins for the MMC).

User Mode — The condition of a console that prevents adding or removing snap-ins or re-saving the console file.

virtual memory — The combination of physical RAM and pagefile space used by the operating system to enlarge usable memory for processes.

Wizard — A tool or utility that has an interactive step-by-step guide to walk you through a complex or detailed configuration process.

3

REVIEW QUESTIONS

1. Which of the following tools is the primary interface through which most Windows XP administration tasks are performed?

   a. Control Panel

   b. Computer Management

   c. Scheduled Tasks

   d. My Computer

2. The MMC offers native administration controls without snap-ins. True or False?

3. In the context of the MMC, what are extensions used for? (Choose all that apply.)

   a. Alter the display of the MMC

   b. To restrict controls based on user accounts

   c. To add additional functionality to stand-alone snap-ins

   d. To allow remote administration of services and objects

4. The MMC can be used to manipulate services and objects on local and remote systems. True or False?

5. Which .msc mode allows users to create new windows but prevents them from viewing some parts of the console tree? (Choose all that apply.)

   a. Author Mode

   b. User Mode: Full Access

   c. User Mode: Delegated Access, Multiple Windows

   d. User Mode: Delegated Access, Single Window

6. Which of the following are tools found in the Administrative Tools section of the Control Panel? (Choose all that apply.)

   a. Computer Management

   b. My Computer

   c. Event Viewer

   d. Utility Manager

7. What is the best tool in Windows XP for automating a recurring task?

   a. AT

   b. CRON

   c. Scheduled Tasks

   d. Event Viewer

8. Which of the following can trigger the launch of an automated event? (Choose all that apply.)

   a. User logon

   b. System idle

   c. Exact time

   d. System startup

9. Automated tasks can be halted when the system switches to battery power. True or False?

10. Which applet is used to configure ToggleKeys and SoundSentry?

    a. Sound and Multimedia

    b. Keyboard

    c. Accessibility Options

    d. System

11. If you want to use the numeric keypad to control the mouse cursor movement, what applet must you open to configure this option?

    a. Sound and Multimedia

    b. Keyboard

    c. Accessibility Options

    d. System

12. The Add Hardware applet can be used to perform which of the following actions? (Choose all that apply.)

    a. Troubleshoot an existing device

    b. Disable a PC Card driver before it is removed

    c. Configure multiple display layout

    d. Install and uninstall drivers for new hardware already present in a Windows XP system

13. Plug and Play devices, although automatically detected by the operating system during bootup, will always require you to employ the Add Hardware applet to install the device driver. True or False?

3

14. What applet should you use to add Windows components distributed on the Windows XP Professional CD?

a. System

b. Add or Remove Programs

c. *Microsoft Windows .NET Server Resource Kit*

d. Regional Settings

15. The Date/Time applet only changes the time as it is seen by Windows XP; the system's BIOS settings must still be changed through DOS. True or False?

16. What applet is used to switch the functions of the mouse buttons?

a. Accessibility Options

b. Regional Settings

c. Mouse

d. System

17. Home/Office Desk, Presentation, and Portable/Laptop are examples of pre-defined _____.

a. Hardware profiles

b. User profiles

c. Power Options settings

d. System profiles

18. Troubleshooting help for an audio card can be accessed through which applet? (Choose all that apply.)

a. Device Manager

b. System

c. Sounds and Audio Devices

d. Accessibility Options

19. What applet can be used to change domain or workgroup membership?

a. System

b. Add Hardware

c. Accessibility Options

d. Workgroup Settings

20. Once you install Windows XP, you must re-install the entire operating system to rename the computer. True or False?

21. When a STOP error occurs, what can the system do? (Choose all that apply.)

    a. Write an event to the system log

    b. Send an administrative alert

    c. Write a memory dump file

    d. Reboot the system

22. What tool is used to ensure that a newly installed device is functioning properly?

    a. System

    b. Add Hardware

    c. Device Manager

    d. Administrative Tools

23. Which of the following system resources may often find themselves in contention for non-Plug and Play devices? (Choose all that apply.)

    a. Paging file space

    b. I/O Port

    c. Priority CPU cycles

    d. IRQ

24. What convention or mechanism is used on Windows XP to manage changing hardware configurations smoothly across reboots?

    a. Plug and Play

    b. User Profiles

    c. Manually installing and removing drivers

    d. Hardware Profiles

25. A hardware profile can be chosen automatically by the system during boot-up. True or False?

HANDS-ON PROJECTS

Project 3-1

To create an MMC console for system management:

1. Type **mmc.exe** into the Open textbox in the **Start|Run** command.

2. Select **File|Add/Remove Snap-in**.

3. Click **Add**.

4. Locate and select **Computer Management** from the **Add Standalone Snap-in** dialog box.

5. Click **Add**.

3

6. Select **Local computer**.

7. Click **Finish**.

8. Click **Close**.

9. Select the **Extensions** tab.

10. Ensure the **Add all extensions** checkbox is selected.

11. Click **OK** to return to the MMC. Notice the Computer Management snap-in is listed in the console tree.

12. Maximize the console root window by double-clicking its title bar.

13. Select **File | Save As**.

14. Change to the directory where you want to store the console file.

15. Give the console file a name, such as **COMPMGT.MSC**. Click **Save**.

16. Select **File | Exit**.

Project 3-2

 This hands-on project assumes the Control Panel is in Classic View.

To create an automated task:

1. Open the Control Panel (**Start | Control Panel**).

2. Open the **Scheduled Tasks** item (double-click on its icon).

3. Launch the Scheduled Tasks wizard by double-clicking **Add Scheduled Task**.

4. Click **Next**.

5. Select **Calculator** from the list.

6. Click **Next**.

7. Select **One time only**.

8. Click **Next**.

9. Set the time to **3 minutes** from the present.

10. Click **Next**.

11. If you want to launch the task with the context of another user account, provide the username and password; otherwise, click **Next**.

12. Click **Finish**.

13. Wait the remainder of the three minutes to see Calculator launch automatically.

14. Close the calculator application.

Project 3-3

This hands-on project assumes the Control Panel is in Classic View.

To add a Windows component:

1. Open the Control Panel (**Start | Control Panel**).
2. Open the **Add or Remove Programs** applet (double-click the applet's icon).
3. Select **Add or Remove Windows Components**.
4. The Windows Components Wizard displays the list of available components. Locate and select the **Other Network File and Print Services**. Click **Next**.
5. Click **Finish**.
6. Close the Add or Remove Programs applet by clicking **Close**.

Project 3-4

This hands-on project assumes the Control Panel is in Classic View.

To set the calendar date, clock time, and time zone for the system:

1. Open the Control Panel (**Start | Control Panel**).
2. Open the **Date and Time** applet (double-click on the applet's icon).
3. Use the pull-down list to select the correct month.
4. Use the scroll buttons to select the correct year.
5. Select the current date from the displayed month calendar.
6. Click the hours in the time field below the analog clock. Use the up and down arrow buttons to adjust the hour to the current time.
7. Select the minutes in the time field. Use the up and down arrow buttons to adjust the minutes to the current time.
8. Select the seconds in the time field. Use the up and down arrow buttons to adjust the seconds to the current time.
9. Select the AM/PM designation in the time field. Use the up and down arrow buttons to adjust the designation to the current time.
10. Select the **Time Zone** tab.
11. Use the pull-down list to select the time zone for your area.
12. Click **OK** to close the Date and Time applet.

Project 3-5

This hands-on project assumes the Control Panel is in Classic View.

3

To create a custom sound scheme:
1. Open the Control Panel (**Start | Control Panel**).
2. Open the **Sounds and Audio Devices** applet (double-click the applet's icon).
3. Select the **Sounds** tab.
4. Use the **Sound Scheme** pull-down list to select **Windows Default**.
5. If prompted to save the previous scheme, click **No**.
6. Select **Asterisk** from the list of **Program events**.
7. Use the **Sounds** pull-down list to select **(None)**.
8. Select **Exit Windows** from the list of Program Events.
9. Use the **Sounds** pull-down list to select **Windows Logoff Sound.wav**.
10. Click the **Save As** button.
11. Give the sound scheme a name, such as **Windows Example 1**. Click **OK**.
12. Click **OK** to close the Sounds and Audio Devices applet.
13. Save any work that may be open, and select **Start | Turn Off Computer**, then click the **Restart** button. Notice the sound that plays as Windows shuts down.

Project 3-6

This hands-on project assumes the Control Panel is in Classic View.

To configure Windows XP Professional for stand-alone home use:
1. Open the Control Panel (**Start | Control Panel**).
2. Open the **System** applet (double-click on the applet's icon).
3. Select the **Computer Name** tab.
4. Click the **Network ID** button.
5. On the **Network Identification Wizard**. Click **Next**.
6. Select **This computer is for home use and is not part of a business network**. Click **Next**.
7. Click **Finish**.
8. Click **OK** on the message that states you must reboot for the changes to take effect.
9. Reboot the computer (**Start | Turn Off Computer | Restart**).

Project 3-7

This hands-on project assumes the Control Panel is in Classic View.

To create a hardware profile for a mobile computer:

1. Open the Control Panel (**Start|Control Panel**).
2. Open the **System** applet (double-click on the applet's icon).
3. Select the **Hardware** tab.
4. Click the **Hardware Profiles** button.
5. Select an existing hardware profile.
6. Click **Copy**, provide a new name, such as **Mobile Profile - no NIC**, click **OK**.
7. Click **OK** to close the Hardware Profiles dialog box.
8. Click **OK** to close the System Properties dialog box.
9. Reboot the system (**Start|Turn Off Computer|Restart**).
10. When prompted, select the new hardware profile using the arrow keys and press **Enter**.
11. Log into the system (**Ctrl+Alt+Delete**), providing your username and password if applicable.
12. Open the **Device Manager** (System applet, Hardware tab, Device Manager button).
13. Expand the **Network adapters** item by clicking the plus sign.
14. Select the listed NIC.
15. Right-click over the NIC, select **Properties** from the pop-up menu.
16. Change the **Device Usage** pull-down menu to read **Do not use this device (disable)**.
17. Click **OK**.
18. Close the Device Manager by clicking on the **X** in the upper right corner of the title bar.
19. Now your system has a normal hardware profile and a profile that has the NIC disabled for use when not connected to the network. Upon each reboot you can select the appropriate hardware profile.

Project 3-8

This hands-on project assumes the Control Panel is in Classic View.

3

To monitor and manage a device via the Device Manager:

1. Open the Administrative Tools (**Start|Control Panel|Administrative Tools**).

2. Launch **Computer Management** by double-clicking on its icon.

3. From the System Tools section in Computer Management, select **Device Manager**.

4. Double-click the **DVD/CD-ROM drive** item to expand its contents.

5. Select one of the items that appear.

6. Select **Action|Properties**.

7. Notice the Device Status message. If all is well, the message should state that the device is working properly. If there were a problem with this device, information about the problem would be listed and you'd be instructed to press the **Troubleshooter** button to access the troubleshooting Wizard.

8. Select the **Properties** tab. This is where you configure specific hardware device settings.

9. Select the **Driver** tab. This is where you can obtain information about the current driver as well as details on updating, replacing, or removing the current driver.

10. Click **OK**.

11. Close the Computer Management tool by clicking on the **X** button in the right corner of the title bar.

CASE PROJECTS

1. You need to delegate administrative tasks to non-administrative users, but you are concerned about granting too much power to users. What can you do?

2. You want to participate in the SETI@home project (*http://setiathome.ssl.berkeley.edu/*). However, the utility consumes most of the CPU cycles when it is active. How can you participate in this project but still be able to get other work done on your computer?

3. You have a notebook computer with a docking station. The docking station hosts a 21" monitor, a DVD drive, a tape backup, and a color printer. What is the best method to enable your notebook computer to use the devices on the docking station while avoiding problems when not connected to the docking station?

4

MANAGING WINDOWS XP FILE SYSTEMS AND STORAGE

After reading this chapter and completing the exercises, you will be able to:

♦ Understand basic and dynamic storage

♦ Understand the drive configurations supported by Windows XP

♦ Understand the FAT, FAT32, and NTFS file systems

♦ Understand permissions, sharing, and other security issues related to file systems

♦ Understand Windows XP drive, volume, and partition maintenance and administration

The Windows XP file storage subsystem offers a versatile disk management system. Windows XP supports both basic and dynamic storage, large disk volumes, fault tolerant drive configurations, and secure access controls. In this chapter, we discuss the basic and dynamic storage methods, the file systems and drive configurations supported by Windows XP, and all of the built-in tools used for disk maintenance.

FILE STORAGE BASICS

Windows XP supports two types of storage: basic and dynamic. **Basic storage** is the storage method with which most Microsoft PC users are familiar. It centers on partitioning a physical disk. **Dynamic storage** is a new method supported only by Windows XP and Windows 2000. Dynamic storage is not based on partitions but on **volumes**. From a user's perspective, the only difference between basic and dynamic storage is the additional ability to create expanded volumes and fault-tolerant configurations on dynamic drives.

Basic Storage

Basic storage is the traditional, industry-standard method of dividing a hard drive into partitions. A partition is a logical division of the physical space on a hard drive. Each partition can be formatted with a different file system. Partitions must be formatted before they can be used by an operating system.

There are two types of partitions: primary and extended. A single hard drive can host up to four **primary partitions**, or it can host up to three primary partitions and a single **extended partition**. An extended partition can be further divided into logical drives. Only primary partitions and logical drives can be formatted with a file system. Thus, a single hard drive can appear as one or more accessible or usable drives (that is, after the partition is properly formatted).

A primary partition can be marked **active**. This informs the computer's BIOS to see operating system booting information on that partition. Only primary partitions can be active and only a single partition can be active at any time. The active partition does not have to be the first partition on the drive.

In basic storage, volumes are two to 32 partitions combined into a single logical structure formatted with a single file system. Volume sets can be extended simply by adding another partition. But volume sets can be reduced in size only by breaking the set and creating a new set. The act of breaking the set destroys (or at least makes inaccessible) all data stored on the volume. A volume set can span multiple partitions on one or more physical drives. A volume set is represented in the operating system by a single **drive letter**. A volume set provides no fault tolerance. If a single drive or partition in a volume set fails, all data in the set is destroyed.

 The new dynamic storage method uses a slightly different definition for the term "volume," so be careful to review the context when it is discussed.

Typically, you'll want to create partitions or volumes as large as the operating system and file system allow. Under Windows XP, those sizes are as follows:

- *FAT*—4 GB
- *FAT32*—32 GB
- *NTFS*—4 TB

Each formatted partition or volume set is assigned a drive letter. Letters A and B are typically reserved for floppy drives, but letters C through Z can be used for formatted partitions and volumes hosted on the hard drive. Thus, only 24 formatted partitions can be accessed from Windows XP. This limitation does not impose a serious restriction in most situations.

The basic storage type supports a wide range of disk configurations, from single, formatted partitions (often called drives or logical drives) to fully fault-tolerant Redundant Array of Inexpensive Disks (RAID-5) configurations. The main difference between basic storage and dynamic storage is that basic storage disk structures require a system reboot when changed.

Windows XP supports this traditional method of storage for backward compatibility. In other words, Windows XP can take over control of drive configurations (see the "Drive Configurations" section later in this chapter) from previous operating systems (Windows 2000, NT, 95, 98, Me, and DOS), provided that the structure conforms to the current restrictions of the file systems they host and that the hosted file system is supported by Windows XP (FAT, FAT32, or NTFS). However, Windows XP does not support creation of basic storage-type drive structures beyond single, formatted partitions. It can manage only existing structures.

Windows XP can be installed only onto basic storage type partitions. There are two partitions associated with Windows XP: **system partition** and **boot partition**. Take careful note of their descriptions, because in our opinion they are labeled backward. The system partition is the active partition where the boot files (required to display the boot menu and initiate the booting of Windows XP) are stored. The boot partition hosts the main Windows XP system files and is the initial default location for the paging file (these are generally the \WINDOWS and \WINNT directories). The boot partition can be the same partition as the system partition, or it can be any other partition (or logical drive in an extended partition) on any drive hosted by the computer. Neither the system partition nor the boot partition can be a member of a volume set or stripe set. They both can be the source of original partition/drive in a disk mirror or disk duplexing configuration. The drive letters of the system partition and boot partition cannot be changed.

Once Windows XP is installed, the boot partition drive can be transformed into a dynamic storage device, but the system partition host must remain a basic storage device.

Dynamic Storage

Dynamic storage is a new type of storage technique (Microsoft documentation labels it as a new standard) introduced in Windows 2000 that does not use partitions. Instead, this method views an entire physical hard drive as a single entity. This entity can be divided into one or more volumes. This storage method offers drive structures from **simple volumes** (entire hard drives as a single formatted entity) to fully fault tolerant RAID-5 configurations. The main difference between dynamic storage and basic storage is that dynamic storage structures can be expanded on the fly without rebooting Windows XP. Furthermore, only Windows 2000 and XP Professional systems can access data on dynamic storage volumes; most other operating systems, including Windows 95, 98, Me, XP Home, and NT on a multi-boot system cannot access dynamic volumes.

Unlike basic storage drives, dynamic storage drives belong to the OS on which they were created. A dynamic storage volume created by Windows XP must be imported into Windows 2000 on a multi-boot system for Windows 2000 to access its contents. However, this process changes its ownership. The volume must be re-imported into Windows XP to return it to its original owner.

New drives (including existing drives with all partitions deleted) can be transformed into dynamic storage hosts through a selection Wizard. This Wizard is launched when the **Disk Management** tool is accessed (Start | Control Panel | Switch to Classic View | Administrative Tools | Computer Management; Storage; Disk Management) and a physical hard drive is present with no predefined partitions. This Wizard appears only the first time Disk Management is accessed after booting, after adding a new drive or deleting all partitions on a drive. You are prompted whether to enable dynamic storage.

Existing drives with partitions can be upgraded to dynamic storage by using the Convert to Dynamic Disk command. Converting a drive does not cause data loss or any change in the existing partition structure (other than converting them into volumes). Plus, existing drive configurations (mirror, duplex, stripe, and spanned volumes) can be upgraded to a dynamic volume. This command appears in the pop-up menu when you right-click a drive header—not a volume—in Disk Management. The drive(s) must have at least 1 MB of unallocated space, and you must reboot for the changes to take effect.

Once a drive is converted to host dynamic storage, it is labeled as such in Disk Management (see Figure 4-1).

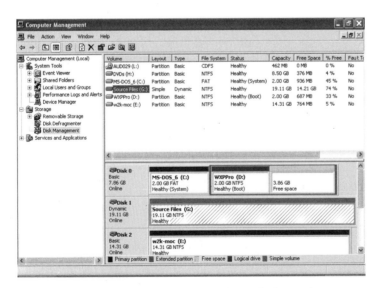

Figure 4-1   A dynamic volume seen through the Disk Management portion of Computer Management

Once you have a dynamic storage host, the next step is to create a volume. A volume is a portion of one or more hard disks that is combined into a single logical structure, formatted with a single file system, and accessed through a single drive letter (also called a **mount point**). To create a volume, perform the following steps:

1. From within Disk Management, right-click an unallocated dynamic storage device and select **New Volume** from the pop-up menu.

2. This launches the New Volume Wizard. Click **Next**.

3. You'll be prompted as to what type of volume to create. Select Simple and click **Next**. (See the section on drive configurations later in this chapter.)

4. Select the available dynamic storage devices and how much of each device to use in the volume being created (see Figure 4-2). Click **Next**.

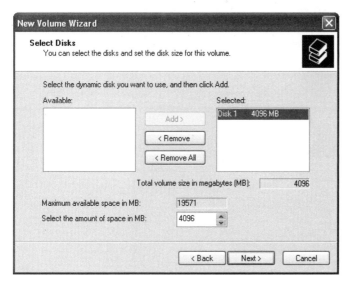

Figure 4-2   Select Disks page of the New Volume Wizard

5. Next, you'll be prompted to select a drive letter, a mount point, or to not assign a drive letter at all (see Figure 4-3). Select the option that suits your purposes and click **Next**. (See the section on drive letters and mount points later in this chapter.)

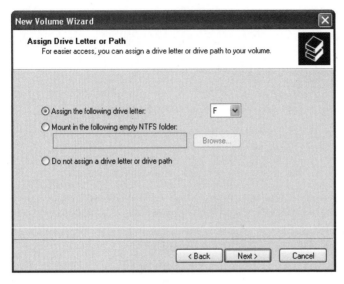

Figure 4-3   Assign Drive Letter or Path page of the New Volume Wizard

6. Select whether to format the volume and with which file system (see Figure 4-4). Click **Next**.

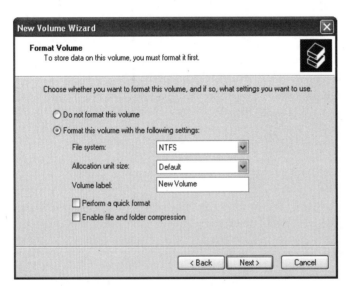

Figure 4-4   Format Volume page of the New Volume Wizard

7. Click **Finish** to implement volume creation.

Table 4-1   Functions and capabilities of basic and dynamic disks

Tasks	Basic Disk	Dynamic Disk
Create and delete primary and extended partitions	X	
Create and delete logical drives within an extended partition	X	
Format and label a partition and mark it as active	X	
Delete a volume set	X	
Break a mirror from a mirror set	X	
Repair a mirror set	X	
Repair a stripe set with parity	X	
Upgrade a basic disk to a dynamic disk	X	
Create and delete simple, spanned, striped, mirrored, and RAID-5 volumes		X
Extend a volume across one or more disks		X
Add a mirror to or remove a mirror from a mirrored volume		X
Repair a mirrored volume		X
Repair a RAID-5 volume		X
Check information about disks, such as capacity, available freespace, and current status	X	X
View volume and partition properties such as size	X	X
Make and change drive-letter assignments for hard disk volumes or partitions and CD-ROM devices	X	X
Create volume mount points	X	X
Set or verify disk sharing and access arrangements for a volume or partition	X	X

Table 4-1 compares the functions and capabilities of basic and dynamic storage devices.

 This table was reproduced from the *Microsoft Windows XP Professional Resource Kit* from Microsoft Press.

Dynamic drives can be returned to basic storage by deleting all volumes and issuing the Convert to Basic Disk command on the drive through Disk Management. Because you must delete the volumes first, converting a disk back to basic storage destroys all data on that drive. Therefore, you should always back up all your data before returning to basic storage.

Removable Storage Devices

The inclusion of Plug and Play technology in Windows XP brings support for removable media and storage devices. These **removable storage devices** or storage media can contain only a single primary partition. They cannot participate in dynamic storage. They cannot host extended partitions. They cannot be marked active.

Drive Configurations

Windows XP supports several drive configurations. While maintaining management capabilities for configurations using basic storage type partitions, Windows XP can create new drive configurations using only dynamic storage devices. There are five drive configurations or structures used by Microsoft operating systems, but only the following three are supported by Windows XP:

- *Simple volume*—All or part of a single drive. Does not provide any fault tolerance. NTFS volumes can be extended; FAT and FAT32 volumes cannot be extended.

- *Spanned volume*—A volume configuration of two or more parts (up to 32) of one or more drives, or a volume configuration of two or more entire drives. Elements of the **spanned volume** do not have to be equal in size. Data is written to the first drive in the volume until it is full, then it continues on with the next drive. This is also called an extended volume. Spanned volumes don't provide any fault tolerance: If one partition or volume in the set fails, all data is lost. Spanned volumes cannot be part of a **striped volume** or a **mirrored volume**. NTFS spanned volumes can be extended, FAT and FAT32 spanned volumes cannot. The system volume and boot volume cannot be extended. Volume sets can be reduced in size only by breaking the set and creating a new set. The act of breaking the set destroys all data stored on the volume.

- *Striped volume*—Two or more volumes (up to 32) of one or more drives or two or more entire drives (up to 32). Data is written to all drives in equal amounts (in 64 KB units) to spread the workload and improve performance. Each part or drive must be roughly equal in size. Striped volumes do not provide any fault tolerance: If one partition or drive in the set fails, all data is lost. Striped volumes cannot be mirrored or extended. Boot and system partitions cannot be part of a striped volume.

 No matter what disk configuration is used, always protect your data by using a regularly scheduled backup system.

File Systems

Windows XP supports the **File Allocation Table** (**FAT**; also called **FAT16**), **FAT32**, and **New Technology File System (NTFS)** file systems. Windows XP retains FAT for backward compatibility with other operating systems. This allows easy upgrade from another operating system to Windows XP and enables multi-boot systems to **share** data drives (when basic storage is used). FAT32 is used to support larger volumes and offer multi-boot shared drives with Windows 98, Me, and Windows 95 OSR2. NTFS is the preferred file system to use with Windows XP. It offers, among other things, significantly larger volume support, file by file compression, and file by file security. Windows XP NTFS volumes can be accessed by Windows NT 4.0 with Service Pack 4 applied and Windows 2000 systems. However, Windows NT 4.0 will be unable to access files that are using features not present with NTFS when NT 4.0 was released (such as encryption via EFS).

FAT and FAT32 are both collectively referred to as FAT in most Microsoft documentation. The separate terms are used only when the distinctions between FAT and FAT32 are important.

FAT, FAT32, and NTFS all support **long file names (LFNs)** with lengths up to 256 characters. FAT and FAT32 store 8.3 equivalents of LFNs for compatibility with DOS-based utilities that do not recognize LFNs. It is important to use LFN supporting utilities when performing any disk or file operation involving LFNs.

FAT and FAT32

FAT, also known as FAT16, was originally developed for DOS. It has experienced several revisions and upgrades as support for FAT was included in newer operating systems. FAT under Windows XP maintains backward compatibility with previous operating systems while supporting newer features or capabilities. In addition, on Windows XP, FAT is most often used to format floppies and other removable media.

Here are the important features of FAT (under Windows XP):

- Supports volumes up to 4 GB in size
- Most efficient on volumes smaller than 256 MB
- Root directory can contain only 512 entries
- No file-level compression
- No file-level security
- Maximum file size is 2 GB

FAT32 is simply an enhanced version of FAT originally released with Windows 95 OSR2. FAT32's main feature change is its volume size. Windows XP can support and access FAT32 volumes up to 2 TB in size, but only volumes up to 32 GB can be created. FAT32 volumes have a minimum size of 512 MB, with a maximum file size of 4 GB.

A FAT volume is divided into clusters. A **cluster** is a group of one or more **sectors** divided into a single non-divisible unit. A sector is the smallest division (512 bytes) of a drive's surface. Due to the limitations of the file system, only a maximum number of clusters can be addressed. For FAT16, the maximum number of clusters is 65,536. For FAT32, the maximum number of clusters is 268,435,456 (see Table 4-2).

Table 4-2   FAT16 and FAT32 Cluster Sizes

Drive Size	FAT16 Cluster Size	FAT32 Cluster Size
260 to 511 MB	8 KB	Not supported
512 to 1023 MB	16 KB	4 KB
1024 MB to 2 GB	32 KB	4 KB
2 to 4 GB	64 KB	4 KB
4 to 8 GB	Not Supported	4 KB
8 to 16 GB	Not Supported	8 KB
16 to 32 GB	Not Supported	16 KB
>32 GB	Not Supported	32 KB

Before the release of Windows 95, the maximum allowable FAT volume size was 2 GB. But with the use of 64 KB clusters, this was extended to 4 GB. However, 64 KB clusters caused problems with some older drive utilities. Thus, Windows XP always warns you when you attempt to format a 2 GB to 4 GB partition with FAT16.

NTFS

NTFS is the preferred file system of Windows XP. Here are the important features of NTFS under Windows XP:

- Supports volumes up to 2 TB in size
- Most efficient on volumes larger than 10 MB
- Root directory can contain unlimited entries
- File-level compression
- File-level security
- File-level encryption (see Chapter 6, "Windows XP Security and Access Controls")
- **Disk quotas**
- POSIX support (POSIX subsystem support is not included in Windows XP Professional)
- File size is limited only by the size of the volume

The version of NTFS included with Windows XP (NTFS v5) is different from that of Windows NT out of the box (NTFS v4). In fact, you must have Service Pack 4 installed on Windows NT to access Windows XP NTFS volumes. Microsoft does not recommend a multi-boot system with pre-SP4 Windows NT and Windows XP for this reason.

FAT and FAT32 volumes on a system can be migrated to the NTFS format without losing data. However, to return to FAT, the volume must be deleted, re-created, and formatted, and the data must be copied back onto the new volume.

NTFS manages clusters more efficiently than FAT32, see Table 4-3.

Table 4-3   NTFS Default Cluster Sizes

Volume Size	Sectors Per Cluster	Cluster Size
512 MB or less	1	512 bytes
513 to 1024 MB	2	1 KB
1025 to 2048 MB	4	2 KB
2049 to 4096 MB	8	4 KB
4097 to 8192 MB	16	8 KB
8193 to 16,384 MB	32	16 KB
16,385 to 32,768 MB	64	32 KB
> 32,768 MB	128	64 KB

File-level compression cannot be used on volumes with a cluster size greater than 4 KB.

Converting File Systems

When you first format a drive in Windows XP, you have the option of selecting FAT, FAT32, or NTFS. If at a later date you decide you need to change the format, you have only two options: reformat with the new file system or convert from FAT/FAT32 to NTFS. A backup should precede either process to ensure that you will not lose data.

The first option of reformatting is easy; simply employ one of the disk tools, such as Disk Management, and format the volume with a new file system. Remember that all data stored on the drive will be lost, so without a backup you will not be able to recover from a format. The second option employs the CONVERT.EXE command line tool. This tool can be used to convert FAT or FAT32 volumes to NTFS. It has two command line parameters: /fs:ntfs and /v. The first specifies the conversion that should result in the NTFS file system (it is strange to have this parameter because it only supports conversion to NTFS). The second turns on verbose mode so all messages regarding the conversion are displayed. When launched, CONVERT attempts to convert the drive immediately. If the drive is locked (i.e., a process has an open file from the volume to be converted), the conversion will occur the next time the system is booted up.

If you use the CONVERT command to initiate a conversion to NTFS, and decide before the reboot that you don't want to convert the volume, you can cancel the process. To cancel a CONVERT action, you must edit the Registry. Using REGEDT32, locate the BootExecute value entry in the \SYSTEM\CurrentControlSet\Control\Session Manager key. Change the content of that value entry from "autoconv \DosDevices\x: /FS:NTFS" (where x is the drive letter of the volume) to "autocheck autochk *". This action prevents the NTFS conversion.

File Compression

File-level compression is the ability to compress data on the basis of single files, folders, or entire volumes. File compression offers the benefit of being able to store more data in the same space, but at the cost of some performance. The amount of compression achieved depends on the data stored in the object (that is, text can often be compressed significantly, whereas executables cannot). Windows XP Professional manages the compression through the NTFS file system drive. Each time a compressed file is read, it must be uncompressed while it is being read. Likewise, when saving a compressed file, copying a file into a compressed folder, or creating a new file in a compressed folder, the data to be stored must be compressed in memory before it is written to the drive.

Configuring and managing file compression involves enabling or disabling the file compression attribute on one or more files or folders. File compression appears as just another attribute of NTFS file/folder objects on the Advanced Attributes dialog box. And, just like all other attributes, file compression can be set on a file by file basis or by setting the attribute on a container. When the "Compress contents to save disk space" checkbox is selected, the object(s) are compressed. When this checkbox is cleared, the object(s) are expanded back to their original size. Troubleshooting compression usually involves either recompressing or removing compression from files or restoring files that were damaged during the compression process from backup.

DISK MANAGEMENT ACTIONS

In addition to creating volumes and transforming devices into dynamic storage, the Disk Management tool offers several other useful features. The All Tasks submenu of the Action menu is context-based, depending on the type of object selected. The All Tasks submenu is the same menu that pops up when you right-click a drive/partition/volume object. Here are the commands that appear in this menu:

- *Change Drive Letter and Paths*—Changes the drive letter of basic disks and dynamic disks or the mount point of dynamic disks.

- *Convert to Basic Disk*—Transforms a dynamic disk into a basic disk; requires that all volumes be deleted.

- *Convert to Dynamic Disk*—Transforms a basic storage device into a dynamic storage device.

- *Delete Partition*—Destroys a partition and returns the space to unallocated status.

- *Explore*—Opens the selected volume or partition in a Windows Explorer window.

- *Extend Volume*—Adds additional unallocated space to an existing volume.

- *Format*—Formats a volume or partition with a file system.

- *Help*—Opens the Help utility.

- *Import Foreign Disks*—Imports a dynamic disk when moved from one Windows XP computer to another.

- *Mark Partition as Active*—Marks a primary partition active.

- *New Logical Drive*—Creates a new logical drive within an extended partition.

- *New Partition*—Creates a partition on a basic disk.

- *New Volume*—Launches a Wizard to create a new simple, spanned, or striped volume.

- *Open*—Opens the selected volume or partition into a new window.

- *Properties*—Opens the Properties dialog box for the selected object.

- *Reactivate Disk*—Brings dynamic disks back online after being powered down, disconnected, or corrupted.

- *Reactivate Volume*—Recovers volumes from a failed status.

- *Remove Disk*—Deactivates a removable drive.

The Action menu itself has two other non-context sensitive commands:

- *Refresh*—Updates drive letters, file system, volume, and removable media information and determines which previously unreadable volumes are now readable.

- *Rescan Disks*—Updates hardware information by rescanning all attached storage devices (including removable media) for changes in configuration. This command is useful if you've added or removed a drive and the display has not been updated to accommodate the change.

Disk Management can be used to manipulate storage devices on remote computers. Simply select the "Computer Management (Local)" item in the console tree and issue the "Connect to another computer" command from the Action menu. This opens a list of all known networked systems. Once you've selected another system, you can perform the same disk management functions as if you were sitting at that machine.

The Properties dialog boxes of drives, volumes, and partitions offer additional details and configuration settings. A drive's (not volume or partition) Properties dialog box (see Figure 4-5) has four tabs: General, Policies, Volume, and Driver. This Properties dialog box is the same one accessible from the Device Manager. The General tab displays details about the drive's model, device type, manufacturer, location in drive chain, and status. At the bottom of this tab, you can access the Troubleshooter by clicking the Troubleshoot button and set whether this device is enabled or disabled in the current hardware profile.

Figure 4-5 A drive Properties dialog box, General tab

The Policies tab is used to configure the write caching and safe removal settings for the device. There are two radio buttons: Optimize for quick removal and Optimize for performance. Fixed hard drives are set automatically to "Optimize for performance and allow only the Enable write caching on the disk" checkbox to be controlled (it is marked by default). Removable drives can be configured with either of the two radio button options. However, the latter setting requires the use of the Safely Remove Hardware icon in the taskbar to avoid losing data, whereas the former allows for instant device removal.

The Volume tab (see Figure 4-6) displays additional details about the device and its hosted volumes, including the following:

- *Disk*—The ordinal number of the disk, such as Disk 0, Disk 1, etc.
- *Type*—The storage type: basic, dynamic, or removable.
- *Status*—The status of the device: online, offline, foreign, unknown.
- *Partition Style*—The partitioning scheme used on the drive; options are MBR (Master Boot Record) on x86 systems, GPT (GUID Partition Table) on Itanium systems, or Not Applicable for unknown or uninitialized devices.
- *Capacity*—The maximum storage capacity of the drive.
- *Unallocated Space*—The amount of space not used in a partition or volume.
- *Reserved Space*—The amount of space reserved for use by the operating system.
- *Volumes contained on this disk*—The volumes and capacity of each volume or partition on the drive.

Figure 4-6   A drive Properties dialog box, Volumes tab

The Driver tab displays details about the device driver used by the drive. From this tab, you can: find details about how the driver can be accessed; update the driver or roll back to the previous driver; or uninstall the device driver (that is, remove the device from the system).

You can right-click a partition or volume to access the Properties dialog box. However, an NTFS-formatted partition or volume in a domain has two additional tabs that are not present on FAT/FAT32-formatted partitions or volumes. The tabs of the Properties dialog box are: General, Tools, Hardware, Sharing, Security, and Quota (the later two are NTFS only).

The General tab (see Figure 4-7) of a partition or volume Properties dialog box displays the following:

- *Label*—The customizable name of the volume or partition. FAT drives can be labeled with up to 11 characters, whereas NTFS's labels can contain 32 characters.

- *Type*—The type of disk: local, network connection, floppy disk drive, CD-ROM drive, RAM disk, removable drive, or mounted disk.

- *File System*—The file system used on the disk: CDFS (for CDs), FAT, FAT32, NTFS, and UDF (Universal Disk Format common on DVD and compact discs).

- *Used Space*—The amount of space used by stored files.

- *Free Space*—The amount of space still available in the partition.

- *Capacity*—The total amount of space in the partition.

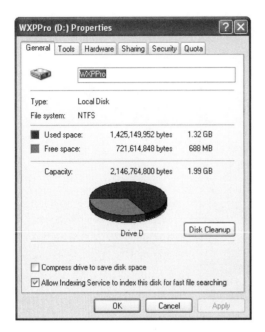

Figure 4-7   A volume Properties dialog box, General tab

- *Graph*—A graphical pie chart representation of used and free space.

- *Disk Cleanup*—A button to access the Disk Cleanup tool (see the "Disk Cleanup" section later in this chapter).

- *Compress drive to save disk space*—By default, files in the root of a drive are compressed automatically; the entire drive will be compressed only when this option is selected.

- *Allow Indexing Service to index this disk for fast file searching*—Indexes the disk.

The Tools tab (see Figure 4-8) offers access to the following:

- *Error-checking*—Accesses the Check Disk tool to find and repair errors on a drive.

- *Defragmentation*—Accesses the **Defragmentation** tool to reduce file fragmentation.

- *Backup*—Accesses the NT Backup utility to back up files (see Chapter 14, "Windows XP Professional Fault Tolerance").

The Hardware tab (see Figure 4-9) lists all physical storage devices and their type. This dialog box accesses the same Troubleshooting and Properties (for drivers) utilities that the Device Manager accesses.

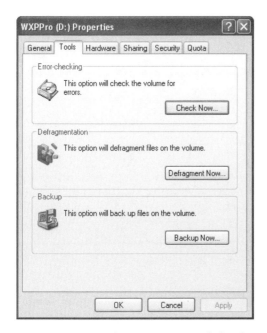

Figure 4-8   A volume Properties dialog box, Tools tab

Figure 4-9   A volume Properties dialog box, Hardware tab

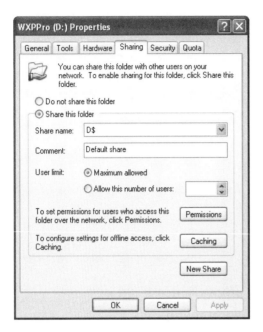

Figure 4-10   A volume Properties dialog box, Sharing tab

The Sharing tab (see Figure 4-10) is used to share partitions with the network. The Security tab (see Figure 4-11) is used to set the NTFS access permissions on the volume or partition as a whole. Individual users or groups can be defined with unique permissions of Allow or Deny for each of the listed object specific actions.

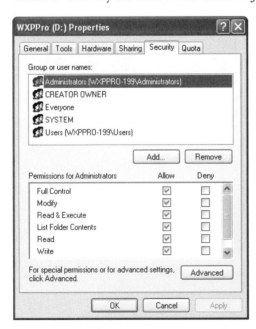

Figure 4-11   A volume Properties dialog box, Security tab

The Quota tab (see Figure 4-12) is used to define disk-use limitations on NTFS volumes and partitions. The quota is defined on a general basis and/or fine-tuned for each individual user. The options include the following:

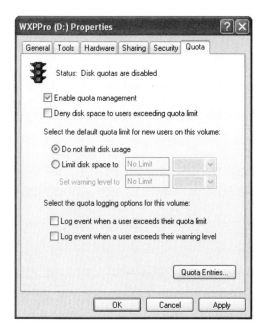

Figure 4-12   A volume Properties dialog box, Quota tab

- *Enable quota management*—Turns on the quota system.

- *Deny disk space to users exceeding quota limit*—Prevents users from gaining more space when in violation of the quota.

- *Do not limit disk usage*—Disables system-wide quota level.

- *Limit disk space to*—Sets maximum amount of drive space that can be accessed by a single user.

- *Set warning level to*—Sets a threshold that, when exceeded, warns users about nearing their quota limit.

- *Log event when users exceed their quota limit*—Adds an item to the Event Viewer.

- *Log event when users exceed their warning level*—Adds an item to the Event Viewer.

- *Quota Entries*—Opens a dialog box where individual quota settings for each user can be fine-tuned.

Drive Letters and Mount Points

Windows XP uses drive letters to grant applications and user interface utilities access to file system resources. Drive letters A and B are typically used for floppy disks, but in the absence of floppy drives, these letters can be employed as mappings for network shares. Drive letters C through Z are used for local hard drives or mappings for network shares. Even without floppies, the first hard drive is always labeled with C. The drive letters assigned to the system and boot partitions/volumes cannot be changed, but all other drive letters can be changed. The Disk Management command of "Change Drive Letter and Paths" is used to alter a drive letter, apply a mount point path, or remove a drive letter. This command is accessed by selecting a volume or partition, and then right-clicking to open the pop-up menu.

A mount point is an alternative to drive letters. A mount point connects a FAT/FAT32 or NTFS volume or partition to an empty directory on an NTFS volume or partition. This allows more than 24 (or 26) volumes to be present on a single machine. The empty directory becomes the gateway to the linked volume. A mount point is created by following this procedure:

1. Create an empty directory.

2. Open the **Disk Management** tool (**Start|Control Panel|Switch to Classic View|Administrative Tools|Computer Management; Storage; Disk Management**).

3. Right-click the volume or partition to be mapped, select **Change Drive Letter and Paths** from the pop-up menu.

4. Click **Add**.

5. Select **Mount in the following empty NTFS folder**.

6. Click **Browse**.

7. Locate and select the empty folder, click **OK**.

8. Click **OK**.

9. To verify that the mount point was defined, use Windows Explorer or My Computer to explore the "empty directory" from step 7. You should discover the directory structure from the mapped volume in step 3.

 It is possible to create an infinite-regression mount point by mapping a volume to an empty directory that it hosts. Although this is valid, it can cause system overflows when disk utilities attempt to follow the infinite path.

Disk Cleanup

Disk Cleanup is a tool used to free up space on hard drives by removing deleted, orphaned, temporary, or downloaded files. The utility can be launched from the General tab of the

Properties dialog box from any drive or through Start | All Programs | Accessories | System Tools | Disk Cleanup. When launched from a drive's properties, it automatically scans that drive for space that can be freed. When launched from the Start menu, you are prompted to select the drive to scan for cleaning. The scanning process can take several minutes, especially on large drives that have an excessively large amount of files.

When scanning is complete, the Disk Cleanup for (drive:) dialog box is displayed (see Figure 4-13). The Disk Cleanup tab lists the file types that can be removed and how much space they currently consume. The View Files button can be used to see the selected file type's details through the My Computer window. Selecting the checkbox beside a listed file type causes those files to be deleted (not placed in the Recycle Bin) when OK is clicked.

4

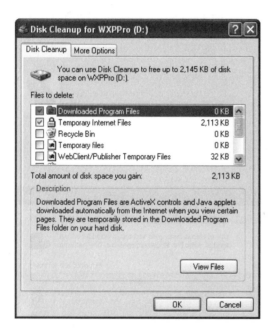

Figure 4-13 Disk Cleanup dialog box

The More Options tab offers access to the Add/Remove Windows Components utility, the Change or Remove Programs utility, and the System Restore utility. The first two of these are the same utilities that can be accessed through the Add/Remove Programs applet in the Control Panel. The System Restore item deletes all but the most recent restore point. See Chapter 14 for more information on System Restore.

Check Disk

Check Disk (Error-checking) is an inspection utility used to examine disk integrity and locate both logical and physical errors on a hard drive. In some cases, logical errors can be corrected. Physical errors are marked and avoided in all future drive accesses by the operating system. Logical errors are bad pointers in the directory structure of a file system, whether FAT, FAT32, or NTFS. Often these errors can be corrected. However, in those cases where correction is not possible, Check Disk saves the data of orphaned fragments to text files in the root directory of the drive using incremental filenames of FILE0001, FILE0002, etc.

Error-checking—called ScanDisk Check Disk in earlier versions of Windows—is accessed by clicking the Check Now button on the Tools tab of a drive's Properties dialog box. Once launched, it prompts you to Automatically fix file system errors or to Scan for and attempt recovery of bad sectors. Check Disk usually requires rebooting the system to scan NTFS volumes.

The system uses Check Disk when it detects an improper system shutdown or errors in the directory structure of a drive. This usually occurs during boot-up and execution processes, and results are displayed on a blue screen (the one where the operating system name, version, build, number of processors, and memory size is detailed).

 The Error-checking tool that ships with Windows XP is specifically designed to manage the file systems supported by Windows XP. Do not use Check Disk or ScanDisk from any other operating system to attempt repairs on Windows XP hard drives.

Defragmentation

As files are written, altered, deleted, rewritten, etc, the storage device develops gaps between used and unused space. As gaps are used to store files instead of contiguous free space, fragmentation occurs. **Fragmentation** is the division of a file into two or more parts where each part is stored in a different location on the hard drive. As the level of fragmentation on a drive increases, the longer it takes for read and write operations to occur. Defragmentation is the process of re-organizing files so they are stored contiguously and no gaps are left between files.

The Windows XP defragmentation utility is designed for FAT, FAT32, and NTFS volumes. Thus, it can reduce or eliminate fragmentation on your hard drives. The defragmentation utility is accessed either from the Tools tab of a drive's Properties dialog box or through Start | All Programs | Accessories | System Tools | Disk Defragmenter.

The Disk Defragmenter (see Figure 4-14) lists all drives in the system. By selecting a drive, you can select one of the following options: Analyze the drive for fragmentation or Defragment the drive. Both processes display a graphical representation of the file storage condition of the drive. Once either process is complete, you can view a report that details the findings of the procedure.

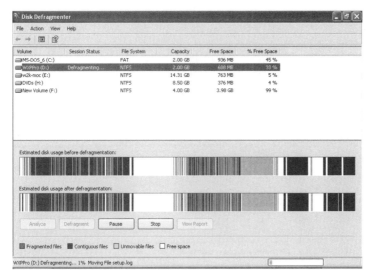

Figure 4-14   Disk Defragmenter

The Disk Defragmenter does not offer a built-in scheduling feature; nor can it be executed from a command line. You must manually defragment or deploy a third-party utility that automates scheduled defragmentation.

FSUTIL

FSUTIL (file system utility) is a powerful command-line utility that can perform a wide range of functions. This tool can be only used by administrators, and even then it should be used with caution. The syntax and parameters of FSUTIL are fairly complex, so take the time to fully review and understand each command before you execute it. For this reason, we are not including an exhaustive list of the syntax and parameters of this tool; instead, we encourage you to use the Help and Support Center to access the online documentation by searching on FSUTIL. The basic commands and actions of FSUTIL are as follows (note: these are the top-level commands, all of them have numerous additional parameters not listed here):

- *behavior*—Defines whether 8.3 character filenames are generated, whether extended characters are accepted in 8.3 filenames on NTFS, how to update the last access timestamp on NTFS volumes, how often quota events are written to the system log, and how much drive space is reserved for the MFT zone.

- *dirty*—Queries, sets, and clears the dirty bit for a volume, which causes autochk to scan the volume for errors upon the next bootup.

- *file*—Finds files by security IDs, sets the 8.3 name of a file, sets the file's valid data length, etc.

- *Preferences*—A user's environmental settings and configuration preferences can be stored as a **profile**, so no matter where a user connects to the network, the preferred desktop and resources are available.

In addition to these items, a Windows XP Professional system maintains a wide range of security settings and preferences that affect a user account. These include **password policy**, **account lockout policy**, **audit policy**, user rights assignment, **security options**, public key policies, IP security policies, and more. Many of these topics are discussed throughout this chapter.

Operating systems such as Windows XP that can support more than one user are called **multiple-user systems**. Maintaining separate and distinct user accounts for each person is the common feature of all multiple-user systems. Windows XP implements its multiple-user system through the following:

- *Groups*—**Groups** are named collections of users. Each member of a group takes on the access privileges or restrictions defined for that group. Through the use of groups, administrators can manage many users at one time because a group's settings can be defined once and apply to all members of that group. When the group settings are changed or modified, those changes automatically affect every member of that group. Thus, changing each user's account is not necessary. Later in this chapter, you will learn how to create and manage groups.

- *Resources*—On a network or within a standalone system, resources are defined as any useful service or object, including printers, shared directories, and software applications. A resource can be accessible by everyone across the network or be limited to one person on a single machine, and at any level in between. The range of control over resources within Windows XP is astounding. Details on how to manage resources and control who has and who doesn't have access are presented later in this chapter.

- *Policies*—A policy is a set of configuration options that define aspects of Windows XP's security. Security policies are used to define password restrictions, account lockouts, user rights, and event auditing. System policies are defined for a user, computer, or a group to restrict the computing environment. Details on both types of policies are discussed later in this chapter.

- *Profiles*—A profile is a stored snapshot of the environmental settings of a user's desktop, Start menu, and other user-specific details. Profiles can exist on a single computer or be configured to follow a user around a network no matter what workstation is used. **User profiles** are discussed in detail later in this chapter.

Now that you've had a brief overview of the multiple-user system of Windows XP, you'll learn about these topics in more detail.

Logging Onto Windows XP

Windows XP uses **logon authentication** for two purposes: first, to maintain security and privacy within a network; and second, to track computer usage by user account. Each Windows XP user can have a unique user account that identifies that user and contains or references all the system preferences for, access privileges of, and private information about that one user. Thus, Windows XP can provide security and privacy for all users through the mandatory requirement of logon authentication.

Windows XP supports two types of logon: Windows Welcome and classic. The Windows Welcome logon is a completely new logon method to the Windows product line. Windows Welcome is designed for use on standalone or workgroup member systems. When the system boots, a list of user accounts with icons is displayed. To logon, you point and click at a user name. If a password is defined for the account, you'll be prompted to enter it before access is granted. If no password is defined for the account, access is granted immediately. Windows Welcome can be used only on standalone or workgroup Windows XP systems; it is not available for use on domain members.

Another feature of Windows Welcome logon is Fast User Switching, which allows Windows XP Professional to switch users without logging off. User switching is accomplished by clicking Start, Log Off, then clicking Switch User. This returns you to the Windows Welcome logon screen, where you can select another user account. You should notice that the user account you just switched from now has a listing under the account name indicating how many programs are still active. The programs of the account that is not in use are still active and running. Once you finish with the second user account, you can switch to any other account or log off. Logging back onto the system with the user account previously in use restores that desktop environment and all active programs.

The classic logon method is to press Ctrl+Alt+Delete to access the WinLogon security dialog box. However, the Ctrl+Alt+Delete key sequence can be disabled, so the WinLogon security dialog box appears by default upon bootup or user logout. If the system is a domain member, this is the only logon method allowed. By simultaneously pressing the Ctrl, Alt, and Delete keys at the default splash screen, the Logon Information dialog box appears. Here users enter the logon information—user name, password, and domain—then click OK to have the security system validate their information and grant access to the computer. Once users have completed their work, they can log off the computer to make it available for the next user. There is no user-switching available when classic logon is used.

The logon mode is set to classic logon automatically when the Windows XP system becomes a domain member. On a standalone or workgroup member Windows XP system, the logon method is set through the User Accounts applet. Just click the "Change the way users log on or off" command in the quick list, then on the "Select logon and logoff" page, select "Use the Welcome screen" or "Use classic logon." When the

Welcome screen option is selected, you can also optionally select to enable Fast User Switching.

When Windows XP Professional is installed, it automatically creates two default user accounts: Administrator and Guest.

Administrator

The **Administrator account** is the most powerful user account possible within the Windows XP environment. This account has unlimited access and unrestricted privileges to every aspect of Windows XP. The Administrator account has unrestricted ability to manage all security settings, other users, groups, the operating system environment, printers, shares, and storage devices. Due to these far-reaching privileges, the Administrator account must be protected from misuse. Defining a complicated password for this account is highly recommended. You should also rename this account, thereby increasing the difficulty for hackers attempting to discover a valid user name and password.

The Administrator account has the following characteristics:

- It cannot be deleted
- It cannot be **locked out**
- It can be **disabled**
- It can have a blank password (however, this is not recommended)
- It can be renamed
- It cannot be removed from the Administrators local group

Guest

The **Guest account** is one of the least privileged user accounts in Windows XP. This account has limited access to resources and computer activities. Even so, you should set a new password for the Guest account, and it should be used only by authorized one-time users or users with low-security access. Any configuration changes made to the desktop or Start menu are not recorded in the Guest's user profile. If you do allow this account to be used, you should rename it.

The Guest account has the following characteristics:

- It cannot be deleted
- It can be locked out
- It can be disabled (it is disabled by default)
- It can have a blank password (it is blank by default)
- It can be renamed
- It can be removed from the Guests local group

NAMING CONVENTIONS

Before creating and managing user accounts, you need to understand naming conventions. A **naming convention** is simply a predetermined process for creating names on a network or standalone system. A naming convention should incorporate a scheme for user accounts, computers, directories, network shares, printers, and servers. These names should be descriptive enough so that anyone can figure out to which type of object the name corresponds. For example, you should name computers and resources by department or by use, to simplify user access.

This stipulation of always using a naming convention seems pointless for small networks, but it is rare for small networks to remain small. Most networks grow at an alarming rate. If you begin naming network objects at random, you'll soon forget which resource corresponds to which name. Even with Windows XP's excellent management tools, you'll quickly lose track of important resources if you don't establish a standard way of naming network resources.

The naming convention your organization settles on ultimately doesn't matter, as long as it can always provide you with a useful name for each new network object. To give you an idea of a naming scheme, here are two common rules:

- User names are constructed from the first and last name of the user, plus a code identifying his or her job title or department (i.e., BobScottAccounting).

- Group names are constructed from resource types, department names, location names, project names, and combinations of all four (i.e., Accounting01, AustinUsers, BigProject01, etc.).

No matter what naming convention is deployed, it needs to address the following four elements:

- It must be consistent across all objects.

- It must be easy to use and understand.

- New names should be easily constructed by mimicking the composition of existing names.

- An object's name should clearly identify that object's type.

MANAGING USER ACCOUNTS

Windows XP Professional actually has two user management interfaces. The first is the User Accounts applet, accessed through the Control Panel, and the second is Local Users and Groups, accessed through the Advanced button on the Advanced tab of the User Accounts applet. The User Accounts applet is used to create a local user account out of an existing domain account. The Local Users and Groups snap-in is used to create local user accounts from scratch.

User Accounts Applet

The User Accounts applet (see Figure 5-1) is used to perform several functions on local user accounts. This applet can be opened only if you are logged into the Windows XP Professional system with the Administrator account, logged with a user account that is a member of the Administrators group, or by providing the username, password, and domain when attempting to launch the applet. (This last method is known as Secondary Logon.) The User Accounts applet has two tabs, Users and Advanced. The Users tab displays all active (i.e., non-disabled) user accounts that can be employed to gain local access. This list details the user name, the domain, and the group memberships of the user account. The term domain in this instance refers to the logical environment where the user account originated. All user accounts created on the Windows XP Professional system have the local computer name listed as its domain (as in WXPPRO-199 in Figure 5-1). All user accounts from a domain (such as created by Windows NT, Windows 2000, or Windows .NET Server) or other networking environment have the name of that domain listed as its domain.

 This section on managing user accounts focuses on local user account management while the computer is a domain member. The User Accounts interface functions differently when the system is a stand-alone system or a workgroup member. In those cases, the User Accounts utility becomes a task Wizard where user maintenance is performed through easy to follow task selections.

Figure 5-1   User Accounts applet, Users tab

To create new local user accounts, you must decide what type of user account to create. On a Windows XP Professional system, there are local user accounts created from scratch locally and there are local user accounts that are just local representations of domain/network user accounts. To create a new local user account from scratch, you'll need to employ Local Users and Groups. To create a local representation of an existing domain/network user account, use the Add button on the User Accounts applet.

Creating a local representation of an existing domain/network user account grants a network user the ability to access resources hosted by the Windows XP Professional system whether or not it is a member of the domain/network. These important user accounts cannot be used to log onto a Windows XP Professional system; they can be used only to access resources over the network hosted on a Windows XP Professional system (i.e., the domain user is authenticated by the domain controller and the local representation of that account is used to gain access to the resources on the client). Plus, the use of local representations allows the administrator or user of a Windows XP Professional system to create a local security configuration of users and groups that does not rely upon the group memberships of the domain/network. However, it is still possible to add domain users and domain groups to local groups.

Clicking the Add button reveals the Add New User Wizard (see Figure 5-2). If you know the name of the user account and the domain of which it is a member, you can type this information in manually. You can also click the Browse button to access the Select User dialog box where you can perform an LDAP query to locate a user. Clicking Next prompts you for the access level to grant the imported user (see Figure 5-3). The selections are:

Figure 5-2   Add New User Wizard, user name and domain page

- *Standard user*—Grants the imported user membership into the local Power Users group.

- *Restricted user*—Grants the imported user membership into the local Users group.

- *Other*—Grants the imported user membership into the existing local group selected from the pull-down list.

Once you click Finish on the Wizard, the imported user is added to the list of local users for this computer. To remove an existing user, just select it from the list and click Remove. You'll be prompted to confirm the user account deletion.

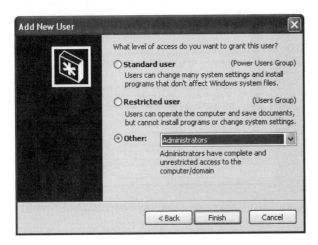

Figure 5-3   Add New User Wizard, level of access page

The Properties button is used to access basic properties for the selected user account. A locally created user account's Properties dialog box has two tabs, General and Group Membership. The General tab is used to change the user name, full name, and description. The Group Membership tab allows you to change a users group membership. An **imported user account's** Properties only has a Group Membership tab; it does not have a General tab. An imported user account can only be a member of a single group. A locally created group can be a member of more than one group, but the Group Membership tab of the Properties for the user account allow only a single group to be selected. To add a user account to multiple groups requires the use of Local Users and Groups.

The password for locally created users can be changed using the Reset Password button at the bottom of the User Accounts applet (be sure to select the user account first). You'll be prompted only for the new password and a confirmation of the new password.

Imported user accounts appear in this applet whether or not the Windows XP Professional system is logged into the domain from which the accounts are imported. The only requirement is that the applet be able to communicate with the domain through a network connection. If the Windows XP Professional system is physically disconnected from the network media or the domain is not available, the imported user accounts won't be listed. Once the domain of origin returns, the user accounts reappear.

The Advanced tab of the User Accounts applet grants you access to password and .NET passport management, advanced user management, and secure logon settings. Manage Passwords is used to add, remove, or edit logon credentials for various networks and Web sites. The .NET Passport Wizard is used to define your Microsoft passport account for use in messaging, Microsoft personalized Web pages, and using passport restricted Web sites. Advanced user management is discussed in detail in the next section. The Secure logon setting is just a single checkbox that determines whether the Ctrl+Alt+Delete key sequence is required before the logon dialog box is displayed for the classic logon method.

Local Users and Groups

The Local Users and Groups tool (see Figure 5-4) is accessed by pressing the Advanced button on the Advanced tab of the User Accounts applet or through Computer Management in Administrative Tools. This tool is used to create and manage local users; imported users do not appear in this interface. The console tree hosts only two nodes: Users and Groups. The Users node contains all local user accounts. The Groups node contains all local group accounts.

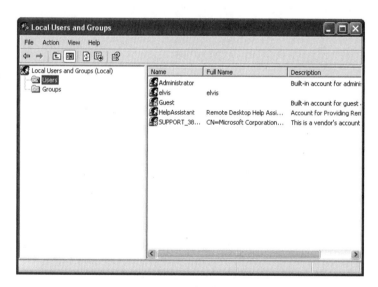

Figure 5-4   Local Users and Groups, Users node

Users

Selecting the Users node displays all existing local user accounts. Initially, the Administrator and Guest account (as seen in Figure 5-4) are displayed. The HelpAssistant and Support accounts are used to enable Remote Assistance and online Help and Support Services, respectively. The details pane lists the name of the user account, the full name of the user, and the description of the account. By selecting a user account and right-clicking, you can access the account's Properties. The Properties dialog box for a local user account has three tabs: General, Member Of, and Profile.

All of the right-click pop-up menu commands described in this chapter also appear in the Action drop-down menu when the appropriate object is selected.

The General tab (see Figure 5-5) of a user account's Properties offers the following:

Figure 5-5   A user account's Properties dialog box, General tab

- *Name of user account*—Not customizable through this dialog box.

- *Full Name*—Customizable full name of the person using the account.

- *Description*—Customizable text field to describe the purpose or use of the account.

- *User must change password at next logon*—A checkbox used to force a user to change their password the next time they log onto the system.

- *User cannot change password*—A checkbox that prevents the user from altering his current password.

- *Password never expires*—A checkbox that exempts this user from the account policy that defines the maximum lifetime of a password.

- *Account is disabled*—A checkbox used to turn off an account. This prevents the account from being used but retains it for security auditing purposes.

- *Account is locked out*—A checkbox used by the lockout policy when an account meets the lockout parameters.

The Member Of tab (see Figure 5-6) lists the groups of which this user account is currently a member. To add group memberships, click the Add button. This opens the Select Groups dialog box. From this dialog box, you can type in the name of an existing local group to add this user account to. Or, you can click the Advanced tab, which opens a dialog box that searches for groups and displays a list to select from. To remove a group membership, select it on the Member Of tab and click Remove.

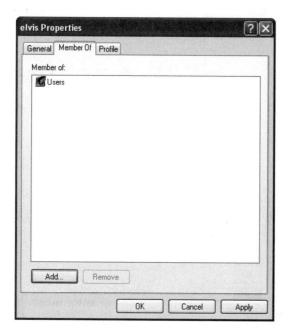

Figure 5-6   A user account's Properties dialog box, Member Of tab

The Profile tab (see Figure 5-7) is used to define the user profile path, logon script, and home folder. Because this is a Windows XP Professional local user, most of the paths used on this tab should be local (i.e., residing on the local computer). Profiles are discussed in detail later in this chapter. The Profile path defines the alternate location where a user's profile is to be stored. By default, user profiles are stored in \Documents and Settings\<*username*>, where <*username*> is the name of the user to whom the profile belongs or applies. The logon script is the local path to a logon script that can map drive letters, launch applications, or perform other command-line operations each time the system boots. The home folder is the default location for the storage of user-created documents and files. By default the home folder is the \Documents and Settings\<*username*>\My Documents folder, but this setting can be used to define an alternate location with either a path statement or with a mapped drive letter to a network share (such as K and \\mainserver\users\steve).

Figure 5-7   A user account's Properties dialog box, Profile tab

From within the Local Users and Groups tool, the Properties command from the pop-up menu of a user account is only one of several commands available. The others are:

- *Set Password*—Provides a new password and confirmation; the original password is not required.

- *Delete*—Completely removes a user account from the system, which, once deleted, is not recoverable. Recreating a new account, even with the same name and configuration, is seen as a different account by the system because its SID (security identifier) has changed.

- *Rename*—Changes the name of the user account.

- *Help*—Accesses context-sensitive help.

All other controls on a Windows XP Professional system are defined through the **Local Security Policy** tool (discussed later in this chapter). Microsoft Windows NT, 2000, and .NET Server user management tools offer several other configuration options due to the resources and services available on a domain level. Consult Windows NT, Windows 2000, or Windows .NET Server documentation for details on managing domain users.

Groups

Selecting the Groups node in the Local Users and Groups interface displays all existing local groups, which are named collections of users. All members of a group share the privileges or restrictions of that group. Groups are used to give a specific level of access to multiple users through a single management action. Once a group has access to a resource, users can be added to or removed from that group as needed. The group concept is key to managing large numbers of users and their access to any number of resources. In fact, if you use the group concept effectively, there should be little need to assign access rights to an individual user.

A local user can be a member of multiple groups. Different groups can be assigned different levels of access to the same resources. In such cases, the most permissive of all granted access levels is used, except when access is specifically denied by one or more groups.

As you plan your network security (covered in detail in Chapter 6, "Windows XP Security and Access Controls"), user base, and resource allocation, remember to keep in mind how you will be managing each of these groups. Think about how groups can be paired with resources to provide a wide range of administrative control. Once your resources are in place and all the required groups have been created, most of your administrative tasks involve adding users to or removing them from these groups.

To provide the highest degree of control over resources, Windows XP uses two types of groups: local and global. Local groups exist only on the computer where they are created. **Global groups** exist throughout a domain. Windows XP Professional can create and manage local groups, but not global groups. Windows XP Professional can add only existing global groups to its local groups to grant access to resources. This distinction is very important, as you'll soon see. Local groups can have members who are users or global groups.

To create and manage groups that can be used both within the domain and in trusting domains, you must have a Windows NT, 2000, or .NET Server in a client/server environment. If a Windows XP Professional system is part of a domain, its user tools can add global groups to local groups as members.

On a domain scale, a complete system of links from resources to users can be established. Each resource has one or more local groups assigned to it. Each user is assigned to one or more global groups. Global user groups are assigned to local resource groups. Each local group can be assigned different levels or types of access to the resource. By placing a global group in a local group, you assign all members of that global group the privileges of the local group, i.e., access to a resource. In other words, domain users are members of global groups that are members of local groups that are assigned access permissions to resources. On a standalone or workgroup system, local users are members of local groups that are assigned access permissions to resources.

You should plan your group management scheme long before you begin implementation. Planning such a scheme involves applying a naming scheme, dividing users into meaningful groups, and understanding the various levels of access your resources offer. For the group method to be effective, you need to manage all access to resources through groups. Never succumb to the temptation to assign access privileges directly to a user account.

Defining group members is often the most time-consuming process of group management. A group should be formed around a common job position, need of resource, or even geographic location. Some existing groupings you can transform into Windows XP groups are:

- Organizational functioning units, workgroups, or departments
- Authorized users of network programs and applications
- Events, projects, or special assignments
- Authorized users of network resources
- Location or geography
- Individual function or job description

As stated, local groups exist only on the computer where they are created. On each computer, all local groups must have a unique name. You can duplicate the names of local groups on different computers, but they are still separate, distinct groups. We don't recommend using the same name twice on any network, even if the architecture allows it.

Windows XP Professional has several default groups. When the groups node is selected in the Local Users and Groups interface, these default groups (as seen in Figure 5-8) are displayed. The default groups are:

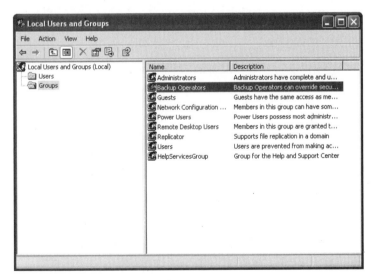

Figure 5-8   Local Users and Groups, Groups node

- *Administrators*—Members of this group have full access to the computer. The Local Administrator is always a member; additionally, if the system is a member of a domain, the Domain Admins group is a member.

- *Backup Operators*—Members of this group can back up and restore all files and folders on a system. It has no default members.

- *Guests*—Members can operate the computer and save files, but cannot install programs or alter system settings. Default member is the Guest account.

- *Network Configuration Operators*—Members can configure network components. It has no default members.

- *Power Users*—Members can modify the computer, create user accounts, share resources, and install programs, but cannot access files that belong to other users. It has no default members.

- *Remote Desktop Users*—Members can logon remotely.

- *Replicator*—This group is used by special user accounts to facilitate directory replication between systems and domains. It has no default members.

- *Users*—Members can operate the computer and save files, but cannot install programs, modify user accounts, share resources, or alter system settings. Default members are the Authenticated Users group (a non-configurable default group) and the Domain Users group if connected to a domain. By default, Windows XP adds all new local user accounts to this group.

- *HelpServicesGroup*—A specialty group used by the Help and Support Center.

The Properties dialog box for a user group allows you to change its description and alter its membership. You can add members to a group from the list of local user accounts or from the list of domain users accounts. Imported user accounts are not listed in this interface. Groups can also be deleted or renamed by selecting the command from the right-click pop-up menu.

New groups are created using the New Group command that appears in the right-click pop-up menu when the cursor is over a blank area of the details pane. When creating a new group, you must provide the group name, a description of the group, and add members.

System Groups and Other Important Groups

Windows XP Professional has several built-in system-controlled groups. System-controlled groups are pre-existing groups that you cannot manage but that appear in dialog boxes when assigned group membership or access permissions. These groups are used by the system to control or place restrictions on specific groups of users based on their activities. These groups include: Anonymous Logon, Batch, Creator Group, Creator Owner, Dialup, Everyone, Interactive, Local Service, Network, Network Service, Remote Interactive Logon, Service, System, and Terminal Server User.

USER PROFILES

A user profile is a collection of desktop and environmental configurations on a Windows XP system for a specific user or group of users. By default, each Windows XP computer maintains a profile for each user who has logged on to the computer, except for Guest accounts. Each user profile contains information about a particular user's Windows XP configuration. Much of this information is about settings the user can configure, such as color scheme, screen savers, and mouse and keyboard layout.

The material stored in a user profile includes:

- *Application Data*—A directory containing user-specific data, such as for Internet Explorer or Outlook

- *Cookies*—A directory containing cookies accepted by the user through their browser

- *Desktop*—A directory containing the icons displayed on the user's desktop

- *Favorites*—A directory containing the user's list of URLs from Internet Explorer

- *Local Settings*—A directory containing user-specific history information and temporary files

- *My Documents*—A directory containing user-created data

- *NetHood*—A directory containing user-specific network mappings

- *PrintHood*—A directory containing user-specific printer mappings

- *My Recent Documents*—A directory containing user-specific links to last accessed resources

- *SendTo*—A directory containing user-specific links used in the Sent To command of the right-click pop-up menu

- *Start Menu*—A directory containing the user-specific Start menu layout

- *Templates*—A directory containing user-specific templates

- *NTUSER.DAT*—A file containing Registry information specific to the user

- *NTUSER.DAT.LOG*—A transaction log file that ensures the profile can be re-created in the event of a failure

- *NTUSER.INI*—A file containing profile-related settings, such as what directories should not be uploaded to a roaming profile

Optionally, an administrator can force users to load a so-called **mandatory profile**. Users can adjust this profile while they're logged on, but all changes are lost as soon as they log off—that is, the settings assigned by the mandatory profile are restored the next time that user logs on. A mandatory profile is created by manually renaming the

NTUSER.DAT file to NTUSER.MAN. This technique provides a way for administrators to control the look and feel of shared accounts, or to restrict non-power users from exercising too much influence over their desktops.

User profiles are managed through the System applet. On the Advanced tab, clicking the Settings button under the User Profiles heading opens the User Profiles dialog box (see Figure 5-9). This dialog box lists all profiles for users who have logged into the Windows XP Professional system. This dialog box displays the name of the user account, along with defining its domain of origin, the disk space consumed by the profile, the profile type, status, and when it was last changed. Profiles can be of two types: local or roaming.

Anytime a user logs onto the system and that user account does not already have a user profile, one is created for them. This is done by duplicating the contents of the Default User profile. The All Users profile contains common elements that will appear in every user's environment, such as common Start menu items.

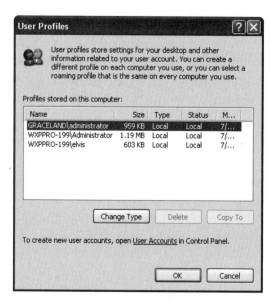

Figure 5-9   User Profiles dialog box

Local Profiles

A local profile is a set of specifications and preferences for an individual user, stored on a local machine. Windows XP provides each user with a folder containing their profile settings. Individual profiles are stored in the \Documents and Settings directory. A different location for the Profiles directory can be specified through the Local Users and Groups tool.

Local profiles are established by default for each user who logs onto a particular machine, and reside in the *%username%* subdirectory beneath the \Documents and Settings directory.

There is no single tool that permits all user profile information to be manipulated abstractly. There are only two ways to create a user profile. The first method is to logon as a user and arrange information as needed. Upon logout, this information becomes that user's local profile, which can then be transformed into a roaming profile. The second method is to assign a mandatory profile to that user from an existing definition. Even this must be set up by example, rather than through explicit controls.

Windows XP Professional local users (including imported users) have only local profiles. It is not possible to transform a local user's local profile to a roaming profile. However, a domain user account that logs onto a Windows XP Professional system will have a local profile created the first time they log on (assuming that user does not already have a roaming profile on the network). This local profile for the domain user can be transformed into a roaming profile.

Roaming Profiles

A roaming profile resides on a network server to make it broadly accessible. When a user whose profile is designated as roaming logs onto any Windows XP system on the network, that profile is automatically downloaded when the user logs on. This process avoids having to store a local profile on each workstation that a user uses. The disadvantage to using this kind of profile is that if a user's roaming profile is large, logging on to the network can take a long time because that information must be copied across the network each time that user logs on. In addition, any changes made to the user's profile are uploaded across the network when the user logs off.

The default path designation for a roaming profile is *computername**username* (*computername* is typically a network server, but not necessarily a domain controller). To create a roaming profile, it is necessary to use the "Copy to" button that appears in the User Profile tab of the System applet on a machine where a local profile for the user already exists. The destination for that copy operation must match the path that defines where the roaming profile resides (as manually defined in the user account); this is the mechanism that tells the startup module where to find a user's roaming profile. Once a local profile is present on a client, such as a Windows XP Professional system, you must use the System applet on that system to copy the profile to a network file server. Then, you must access the Active Directory Users and Computers tool on a domain controller to alter the profile path for the domain user account. You can create a roaming user profile for a local user by modifying the profile path for that user account through the Local Users and Groups tool.

LOCAL SECURITY POLICY

Windows XP has combined several security and access controls into a centralized policy. This centralized policy is called the group policy. There is a local security policy (i.e., a local group policy) for the local system and within a domain. Group policies can be defined for the domain, sites, and organizational units (OUs). All of these group policy types can be managed from a Windows 2000 or .NET Server system, but only the local computer group policy can be managed from a Windows XP Professional system.

Group policies are applied in the following manner:

1. Any existing legacy Windows NT 4.0 NTCONFIG.POL file is applied.

2. Any unique local group policy is applied (read local group-policy instead of local-group policy).

3. Any site group policies are applied.

4. Any domain group policies are applied.

5. Any organizational units (OU) group policies are applied.

Group policies are applied upon bootup and each time a user logs on. Group policies are refreshed every 90 minutes on Windows XP Professional if there are any changes and every 16 hours if there aren't.

The order of application of these policies is important because contradictory settings in the latter policies override the settings of the former policies. The cumulative result of this priority application of group policy is known as the effective policy. On Windows XP Professional systems, the effective policy is either all of these group policies properly combined when logged on with a domain user account or only the local group policy (the local group policy applies whether or not a user is logged on).

The Local Security Policy tool is used to edit the local group policy on a Windows XP Professional system. This tool is accessed from the Administrative Tools applet from the Control Panel. The local group policy consists of several sub-policies, including password, account lockout, audit, user rights, security options, public key, and IP security (see the "Windows XP Security and Access Controls" section in Chapter 6 for details on public key and IP security).

In the details section of the Local Security Policy tool, notice that each specific policy item is listed with both its local setting and its effective setting. Local settings apply when no one is logged on or when logged on with a local user account. Effective settings apply when logged on with a domain user account. For all policy items, only the local default setting is listed because the effective setting varies based on network configuration.

Password Policy

The Password Policy (see Figure 5-10) defines the restrictions on passwords. This policy is used to enforce strong passwords for a more secure environment. The items in this policy are:

- *Enforce password history: 0 Passwords*—Maintaining a password history prevents reuse of old passwords; a setting of 5 or greater for this item is recommended.

- *Maximum Password Age: 42 Days*—Defines when a password expires and must be replaced; a setting of 30, 45, or 60 days is recommended.

- *Minimum Password Age: 0 Days*—Defines the least amount of time that can pass between password changes; a setting of 1, 3, or 5 days is recommended.

- *Minimum Password Length: 0 Characters*—Sets the number of characters that must be present in a password; a setting of 6 or more is recommended.

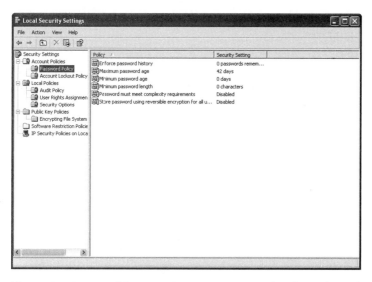

Figure 5-10   Local Security Settings, Password Policy selected

- *Passwords must meet complexity requirements of installed password filter: Disabled*— Determines whether passwords must comply with installed password filters. See the *Microsoft Windows .Net Server Resource Kit* for details.

- *Store passwords using reversible encryption for all users in the domain: Disabled*— Determines whether CHAP (Challenge Handshake Authentication Protocol) is used to encrypt passwords; leave this disabled unless required by a client.

Account Lockout Policy

The Account Lockout Policy defines the conditions that result when a user account is locked out. Lockout is used to prevent brute force attacks against user accounts. The items in this policy are:

- *Account lockout threshold: 0 Invalid logon attempts*—Defines the number of failed logons that must occur before an account is locked out; a setting of 3 to 5 is recommended.

- *Account lockout duration: Not Applicable (defaults to 30 minutes once Account Lockout Threshold is defined)*—Defines the length of time an account remains locked out; a value of 0 causes locked-out accounts to require administrative action to unlock, a setting of 30 minutes to 2 hours is recommended.

- *Reset account lockout counter after: Not Applicable (defaults to 30 minutes once Account Lockout Threshold is defined)*—Defines the length of time that must expire before the failed logon attempts for a user account is reset; a setting of 15 minutes is recommended.

Audit Policy

The Audit Policy defines the events that are recorded in the Security log of the Event Viewer. Auditing is used to track resource usage. Each item in this list can be set to audit the Success and/or Failure of the event. The items in this policy are as follows:

- *Audit account logon events: No auditing*—Audits authentication of a user account on this system when it is used to logon or off another system.

- *Audit account management: No auditing*—This item audits the changes to user accounts and group memberships.

- *Audit directory service access: No auditing*—Audits access to Active Directory objects.

- *Audit logon events: No auditing*—Audits user account logins, logoffs, and establishment of network connections.

- *Audit object access: No auditing*—Audits resource access.

- *Audit policy change: No auditing*—Audits changes to the security policy.

- *Audit privilege use: No auditing*—Audits use of special rights or privileges.

- *Audit process tracking: No auditing*—Audits the activity of processes.

- *Audit system events: No auditing*—Audits system-level activities.

 For more details about auditing, see Chapter 6.

User Rights Policy

The **User Rights Policy** defines which groups or users can perform the specific privileged action. The items in this policy are:

- *Access this computer from the network*—Everyone, Users, Power Users, Backup Operators, Administrators

- *Act as part of the operating system*—None

- *Add workstation to domain*—None

- *Adjust memory quotas for a process*—Local Service, Network Service, Administrators

- *Allow logon through Terminal Services*—Administrators, Remote Desktop Users

- *Back up files and directories*—Backup Operators, Administrators
- *Bypass traverse checking*—Everyone, Users, Power Users, Backup Operators, Administrators
- *Change the system time*—Power Users, Administrators
- *Create a pagefile*—Administrators
- *Create a token object*—None
- *Create permanent shared objects*—None
- *Debug programs*—Administrators
- *Deny access to this computer from the network*—Guest, SUPPORT
- *Deny logon as a batch job*—SUPPORT
- *Deny logon as a service*—None
- *Deny logon locally*—Guest, SUPPORT
- *Deny logon through Terminal Services*—None
- *Enable computer and user accounts to be trusted for delegation*—None
- *Force shutdown from a remote system*—Administrators
- *Generate security audits*—Local Services, Network Service
- *Increase quotas*—Administrators
- *Load and unload device drivers*—Administrators
- *Lock pages in memory*—None
- *Logon as a batch job*—None
- *Logon as a service*—Network Service
- *Logon locally*—Guest account, Users, Power Users, Backup Operators, Administrators
- *Manage auditing and security log*—Administrators
- *Modify firmware environment values*—Administrators
- *Perform volume maintenance tasks*—Administrators
- *Profile single process*—Power Users, Administrators
- *Profile system performance*—Administrators
- *Remove computer from docking station*—Users, Power Users, Administrators
- *Replace a process level token*—LOCAL SERVICE, NETWORK SERVICE
- *Restore files and directories*—Backup Operators, Administrators

- *Shut down the system*—Users, Power Users, Backup Operators, Administrators
- *Synchronize directory service data*—None
- *Take ownership of files or other objects*—Administrators

User Rights are enabled as defined in the previous list by default. You can alter this configuration through the User Rights Assignment section of the Local Security Policy. Troubleshooting user rights is a process of test, re-configure, and retest. If you suspect an action cannot be performed that should be possible, test, re-set the associated user right, re-log on that user, and try the action again. Be sure to double-check any file or object permissions associated with the action because it can be blocked by lack of access rather than a user right.

For more details on these user rights, consult the *Microsoft Windows XP Professional Resource Kit*.

Security Options

Security Options defines and controls various security features, functions, and controls of the Windows XP environment. The items in this policy are:

- Accounts: Administrator account status: Enabled
- Accounts: Guest account status: Disabled
- Accounts: Limit local account use of blank passwords to console logon only: Enable
- Accounts: Rename administrator account: Administrator
- Accounts: Rename guest account: Guest
- Audit: Audit the access of global system objects: Disabled
- Audit: Audit use of Backup and Restore privilege: Disabled
- Audit: Shut down system immediately if unable to log security audits: Disabled
- Devices: Allow undock without having to logon: Enabled
- Devices: Allowed to format and eject removable media: Administrators
- Devices: Prevent users from installing printer drivers: Disabled
- Devices: Restrict CD-ROM access to locally logged-on user only: Disabled
- Devices: Restrict floppy access to locally logged-on user only: Disabled
- Devices: Unsigned driver installation behavior: Warn but allow installation
- Domain controller: Allow server operators to schedule tasks: Not defined
- Domain controller: LDAP server signing requirements: Not defined

- Domain controller: Refuse machine account password changes: Not defined
- Domain member: Digitally encrypt or sign secure channel data (always): Enabled
- Domain member: Digitally encrypt secure channel data (when possible): Enabled
- Domain member: Digitally sign secure channel data (when possible): Enabled
- Domain member: Disable machine account password changes: Disabled
- Domain member: Maximum machine account password age: 30 days
- Domain member: Require strong (Windows 2000 or later) session key: Disabled
- Interactive logon: Do not display last user name: Disabled
- Interactive logon: Do not require CTRL+ALT+DEL: Not defined
- Interactive logon: Message text for users attempting to logon: blank
- Interactive logon: Message title for users attempting to logon: Not defined
- Interactive logon: Number of previous logons to cache (in case domain controller is not available): 10 logons
- Interactive logon: Prompt user to change password before expiration: 14 days
- Interactive logon: Require Domain Controller authentication to unlock workstation: Disabled
- Interactive logon: Smart card removal behavior: No Action
- Microsoft network client: Digitally sign communications (always): Disabled
- Microsoft network client: Digitally sign communications (if server agrees): Enabled
- Microsoft network client: Send unencrypted password to third-party SMB server: Disabled
- Microsoft network server: Amount of idle time required before suspending session: 15 minutes
- Microsoft network server: Digitally sign communications (always): Disabled
- Microsoft network server: Digitally sign communications (if client agrees): Disabled
- Microsoft network server: Disconnect clients when logon hours expire: Enabled
- Network access: Allow anonymous SID/Name translation: Disabled

5

- Network access: Do not allow anonymous enumeration of SAM accounts: Enabled

- Network access: Do not allow anonymous enumeration of SAM accounts and shares: Disabled

- Network access: Do not allow storage of credentials or .NET Passports for network authentication: Disabled

- Network access: Let Everyone permissions apply to anonymous users: Disabled

- Network access: Named Pipes that can be accessed anonymously: COMNAP, COMNODE, SQL/QUERY, SPOOLSS, LLSRPC, EPMAPPER, LOCATOR, TrkWks, TrkSvr

- Network access: Remotely accessible Registry paths: System\CurrentControlSet\Control\ProductOptions, System\CurrentControlSet\Control\Print\Printers, System\CurrentControlSet\Control\Server Applications, System\CurrentControlSet\Services\Eventlog, Software\Microsoft\OLAP Server, Software\Microsoft\Windows NT\Current Version, System\CurrentControlSet\Control\ContentIndex, System\CurrentControlSet\Control\Terminal Server, System\CurrentControlSet\Control\Terminal Server\UserConfig, System\CurrentControlSet\Control\Terminal Server\DefaultUserConfig

- Network access: Shares that can be accessed anonymously: COMCFG, DFS$

- Network access: Sharing and security model for local accounts: Guest only— local users authenticate as Guest

- Network security: Do not share LAN Manager has value on next password change: Disabled

- Network security: Force logoff when logon hours expire: Disabled

- Network security: LAN Manager authentication level: Send LM & NTLM responses

- Network security: LDAP client signing requirements: Negotiate signing

- Network security: Minimum session security for NTLM SSP based (including secure RPC) clients: No minimum

- Network security: Minimum session security for NTLM SSP based (including secure RPC) servers: No minimum

- Recovery console: Allow automatic administrative logon: Disabled

- Recovery console: Allow floppy copy an access to all drives and all folders: Disabled

- Shutdown: Allow system to be shut down without having to logon: Enabled

- Shutdown: Clear virtual memory pagefile: Disabled

- System cryptography: Use FIPS compliant algorithms for encryption, hashing, and signing: Disabled

- System objects: Default owner for objects created by members of Administrators group: Object creator

- System objects: Require case insensitivity for non-Windows subsystems: Enabled

- System objects: Strengthen default permissions of internal system objects (e.g., Symbolic Links): Enabled

For more details on these security options, consult the *Microsoft Windows XP Professional Resource Kit.*

TROUBLESHOOTING CACHED CREDENTIALS

Windows XP Professional automatically caches a user's credentials in the Registry when a domain logon or .NET passport logon is performed. Caching of credentials is used to enable a single sign-on requirement. This process allows a user access to shared resources from the network without having to re-authenticate each time. By default, Windows XP caches credentials for the last 10 users who logged on. Caching of credentials can be disabled through two means from the Windows XP Professional client. One method is to enable the following group policy setting: Network access: Do not allow Stored User Names and Passwords to save passwords or credentials for domain authentication (this setting is located within Computer Configuration, Windows Settings, Security Settings, Local Policies, Security Options). The second method is to set the "cachedlogonscount" Registry value within the HKEY_LOCAL_MACHINE\SOFTWARE\Microsoft\ Windows NT\CurrentVersion\WinLogon key to 0. It is set to 10 by default. Troubleshooting credential caching typically involves disabling the feature and rebooting the system to clear out the previously cached information. Not caching credentials is a more secure configuration.

In addition to caching logon credentials, Windows XP also retains usernames and passwords for resources. These cached resource access credentials are managed through a utility called "Stored User Names and Passwords." This utility is accessed through the User Accounts applet. If you are a domain member, select the Advanced tab and click Manage Passwords. If you are not a domain member, click the account name and click Manage my network passwords from the Related Tasks lists. From this simple window, you can add, remove, or edit stored credentials. If either of the changes to disable caching of credentials is implemented, Windows XP will also disable Stored User Names and Passwords from retaining resource access logon credentials.

If you discover that you are being authenticated as the wrong user account or with the wrong access level, you should remove the stored account information for that server or domain. The next time you attempt to access the resource, you should be prompted for your credentials. Another problem is being unable to access resources to which you previously had access. In many cases, this may indicate that your account has expired or your password must be changed. To remedy this type of situation, edit your account credentials to reflect the updated account information. Yet another problem might occur when you obtain access to a resource to which you should not have access. In most cases, this indicates that stored credentials should be deleted to remove this unauthorized access. You should even consider disabling the storage of credentials by enabling the security option within group policy.

FILE AND SETTINGS TRANSFER WIZARD

The Files and Settings Transfer Wizard is used to move your data files and personal desktop settings from another computer to your new Windows XP Professional system. You must have some sort of network connection between the two systems; this can be a standard LAN connection, a direct cable connection, or a dial-up connection. Using this Wizard, you can transfer files from Windows 95, 98, SE, Me, NT, 2000, or XP systems. To launch this Wizard, select Start | All Programs | Accessories | System Tools.

To use the Wizard, you must be able to execute it on both the new and old systems. If you have the Windows XP Professional CD on hand, you can launch the Wizard from the \Support\Tools folder (it's called FASTWiz.exe). If you don't have the CD, you can create a Wizard disk from which you can launch the Wizard on the old system. The process involved in using the Files and Settings Transfer Wizard is put to use in Hands-on Project 5-10.

The transfer process can take considerable time. The default settings are to grab nearly every file that is not native to the Windows OS or installed applications. This means every document, sound, movie, image, or other file type will be included in the default file selection. There is an option to custom-select the files to transfer. If you have a significant amount of files, you may want to use this option to reduce the time and space consumed by the transfer process.

CHAPTER SUMMARY

❑ In this chapter, you learned about local users and groups. Windows XP Professional can employ three types of users: locally created users, imported users, and domain users. A user account stores preference settings for each individual who uses a computer. Each user can have his own profile that retains all of his preferred desktop settings. Users are collected into groups to simplify management and grant access or privileges. Users and groups are managed through the User Accounts applet and the Local Users and Groups utility. Windows XP Professional has two built-in users:

Administrator and Guest, and several built-in groups. Some groups allow you to customize their membership; others are system-controlled groups with memberships that cannot be customized.

❑ User profiles can be local or roaming. User profiles store a wide variety of personalized or custom data about a user's environment. A user profile can be mandatory just by changing NTUSER.DAT to NTUSER.MAN.

❑ The Local Security Policy is used to manage password, account lockout, audit, user rights, security options, and more. These controls aid in enforcing security and controlling who is able to perform specific actions on the system.

5

KEY TERMS

account lockout policy — Defines the conditions that result in a user account being locked out.

Administrator account — The most powerful account possible within the Windows XP environment.

audit policy — Defines the events that are recorded in the Security log of the Event Viewer.

disabled — The state of a user account, which is retained on the system but cannot be used to logon.

domain user account — A user account that can be used throughout a domain.

global group — A group that exists throughout a domain. A global group can be created only on a Windows Server system.

groups — A named collections of users.

Guest account — One of the least privileged user accounts in Windows XP.

imported user account — A local account created by duplicating the name and password of an existing domain account. An imported account can be used only when the Windows XP Professional system is able to communicate with the domain of the original account.

local groups — A group that exists only on the computer where it was created. A local group can have users and global groups as members.

Local Security Policy — The centralized control mechanism that governs password, account lockout, audit, user rights, security options, public key, and IP security.

local user account — A user account that exists on a single computer.

locked out — The state of a user account that is disabled due to logon attempts that have repeatedly failed.

logon authentication — The requirement to provide a name and password to gain access to the computer.

mandatory profile — A user profile that does not retain changes once the user logs out. Mandatory profiles are used to maintain a common desktop environment for users.

multiple-user system — An operating system that maintains separate and distinct user accounts for each person.

naming convention — A standardized regular method of creating names for objects, users, computers, groups, etc.

password policy — Defines the restrictions on passwords.

profile — See *user profile*.

security options — Defines and controls various security features, functions, and controls of the Windows XP environment.

user account — A named security element used by a computer system to identify individuals and to record activity, control access, and retain settings.

user profile — A collection of user-specific settings that retain the state of the desktop, Start menu, color scheme, and other environmental aspects across logons.

User Rights Policy — Defines which groups or users can perform the specific privileged action.

REVIEW QUESTIONS

1. Windows XP Professional is able to create and manage what types of user accounts?

   a. Local

   b. Domain

   c. Imported

   d. Global

2. What types of user accounts can be used on a Windows XP Professional system?

   a. Local

   b. Domain

   c. Imported

   d. Global

3. When not connected to a network, what types of user accounts can be employed on a Windows XP Professional system?

   a. Local

   b. Domain

   c. Imported

   d. Global

4. A Windows XP Professional is an operating system that can allow more than one user account to log onto a single system simultaneously. True or False?

5. Which of the following are true of groups?

   a. Several default groups are built into Windows XP

   b. Are named collections of users

   c. The system groups can be deleted through the Local Users and Groups tool

   d. Used to simply the assignment of permissions

6. Why does Windows XP require logon authentication?

   a. To prevent the spread of viruses

   b. To track computer usage by user account

   c. To maintain security

   d. To promote a naming scheme

7. Which of the following are true for both the Administrator account and the Guest account?

   a. Cannot be deleted

   b. Can be locked out

   c. Cannot be disabled

   d. Can be renamed

8. When logged on under the Guest account, a user has the same access as other members of what group?

   a. Authenticated Users

   b. Users

   c. Power Users

   d. Everyone

9. Imported user accounts can be managed through what interface?

   a. User Manager for Domains

   b. User Accounts

   c. Local Users and Groups

   d. Active Directory Users and Computers

10. Which of the following are true of imported users?

   a. Can only be a member of a single group

   b. You can change their password

   c. Exist only when their domain of origin is present online

   d. Are used to grant domain users access to the local resources

11. When creating a new user through the User Accounts applet, the Restricted user selection makes the new user a member of what group?

    a. Guests

    b. Power Users

    c. Users

    d. Backup Operators

12. To configure more than one group membership for a local user account requires the use of the User Accounts applet. True or False?

13. When the control item under Secure logon on the Advanced tab of the Users and Password applet is selected, not only is Ctrl+Alt+Delete not required, but the last user account to successfully logon is automatically re-used to log onto the system. True or False?

14. You create several new user accounts. You tell everyone they need to logon and change their password to something other than the dummy password you entered to create the account. In the past you've discovered that most users forget to change the password. How can you force them to make this change?

    a. User cannot change password

    b. User must change password at next logon

    c. Password never expires

    d. Account is disabled

15. On a Windows XP Professional client, what types of profiles can be used?

    a. Local

    b. Roaming

    c. Mandatory

    d. Dynamic

16. User profiles are stored by default in a sub-directory named after the user account in what default directory on a Windows XP Professional system?

    a. \Winnt\Profiles

    b. \Users

    c. \Profiles

    d. \Documents and Settings

17. The user account Properties dialog box from the Local Users and Groups tool can be used to change the password. True or False?

18. The user tools of Windows XP Professional can create and manage both local and global groups. True or False?

19. Local groups can have global groups as members. True or False?

20. Which of the following groups are not configurable?

    a. Administrators

    b. Interactive

    c. Backup Operators

    d. Creator Owner

    e. Authenticated Users

21. What makes a profile mandatory?

    a. Checkbox setting through the user account's Properties dialog box

    b. Storing it locally

    c. Renaming a file with the extension .MAN

    d. By not connecting to a network

22. The effective policy is the result of applying all network- or domain-hosted security policies then finally applying the local security policy. True or False?

23. The local security policy is a collection of what individual policies?

    a. password

    b. account lockout

    c. audit

    d. user rights

    e. computer settings

    f. security options

    g. public key

    h. IP security

24. To prevent malicious users from breaking into your computer system by repeatedly trying to guess a password, what built-in security tool can you use?

    a. Password policy

    b. IP security

    c. Lockout

    d. Encryption

25. What control element in Windows XP is used to assign specific privileged actions to users and groups?

    a. Auditing

    b. User rights

    c. Profiles

    d. Security options

5

HANDS-ON PROJECTS

Project 5-1

To import a user account:

This hands-on project requires that a domain be accessible over a network connection.

1. Open the Control Panel (**Start | Control Panel**).
2. Double-click **User Accounts**.
3. Click **Add**.
4. In the Add New User Wizard, click **Browse**.
5. Select a user account from the list. Click **OK**.
6. Click **Next**.
7. Select **Standard User** when prompted about the level of access to grant this user, click **Finish**.
8. Notice the imported user appears in the list of users on the User Accounts applet.

Project 5-2

To change group membership of an imported user:

This hands-on project requires that Hands-on Project 5-1 be completed.

1. In the User Accounts applet, select the imported user created in Hands-on Project 5-1.
2. Click **Properties**.
3. On the Group Membership tab, select the **Other** radio button.
4. From the pull-down list, select **Power Users**.
5. Click **OK**.

Project 5-3

To delete a user account:

1. In the User Accounts applet, select the imported user created in Hands-on Project 5-1.
2. Click **Remove**.
3. When asked to confirm, click **Yes**.

Project 5-4

To create a new local user account:

1. Select the **Advanced** tab on the User Accounts applet.
2. Click the **Advanced** button.
3. Select the **Users** node in the console tree of Local Users and Groups.
4. Select **Action|New User**.
5. In the New User dialog box, enter a user name (such as **BobTemp**), full name (such as **Bob Smith**), and description (such as **A temporary account for Bob**).
6. Provide a password and confirm that password.
7. Deselect the **User must change password at next logon** checkbox.
8. Click **Create**.
9. Click **Close**.
10. The BobTemp user account is now listed in the details pane.

Project 5-5

To change group membership for a local user account:

This hands-on project requires that Hands-on Project 5-4 be completed.

1. Select the **BobTemp** user account created in Hands-on Project 5-4.
2. Select **Action|Properties**.
3. Select the **Member Of** tab.
4. Click the **Add** button.
5. Click the **Advanced** button.
6. Click **Find Now**.
7. Select the **Power Users** group.
8. Click **OK**.

9. Click **OK**.

10. Select the **Users** group.

11. Click **Remove**.

12. Click **OK** to close the Properties dialog box.

Project 5-6

To create a local group:

This hands-on project requires that Hands-on Project 5-4 be completed.

1. Select the **Groups** node in the console tree.

2. Select **Action | New Group**.

3. In the New Group dialog box, provide a group name (such as **SalesGrp**) and description (such as **Members of the sales department**).

4. Click **Add**.

5. Click **Advanced**.

6. Click **Find Now**.

7. Select the **BobTemp** user.

8. Click **OK**.

9. Click **OK**.

10. Click **Create**.

11. Click **Close**.

Project 5-7

To delete a group:

This hands-on project requires that Hands-on Project 5-5 be completed.

1. Select the **SalesGrp** created in Hands-on Project 5-5.

2. Select **Action | Delete**.

3. When prompted to confirm, click **Yes**.

might audit access to certain network resources such as files or printers by different users and/or groups. To set an object's auditing controls, perform the following steps:

 Auditing can be configured only for users and resources that belong to a domain, not a work group.

1. Open the Properties dialog box for an NTFS object (such as a file, folder, or printer). Right-click the object, then select **Properties** from the pop-up menu.

2. Select the **Security** tab.

3. Click the **Advanced** button.

4. Select the **Auditing** tab. This displays all of the currently defined audit events for this object. It is blank by default.

5. Click the **Add** button.

6. Click the **Advanced** button.

7. Click the **Find Now** button.

8. Select a computer, group, or a user from the Select User, Computer, or Group dialog box.

9. Click **OK**.

10. Click **OK**.

11. Select either **Successful** or **Failed** for any of the listed actions for this object type. The selections made here are the actions that are recorded in the Security Log.

 If you selected to record only Failures in the Local Security Policy, selecting Successful actions on this dialog box does not record items in the Security Log.

12. Click **OK**.

13. Repeat steps 5 through 12 for all users, computers, or groups.

14. Repeat steps 1 through 13 for all objects.

 Auditing numerous objects or events can result in a large Security Log and can slow down network or computer performance.

The Event Viewer can be configured to monitor the size of the Security Log and to take action when it reaches a target size. The actions are Overwrite events as needed, Overwrite events older than XX days, or Do not overwrite events. If the maximum size is reached and Do not overwrite events is selected, an alert appears stating that the log needs to be cleared. To access these controls, select Properties from the menu that appears when right-clicking over the Security Log node in the Event Viewer.

ENCRYPTED FILE SYSTEM

Microsoft has extended the native NTFS file system to include encrypted storage. This new security measure, the **Encrypted File System (EFS)**, allows you to encrypt data stored on NTFS drive. When EFS is enabled on a file, folder, or drive, only the enabling user can gain access to the encrypted object. EFS is enabled through a checkbox accessed through the Advanced button on the General tab of an object's Properties dialog box.

EFS uses a public and private key encryption method. The private key is assigned to a single user account. No other user, computer, or operating system can gain access to the encrypted files. For the authorized user (i.e., the user with the correct private key), access to the encrypted files is unhindered. In fact, the entire encryption process is invisible to the user.

Note

Encryption is just another attribute of NTFS; therefore, you should treat encryption in the same manner as attributes and permissions. Any new file created or copied into an encrypted folder assumes the settings of that folder. Moving an encrypted file to a nonencrypted folder allows the file to retain its original settings, but copying the encrypted file causes the file to assume the settings of the destination folder. Because EFS is an additional level of processing required by the operating system to grant access to file-level objects, the performance of the file system can be noticeably impaired. You'll need to perform your own baseline comparison of your storage system's performance to determine exactly how much degradation is caused by EFS.

If the encryption key is lost or the user account is deleted, there is a mechanism to recover encrypted files. This mechanism is called the recovery agent, which is defined through Group Policy under the Public Key Policies. EFS does not function without a recovery agent. In fact, Windows XP (and Windows 2000) automatically designates the local Administrator as the recovery agent until you specifically define another recovery agent. The recovery agent is able to decrypt files by logging onto the system where the files are stored and de-selecting the Encrypt checkbox on the files and folder's Advanced Properties dialog box. For more details on the Recovery agent, please consult the *Microsoft Windows XP Professional Resource Kit*.

Windows XP includes a command-line tool for batch-processing of encryption (i.e., encrypting or decrypting large numbers of files or folders through a command line or batch file). The CIPHER command has the following syntax:

```
CIPHER [/E|/D] [/S[:directory]] [/A] [/I] [/F] [/Q]
       [/H] [pathname [...]]
CIPHER /K
CIPHER /R:pathname
CIPHER /U [/N]
CIPHER /W:directory
```

The following list defines each of the CIPHER command's parameters:

- /A—Forces operation on files and folders.

- /D—Decrypts the listed filename(s).

- /E—Encrypts the listed filename(s).

- /F—Forces encryption, even on already encrypted files.

- /H—Shows files with the hidden or system attributed set.

- /I—Ignores errors and proceeds with processing.

- /K—Creates a new encryption key for the user.

- /N—Prevents encryption keys from being updated. Must be used with /U.

- /Q—Silences activity except for essential feedback.

- /R—Generates a recovery agent key and certificate into .PFX and .CER files.

- /S—Performs the action on all subcontents.

- /U—Scans for all encrypted files on local drives to update user's encryption key.

- /W—Removes deleted data in the available disk space.

- *Pathname*—Specifies a pattern, file, or directory. Wildcards can be used; each pattern must be separated by a space.

- *Directory*—Specifies a directory.

When CIPHER is used with only a filename and without parameters, the status of the object is displayed, indicating whether the object is encrypted and whether new files added to a folder will be encrypted.

The primary benefit of EFS is that if your computer is either physically accessed or stolen, the data is protected as long as the malicious user does not gain access to the username and password that holds the private key for the encrypted files. The primary drawback is the increased processing power required to encrypt all writes and decrypt all reads on the fly. This process negatively affects performance to a noticeable extent on many systems.

6

INTERNET SECURITY

Connecting to the Internet requires that you accept some risk. That risk includes downloading Trojan horses or viruses, accepting malicious e-mail, or even allowing a remote cracker to take complete control of your computer. Most of the security features used to protect data within a LAN or even on a standalone system can also be leveraged to protect against Internet attacks. Plus, Microsoft has added the Internet Connection Firewall to Windows XP. The Internet Connection Firewall (ICF) is a simple firewall used to protect any network connection, especially dial-up or dedicated Internet links. ICF is discussed in detail in Chapter 8, "Internetworking with Remote Access."

CHAPTER SUMMARY

❑ Windows XP has object-level access controls that provide the foundation on which all resource access rest. By comparing the access control lists associated with individual objects to the access tokens that define the rights of any user process, Windows XP decides which object access requests to grant and which to deny.

❑ The Windows XP logon process (WinLogon) strictly controls how users identify themselves and log onto a Windows XP machine. The attention sequence (Ctrl+Alt+Delete) prevents an unauthorized user from obtaining system access to domain clients or properly configured standalone clients. Likewise, WinLogon's protected memory structures keep this all-important gatekeeper function from being replaced by would-be system crackers. Authentication can take place using various encryption schemes, including Kerberos, SSL, or NTLM.

❑ WinLogon also supports a number of logon controls: handling of a default logon name, providing security notices, changing the default shell, handling system shutdown options, and enabling automatic logon. Key Local Computer Policy settings can be used to block unauthorized break-in attempts.

❑ The local computer policy controls many aspects of the security system as well as enabling or restricting specific functions and features of the operating system. You can use Windows XP auditing capabilities to track down errant behavior or detect when system problems may be occurring. Encrypted File System (EFS) protects your data with an encryption system. All in all, Windows XP offers a reasonably secure operating environment that is designed to help administrators keep their important assets safe from harm and unwanted exposure.

KEY TERMS

access control list (ACL) — A list of security identifiers that are contained by a resource object. Only those processes with the appropriate access token can activate the services of that object.

access token — Objects containing the security identifier of an active process. These tokens determine the security context of the process.

auditing — This is the process of tracking events by recording selected types of events in the Security Log.

authentication — The process of validating a user's credentials to allow access to certain resources.

certificate — An electronic identity verification mechanism. Certificates are assigned to a client or server by a Certificate Authority. When communications begin, each side of the transmission can decide to either trust the other party based on their certificate and continue the communications or not to trust and terminate communications.

domain — A collection of computers with centrally managed security and activities.

domain controller — A specified computer role of WindowsNT, 2000, or .NET Servers that authenticates domain logons and maintains the security policies and the account database for a domain.

domain security — The control of user accounts, group memberships, and resource access for all members of a network instead of for only a single computer.

Encrypted File System (EFS) — A security feature of NTFS under Windows XP that allows files, folders, or entire drives to be encrypted. Once encrypted, only the user account that enabled the encryption has the proper private key to decrypt and access the secured objects.

event — Any significant occurrence in the system or in an application that requires users to be notified or a log entry to be added. Types of events include audits, driver failures, user logon, process launching, system shutdown, etc.

Event Viewer — The utility that maintains application, security, and system event logs on your computer, enabling you to view and manage the event logs, gather information about hardware and software problems, and monitor Windows XP security events.

identification — The process of establishing a valid account identity on a Windows XP machine by supplying a correct and working domain name (if necessary) and account name.

IPSec (IP Security) — An encrypted communication mechanism for TCP/IP to create protected communication sessions. IPSec is a suite of cryptography-based protection services and security protocols.

Kerberos version 5 — An authentication encryption protocol employed by Windows XP to protect logon credentials.

Local Computer Policy — A Windows XP security control feature used to define and regulate security-related features and functions.

network authentication — The act of connecting to or accessing resources from some other member of the domain network. Network authentication is used to prove that you are a valid member of the domain, that your user account is properly authenticated, and that you have access permissions to perform the requested action.

NTLM (NT LAN Manager) authentication — The authentication mechanism used on Windows NT that is retained by Windows XP for backward compatibility.

object — Everything within the Windows XP operating environment is an object. Objects include files, folders, shares, printers, processes, etc.

6

password — A unique string of characters that must be provided before a logon or an access is authorized. Passwords are a security measure used to restrict initial access to Windows XP resources.

process — The primary unit of execution in the Windows XP operating system environment. A process may contain one or more execution threads, all associated with a named user account, SID, and access token. Processes essentially define the container within which individual applications and commands execute under Windows XP.

public key policy — A security control of Windows XP where recovery agents for EFS and domain-wide and trusted certificate authorities are defined and configured. These policies can be enforced on a user by user basis.

Secure Socket Layer/Transport Layer Security (SSL/TLS) — A mechanism used primarily over HTTP communications to create an encrypted session link through the exchange of certificates and public encryption keys.

security ID (SID) — A unique number that identifies a logged-on user to the security system. SIDs can identify one user or a group of users.

shell — The default user process that is launched when a valid account name and password combination is authenticated by the WinLogon process for Windows XP. The default shell of Windows XP is Windows Explorer. The default shell process manages the desktop, Start menu, taskbar, and other interface controls. The shell process defines a logged on user's runtime environment from this point forward, and supplies all spawned processes or commands with its access token to define their access permissions until that account logs out.

user account — This entity contains all of the information that defines a user to the Windows XP environment.

WinLogon — The process used by Windows XP to control user authentication and manage the logon process. WinLogon produces the logon dialog box where user name, password, and domain are selected, controls automated logon, warning text, the display of the shutdown button, and the display of the last user to log onto the system.

REVIEW QUESTIONS

1. Which of the following should be used to define IPSec policies for a domain?

   a. TCP/IP Properties

   b. Local Computer Policy

   c. Event Viewer

   d. Group Policy

2. All processes in Windows XP require an access token. True or False?

3. A SID is a unique number and is never duplicated. True or False?

4. Permissions that are changed while the user is actively logged on do not take effect until that user logs on to the system again. True or False?

5. The default Windows XP authentication method is to supply valid domain and account names, plus a valid password; however, Windows XP permits use of alternate authentication techniques. True or False?

6. What is the first thing the security system looks for when it scans an ACL for an object?

   a. A Deny to the object for the requested service, at which point access is immediately denied

   b. Any Allow permission that provides the requested permission

   c. It checks the default, and if access is permitted thereby, allows the request to proceed

   d. None of the above

7. What is the default access level that Windows XP assigns to new objects by default?

   a. Restrict

   b. Allow

8. Which of the following is a good reason for adding DontDisplayLastUserName to the Windows XP Registry? (Choose all that apply.)

   a. To prevent easy discovery of user account names

   b. To improve security on a shared machine

   c. To reduce burnout on the machine's monitor

   d. To force users to provide a valid user name in addition to a password to logon

9. The Windows XP authentication process can be automated by adding default user information and the _____ value to the Registry.

   a. DontDisplayLastUsername

   b. AutoAdminLogon

   c. Legal Notice Caption

   d. AutomateLogon

10. Which of the following is the most likely reason for a security notice that appears when users attempt to logon to a Windows XP machine at the National Security Agency?

   a. To make sure that outsiders don't try to break into the system.

   b. To inform unauthorized users that they are subject to legal action if they obtain unauthorized access to the system.

   c. To remind valid system users about Acceptable Use Policies.

   d. None of the above

11. The default shell process for Windows XP is called the:

    a. Windows Explorer

    b. Program Manager

    c. Command shell

    d. C shell

12. The _____ is created by the Windows XP security subsystem at logon and identifies the current user to the subsystem.

    a. Access ID

    b. Security ID

    c. Group ID

    d. access token

13. The _____ key sequence initiates the classic logon process.

    a. Ctrl+Esc

    b. Alt+Tab

    c. Ctrl+Break

    d. Ctrl+Alt+Delete

14. An access token is required to access any Windows XP object. True or False?

15. To customize the security structure of your Windows XP system, you can change the behavior of the logon process. True or False?

16. What is the primary protocol that Windows XP uses for authentication?

    a. NTLM

    b. Secure Socket Layer

    c. Kerberos

    d. NetBIOS

17. Which of the following statements are true about the Local Computer Policy? (Choose all that apply.)

    a. It is used to control aspects of the Windows XP security system.

    b. It is used to assign user accounts to groups.

    c. It can be customized by third-party applications.

    d. It can be superceded by a domain's Group Policy.

18. What is the special-purpose application invoked by the Windows XP attention sequence that serves as the logon process?

    a. WINPOPUP

    b. WINLOGON

    c. USERMGR

    d. EXPLORER

19. What security feature is included in Windows XP specifically to protect TCP/IP communications between two systems?

    a. Kerberos version 5

    b. IPSec

    c. Strong passwords

    d. EFS

20. What is EFS used to protect?

    a. Passwords

    b. Data files

    c. Group Policy

    d. Communication sessions

21. If the Windows Explorer shell is replaced with the Program Manager shell, which of the following side effects will occur? (Choose all that apply.)

    a. No access to the Start menu

    b. No task bar

    c. No access to the Task Manager

    d. No more DOS Command prompt

22. Only the user who encrypted a file through EFS can access that file later. True or False?

23. What predefined IPSec policy should you use to employ encryption only when required by a remote system?

    a. Client (Respond Only)

    b. Server (Request Security)

    c. Secure Server (Require Security)

24. Auditing can be defined for an object for specific users and groups for one or more individual services or actions. True or False?

25. Audit events are recorded in the System log. True or False?

Hands-on Projects

Project 6-1

To open the Local Computer Policy:

    1. Open the **Run** command (**Start|Run**).

    2. Type **mmc**, then click **OK**. This launches the Microsoft Management Console.

    3. Select **Add/Remove Snap-in** from the File menu.

4. Click the **Add** button.

5. Locate and select **Group Policy**.

6. Click **Add**.

7. On the Select Group Policy object dialog box, notice that Local Computer is listed by default. Click **Finish**.

8. Click **Close** on the Add Standalone Snap-in dialog box.

9. Click **OK** on the Add/Remove Snap-in dialog box.

10. The Local Computer Policy node should now appear in the MMC.

Project 6-2

To disable the display of the last user name on the logon screen:

This hands-on project requires that you first complete Hands-on Project 6-1.

1. In the Local Computer Policy console, click the **boxed plus sign** beside Local Computer Policy to expand its contents.

2. Locate the **Computer Configuration** node. Click its **boxed plus sign** to expand its contents.

3. Locate the **Windows Settings** node. Click on its **boxed plus sign** to expand its contents.

4. Locate the **Security Settings** node. Click on its **boxed plus sign** to expand its contents.

5. Locate the **Local Policies** node. Click on its **boxed plus sign** to expand its contents.

6. Locate and select the **Security Options** node.

7. In the Details pane, locate and select **Interactive logon: Do not display last user name**.

8. Select the **Action** menu, then click **Properties**. The Local Security Policy Setting dialog box for the selected control is displayed.

9. Select the **Enable** radio button.

10. Click **OK**.

11. Log off and log back in. Notice that the last logged on user name is no longer displayed.

Project 6-3

To display a legal warning message at logon:

This hands-on project requires that you first complete Hands-on Project 6-1.

1. In the Local Computer Policy console, locate and select the following subnode: **Computer Configuration|Windows Settings|Security Settings|Local Policies|Security Options**.
2. Locate and select **Interactive logon: Message title for users attempting to log on**.
3. Select the **Action** menu, then click **Properties**.
4. Type **Warning!** in the field. Click **OK**.
5. Select **Interactive logon: Message text for users attempting to log on**.
6. Select the **Action** menu, then click **Properties**.
7. In the field type a warning message similar to the following: (Note: This excellent security warning message is reproduced from *The Windows NT Security Handbook*, by Tom Sheldon, Osborne/McGraw-Hill: Berkeley, 1997) **"Authorized Users Only! The information on this computer and network is the property of [name organization here] and is protected by intellectual property law. You must have legitimate access to an assigned account on this computer to access any information. You are permitted only to access information as defined by the system administrators. Your activities may be monitored. Any unauthorized access will be punished to the full extent of the law."**
8. Click **OK**.
9. Log off then log back in to see the warning message displayed between pressing Ctrl+Alt+Delete and the display of the WinLogon dialog box.

Project 6-4

To change the default shell:

Changing the shell will result in a new user interface. The Program Manager does not offer a Start menu, taskbar, Task Manager, and many other interface controls you are accustomed to from Windows XP. Employ this hands-on project with caution.

1. Open the **Run** command (**Start|Run**).
2. Type **regedit**. Click **OK**.

6

3. Locate and select the key: **HKEY_LOCAL_MACHINE\SOFTWARE\Microsoft\Windows NT\CurrentVersion\Winlogon.**

4. Locate and select the **Shell** value.

5. Select **Modify** from the Edit menu.

6. Change the value data from EXPLORER.EXE to **PROGMAN.EXE**.

7. Click **OK**.

8. Select **Exit** from the Registry menu.

9. The system is now configured to launch the Windows NT 3.51 Program Manager as the shell. To return the shell to Windows Explorer, either reopen the Registry editor now and change the Shell value back to its original setting (EXPLORER.EXE), or, if you have already logged in with Program Manager as the shell, use the Run command from the File menu of the Program Manager to launch Regedit and make the change.

Project 6-5

To encrypt a folder with EFS:

The folder must be on an NTFS file system to complete this exercise.

1. Launch Windows Explorer (**Start | All Programs | Accessories | Windows Explorer**).

2. Expand My Computer and select the **C** drive in the left column. (If drive C is not formatted with NTFS, select some other drive that is formatted with NTFS).

3. Select the **File** menu, then **New**, and select **Folder** from the submenu.

4. Type in a name for the folder (such as **EFStemp**), then press **Enter**.

5. Right-click the new folder, then select **Properties** from the menu.

6. On the **General** tab, click the **Advanced** button.

7. Click to place a check in the **Encrypt contents to secure data** checkbox.

8. Click **OK**.

9. Click **OK**.

10. Log off (**Start | Log Off | Log Off**)

11. Logon to the system with a different user account (**Ctrl+Alt+Delete**, then provide a different user name and password).

12. Launch Windows Explorer (**Start | All Programs | Accessories | Windows Explorer**).

13. Locate and try to access the EFStemp folder. Notice that you are unable to gain access.

14. Log off (**Start | Log Off | Log Off**)

15. Logon with the user account used to encrypt the folder (**Ctrl+Alt+Delete**, then provide user name and password).

16. Locate and try to access the **EFStemp** folder. Notice that you are able to gain access.

17. Right-click the **EFStemp** folder, then select **Properties** from the menu.

18. On the **General** tab, click the **Advanced** button.

19. Deselect (uncheck) the **Encrypt contents to secure data** checkbox.

20. Click **OK**.

21. Click **OK**.

Project 6-6

To explore the Local Computer Policy:

This hands-on project requires that you first complete Hands-on Project 6-1.

1. Expand the **Computer Configuration** node of the Local Computer Policy.

2. Expand the **Administrative Templates** node.

3. Expand each of the **Windows Components**, **System**, **Network**, and **Printers** subnodes.

4. Select each subnode one by one. Review the control details contained in each.

5. To open the Properties of a control detail, select it then select the Action menu, then click **Properties**.

6. View the Policy and Explain tabs of all control details that interest you.

7. Expand the **User Configuration** node and all of its subnodes.

8. Perform the same expansion and exploration as you did under the Computer Configuration node.

9. Select the **Exit** command from the Console menu of the MMC to close the utility. Click **Cancel** to discard any changes, if prompted.

Project 6-7

To set permissions on a file or folder:

This hands-on project requires that Windows XP be installed and an NTFS partition is present. Additionally, the computer must be a member of a domain.

1. Open Windows Explorer (**Start**|**All Programs**|**Accessories**|**Windows Explorer**).
2. In the left pane, select a drive formatted with NTFS within My Computer.
3. In the right pane, select a file or folder.
4. From the File menu, select **Properties**.
5. Select the **Security** tab.
6. Click **Add**.
7. Click the **Advanced** button.
8. Click the **Find Now** button.
9. Select the **Authenticated Users** group.
10. Click **OK**.
11. Click **OK**.
12. Select the **Authenticated Users** group, which now appears in the list of names on the Security tab for the NTFS object.
13. Select the **Modify** checkbox in the Allow column.
14. Select the **Everyone** group. Notice how the defined permissions for these two groups differ.
15. Click **OK**.

Project 6-8

To enable file access auditing:

1. Open the **Control Panel** (**Start**|**Control Panel**), and click **Switch to Classic View**.
2. Open the **Administrative Tools** by double-clicking on its icon.
3. Open the **Local Security Policy** by double-clicking on its icon.
4. Expand the **Local Policies** node by double-clicking on it.
5. Select the **Audit Policy** node.
6. Double-click the **Audit object access** item.
7. Select the **Success** checkbox. Click **OK**.

8. Launch Windows Explorer (**Start | All Programs | Accessories | Windows Explorer**).

9. Locate and select any text document on your computer, such as *%systemroot%\Winnt\setuplog.txt*.

10. Select **File | Properties**.

11. Select the **Security** tab.

12. Click the **Advanced** button.

13. Select the **Audit** tab.

14. Click **Add**.

15. Click the **Advanced** button.

16. Click the **Find Now** button.

17. Select **Authenticated Users**.

18. Click **OK**.

19. Click **OK**.

20. Select the **List Folder/Read Data** checkbox under **Successful**.

21. Click **OK**.

22. Click **OK**.

23. Click **OK**.

24. Double-click the text file to open it.

25. Close Notepad by selecting **File | Exit**.

26. Return to **Administrative Tools** by clicking on its button on the taskbar.

27. Open the **Event Viewer** by double-clicking its icon.

28. Select the **Security** Log.

29. Double-click one of the event details.

30. Using the arrow buttons, scroll through the most recent event details to locate an event dealing with the successful reading of the text file.

31. Click **OK** to close the Event detail.

32. Close the Event Viewer by clicking the **X** button in the title bar.

33. Close Administrative Tools by selecting **File | Close**.

34. Close Windows Explorer by selecting **File | Close**.

35. On the Local Security Settings dialog box, double-click **Audit Object Access**.

36. Deselect **Success**.

37. Click **OK**.

38. Close the Local Security Settings dialog box by clicking the **X** button in the title bar.

6

CASE PROJECTS

1. You've been assigned the task of defining a security policy for your company. You've been given basic guidelines to follow. These include preventing users from installing software, securing the logon process, and enforcing disk quotas. Using the Local Computer Policy, detail the control you should configure and what settings you think would work best to accomplish these goals.

2. You've recently inherited the responsibility of administering a Windows XP network. The last administrator was rather lax in restricting user access. After working through the data folders to correct the access permissions, you suspect that some users still have access to confidential files. What can you do to determine if this type of access is still occurring? Describe the steps involved in enabling this mechanism and examining the results.

7

NETWORK PROTOCOLS

After reading this chapter and completing the exercises, you will be able to:

♦ Understand networking in Windows XP

♦ Understand Windows XP's networking protocols

♦ Configure and use TCP/IP protocols and services

♦ Access NetWare servers and services from Windows XP

♦ Understand Windows XP Remote Tools

In this chapter, we discuss the networking protocols that Windows XP supports, as well as how and when to use them. We discuss TCP/IP (Transmission Control Protocol/Internet Protocol)—probably the most important networking protocol used with any version of Windows—and what is required to configure Windows XP to employ this protocol for network communications. We also discuss NWLink, a protocol historically associated with NetWare, but a valid protocol option under Windows XP as well. We also discuss other protocols that Windows XP Professional supports.

Windows XP Network Overview

Windows XP is the most versatile Windows operating system from Microsoft to date. It is capable of establishing a network connection through myriad devices and technologies. Windows XP was designed specifically to offer easy-to-use networking capabilities for both inexperienced home users and enterprise-level networked organizations. Windows XP is able to act as a standalone system for occasional Internet dial-up, or as a dedicated workgroup connection-sharing server, or even as a client in a domain network.

Windows XP supports local area network (LAN) connections, which are typically established with an expansion card or a PC Card network adapter. The network medium is attached to the network adapter, usually with twisted-pair cabling. Windows XP offers both WAN and LAN support, and can establish VPN and IPSec connections with local and remote systems. Windows XP also supports a wide range of MAN and WAN communication devices.

Windows XP has improved upon the remote access support found in Windows 9x and Windows 2000. It is easier to create and use dial-up Internet connections than in previous versions. Windows XP also supports dedicated connections such as cable modems, or specialty connections such as DSL and ISDN. Through the use of the proper hardware, Windows XP can fully manage any type of remote access connectivity.

Windows XP also supports emerging wireless technologies to eliminate network cables from both home and office networking. In fact, Microsoft is so intent on pushing wireless technologies that it has transformed most of its own Redmond, Washington, campus and many of its branch offices into wireless networks. Microsoft has placed itself firmly behind the IEEE 802.11 wireless standards. Many public facilities, such as airports and hotels, are adopting wireless technologies to offer Internet connectivity and local information to their customers throughout their buildings without tying people down with wires. Once a wireless NIC is installed, you'll find that Windows XP integrates itself seamlessly into a wireless network.

Through its implementation of the NWLink protocol, Windows XP continues its support for the IPX/SPX (Internetwork Packet Exchange/Sequenced Packet Exchange) protocol suite for compatibility with Novell NetWare networks. There is a large installed user base for NetWare; therefore, support for this type of network transmission is important to overall network connectivity.

Windows XP Network Components

Windows XP is designed for networking, with all the elements necessary for interacting with a network without requiring any additional software. Windows XP networking is powerful and efficient, while being relatively easy to configure and use with a graphical user interface and Wizards for configuration support.

Windows XP Professional can function as a network client, as a network server (in a limited sense), or both. It can participate in peer-to-peer, client/server, and terminal/host environments. Windows XP also has everything needed to access the Internet, including all necessary protocols and client capabilities, a Web browser (Internet Explorer), and other Internet tools and utilities.

In Windows XP, numerous components work together to define its networking capabilities. Each component provides one or more individual network functions and defines an interface through which data moves on its way to and from other system components. This allows Windows XP to support multiple protocols easily and transparently; applications need only know how to communicate through a standard application programming interface (API), while the modular organization of the operating system shields them from the complex details that can sometimes be involved.

Networking components can be added to or deleted from a Windows XP system without affecting the function of other components, except in those cases where such components are bound to the other components. (Binding is discussed later in this chapter.) Adding new components brings new services, communications technologies, and other capabilities into existing networks and allows additional protocols to join the mix at any time.

7

NETWORK PROTOCOLS

Windows XP supports two core network transport protocols. Both of these protocols can be used on any network of any size. The major network protocols are the **Transmission Control Protocol/Internet Protocol (TCP/IP)** and **NWLink** (identified in the Local Area Connection Properties window as the NWLink IPX/SPX/NetBIOS Compatible Protocol). These network protocols have associated advantages and drawbacks, as outlined in the sections that follow. The following list sums up the important characteristics of each of these protocols:

- TCP/IP works on almost any scale, from a single-segment network to a global scale, as demonstrated by its use on the global Internet. TCP/IP is complicated yet powerful, and is the most widely used of all networking protocols.

- NWLink works best on networks of medium scope (20 servers or fewer in a single facility). It's also useful on networks that include versions of NetWare that predate NetWare 5.x (the first version of NetWare to incorporate full-blown, native TCP/IP support).

TCP/IP

TCP/IP represents an all-embracing suite of protocols that cover a wide range of capabilities (more than 50 component protocols that belong to the TCP/IP suite have been standardized).

TCP/IP has also been around for a long time; the original version of TCP/IP emerged from research funded by the Advanced Research Projects Agency (ARPA, a division of the U.S. Department of Defense). Work on this technology began in 1969, continued throughout the 1970s, and became broadly available in 1981 and 1982. Today, TCP/IP is the most common networking protocol in use worldwide, and it is the protocol suite that makes the Internet possible.

TCP/IP has become the platform for a staggering variety of network services, including newsgroups (NNTP), electronic mail (SNMP and MIME), file transfer (FTP) remote printing (lpr, lpd, lpq utilities), remote boot (bootp and **DHCP—Dynamic Host Configuration Protocol**), and the World Wide Web (HTTP—Hypertext Transfer Protocol).

To provide **Network Basic Input/Output System (NetBIOS)** support using TCP/IP transports, Microsoft includes an implementation of **NBT (NetBIOS over TCP/IP)** with Windows XP. Microsoft extends the definition of NBT behaviors by defining a new type of NetBIOS network node for the NBT environment, called an "H" (for Hybrid) node. An H node inverts the normal behavior of the standard NBT "N" (or network) node. It looks first for a NetBIOS name service (such as a WINS server), then sends a broadcast to request local name resolution. An N node broadcasts first, then attempts a directed request for name resolution. Microsoft's approach reduces the amount of broadcast traffic on most IP-based networks that use NetBIOS names (as older Microsoft networks that predate Windows 2000 must do).

TCP/IP Advantages

TCP/IP supports networking services better than the other Windows XP protocols through its multiple components (see Figure 7-1). TCP/IP supports multiple routing protocols that in turn support large, complex networks. TCP/IP also incorporates better error detection and handling, and works with more kinds of computers than any other protocol suite. The following is a list of the elements shown in Figure 7-1:

- *Other*—Any of the nearly 40 other service/application-level protocols defined for TCP/IP.

- *FTP (File Transfer Protocol)*—The service protocol and corresponding TCP/IP application that permit network file transfer.

- *Telnet*—The service protocol and corresponding TCP/IP applications that support networked terminal emulation services.

- *SMTP (Simple Mail Transfer Protocol)*—The most common e-mail service protocol in the TCP/IP environment. POP3 (Post Office Protocol version 3) and IMAP (Internet Mail Access Protocol) are also involved in a great deal of Internet e-mail traffic.

- *UDP (User Datagram Protocol)*—A secondary transport protocol on TCP/IP networks, UDP is a lightweight cousin of TCP. It is **connectionless**, has low overhead, and offers best-effort delivery rather than the delivery guarantees offered by TCP. It is used for all kinds of services on TCP networks, including NFS and TFTP.

- *NFS (Network File System)*—A UDP-based networked file system originally developed by Sun Microsystems and widely used on many TCP/IP networks. (Windows XP does not include built-in NFS support, but numerous third-party options are available.)

- **TFTP (Trivial File Transfer Protocol)**—A lightweight, UDP-based alternative to FTP, designed primarily to permit users running Telnet sessions elsewhere on a network to grab files from their "home machines."

- **DNS (Domain Name Service)**—An address resolution service for TCP/IP-based networks that translates between numeric IP addresses and symbolic names known formally as fully qualified domain names (FQDNs).

- **SNMP (Simple Network Management Protocol)**—The primary management protocol used on TCP/IP networks, SNMP is used to report management data to management consoles or applications and to interrogate repositories of management data around a network.

- **TCP (Transmission Control Protocol)**—The primary transport protocol in TCP/IP, TCP is a robust, reliable, guaranteed delivery, **connection-oriented** transport protocol.

- *Routing protocols*—These embrace a number of important IP protocols, including the Routing Internet Protocol (RIP), the Open Shortest Path First (OSPF) protocol, the Border Gateway Protocol (BGP), and others.

- **ARP (Address Resolution Protocol)**—Used to map from a logical IP address to a physical MAC-layer address.

- **RARP (Reverse Address Resolution Protocol)**—Used to map from a physical MAC-layer address to a logical IP address.

- **IP (Internet Protocol)**—The primary protocol in TCP/IP, IP includes network-addressing information that is manipulated when a packet is routed from sender to receiver, along with data integrity and network status information.

- **ICMP (Internet Control Message Protocol)**—The protocol that deals with quality of service, availability, and network behavior information. Also supports the **PING (Packet Internet Groper)** utility, often used to inquire if an address is reachable on the Internet, and if so, to provide a measure of the "round trip time" to send a packet to its destination address, and receive a reply.

- *IEEE 802.X*—Includes the 802.2 networking standard, plus standard networking technologies like Ethernet (802.3) and Token Ring (802.5), among others.

- *FDDI (Fiber Distributed Data Interface)*—A 100 Mbps fiber-based networking technology.

7

- *ATM (Asynchronous Transfer Mode)*—A cell-oriented, fiber- and copper-based networking technology that supports data rates from 25 Mbps to as high as 2.4 Gbps.

- *ISDN (Integrated Services Digital Network)*—A digital alternative to analog telephony, ISDN links support two or more 64 Kbps channels per connection, depending on type.

- *X.25*—An ITU standard for packet-switched networking, X.25 is very common outside the United States where its robust data-handling capability makes it a good match for substandard telephone networks.

- *Ethernet II*—An older version of Ethernet that preceded the 802.3 specification, Ethernet II offers the same 10 Mbps as standard Ethernet, but uses different frame formats.

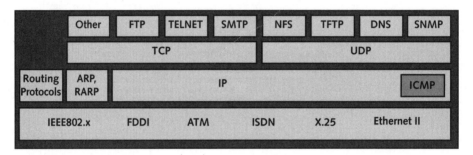

Figure 7-1   TCP/IP protocol stack

In addition to its many services and capabilities, TCP/IP also supports the following:

- Direct Internet access from any TCP/IP-equipped computer, with a link to the Internet by phone, some kind of digital link (ISDN, frame relay, T1, and so forth), or across any network with routed Internet access.

- Powerful network management protocols and services, such as SNMP and the Desktop Management Interface (DMI, which supports interrogation of desktop hardware and software configuration data).

- Dynamic Host Configuration Protocol (DHCP), which provides unique IP addresses on demand and simplifies IP address management.

- Microsoft's **Windows Internet Name Service (WINS)** to enable IP-based NetBIOS name browsing for Microsoft clients and servers, as well as the Domain Name Service (DNS) that is the most common name resolution service used to map FQDNs to numeric IP addresses throughout the Internet. NetBIOS names are limited to 15 characters. FQDNs or HOST names are names comprised of multiple segments, such as mail.adminsys.microsoft.com.

The Internet Network Information Center (InterNIC) manages all TCP/IP domain names, network numbers, and IP addresses, to make the global Internet work correctly and reliably.

TCP/IP Drawbacks

For all the clear advantages of TCP/IP, there are some drawbacks. As network protocols go, TCP/IP is neither extremely fast nor terribly easy to use. Configuring and managing a TCP/IP-based network requires a fair degree of expertise, careful planning, and constant maintenance and attention. Each of the many services and protocols that TCP/IP supports brings its own unique installation, configuration, and management chores. In addition, there's a huge mass of information and detail work involved in establishing and maintaining a TCP/IP-based network. In short, it's a demanding and unforgiving environment, and should always be approached with great care.

NWLink (IPX/SPX)

NWLink is Microsoft's implementation of Novell's **IPX/SPX** protocol stack. Rather than supporting the native Novell **Open Datalink Interface (ODI)**, NWLink works with the **NDIS (Network Device Interface Specification)** driver technology that's native to Windows XP; NDIS defines parameters for loading more than one protocol on a network adapter. NWLink is sufficiently complete to support the most important IPX/SPX APIs.

 Although IPX/SPX is the default protocol for NetWare prior to version 5, TCP/IP is the default protocol in version 5.

NWLink Advantages

NWLink offers some powerful capabilities, including:

- *SPX II*—SPX II is a new version of SPX that has been enhanced to support windowing and can set a maximum frame size.

- *Auto detection of frame types*—NWLink automatically detects which IPX **frame type** is used on a network during initial startup and broadcast advertisement phases. When multiple frame types appear, Windows XP defaults to the industry-standard 802.2 frame type.

- *Direct hosting over IPX*—This is the ability to host ongoing network sessions using IPX transports. Direct hosting over IPX can increase network performance by as much as 20 percent on client computers. This is especially beneficial for client/server applications.

NWLink Drawbacks

On large networks, IPX may not scale well. IPX lacks a built-in facility for centralized name and address management like the service that DNS provides for TCP/IP. This omission allows address conflicts to occur—especially when previously isolated networks that employed identical defaults or common addressing schemes attempt to interoperate. Novell established an address Registry in 1994 (IPX was introduced in 1983), but it is generally neither used nor acknowledged. The InterNIC and its subsequent assigns have managed all public IP addresses since 1982. IPX fails to support a comprehensive collection of network management tools. Finally, IPX imposes a greater memory footprint on DOS machines and runs less efficiently across slow serial connections.

NetBEUI and DLC

Both **NetBIOS Extended User Interface (NetBEUI)** and **Data Link Control (DLC)** have been greatly de-emphasized in Windows XP. In fact, you won't even find them as available options when attempting to install new protocols. Microsoft has finally seen the light. NetBEUI is not often used anymore, owing to its limitations on the number of addressable nodes per network and its inability to be routed. Likewise, DLC has been replaced by SNA for mainframe interaction and TCP/IP or proprietary protocols for network attached printers. If your current network relies upon either of these protocols, you need to consider other alternatives before deploying Windows XP.

INTERPROCESS COMMUNICATION

In the Windows XP environment, communication among processes is quite important because of the operating system's multitasking, multithreaded architecture. **Interprocess communication (IPC)** defines a way for such processes to exchange information. This mechanism is general-purpose so it doesn't matter whether such communications occur on the same computer or between networked computers. IPC defines a way for client computers to request services from some servers and permits servers to reply to requests for services. As shown in Figure 7-2, IPC operates directly below the redirector on the client side and the network file system on the server side to provide a standard communications interface for handling requests and replies.

In Windows XP, IPC mechanisms fall into two categories: programming interfaces and file system mechanisms. Programming interfaces permit general, open-ended client/server dialog, as mediated by applications or system services. Normally, such dialog is not strictly related to data streams or data files. File system mechanisms support file sharing between clients and servers. Where programming interfaces are concerned, individual APIs differ depending on what kinds of client-server dialog they support. Where file systems are concerned, they must behave the same way, no matter how (or where) they employ Windows XP networked file systems and services.

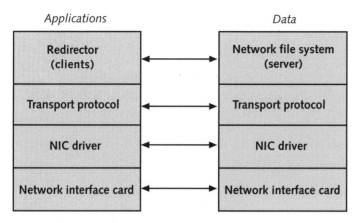

Applications   *Data*

Figure 7-2   Interprocess communication between client and server

7

IPC File System Mechanisms

Windows XP includes two IPC interfaces for file system access: named pipes and mail-slots. These mechanisms work through the Windows XP redirector, which distinguishes between local and network resource requests. This process permits one simple set of file I/O commands to handle both local and network access to file system data.

Named Pipes

Named pipes support a connection-oriented message-passing service for clients and servers. To be connection-oriented, a message's receiver must acknowledge each message it receives. Named pipes offer a reliable method for clients and servers to exchange requests, replies, and associated files. Named pipes provide their own methods to ensure reliable data transfer, which makes them a good match for lightweight, unreliable transport protocols like the User Datagram Protocol (UDP). In short, named pipes delivery guarantees make transport-level delivery guarantees less essential.

The Windows XP version of named pipes includes a security feature called impersonation, which permits the server side of the named pipes interface to masquerade as a client that requests a service. This allows the interface to check the client's access rights and to make sure that the client's request is legal, before returning any reply to request for data.

Mailslots File System

Mailslots are like a connectionless version of named pipes; mailslots offer no delivery guarantees, nor do they acknowledge successful receipt of data. Windows XP uses mailslots internally to support nonessential system-to-system communications. Such things as registering names for computers, domains, and users across a network, passing messages related to the Windows XP browser service, and providing support for broadcasting text messages across the network fall into this category. Outside such lightweight uses, mailslots are used less frequently than named pipes.

IPC Programming Interfaces

For communications to succeed, the client and server sides of an application must share a common programming interface. Windows XP offers a number of distinct interfaces to support IPC mechanisms for various kinds of client/server applications. Windows XP supports several programming interfaces, including NetBIOS, Windows Sockets, RPC, NetDDE, DCOM, Wnet, and WinInet.

 External applications can support other programming interfaces or implement private interfaces.

NetBIOS

NetBIOS is a widely used, but simple PC client/server IPC mechanism. Because it is so easy to program, it has remained quite popular ever since IBM published its definition in 1985. NetBIOS services are required to permit older Windows networks to operate, or to permit older clients and servers (those that predate Windows 2000 and Windows XP) to operate on a Microsoft Windows network.

Fortunately, NetBIOS works with all TDI-compliant transports, including NWLink (NetBIOS over NWLink, or NWNBLink) and TCP/IP (NetBIOS over TCP/IP, or NBT). Windows XP uses TCP/IP as its primary network protocol by default, but Windows XP may also use NBT. By default, Windows XP's TCP/IP is configured to use the NetBIOS setting defined by a local DHCP server. However, when statically defined IP addresses are used, NetBIOS is enabled by default. This setting is configured on the WINS tab of the Advanced TCP/IP Properties dialog box. The options here are:

- Use NetBIOS setting from the DHCP server. If a static IP address is used or the DHCP server does not provide NetBIOS setting, enable NetBIOS over TCP/IP (selected by default)
- Enable NetBIOS over TCP/IP
- Disable NetBIOS over TCP/IP

Windows Sockets

Windows Sockets (WinSock) define a standardized and broadly deployed interface to network transports such as TCP/IP and IPX. WinSock was created to migrate UNIX applications written to the Berkeley Sockets specification into the Windows environment. WinSock also makes it easier to standardize network communications used on multiple platforms because one socket interface is much like another, even if one runs on UNIX and the other on some variety of Windows (such as Windows XP, where WinSock 2.0 is the standard sockets API).

Windows Sockets appear in many programs that originated as UNIX programs and include the majority of Internet utilities, especially the most popular IP utilities, such as Web browsers, e-mail software, and file transfer programs.

RPC

Remote Procedure Call (RPC) implements IPC tools that can invoke separate programs on remote computers, supply them with input, and collect whatever results they produce. This permits the distribution of a single processing task among multiple computers, a process that can improve overall performance and help balance the processing load across numerous machines.

RPC is indifferent to where its client and server portions reside. It's possible for both client and server portions of an application to run on a single computer. In that case, they communicate using local procedure call (LPC) mechanisms. This makes building such applications easy because they can be constructed on one computer, while allowing processing to be distributed on one machine or across many machines, as processing needs dictate. This creates an environment that is both flexible and powerful.

RPC consists of four basic components:

- A remote stub procedure that packages RPC requests for transmission to a server. It's called a stub because it acts as a simple, extremely compact front end to a remote process that may be much larger and more complex elsewhere on the network.

- An RPC runtime system to pass data between local and remote machines or between client and server processes.

- An application stub procedure that receives requests from the runtime RPC system. Upon such receipt, this stub procedure formats requests for the designated target RPC computer and makes the necessary procedure call. This procedure call can be either a local procedure call (if both client and server components are running on the same computer) or a remote procedure call (if client and server components are running on two machines).

- One or more remote procedures that may be called for service (whether locally or across the network).

NetDDE

Network Dynamic Data Exchange (NetDDE) creates ongoing data streams called exchange pipes (or simply, pipes) between two applications across a network. This process works just like Microsoft's local **DDE**, which creates data exchange pipes between two applications on the same machine. DDE facilitates data sharing, object linking and embedding (OLE), and dynamic updates between linked applications. NetDDE extends local DDE across the network.

NetDDE services are installed by default during the base Windows XP installation, but they remain dormant until they are started explicitly. NetDDE services must be started using the Services control in Computer Management, where they appear under the headings Network DDE (the client side of NetDDE) and Network DDE DSDM (DDE Share Database Manager, the server side of NetDDE).

Distributed Component Object Model

Distributed Component Object Model (DCOM) (previously known as Network OLE) is a protocol that facilitates the communication of application components over a network by providing a reliable, secure, and efficient mechanism for exchanging information. DCOM can operate over most network transport mechanisms, including HTTP. Microsoft based its implementation of DCOM on the Open Software Foundation's DCE-RPC specification, but expanded its capabilities to include Java and ActiveX support.

Windows Network Interface

The Windows Network (Wnet) interface allows applications to take advantage of Windows XP networking capabilities through a standardized API. This means that the application does not require specific control data about the network provider or implementation, allowing applications to be network-independent while still able to interact with network-based resources.

Win32 Internet API

The WinInet API (WinInet) is a mechanism that enables applications to take advantage of Internet functionality without requiring extensive proprietary programming. Through WinInet, applications can be designed to include FTP, Web, and Gopher support with a minimal of additional coding. WinInet makes interacting with Internet resources as simple as reading files from a local hard drive without requiring programming to WinSock or TCP/IP.

REDIRECTORS

A redirector examines all requests for system resources and decides whether such requests are local (they can be found on the requesting machine) or remote. The redirector handles transmission of remote requests across the network so that the requests are filled.

Windows XP's file and print sharing are regarded as the most important functions supplied by any network operating system. Windows XP delivers these services through two critical components: the Workstation service and the Server service. Both of these services are essentially file system drivers that operate in concert with other file system drivers that can access local file systems on a Windows XP machine. The following components are redirectors that operate at this level: Workstation service, Server service, **Multiple Universal Naming Convention Provider (MUP)**, and **Multi-Provider Router (MPR)**.

All of these system components take client requests for service and redirect them to an appropriate network service provider. Redirectors interact and interface directly with user applications. The sections that follow explain more about each of these components and their roles in the Windows XP networking environment.

Workstation Service

The Workstation service supports client access to network resources and handles functions such as logging in, connecting to network shares (directories and printers), and creating links using Windows XP's IPC options. The Workstation service has two elements, the User mode interface and the redirector. The User mode interface determines the particular file system that any User mode file I/O request is referencing. The redirector recognizes and translates requests for remote file and print services and forwards them to lower-level boundary layers aimed at network access and delivery.

This service encompasses a redirector file system that handles access to shared directories on networked computers. The file system is used further to satisfy remote access requests, but if any request uses a network name to refer to a local resource, it will instead pass that request to local file system drivers.

The Workstation service requires that at least one TDI-compliant transport and at least one MUP are running. Otherwise, the service cannot function properly because it supports connections with other Windows XP machines (through their Server services), LAN Manager, LAN Server, and other MS-Net servers, which require an MUP to be running. The Workstation service, like any other redirector, communicates with transport protocols through the common TDI boundary layer.

Server Service

The Windows XP Server service handles the creation and management of shared resources and performs security checks against requests for such resources, including directories and printers. The Server service allows a Windows XP computer to act as a server on a client/server network, up to the maximum number of licensed clients. This limits the number of simultaneous connections possible to a Windows XP Professional machine to 10, in keeping with its built-in connection limitations.

Just as with the Workstation service, the Server service operates as a file system driver. Therefore, it also uses other file system drivers to satisfy I/O requests. The Server service is also divided into two elements:

- *SERVER.EXE*—Manages client connection requests.
- *SRV.SYS*—The redirector file system that operates across the network, and that interacts with other local file system drivers when necessary.

Multiple Universal Naming Convention Provider

Windows XP supports multiple redirectors that can be active simultaneously. As an example, both the Workstation and Server services and the NetWare redirector built into Windows XP's **Client Service for NetWare (CSNW)** can be active at the same time. Like the Server service, the NetWare redirector handles Microsoft Windows Network shares, but exposes them to NetWare clients instead of Microsoft Network clients. As with other boundary layers, the ability to support multiple clients uniformly is possible because a common provider interface allows Windows XP to treat all redirectors the same way.

The boundary layer called the Multiple Universal Naming Convention Provider (MUP) defines a link between applications that make UNC requests for different redirectors. MUP allows applications to remain oblivious to the number or type of redirectors that might be in use. For incoming requests, the MUP also decides which redirector should handle that request by parsing the UNC share name that appears within the request.

Here's how it works: When the I/O subsystem receives any request that includes a UNC name, it turns that request over to the MUP. The MUP first checks its internal list of recently accessed shares, which it maintains over time. If the MUP recognizes the UNC name, it immediately passes the request to the required redirector. If it doesn't recognize the UNC name, the MUP sends the request to each registered redirector and requests that it service the request.

The MUP chooses redirectors on the basis of the highest registered response time during which the redirector claims it can connect to a UNC name, information that can be cached until no activity occurs for 15 minutes. This can make trying a series of redirectors incredibly time-consuming and helps explain why the binding order of protocols is so important, because that also influences the order in which name resolution requests will be handled.

Universal Naming Convention Names

Universal Naming Convention (UNC) names represent the format used in NetBIOS-oriented name resolution systems. UNC names precede the computer portion of a name with two slashes, followed by a slash that precedes (and separates elements of) the share name and the directory path, followed by the requested file name. Thus this string

```
\\computername\sharename\dir-path\filename.ext
```

represents a valid UNC name. In this example, the name of the computer is *computername*, the name of the share is *sharename*, the directory path is named *dir-path*, and the file is named *filename.ext*.

Multi-Provider Router

Not all programs use UNC names in the Windows XP environment. Programs that call the Win32 API must use the file system service called the **Multi-Provider Router**

(MPR) to designate the proper redirector to handle a resource request. The MPR lets applications written to older Microsoft specifications behave as if they were written to conform to UNC naming. The MPR is able to recognize the UNCs that represent drive mappings, so it can decide which redirector can handle a mapped network drive letter (such as X:) and make sure that a request that references that drive can be properly satisfied. The MPR handles all Win32 Network API calls, passing resource requests from that interface to those redirectors that register their presence through special-purpose dynamic link libraries (DLLs). That is, any redirector that wants to support the MPR must provide a DLL that communicates through the common MPR interface. Normally this means that whichever network developer supplies a redirector must also supply this DLL. Microsoft implemented CSNW as a DLL that supports this interface. This allows the NetWare redirector to provide the same kind of transparent file system and network resource access as other Windows XP redirectors.

7

NETWORKING UNDER WINDOWS XP

The Windows XP networking system is controlled by a single multifaceted interface that combines networking access for LAN, Internet, and modem. The interface is called Network Connections (see Figure 7-3), and is accessed through the Control Panel (in Classic View, or through the Network and Internet Connections category in Category View). A Connect To submenu is added to the Start menu if you create dial-up or VPN connection objects. Through this menu, you can also access the Network Connections tool by selecting the Show all connections command.

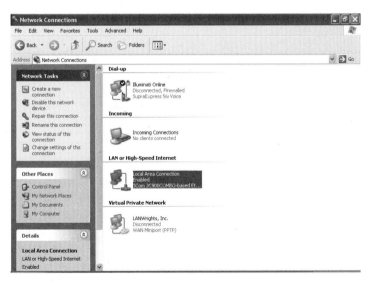

Figure 7-3   The Network Connections utility

Network Connections is used to create and configure network connections. The "Create a new connection" command in the Network Tasks list launches a Wizard that takes the user through the process of establishing new network links. The Wizard is used for any network links employing modems, virtual private networks (VPNs) over the Internet, or serial, parallel, or infrared ports. Windows XP automatically enables all normal network links achieved through a network adapter and an attached cable. A Local Area Connection icon is listed in the Network Connections window for each installed adapter card. If there are two or more LAN connections, we recommend renaming the Local Area Connection icons to reflect the domain, network, or purpose of the link.

Existing Local Area Connections can be configured by opening the Properties for that object either through the File menu or the right-click pop-up menu. A typical default configuration of a Local Area Connection Properties dialog box is shown in Figure 7-4, listing the adapter in use as well as all installed protocols and services that can function over this interface. The Configure button is used to access the Properties dialog box for the adapter. Each listed service or protocol has a checkbox. When checked, the protocol or service is bound to the adapter (that is, it can operate over the network link established by the adapter). When unchecked, the protocol or service is not bound to the adapter.

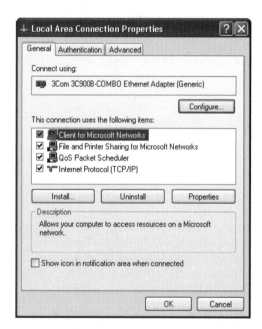

Figure 7-4   A Local Area Connection Properties dialog box, General tab

The Install button is used to add new client interfaces, protocols, and services that any of the Connection objects can use. When a new element is added, all possible bindings are enabled by default. The following are the available elements that can be installed onto Windows XP Professional:

- *Client: Client for Microsoft Networks*—Used to gain access to Microsoft network resources. This component is installed by default.

- *Client: Client Service for NetWare*—Used to gain access to NetWare resources.

- *Service: QoS Packet Scheduler*—An extension service for Winsock used to reserve bandwidth for communications. This component is installed by default.

- *Service: File and Printer Sharing for Microsoft Networks*—Enables a system to share its files and printers with a Microsoft network. This component is installed by default.

- *Service: Service Advertising Protocol*—Used by Windows XP to participate actively in NetWare networks.

- *Protocol: Internet Protocol (TCP/IP)*—Protocol used on networks connected to the Internet or using Internet Information Services (IIS) privately. This component is installed by default.

- *Protocol: Network Monitor Driver*—Driver used to allow full versions of Network Monitor to obtain network activity information from Windows XP Professional systems.

- *Protocol: NWLink IPX/SPX/NetBIOS Compatible Transport Protocol*—Protocol most often used on NetWare networks.

The Uninstall button is used to remove a client, protocol, or service. Once an element is removed, it is removed for all Connection objects. The Properties button opens the Properties dialog box for the selected installed component (client, service, or protocol). Note that not all components have configurable options. This dialog box also offers a checkbox control to display an icon in the icon tray when the Connection object is in use.

The Network Connections interface's File and Advanced drop-down menus include the following functions:

- *File: Disable*—Prevents the selected Connection object from being used to establish a communications link. This command is for automatic connections, such as those for a LAN.

- *File: Enable*—Allows the selected Connection object to be used to establish a communications link. This command is for automatic connections, such as those for a LAN.

- *File: Connect*—Launches the selected Connection object to establish a communications link. This command is for manual connections, such as those over a modem.

- *File: Status*—Displays a Status window for the selected Connection object that lists whether the object is connected, how long the connection has been active, the speed of the connection, and the packet counts. This window offers Properties and Disable buttons to perform the same functions as the File menu commands.

- *File: Repair*—Attempts to repair a connection object by clearing the ARP cache and resetting buffers or ports. This is often a good first step to try before changing configuration data. This command also forces a new DHCP lease request if the interface is configured to use DHCP.

- *File: New Connection*—Launches the Make New Connection Wizard.

- *Advanced: Operator-Assisted Dialing*—Used to manually dial a connection number then have the computer take over control of the line once the remote system answers the call.

- *Advanced: Dial-up Preferences*—Opens a dialog box in which RAS-related controls are set (see Chapter 8, "Internetworking with Remote Access").

- *Advanced: Network Identification*—Opens the Computer Name tab of the System applet that displays the current computer name and workgroup/domain name. To join a domain and create a local user, click Network ID.

- *Advanced: Bridge Connections*—Used to create a virtual bridge between two or more network segments.

- *Advanced: Advanced Settings*—Opens a dialog box where bindings and provider order can be managed; see the "Managing Bindings" section later this chapter.

- *Advanced: Optional Networking Components*—Adds other networking components, such as Monitoring and Management Tools, Networking Services, and Other Network File and Print Services.

Some of these commands appear only when a specific Connection object type is selected.

For most networks, the default Local Area Connection Windows XP creates automatically is sufficient for LAN activity. As shown earlier in Figure 7-4, this Connection object is designed to link up with a Microsoft-based network (workgroup or domain), allows file and printer sharing, and employs the TCP/IP protocol.

To change TCP/IP settings, select the protocol from the list of components in the Properties window of a Local Area Connection, then click Properties. This reveals the Internet Protocol (TCP/IP) Properties dialog box (see Figure 7-5). From here you can easily enable DHCP for this computer, or define a static IP address, subnet mask, and gateway. You can also define the preferred and alternate DNS servers. The Advanced button brings up a multi-tabbed dialog box in which multiple IP addresses, additional gateways, DNS and WINS functionality, and TCP/IP service extension properties can be defined.

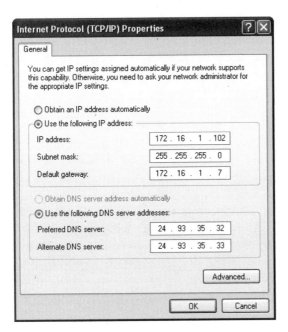

Figure 7-5   The Internet Protocol (TCP/IP) Properties dialog box

Adding new network interfaces to Windows XP Professional is handled in the same fashion as installing any other piece of hardware: physically install it and allow Windows XP to detect it and install drivers, or use the Add Hardware applet to perform the drive installation manually. Both of these procedures are discussed in Chapter 3, "Using the System Utilities." Once a new NIC is installed, Windows XP automatically creates a new Local Area Connection that you can customize for your networking needs.

NETWORK BRIDGE

Windows XP boasts a new networking feature known as network bridge. In essence, network bridge creates a layer 2 bridge between two or more network interfaces, effectively connecting multiple network segments. Network bridge is able to connect network segments even if they use different protocols and different topologies. Microsoft has included the network bridging capability in Windows XP to help encourage the creation of networks both in small offices and at home. Using the Windows XP-based network bridge, there's no need to purchase a separate (and sometimes expensive) hardware bridge or router. Furthermore, no configuration is required. Just select two or more network connections, then issue the Bridge Connections command from the Advanced menu in the Network Connections utility.

Windows XP can support only a single network bridge per system. However, that one bridge can bridge multiple networks together. The only restrictions on connections that may be bridged apply to those that the Internet Connection Sharing (ICS) or Internet Connection Firewall (ICF) control. Another restriction is that only similar interfaces can be bridged. That is, a dial-up connection can be bridged only to other dial-up connections.

 See Chapter 8, "Internetworking with Remote Access," for details on ICS and ICF.

Once a bridge is created, it appears as a connection object named Network Bridge within the Network Connections utility. To add other connections to this bridge, mark their respective checkboxes in the list of adapters available in the Properties dialog box of the Network Bridge. To remove a connection from a bridge, de-select the appropriate checkbox from this dialog box. To remove the bridge altogether, select it within the Network Connections and press the Delete key.

NETWORKING WIZARD

The Network Setup Wizard (previously known as the Home Networking Wizard) is used to configure non-domain networks for small offices or home use of Windows XP. This step-by-step walk-through tool allows easy configuration of:

- Friendly computer names, such as "Study Computer" or "Den System"
- Your Internet connection, be it dial-up or dedicated
- Internet Connection Sharing (ICS)
- Internet Connection Firewall (ICF)
- Configure TCP/IP for networking

The Network Setup Wizard can be launched from the network tasks list from within the Network Connection utility, or through the Network and Internet Connections category of the Control Panel. For best results, use the Wizard on the system to be the ICS host first. All other systems on the network automatically configure themselves against the ICS host to gain access to the shared Internet link and to share resources between networked systems.

During the Network Setup Wizard's operation, you are asked whether to create a floppy disk to run the Network Setup Wizard on Windows 98, 98 SE, or Me. If you are using any of these systems on your network, creating the floppy disk is a good idea. The Wizard will not function on any other system, thus, Windows 2000 and NT systems must be configured manually to participate in this type of network.

By default, NetWare versions before 5.0 do not support long filenames. To ensure that long Windows filenames are not truncated when they are copied to NetWare servers, those servers must load the OS/2 name space. This is done on the NetWare server itself and ensures that all files retain their settings when stored on the server.

NWLink and CSNW also support IPX burst mode, which enhances bulk data transfer over an IPX network. By design, IPX is best suited to handle small- to medium-sized packets and numerous network communications. When tasked with transferring large amounts of data, IPX loses efficiency and creates excessive network traffic. Burst mode allows routed network connections to negotiate the largest possible packet size so that fewer packets are sent to transmit large data files. This improves bandwidth utilization and reduces network overhead.

Bindery and NDS Support

To effectively ensure that client computers can attach to any server on the network, Client Service for NetWare includes support for both bindery and NDS servers. As mentioned, versions of NetWare prior to 4.0 used the bindery to store their configuration information, including user and group lists, printers, and security settings. When users logon to a bindery-based NetWare server, they access the bindery for logon authentication, confirmation of security authorizations, group memberships, and so forth. One of the primary limitations of bindery-based NetWare is that each server on the network has its own bindery. Users that access resources on multiple servers are required to logon to each server individually.

NetWare 4.0 uses a Novell Directory Services (NDS) database to store and maintain information that was previously stored in the bindery. The NDS database is much more dynamic and supports enterprise-wide networks. The NDS database is a hierarchical tree stored on many servers on the network that provides single-logon access to resources. In addition, centralized administration and resource management is possible with NDS—a real improvement over earlier versions of NetWare.

Because NDS is a hierarchical database that can be stored on multiple servers on the network, an NDS implementation resembles a tree and is referred to as the **NDS tree**. At the base of the tree is the Root object, which generally represents the largest organization connected to the network, often the entire corporation. Working down through the tree, each department may have a container, then each group within the department can have another container. In NDS, each network resource, whether a user, group, file server, printer, or storage area, is represented as an object. Objects are stored in containers representing their function on the network. A network object's location in the NDS tree is called its **context**. Figure 7-10 is an example of an NDS tree.

In the example shown in Figure 7-10, the Phillip user object resides in the Sales container, which in turn resides in the Sales/Marketing container, which resides under the DJNet Enterprises Root object. The context for the Phillip user is DJNet Enterprises.Sales/Marketing.Sales.

7

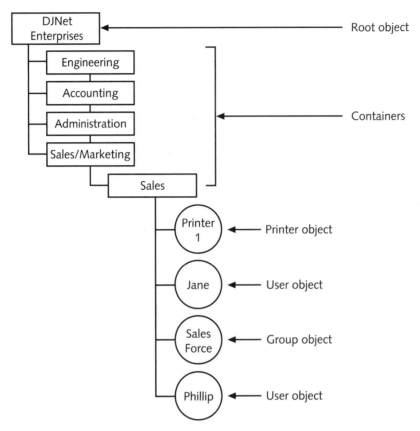

Figure 7-10   Illustration of an NDS tree structure

Installing and Configuring Client Service for NetWare

Like NWLink, installation of Client Service for NetWare occurs in the Local Area Connection Properties dialog box. Once in that window for the appropriate connection object, click Install; you will be asked whether to install a Client, Service, or Protocol. As its name implies, Client Service for NetWare is a client component. Select Client and click Add. If the default configuration is installed, the only client available for installation is CSNW. Ensure that Client Service for NetWare is selected and click OK to continue the installation. Once installation is complete, you will be asked to restart your computer. You must do so before CSNW can be used. Click Yes to reboot your computer.

 Client Service for NetWare relies on NWLink to operate. If NWLink is not loaded when CSNW is installed, it will be installed automatically.

Assigning a Default Tree and Context Using CSNW

After the computer has restarted, you will be presented with the Select NetWare Logon dialog box. It is through this dialog box that you assign a default NetWare tree and context on the NDS-enabled NetWare network to which the Windows XP Professional computer will connect. Unlike most areas of Windows XP, you cannot browse for tree and context data. You must have this information available to type into the dialog box. If this information is not available the first time the computer is restarted, you can click Cancel and enter the information later.

Unlike many networking components, CSNW is not configured through the Local Area Connection Properties dialog box. When CSNW is installed, a separate utility is placed in the Control Panel, and represented by the CSNW icon. If at any point you need to change the default tree and context settings, or any CSNW settings, double-click the CSNW icon to access the Client Service for NetWare configuration dialog box. When accessed by this method, additional configuration options are available, as discussed in later sections.

The CSNW applet appears in the Control Panel only in Classic View; it is not available in Category View.

Preferred Server vs. Directory Tree

Should you need to connect a Windows XP Professional computer to a bindery-based NetWare server, you must to use the Preferred Server configuration options available in the Client Service for NetWare applet (see Figure 7-11). Unlike the Default Tree and Context settings where you must type in the tree and context manually, clicking the down arrow next to the Preferred Server box displays a list of all servers that advertise themselves on your network. From that list, select the name of the NetWare server to which you want to attach. You can also enter the server's name in the Preferred Server box directly. If making a manual entry, be sure the server's name is spelled correctly. If an incorrect server name is entered, the dialog box shown in Figure 7-12 appears, informing you that you could not be authenticated on the selected server because the network path could not be found. Clicking No returns you to the Select NetWare Logon dialog box, whereas clicking Yes accepts the configuration anyway.

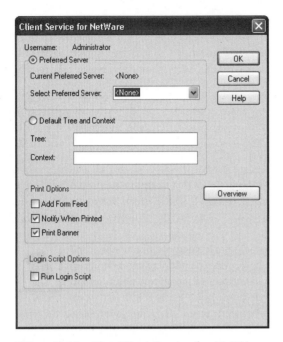

Figure 7-11   The Client Service for NetWare applet

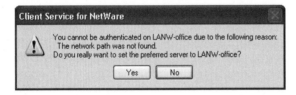

Figure 7-12   Client Service for NetWare error (incorrect server path)

Regardless of the configuration changes you make, a dialog box is invoked notifying you that the changes will take effect the next time you log in. Click OK to continue. The computer must be restarted manually, because the configuration program does not automatically restart the computer after the dialog box is closed.

Other Configuration Settings

When you use the Client Service for NetWare applet to configure networking components, configuration options are available that are not presented when the client is first installed. As shown in Figure 7-11, these options make up the bottom half of the dialog box, in the Print Options and Login Script Options section.

The settings available in the Print Options section determine whether a computer sends a form feed command to the printer when the print job is finished, sends a notification message to the user when the print job is complete, or prints a banner before the print job itself. Form feed commands are generally necessary only on older printers, usually those that use tractor-feed paper; most laser and inkjet printers do not require form feed commands to end a print job. If this option is used on a laser printer, for example, a blank sheet of paper is ejected from the printer after the job. Many users in a networked environment are not within eyesight of the printers they are using. For that reason, the Client Service for NetWare can be configured to send a network notification to the user after a job is complete. If that option is selected, a pop-up box appears on the user's computer when the print job is done. The banner page is also used in many larger networks. A banner page identifies the user who initiated the print job and the name of the job. Thus, users can easily identify their print jobs when they go to pick them up from the printer.

When the Run Login Script option is selected, the computer runs the NetWare logon script specified for the user by the administrator. This preserves logon scripts that network administrators have developed for their clients and provides easy, centralized administration for all client computers. This is especially important to standardize client behavior, regardless of the client type. However, many of the functions that logon scripts provide also work using Windows XP functions such as Map Network Drive. As more client computers are converted to Windows XP Professional, it may no longer be necessary to use logon scripts, and this option can be disabled.

 Note that Novell uses the terms "log in" and "login," whereas Microsoft uses "log on" and "logon."

CONNECTING TO NETWARE RESOURCES

Because Client Service for NetWare integrates so closely with Windows XP, connecting to NetWare resources works the same way as connecting to other resources. Most often, this is accomplished through My Network Places. In an NDS environment, if the resources to which you are connecting are in the same NDS tree, your initial logon provides you access to available resources. However, on bindery-based networks, you must logon to each server to access the resources on that server. Once you have logged on to the appropriate server or directory tree, the NetWare security system determines whether you should be granted access to the requested resources.

Through the Computers Near Me icon in My Network Places, you can connect to resources on servers or trees to which you have already logged on. To search for other servers or NDS trees, double-click the Entire Network icon, and click the Entire Contents link shown in the lower-left corner.

After clicking on the link, you will be presented with icons for each type of client installed, usually Microsoft Windows Network and NetWare or Compatible Network. To browse for additional NetWare resources, double-click the NetWare or Compatible Network icon.

Choosing Appropriate NetWare Client Software

Because Novell also offers its Novell 32-bit Client for Windows, you may sometimes find yourself forced to choose between the Windows Client for NetWare Networks or the Novell equivalent when setting up Windows XP Professional workstations for network access. In that case, we urge you to consider the following list of factors to help you choose an appropriate client:

- On networks where NetWare servers outnumber Windows servers, or where clients need native NDS or NetWare-aware applications support, it's sensible to use the Novell 32-bit client for Windows.

- On networks where Windows servers outnumber NetWare servers, or where clients need native Active Directory and Windows applications support, it may make more sense to use the Microsoft Client for NetWare networks.

- In situations where an equal number of servers of each type occur, or where NDS or NetWare-aware applications aren't necessary, it's far easier to install and use the Microsoft Client for NetWare networks.

- When all that's required for Windows XP clients is access to file and print services on NetWare servers, you may want to consider installing Gateway Services for NetWare on Windows servers, because they can mediate access to NetWare file and print services. In that case, no NetWare client software of any kind is needed.

If you let your circumstances dictate the choice of client, remember also the principle of "least administrative effort." This means that you should evaluate which approach involves the least amount of effort to implement, and weigh its pros and cons very carefully. Only when the balance firmly tilts toward the cons should you consider a different implementation approach!

 If you decide to install the Novell 32-bit Windows client, you may not also install NWLink or CSNW (in fact, if you've installed those Microsoft components, you must first uninstall them before you attempt to install the Novell components).

CHAPTER SUMMARY

❑ Windows XP Professional provides network access primarily by using TCP/IP. TCP/IP is routable, supports enterprise-level networks, and has been designed to interconnect dissimilar types of computers, which helps to explain why it's the protocol of choice on the Internet. TCP/IP is an industry-standard protocol that provides easy cross-platform communication.

❐ Windows XP includes a number of applications that utilize TCP/IP and provide Internet connectivity. In spite of TCP/IP's complexity, configuring Windows XP to employ this protocol is not difficult.

❐ Windows XP includes several new networking features and utilities; these include network bridging, Remote Assistance, Remote Desktop, greater support for wireless networking, and support for the upcoming IPv6 protocol.

❐ Windows XP includes the NWLink protocol and Client Service for NetWare (CSNW) to enable users to access resources and services from NetWare-based networks. This implementation supports older, bindery-based NetWare servers (3.x and older) as well as newer, Novell Directory Services-based NetWare servers (4.x and newer).

❐ When choosing NetWare client software for use on Windows XP clients, pick the client that fits the majority of servers in use, or that provides native support for the most important directory and application services.

7

Key Terms

Address Resolution Protocol (ARP) — The IP protocol used to resolve numeric IP addresses into their MAC layer physical address equivalents.

bindery — The database used by versions of NetWare before 4.0 to store network resource configuration information.

binding — The process of developing a stack by linking together network services and protocols. The binding facility allows users to define exactly how network services operate for optimal network performance.

Client Service for NetWare (CSNW) — Service included with Windows XP Professional that provides easy connection to NetWare servers.

Common Internet File System (CIFS) — An enhanced version of SMB used for file and print services.

connectionless — A class of network transport protocols that makes only a "best-effort" attempt at delivery, and that includes no explicit mechanisms to guarantee delivery or data integrity. Because such protocols need not be particularly reliable, they are often much faster and require less overhead than connection-oriented protocols.

connection-oriented — A class of network transport protocols that includes guaranteed delivery, explicit acknowledgement of data receipt, and a variety of data integrity checks to ensure reliable transmission and reception of data across a network. Although reliable, connection-oriented protocols can be slow because of the overhead and extra communication.

context — The location of an NDS object in the NDS tree.

Data Link Control (DLC) — A network transport protocol that allows connectivity to mainframes, printers, and servers running Remote Program Load software.

Domain Name Service (DNS) — TCP/IP service that is used to resolve names to IP addresses.

Dynamic Data Exchange (DDE) — A method of interprocess communication within the Windows operating system.

Dynamic Host Configuration Protocol (DHCP) — An IP-based address management service that permits clients to obtain IP addresses from a DHCP server. This allows network administrators to control and manage IP addresses centrally, rather than on a per-machine basis.

File Transfer Protocol (FTP) — The protocol and service that provides TCP/IP-based file transfer to and from remote hosts and confers the ability to navigate and operate within remote file systems.

frame type — One of four available packet structures supported by IPX/SPX and NWLink. The four frame types supported are Ethernet 802.2, Ethernet 802.3, Ethernet II, and Ethernet SNAP.

HOSTS — A static file placed on members of a network to provide a resolution mechanism between host names and IP addresses.

Internet Control Message Protocol (ICMP) — The protocol in the TCP/IP suite that handles communication between devices about network traffic, quality of service, and requests for specific acknowledgments (such as those used in the PING utility).

Internetwork Packet Exchange (IPX) — The protocol developed by Novell for its NetWare product. IPX is a routable, connection-oriented protocol similar to TCP/IP but much easier to manage and with lower communication overhead.

Internetwork Packet Exchange/Sequenced Packet Exchange (IPX/SPX) — The name of the two primary protocols developed by Novell for its NetWare network operating system. IPX/SPX is derived from the XNS protocol stack and leans heavily on XNS architecture and functionality. See also IPX and SPX.

Internet Protocol (IP) — The protocol that handles routing and addressing information for the TCP/IP protocol suite. IP provides a simple connectionless transmission that relies on higher layer protocols to establish reliability.

interprocess communication (IPC) — The mechanism that defines a way for internal Windows processes to exchange information.

LMHOSTS — File is used in Microsoft networks to provide NetBIOS name-to-address resolution.

mailslots — A connectionless version of named pipes; mailslots offer no delivery guarantees, nor do they acknowledge successful receipt of data.

Multiple Universal Naming Convention Provider (MUP) — A Windows XP software component that allows two or more UNC providers (for example, Microsoft networks and NetWare networks) to exist simultaneously. The MUP determines which UNC provider will handle a particular UNC request and forwards the request to that provider.

Multi-Provider Router (MPR) — A file system service that can designate the proper redirector to handle a resource request that does not use UNC naming. The MPR lets applications written to older Microsoft specifications behave as if they used UNC naming. The MPR is able to recognize those UNCs that correspond to defined drive mappings receive copies of the domain security database or Active Directory.

named pipes — Provides support for a connection-oriented message passing service for clients and servers.

NDS tree — The hierarchical representation of the Novell Directory Services database on NetWare 4.0 and higher networks.

NetBIOS Extended User Interface (NetBEUI) — A simple transport program developed to support NetBIOS installations. NetBEUI is not routable, so it is not appropriate for larger networks.

NetBIOS over TCP/IP (NBT) — A network protocol in the TCP/IP stack that provides NetBIOS naming services.

NetWare Core Protocol (NCP) — The protocol used by CSNW to make file and print services requests of NetWare servers.

Network Basic Input/Output System (NetBIOS) — A client/server interprocess communication service developed by IBM in 1985. NetBIOS presents a relatively primitive mechanism for communication in client/server applications, but allows an easy implementation across various Microsoft Windows computers.

Network Device Interface Specification (NDIS) — Microsoft specification that defines parameters for loading more than one protocol on a network adapter.

Network Dynamic Data Exchange (NetDDE) — An interprocess communication mechanism developed by Microsoft to support the distribution of DDE applications over a network.

network number — The specific network identifier used by IPX for internal and network communication.

Novell Directory Services (NDS) — The hierarchical database used by NetWare 4.0 and higher servers to store network resource object configuration information.

NWLink — Microsoft's implementation of Novell's IPX/SPX protocol suite.

Open Datalink Interface (ODI) — Novell's specification for network device communication.

Packet Internet Groper (PING) — An IP-based utility that can be used to check network connectivity or to verify whether a specific host elsewhere on the network can be reached.

Reverse Address Resolution Protocol (RARP) — The IP protocol used to map from a physical MAC-layer address to a logical IP address.

remote execution (rexec) — The IP-based utility that permits a user on one machine to execute a program on another machine elsewhere on the network.

remote shell (rsh) — The IP-based utility that permits a user on one machine to enter a shell command on another machine on the network.

Sequenced Packet Exchange (SPX) — A connection-oriented protocol used in the NetWare environment when guaranteed delivery is required.

Simple Mail Transport Protocol (SMTP) — The IP-based messaging protocol and service that supports most Internet e-mail.

7

Simple Network Management Protocol (SNMP) — The IP-based network management protocol and service that makes it possible for management applications to poll network devices and permits devices to report on error or alert conditions to such applications.

subnet — A portion of a network that might or might not be a physically separate network. A subnet shares a network address with other parts of the network but is distinguished by a subnet number.

subnet mask — The number used to define which part of a computer's IP address denotes the host and which part denotes the network.

Telnet — The TCP/IP-based terminal emulation protocol used on IP-based networks to permit clients on one machine to attach to and operate on another machine on the network as if the other machines were terminals locally attached to a remote host.

Transmission Control Protocol/Internet Protocol (TCP/IP) — A suite of Internet protocols upon which the global Internet is based. TCP/IP is the default protocol for Windows XP.

Transmission Control Protocol (TCP) — The reliable, connection-oriented IP-based transport protocol that supports many of the most important IP services, including HTTP, SMTP, and FTP.

Trivial File Transport Protocol (TFTP) — A lightweight alternative to FTP, TFTP uses UDP to provide only simple get-and-put capabilities for file transfer on IP-based networks.

Universal Naming Convention (UNC) — A multivendor, multiplatform convention for identifying shared resources on a network.

User Datagram Protocol (UDP) — A lightweight, connectionless transport protocol used as an alternative to TCP in IP-based environments to supply faster, lower overhead access, primarily (but not exclusively) to local resources.

Windows Internet Name Service (WINS) — Service that provides NetBIOS-name-to-IP-address resolution.

REVIEW QUESTIONS

1. The _____ enables a system to determine which part of an IP address represents the host, and which part represents the network.

2. _____ is a TCP/IP service used to resolve host or domain names to addresses.

3. The _____ service can be used to automatically assign IP configurations to a computer.

4. The _____ file provides NetBIOS name-to-IP address resolution.

5. _____ is a TCP/IP protocol that is used for file manipulation.

6. By changing the _____, you alter the order in which services are accessed.

7. _____ is the Microsoft service that provides NetBIOS name to address resolution.

8. The current version of TCP/IP (IPv4) uses a/an _____ bit addressing scheme.

9. NDIS allows any number of adapters to be bound to any number of transport protocols. True or False?

10. Which of the following new networking features of Windows XP cannot be used on systems that are domain clients?

   a. Network Bridging

   b. Remote Assistance

   c. Remote Desktop

   d. Wireless networking

11. What are the restrictions for making a network connection part of a network bridge on Windows XP?

   a. Not a dial-up connection

   b. Not controlled by ICF

   c. Not a wireless connection

   d. Not controlled by ICS

12. Which Windows XP networking component allows a system to access shared resources?

   a. TCP/IP

   b. Workstation service

   c. RPC

   d. NetDDE

13. If you are assigned the IP address 172.16.1.1, what full class subnet mask is most likely the correct one to use?

   a. 255.0.0.0

   b. 255.255.0.0

   c. 255.255.255.0

14. Which class of IP addresses offers the most flexibility with regard to subnetting by providing for the most number of hosts?

   a. Class A

   b. Class B

   c. Class C

15. What should be placed on remote systems that connect to routed networks over slow WAN links?

    a. NWLink

    b. LMHOSTS

    c. DNS

    d. HOSTS

    e. WinInet

16. Which TCP/IP command was designed to test the presence of a remote system?

    a. Telnet

    b. PING

    c. ARP

    d. Route

17. Which of the following is the static text-based equivalent of the Windows XP NetBIOS name to IP address resolution service?

    a. HOSTS

    b. LMHOSTS

    c. DNS

    d. WINS

18. If your network hosts the appropriate automatic addressing service, you do not need to manually configure TCP/IP to participate in a network. True or False?

19. Which of the following protocols is used to inquire if an address is reachable on the Internet?

    a. SMTP

    b. UTP

    c. PING

    d. IMAP

20. What IPC interfaces are used by Windows XP for file system access? (Choose all that apply.)

    a. WinSock

    b. named pipes

    c. mailslots

    d. OLE

21. Networking bridging offers what benefits?

    a. Filtering

    b. Communication between subnets without expensive hardware

    c. Communication between networks of differing media and protocol

    d. Full routing control

22. Remote Desktop can be used to invite another user to interact with your desktop environment in order to demonstrate how to perform some activity. True or False?

23. NDIS and ODI are technologies that provide for _____.

    a. dynamic client configuration

    b. distribution of driver software

    c. binding of multiple protocols to multiple adapters

    d. resolution of names to IP addresses

24. Which of the following will reduce broadcasts the most in a TCP/IP environment?

    a. DNS

    b. WINS

    c. NWLink

    d. DLC

25. TCP/IP is the most widely used protocol in the world. True or False?

26. All versions of NetWare utilize NDS. True or False?

27. Which of the following elements is part of Microsoft's NetWare environment for Windows XP Professional? (Choose all that apply.)

    a. NWLink

    b. CSNW

    c. GSNW

    d. NetWare File and Print Services

28. For IPX/SPX communication to succeed on a network, all computers must use the same frame type. True or False?

29. Which of the following NetWare protocols provides guaranteed packet delivery?

    a. NWLink

    b. IPX

    c. SPX

    d. NCP

7

30. When choosing a NetWare client for Windows XP, which of the following conditions should guide that choice? (Choose all that apply.)

    a. Always use the Microsoft Client for NetWare networks.

    b. Always use the Novell 32-bit Windows client.

    c. If there are more NetWare servers than Windows servers, or if native support for NDS and NetWare-aware applications is required, use the Novell 32-bit Windows client.

    d. If there are more Windows servers than NetWare servers, or if native support for Active Directory and Windows applications is required, use the Microsoft Client for NetWare Networks.

HANDS-ON PROJECTS

Project 7-1

To view the status and properties of a Local Area Connection:

This hands-on project assumes your Windows XP Professional system is connected to a network.

1. Open the **Network Connections** dialog box (**Start | Control Panel | Network Connections**). If the Control Panel is in Category View, select the Network and Internet Connections category, then click the Network Connections object.

2. Select the **Local Area Connection** object.

3. Select **File | Status**. This reveals the Local Area Connection Status dialog box. Notice the details provided on this dialog box: Connection Status, Duration, Speed, and Packets.

4. Click the **Properties** button. This reveals the Local Area Connection Properties dialog box for this connection. Notice how this dialog box reveals the NIC involved with this connection and all of the services and protocols associated with this connection.

5. Click **Cancel** to close the Local Area Connection Properties dialog box.

6. Click **Close** to close the Local Area Connection Status dialog box.

Project 7-2

To use PING to test TCP/IP communications:

This hands-on project assumes you are connected to a TCP/IP network. You must know the IP address or host name or FQDN of at least one system on your network (or the Internet if you also have Internet access).

1. Open the **Command Prompt** (**Start** | **All Programs** | **Accessories** | **Command Prompt**).

2. Type **PING** *<IP address or name>* where *<IP address or name>* is the IP address of a system on your network, the name of a system on your network, or the domain name of a system on the Internet. Press **Enter**. You should see a statement similar to "Pinging 172.16.1.7 with 32 bytes of data:" followed by four lines listing whether a reply was received or a timeout occurred.

3. Type **exit** then press **Enter**.

Project 7-3

To view the HOSTS and LMHOSTS sample files:

1. Open Notepad (**Start** | **All Programs** | **Accessories** | **Notepad**).

2. Select **File** | **Open**.

3. Use the Open dialog box to locate and select the **\WINDOWS\system32\-drivers\etc** directory.

4. Change the **Files of type** to **All Files** by using the pull-down list.

5. You should see a list of files in this folder. Select **hosts**, then click **Open**.

6. Scroll down through this file reading the information it provides. Do not make any changes to the file at this time.

7. Select **File** | **Open**. You should still be viewing the \etc directory.

8. Change the **Files of type** to **All Files** by using the pull-down list.

9. You should see a list of files in this folder. Select **lmhosts** or **lmhosts.sam**, then click **Open**.

10. Scroll down through this file reading the information it provides. Do not make any changes to the file at this time.

11. Select **File** | **Exit**.

Project 7-4

To configure TCP/IP:

The IP address of 172.16.1.1 and subnet mask of 255.255.255.0 can be replaced by your own assigned values.

1. Open Network Connections (**Start | Control Panel | Network Connections**).
2. Select the **Local Area Connection** object.
3. Select **File | Properties**. This reveals the Properties dialog box for the selected Local Area Connection object.
4. Select the **Internet Protocol (TCP/IP)** in the list of components.
5. Click **Properties**. This reveals the Internet Protocol (TCP/IP) Properties dialog box.
6. Select the **Use the following IP address** radio button.
7. Type in the IP address of **172.16.1.1**.
8. Type in the subnet mask of **255.255.255.0**.
9. Click **OK**.
10. Click **OK**.
11. Click the **File** menu, then click **Close**.
12. Reboot the system for the changes to take effect.

Project 7-5

To view network bindings:

1. Open Network Connections (**Start | Control Panel | Network Connections**). If the Control Panel is in Category View, select the Network and Internet Connections category, then click the Network Connections object.
2. Click the **Advanced** menu, then click **Advanced Settings**. This reveals the Advanced Settings dialog box where bindings are managed.
3. Select a connection from the connection box.
4. Notice the contents of the lower field where installed services and protocols are listed in their binding order.
5. Notice the items closer to the top of the list are bound in priority to those listed lower on the list.
6. Notice the checkbox beside each item that allows you to disable that service or protocol.
7. Click **Cancel** to ensure you've made no changes.
8. Click the **File** menu, then click **Close**.

Project 7-6

To send an invitation for Remote Assistance:

This hands-on project requires that the system have the Outlook Express or other e-mail system configured. This project also requires that you know the e-mail address of the teacher to invite.

1. Click **Start|Help and Support**. The Help and Support Center is displayed.
2. Click **Invite a friend to connect to your computer with Remote Assistance**. The Remote Assistance help page is displayed.
3. Click on **Invite someone to help you**. The Pick how you want to contact your assistant page is displayed.
4. In the Type an e-mail address text box, type in the e-mail address of the teacher to invite.
5. Click **Invite this person**. The E-mail an invitation page is displayed.
6. In the **From** field, type in the name to appear on the invitation if Administrator is not sufficient.
7. In the **Message** field, type in a message to the invitee, such as "Please help me."
8. Click **Continue**.
9. Define the expiration time limit for this invitation, such as 30 minutes.
10. Be sure the **Require the recipient to use a password** checkbox is marked.
11. Provide a password and confirm the password. Be sure to remember what this password is and to provide it to the teacher. It is not wise to include the password in the e-mail message.
12. Click **Send Invitation**.
13. A confirmation box may appear asking whether you wish to send the message, click **Send** or **Yes**.
14. The Help and Support Center returns you to the Remote Assistance page, click **View invitation status**. A listing of the invitation you've sent appears.
15. Click the radio button beside your invitation, then click **Details**.
16. A dialog box with complete details about the invitation is displayed, click **Close**.

Do not use any of these options now, but for informational purposes, you should know that the Expire button instantly expires the invitation, the Resend button initiates resending the invitation, and the Delete button removes the invitation.

17. Click the **X** button in the title bar to close the Help and Support Center.

You may have to send the message manually from within Outlook.

Project 7-7

To respond to an invitation for Remote Assistance:

This hands-on project requires the following: that you work from another Windows XP system, that you have received the invitation from Hands-on Project 7-6, network connectivity between the teacher/assistant computer and the student/end-user computer, and that both computer system have Internet access.

1. On the teacher's computer, open an e-mail client, such as Outlook Express.
2. Locate the e-mail from the student.
3. Launch the attachment to initiate Remote Assistance.

The messages and attachments from Remote Assistance are easy to impersonate, so be sure that the attachment you launch is a valid Remote Assistance utility and not a malicious hacker tool.

4. The Remote Assistance tool launches, and prompts you for the password; type in the password provided by the student.
5. Click **Yes**.
6. On the student's computer, a pop-up dialog box appears asking if you want to allow the teacher to connect, click **Yes**.
7. The Remote Assistance control bar appears on the student's computer. The Remote Assistance desktop access window and control utility appears on the teacher's computer.
8. From either system, type in a short message in the **Message Entry** section, such as **What may I assist you with?**, then click **Send**.
9. On the teacher's computer, click **Take Control** from the top toolbar.
10. On the student's computer, click **Yes** when prompted whether to grant control of the computer.
11. On the teacher's computer, click **OK** when informed you have taken control.
12. On the teacher's computer open and close **Windows Explorer**. Notice that the movements made on the teacher's computer actually take effect on the student's computer.
13. On the teacher's computer, click **Disconnect** from the top tool bar.
14. On both computers, click **OK** when informed that Remote Assistance has been disconnected.
15. On both computers, click the **X** button on the title bar of Remote Assistance to close the interface.

Project 7-8

To install NWLink:

1. If you have not already done so, log on to your Windows XP Professional computer as Administrator.

2. Click **Start**, then right-click **My Network Places** and then select **Properties**.

3. Right-click **Local Area Connection** and then select **Properties**.

4. In the Local Area Connection Properties dialog box, click **Install**.

5. Select **Protocol** from the list of available components and then click **Add**.

6. Select **NWLink IPX/SPX/NetBIOS Compatible Transport Protocol** from the list.

7. Click **OK** to complete the installation. Note that you do not need to reboot the computer for this addition to take effect.

8. Click **Close** on the Local Area Connection dialog box.

9. Right-click again on the **Local Area Connection** icon and select **Properties** to configure NWLink. Note that NWLink NetBIOS has been added to the installed components list.

10. Select **NWLink IPX/SPX/NetBIOS Compatible Transport Protocol** from the list and then click **Properties**.

11. Enter an internal network number for the computer. Use any combination of up to six numbers and letters A–F. For example, 1FAD or 1999A.

12. Click the down arrow for the **Frame type** dropdown list and select a frame type. If you are in a classroom environment, select the frame type specified by the instructor.

13. Note that you must specify the Network number for the selected frame. Enter a network number in the space provided. If you are in a classroom environment, enter the network number specified by the instructor.

14. Click **OK** twice to complete the configuration. Note that the changes take effect immediately. If you are in a classroom environment, ensure that communications are available to computers with the same frame type and network number.

15. Close the Network and Dial-up Connections window.

Project 7-9

To install and configure Client Service for NetWare:

1. If you have not already done so, logon to your Windows XP Professional computer as Administrator.

2. Click **Start**, then right-click **My Network Places** and then select **Properties**.

3. Right-click **Local Area Connection** and then select **Properties**.

4. In the Local Area Connection Properties dialog box, click **Install**.

5. Select **Client** from the list of available components and then click **Add**. Note that the only client available to be installed is Client Service for NetWare.

6. Select **Client Service for NetWare** and then click **OK**. Click **Yes** to restart your computer when prompted to do so.

7. Logon to the computer as Administrator.

8. When prompted in the Select NetWare Logon window, follow your classroom instructions. You'll either click the Default Tree and Context radio button, and enter the default tree and context for your computer on the network, or provide a name for the Preferred Server to which the computer will connect (this latter element is selected by default).

9. Wait a moment while the configuration changes are made, then, if prompted, click **Yes** to restart the computer.

10. After the computer has restarted, log on to your Windows XP Professional computer as Administrator.

11. Open the Control Panel by selecting **Start|Control Panel**. Note that the CSNW icon appears.

12. Double-click the **CSNW** icon to open the Client Service for NetWare dialog box. Adjust the Print Options and Login Script Options as desired and click **OK**.

13. Note that you receive an information box telling you that the changes will take effect the next time you log in. Click **OK** to continue.

14. Close the Control Panel.

CASE PROJECTS

1. Describe the functions and features of TCP/IP included with Windows XP.

2. As a network administrator at XYZ Corp., you always hear about it when performance problems arise on the network. In the past two weeks, you've been involved in switching the network over from using NWLink exclusively to a mixture of NWLink and TCP/IP. You've installed TCP/IP on all Windows 2000 Server and Windows XP Professional systems, and made sure that all the machines are properly configured. Because the network is growing, and an additional cable segment has been added, with more planned for the future, you plan to switch entirely from NWLink to TCP/IP over time. All of a sudden, your users complain that the network has slowed dramatically. What steps can you take that might improve speed performance? Which machines should you make changes on and why?

8

INTERNETWORKING WITH
REMOTE ACCESS

After reading this chapter and completing the exercises, you will be able to:

♦ Understand remote access under Windows XP

♦ Configure various remote access connection types for a Windows XP Professional system

♦ Install remote access hardware

♦ Understand remote access security

♦ Understand the Internet Options applet

♦ Implement Internet Connection Sharing and the Internet Connection Firewall

♦ Understand the native Internet tools and utilities

♦ Troubleshoot remote access problems

Not all network access occurs from computers that are directly attached to the network where the resources and data reside. For roaming workers, such as salespeople and field engineers, and increasingly for telecommuters, the ability to gain access to a network remotely—that is, from some location other than where the network physically resides—is crucial. This is an area where Windows XP really shines; it is one of the few major network operating systems that includes remote access capabilities with the core software at no additional charge. For Windows XP Professional, this means that part of the package is a single dial-in or dial-out connection that can use a **modem** over a PSTN (Public Switched Telephone Network) connection, DSL (Digital Subscriber Loop), cable modem, an **ISDN (Integrated Services Digital Network)** line, frame relay, or any of the other more exotic digital remote link technology. Since Windows NT became a force to be reckoned with in 1995 with the release of Windows NT 3.51, remote access services have played a central role in the operating system's burgeoning popularity and widespread acceptance up to and including the current Windows XP release.

REMOTE ACCESS

You can use **remote access service** to logon to a Windows XP system for user or administrative access while you're away from the office. For example, a user can access the system from a hotel room while traveling on business. Remote access can be used to dial into another system or to answer incoming connections. A client system is any system that initiates access to a Windows XP system established as a remote access server.

A Windows XP remote access configuration includes the following components:

- *Clients*—Windows XP, Windows 2000, Windows NT, Windows 95/98, Windows for Workgroups, MS-DOS (with Microsoft network client software installed), and LAN Manager remote access clients can all connect to a Windows XP remote access server. "Clients" can also mean any client of a platform that supports the Point to Point Protocol (PPP).

- *Protocols*—Windows XP remote access servers support the PPP protocol, enabling any PPP client to use TCP/IP (Transmission Control Protocol/Internet Protocol) or NWLink (IPX/SPX). Windows XP as a dial-up client can also access the installed base of SLIP (Serial Line Internet Protocol) remote access servers. However, SLIP cannot be used to connect to a Windows XP remote access server system.

- *WAN Connectivity*—Clients can dial in using standard telephone lines with a modem or modem pool employing legacy analog or the new DSL technology. Faster links are possible using ISDN or T-Carrier lines. Remote access clients can also be connected to remote access servers using X.25, ATM (Asychronous Transfer Mode), or an RS-232C null modem. Windows XP also allows for Channel Aggregation with PPP Multilink. Windows XP does support cable modems; however, in most cases proprietary software and drivers from the vendor are used to establish connections over these network adapter-like devices, because they function differently from a modem.

- *Security*—Windows XP logon and domain security, support for security hosts, data encryption, Internet Connection Firewall (ICF), IPSec (IP Security), and callback provide secure network access for remote clients. With Windows XP you also have the option of separating LAN traffic from remote access traffic with the Point-to-Point Tunneling Protocol (PPTP) or the Layer Two Tunneling Protocol (L2TP).

- *Server*—As a remote access server, Windows XP Professional supports only one inbound connection at a time. However, most Windows Server operating systems permit up to 256 remote clients to dial in. The remote access server can be configured to provide access to an entire network or restrict access to the remote access server.

- *LAN protocols*—IP protocol support permits accessing a TCP/IP network like the global Internet. NWLink (IPX/SPX) protocol support enables remote clients to access NetWare servers and printers. You can use NetBIOS applications over IPX or TCP/IP, and Windows Sockets applications over TCP/IP or IPX, named pipes, Remote Procedure Call (RPC), and the LAN Manager API are also supported.

 Remote control and remote access are control technologies that work in different ways. Remote control employs a remote client as a dumb terminal for the answering system, whereas remote access establishes an actual network connection between a remote client and the answering computer system, using a link device (such as a modem) as a network adapter. Remote access keyboard entries and mouse movements occur locally; with remote control, these actions are passed to a host system. Using remote access, computing operations are executed on the client; remote control computing operations are executed on the host with the resulting video signal sent to the client.

 Remote access and Terminal Services are also different mechanisms. Terminal Services allows thin clients—basic computers consisting of a display, keyboard, and mouse, with only enough capability to connect to the terminal server host—to participate in a rich computing environment. Basically, the terminal server host acts as the CPU for the thin client. All operations and calculations are performed on the terminal server host; only display changes are sent to the client and only keyboard and mouse information is sent back to the terminal server. Terminal Services are often employed in situations where budget restrictions prevent the purchase of fully capable desktop systems or when complete security is required (i.e., when data cannot exist outside the secure server). Remote access is a mechanism by which remote computers that exist as independent systems are able to make connections over some type of communication link to a system or standalone machine. This link is used to access data or to gain further access to linked networks.

FEATURES OF REMOTE ACCESS IN WINDOWS XP

Remote access is a standard component of Windows XP and does not require a manual service installation. Some of the impressive features of remote access under Windows XP are discussed in the following sections.

PPP Multilink

PPP remote access multilink allows you to increase overall throughput by combining the bandwidth of two or more physical communication links such as analog modems, ISDN, and other analog/digital links. PPP Multilink is based on Internet Engineering Task Force (IETF) standard RFC 1717, "The PPP Multilink." RFC stands for Request for Comments, designating official standards documents published by the IETF. This standard is located on the Web at *http://www.faqs.org/rfcs/rfc1717.html*.

VPN Protocols

Windows XP supports two virtual private network (VPN) protocols: Point-to-Point Tunneling Protocol and Layer Two Tunneling Protocol. **Point-to-Point Tunneling Protocol (PPTP)** is a networking technology that supports multiprotocol VPNs, allowing users to access corporate networks securely through the Internet. Clients using PPTP can access a corporate LAN by dialing an ISP or directly through the Internet. In both cases, the PPTP tunnel is encrypted and secure and works with any protocol.

Cisco Systems developed a PPTP alternative called **Layer Two Tunneling Protocol (L2TP)**. Similar to PPTP, L2TP encapsulates PPP frames for transport over various networks, including IP, X.25, Frame Relay, and ATM. L2TP is used in combination with IPSec to provide a secure encrypted VPN link over public networks.

Restartable File Copy

The restartable file copy feature automatically retransmits incomplete file transfers produced by interruption of remote access connectivity. This feature provides the following:

- Faster transmission of large files over lower-quality connections

- Reduced cost from avoiding retransmission of the whole file

- Reduced frustration from interrupted transfers

Idle Disconnect

The idle disconnect feature breaks off a remote access connection after a specified period of inactivity. This feature reduces the costs of remote access, helps you troubleshoot by closing dead connections, and frees up inactive remote access ports.

Autodial and Log-on Dial

You can configure remote access to automatically connect and retrieve files and applications stored on a remote system. Users do not have to establish a remote access connection each time they want to transfer a remote object; Windows XP quickly and efficiently handles all remote access events. By maintaining a virtual database of mappings between resources and connection objects, Windows XP remote access is able to re-establish links when previously accessed resources are re-requested.

Client and Server Enhancements

Windows XP remote access includes a number of client and server components that allow third-party vendors to develop remote access and dial-up networking applications.

Look and Feel

Windows XP remote access has undergone some changes since Windows 2000 and is significantly different from similar utilities in Windows NT and Windows 95/98. Remote access capabilities have now been integrated with the networking components, resulting in Network Connections, a multi-purpose management interface where both standard LAN networking links and remote access links are established and configured. Just about everything related to remote access is controlled through this interface. The only exception is that all remote access hardware (such as modems) are installed through the Add Hardware applet if they were not installed automatically by plug and play at bootup.

Callback Security

You can control access to the system from specified phone numbers by using the Callback feature. Calls may originate only from known phone number locations, or the remote access client can set the phone number dynamically. Callback is configured on the Callback tab of the Dial-up Preferences dialog box accessed through the Advanced menu of the Network Connections utility. There are three options: No callback, Ask me during dialing when the server offers, and Always call me back at the number(s) below. Allowing the number to be set dynamically (i.e., during the connection) does not provide any security; security is enforced only when predefined callback numbers are used.

WAN Connectivity

Wide area networks (WANs) link sites that are often a considerable physical distance apart. Using remote access, Windows XP enables you to create a WAN by connecting existing LANs through remote access over telephone, ISDN, cable modems, campus networks, or other communication lines. This is a cost-effective solution if you have minimal-to-moderate network traffic between sites. You can improve the performance of remote access-based WANs in one of three ways:

- Increasing bandwidth of the remote access connection

- Multilinking communication links using PPP Multilink

- Implementing PPTP over the Internet

INTERNET NETWORK ACCESS PROTOCOLS

Windows XP remote access supports all standard protocols for remote Internet access as well as **PPP Multilink**, a variation of PPP that enables you to create one large high-bandwidth pipe by banding together multiple PPP channels. The remote access protocol used in establishing and maintaining a WAN link is dependent on the client and server OS and LAN protocols. Windows XP-supported remote access protocols are outlined in the following sections.

PPP

Point-to-Point Protocol (PPP) is the current standard for remote access. Remote access protocol standards are defined in RFCs published by the IETF and other working groups. The RFCs supported in Windows XP remote access are:

- *RFC 1661*—The Point-to-Point Protocol (PPP)

- *RFC 1549*—PPP in HDLC Framing

- *RFC 1552*—The PPP Internetwork Packet Exchange Control Protocol (IPXCP)

- *RFC 1334*—PPP Authentication Protocols

- *RFC 1332*—The PPP Internet Protocol Control Protocol (IPCP)

Microsoft recommends using PPP because it is flexible and is the industry standard, which means continued compatibility with client and server hardware and software in the future. Remote clients connecting to third-party PPP servers might need to use a post-connect terminal script to logon to the PPP server. The server informs users it is switching to PPP framing mode (users must start the Terminal to complete logon).

 When using a non-Microsoft PPP stack to dial into a Windows Server that is a part of a domain and not a domain controller, the server looks only to its local accounts for the account name and password you specified on dial-in. If the server doesn't find the name and password locally, it won't check the domain accounts; it simply denies access. Because a domain controller does not have local accounts that it can use for verification, it uses the accounts in the domain's Active Directory database to grant or deny access.

PPTP

Point-to-Point-Tunneling Protocol (PPTP) is one of Windows XP's most interesting features. It allows you to establish a secure remote access pipeline over the public Internet and to "tunnel" IPX or TCP/IP traffic inside PPP packets. PPTP can provide real benefits for companies with numerous remote users who now subscribe to a local Internet Service Provider (ISP) for e-mail and Internet access and who use the same connection to access the corporate LAN. These VPNs can support the IPX and TCP/IP LAN protocols and provide private network access from any Internet connection point. PPTP's significant features include:

- *Transmission costs*—Uses the Internet as the primary long-distance connection medium rather than leased lines or long-distance telephone lines, reducing the cost of establishing and maintaining a remote access connection.

- *Hardware costs*—Requires less hardware by letting you locate modems and ISDN hardware on a network rather than directly attaching them to the remote access server.

■ *High*—This is the safest way to browse, but also the least functional. Less secure features are disabled, and appropriate for sites that might have harmful content. This is the default security level of the Restricted zone.

The content of this bulleted list is taken directly from the Security tab of the Internet Options dialog box of Windows XP Professional. Copyright is held by Microsoft.

These restrictions can include controls set for Disable, Enable, or Prompt (or possible custom settings based on security control) over downloading signed ActiveX controls, downloading unsigned ActiveX controls, run ActiveX scripts not marked as safe, run ActiveX controls and plug-ins, run ActiveX scripts marked as safe, file downloads, font downloads, Java permissions, etc.

The Internet zone contains all sites on the Internet or local intranet that have not been placed in any of the three other zones. The Local intranet zone contains those sites within your local intranet. This list is created automatically based on include/exclude selections of three controls: all local sites not in other zones, all sites that bypass the proxy server, and all network UNC paths. The Trusted sites zone includes only those sites that you add to this zone specifically. You should only add sites to this zone that you highly trust. You can force https server verification for all sites in this zone. The Restricted zone includes only those sites that you specifically add to this zone. You should add any site you discover that attempts to cause harm.

The Content Advisor—accessed from the Content tab of the Internet Options dialog box—is used to control site access based on RSACi content ratings. You are able to select the level of language, nudity, sex, and violence which users are allowed to see. Pre-approved sites can be defined using the site's URL as always accessible or never accessible. You can allow users to view all non-rated sites; however, this option is disabled by default. You can also define a supervisor password that allows access to all previously restricted content.

 For details on configuring Internet Explorer, consult the IE Help file or the IE Web site at *http://www.microsoft.com/windows/ie/default.htm*.

INTERNET CONNECTION SHARING

Internet Connection Sharing (ICS) is used to share a single network connection with a small group of networked computers. The shared connection can be a link to the Internet or any type of network. ICS is enabled on the Advanced tab of a connection object's Properties dialog box (refer to Figure 8-10 earlier in the chapter). By enabling sharing for a connection object, you allow other computers on your network to access resources over that external link.

Internet Connection Sharing incorporates the Network Address Translation (NAT) function, a Dynamic Host Configuration Protocol (DHCP) address allocator, and a Domain

Name Service (DNS) proxy. The mechanism hides your internal network configuration (keeping this information secure), provides automatic assignment of unregistered non-routable IP addresses to internal clients, and provides a forwarding hand-off procedure for all requests for external services. Basically, Internet Connection Sharing transforms your Windows XP system into a limited DHCP proxy server. After ICS is enabled, you must set all other clients to use DHCP in order to take advantage of the shared connection. Try Hands-on Project 8-8 to configure Internet Connection Sharing.

Once Internet Connection Sharing is enabled, you can also select whether to enable on-demand dialing. This feature automatically re-establishes the remote link when a client attempts to access external resources over your system through the currently offline connection object. Microsoft recommends using ICF on each ICS link for added security. For further tuning and configuration of the Internet Connection Sharing service, consult the *Microsoft Windows XP Professional Resource Kit*.

Troubleshooting the Internet Connection Service involves two distinct activities. First, verification that the connection is active and functioning can usually be accomplished using a Web browser. Second, verification that communication from other clients can access your system over the network can be achieved either by pinging or by attempting to access a shared resource from your client.

Once ICS is enabled, you can also define which services running on your internal network are accessible to external Internet users. This is performed through the Settings button on the Advanced tab, which opens the Advanced Settings dialog box. If you have enabled only ICS, then the Advanced Settings dialog box has a single tab—Services. However, if you have enabled ICF, then this dialog box has three tabs (discussed in the ICF section, see Figure 8-14). Windows XP is configured by default to allow access to L2TP, PPTP, and IKE (i.e., IPSec) resources. This allows external VPN clients to establish a connection into the network over the dial-up link. If you want to share other resources, you can enable FTP, IMAP, SMTP, POP, Remote Desktop, HTTP, Telnet, and HTTP. Other services can be defined by using the Add or Edit buttons.

ICS should not be used on any network with domain controllers, DNS servers, gateway systems, DHCP servers, or with clients that must have static IP addresses. ICS is designed for use on small workgroup networks, not within domains. ICS and normal DHCP interfere with each other. ICS uses the 192.168.x.x network to assign IP addresses to clients and does not support statically configured clients. For sharing an Internet connection with a domain, use the proxy routing and NAT capabilities of a Windows Server product.

INTERNET CONNECTION FIREWALL

The Internet Connection Firewall (ICF) is a security measure for protecting network connections from unwanted traffic. ICF can set restrictions on traffic in and out of your network to an external network or the Internet. Microsoft recommends that ICF be used on each ICS link, but ICF can be used on LAN connections as well. In fact, Microsoft recommends using ICF on every network connection to an external network except those that host VPN links. ICF is a much needed feature for systems that employ shared broadband connections, such as cable modems or even campus networks. On shared broadband connections, the potential exists for one client customer to infiltrate another client's system. Only a secure personal firewall can prevent such infiltration.

ICF is a stateful firewall, which means each packet that passes ICF is inspected to determine its source and destination addresses. This allows ICF to prevent any external traffic not requested by an internal client from entering the private network. However, ICF can also be configured to allow specific types of traffic to enter the private network without a corresponding internal client request. These features are defined on the Services tab of the Advanced Settings dialog box (see Figure 8-14) accessed through the Settings button on the Advanced tab of a connection object's Properties dialog box (as discussed in the section of this chapter on ICS).

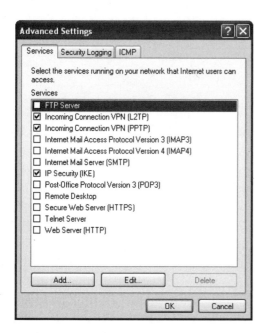

Figure 8-14   Advanced Settings dialog box, General tab.

By default, ICF silently drops all traffic that is not allowed to enter the private network. In other words, it does not record a log file of dropped packets. If you want a record of dropped packets or successful connections, logging can be enabled on the Security

Logging tab. You can use the logging ICF actions to determine which ports or services outside are attempting to connect to and which are succeeding. You might find some surprising footprints in the logs. Such as finding out that you have a Web server running on the default port 80 and some external user is regularly connecting to it. Rogue connections into your system, whether over a LAN or Internet connection can significantly reduce the performance of your system and compromise your security.

The ICMP tab is used to configure to which external system ICMP requests the ICF-protected system will respond.

Try Hands-on Project 8-9 to configure Internet Connection Sharing.

WINDOWS XP AND THE INTERNET

Windows XP Professional features a number of tools to help you access the vast resources of the Internet: Internet Explorer, Outlook Express, FTP client, Telnet client, and Internet Information Server (IIS), Connections can be established through Network Connections to the Internet or an Internet access point (such as a LAN with a proxy server).

Internet Explorer

Microsoft's Internet Explorer (IE) version 6.0 is included with the Windows XP operating system (this was the current release of IE when Windows XP was developed). Newer versions of IE can be obtained from the Microsoft Web site at *http://www.microsoft.com/ie/*.

IE is a state-of-the-art Web browser. In addition to being powerful and easy to use as a Web-surfing tool, IE is tightly integrated with other Windows applications; it can invoke Word to open .doc files or Excel to open .xls files across the Web. The program also includes advanced support for newsgroups and FTP and is tightly integrated with Outlook Express.

Outlook Express

One of the most popular e-mail client utilities is Outlook, a part of the suite of applications known as Microsoft Office. To tempt you with its impressive features and offer you a taste of a multi-function e-mail client, Microsoft has included Outlook Express in Windows XP. Outlook Express is limited only by the types of messaging it supports—it can manage only Internet e-mail involving POP3, IMAP, and SMTP services. Outlook Express can be used to read and write e-mail, file and sort messages, and more. It can act as a contact management tool, is integrated with IE for easy task switching, and offers customizable interfaces and rules (actions to be performed on messages automatically).

If "free" is your first criterion when choosing an e-mail package, Outlook Express is no slouch. However, if you are not above spending a few dollars for a worthwhile product, Outlook is worth the upgrade. For more information on Outlook and Outlook Express, visit *http://www.microsoft.com/outlook/*.

FTP Client

As mentioned earlier, FTP is an IP-based Application layer protocol that handles file transfer and remote file system access and manipulation functions. Microsoft includes a command-line implementation of an FTP client as part of the Windows XP operating system. This client is installed automatically when TCP/IP is installed.

 To learn more about this program, launch a DOS window (Start|All Programs|Accessories|Command Prompt) and enter *ftp* at the command line. When the ftp> prompt appears, enter *help* to read the program's associated list of commands (enter *help <command>* to obtain information about a specific command, where you replace *<command>* with the name of an actual FTP command, like *get* or *put*).

Even though the command-line version of FTP included with Windows XP is perfectly adequate, there are numerous freeware and shareware GUI implementations of FTP that can take its place and are much easier and friendlier to use. For a complete listing of such utilities, visit either of these Web sites, select Windows as the platform, and use "FTP" or "FTP client" as your search string:

- *http://www.shareware.com*
- *http://www.download.com*

The authors are quite partial to the IpSwitch package, WS_FTP Professional. It combines an Explorer-like file interface with easy controls for uploads and downloads. Visit *http://www.ipswitch.com/* to download an evaluation version.

Telnet Client

Telnet is the text-based remote interaction tool commonly used on older UNIX systems to gain access to shell accounts. Some ISPs still offer shell access to customers. The Telnet client included with Windows XP is a simple tool that attempts to establish a Telnet session with a remote system based on domain name or IP address. You can alter the display fonts and record the session for later perusal (it's all text anyway). For more information on Telnet, type telnet at a Command Prompt (Start | All Programs | Accessories | Command Prompt), then select Contents from the Help menu of the Telnet window.

Internet Information Server

A reduced functionality version of Internet Information Server (IIS) is included with Windows XP Professional to allow a system to host Web and FTP services. In most cases, IIS on a client system (such as Windows XP Professional) is used for site development and testing before deployment on an IIS system (such as Windows NT Server, Windows 2000 Server, or Windows .NET Server). When hosted by Windows XP Professional, IIS is limited to the same 10 simultaneous connections as Windows XP Professional itself. Thus, it is not a platform designed or intended for public Web/FTP site hosting.

Perhaps the most important and widely recognized function of IIS is the WWW (World Wide Web) Service. This service allows the user to publish Hypertext Markup Language (HTML) documents for use on the Web. Web browsers like Internet Explorer use the Hypertext Transfer Protocol (HTTP) to retrieve HTML documents from servers.

Overlooking limitations on the number of simultaneous users and the omission of certain site management tools, the two environments (IIS on Windows XP Professional and IIS on a Windows Server) are nearly identical. Certainly they're adequate to facilitate Web site development on a Windows XP Professional system with IIS, for ultimate deployment on Windows Server system with IIS.

The FTP Server installed with IIS is used to transfer files from the server to remote computers. Most installations of FTP on the Internet are used to download drivers and other data or software files.

This code module represents the server side of FTP, whereas the software mentioned earlier in the chapter covered the client side of FTP. In other words, this module permits machines elsewhere on the network to upload files to or download files from an Windows XP Professional system. The client-side software only permits the system to perform the same activities with other FTP servers elsewhere on the network.

Web server resources are managed similarly to any other network resource. You should think of Web and FTP services as a type of share for Internet clients. Thus, troubleshooting Web resource access problems is like troubleshooting typical network shared resource access problems. You need to manage file permissions on an NTFS file object level and general access to resources through the share (or in this case Web or FTP services). If a user is unable to gain access to a resource through the Web or FTP, check the NTFS file object-level permissions first on the file/object/resource itself, then on all of its parent containers. Next, check the setting on the Web or FTP service itself. To access resources over Web or FTP, the user must have at least Read access granted through the service and at least Read access on the file or resource based on group memberships. Keep in mind that most Web access is anonymous, whereas many FTP sites require user authentication for access. However, the logon credentials for FTP are transmitted in clear text. The anonymous user account IUSR_<computername> is a member of the Everyone and the Authenticated Users groups. This account is used to "authenticate" anonymous users on both Web and FTP sites hosted by IIS. Be sure to check the permissions for these groups as well.

A single Windows XP Professional system (or any Windows NT or 2000 system) can be assigned multiple IP addresses. When a system has multiple IP addresses and is the host of IIS as a Web server, each Web site can be assigned its own IP address. Assigning each Web site a different IP address is handled on the Web Site tab of the Properties dialog box. Just set the IP Address field to the specific IP address you want this Web site to use.

If you want to host multiple Web sites from a system that has only a single IP address, you must employ host headers. Host headers are defined through the Advanced button located alongside the IP Address field on the Web Site tab of the Properties dialog box of a Web site. Each unique Web site should be assigned its own host header. A host header is usually a word, short phrase, domain name, or title that the administrator of the Web site wants to use as the distinguishing element for that site. The host header is never seen by the Web user. If host headers are not used, a Web user would always see the first or default Web site hosted by the one-IP address IIS Web server even if they used the URL or domain name of any other Web site hosted by that Web server.

For more information on IIS, consult the *Microsoft Windows XP Professional Resource Kit* or the *Microsoft Windows .NET Server Resource Kit.*

ORDER PRINTS ONLINE

Order Prints Online is a feature of the My Pictures folder and any media folder defined as an image repository (see the "Media Folders and the Customize Tab" section in Chapter 4, "Managing Windows XP File System and Storage"). This command launches the Online Print Ordering Wizard, which walks you through the process of submitting digital images to a printing company. You'll select the images to print, the sizes, quantities, and billing and shipping information. The Wizard requires that Internet access be available. If you need help with the Wizard, use the Help and Support Center of Windows XP.

CLIENTS VS. SERVER-BASED REMOTE ACCESS

Choosing which platform to use as a remote access server is usually straightforward. Windows XP Professional is limited to a single incoming dial-up connection and can support only 10 simultaneous network connections (including LAN and VPN). Windows 2000 Server and Windows .NET Server both support up to 256 concurrent incoming dial-up connections and have no hard restriction on number of simultaneous network connections (restricted by license for LAN and hardware for VPN or Internet connections). Windows XP Professional can share an Internet link with a workgroup, but the workgroup is forced to use DHCP, and the range of IP addresses is assigned by ICS. Windows Servers offer Internet connection sharing through a proxy router that does not restrict the clients to DHCP or a specified IP address range. Windows XP Professional lacks a full-featured version of IIS, which is integrated into Windows Server products.

From these issues, it is clear that a small workgroup network can use Windows XP Professional as its remote access server if it can operate within the connection limitations. If an organization requires greater flexibility and connectivity, a Windows Server should be selected to act as the remote access server.

REMOTE ACCESS TROUBLESHOOTING

Remote access problems can be fairly elusive, but there are several common-sense first steps and several useful Windows XP tools to simplify the process of troubleshooting. Your first approach to a remote access problem should include considerations for:

- Physical connections (phone lines, serial cables, etc.)
- Power to external devices
- Properly installed and updated drivers
- Properly configured settings
- Correct authentication credentials
- Similar encryption or security requirements
- Proper protocol requirements and settings

If reviewing these items still fails to uncover the problem, there are several log files you can examine to hopefully glean more specific information. There are three logs related to remote access events. The first log is a file containing all communications made between the OS and the modem device during connection establishment. This log must be enabled through the Diagnostics tab of the modem's Properties on the Modems tab of the Phone and Modem Options applet. Once enabled, a text file named after the modem (in the format "ModemLog_Practical Peripherals PC288LCD V.34.txt") is stored in the main Windows XP directory. This file can be viewed with Notepad or simply by clicking View Log next to the enable checkbox on the Diagnostics tab.

The second log file, PPP.LOG, records the communications involved in the setup, management, and continuity of a PPP connection. This log is enabled by editing the Registry. The PPP value in the HKEY_LOCAL_MACHINE\SOFTWARE\Microsoft\Tracing\ key should be set to 1 to start the logging. This file is stored in the %systemroot%\tracing folder.

The final log is the System log as viewed through the Event Viewer. This log often records events related to remote access connection failures.

By combining data gleaned from these logs, you should be able to determine the cause of your connection problem and easily discover a simple resolution. If you need further remote access troubleshooting help, consult the *Microsoft Windows XP Professional Resource Kit*.

CHAPTER SUMMARY

- In this chapter, we've introduced you to the Windows XP Remote Access Service, including the significant features of remote access in Windows XP. We've examined remote access WAN connections and protocols, how to install and configure remote access, and how take full advantage of remote access dial-up networking and security features. With all this information, you should be ready to dial into your Windows XP Professional system from the outside or use it to dial out to a service provider. Additionally, we discussed the Internet access features built into Windows XP and how they can be employed to gain access to vast public and private resources. Windows XP is also designed to participate in virtual private networks (VPNs) by establishing an encrypted link between two systems over the Internet.

KEY TERMS

Dynamic Host Configuration Protocol (DHCP) — A method of automatically assigning IP addresses to client computers on a network.

gateway — A computer that serves as a router, a format translator, or a security filter for an entire network.

Integrated Services Digital Network (ISDN) — A direct, digital dial-up PSTN Data Link-layer connection that operates at 64KB per channel over regular twisted-pair cable between a subscriber site and a PSTN central office.

Layer Two Tunneling Protocol (L2TP) — A VPN protocol developed by Cisco Systems, Inc. to improve security over Internet links by integrating with IPSec.

modem (modulator/demodulator) — A Data-link layer device used to create an analog signal suitable for transmission over telephone lines from a digital data stream. Modern modems also include a command set to negotiate connections and data rates with remote modems and to set their default behavior.

Point-to-Point Protocol (PPP) — A Network layer transport that provides connectivity over serial or modem lines. PPP can negotiate any transport protocol used by both systems involved in the link and can automatically assign IP, DNS, and gateway addresses when used with TCP/IP.

Point-to-Point Tunneling Protocol (PPTP) — Protocol used to connect to private networks through the Internet or an ISP.

port — Any physical communication channel to which a modem, direct cable, or other device can be connected to enable a link between two computers.

PPP MultiLink — A capability of remote access to aggregate multiple data streams into one network connection for the purpose of using more than one modem or ISDN channel in a single connection.

Public Switched Telephone Networks (PSTN) — A global network of interconnected digital and analog communication links originally designed to support voice communication between any two points in the world, but quickly adapted to handle digital data traffic.

Remote Access Service (remote access) — The service in Windows XP that allows users to log into the system remotely.

serial — A method of communication that transfers data across a medium one bit at a time, usually adding start and stop bits to ensure reliable delivery.

Serial Line Internet Protocol (SLIP) — An implementation of the IP protocol over serial lines. SLIP has been made obsolete by PPP.

wide area network (WAN) — A geographically dispersed network of networks connected by routers and communications links. The Internet is the largest WAN.

X.25 — A standard that defines packet switching networks.

REVIEW QUESTIONS

1. You have configured a Windows XP Professional client to dial up and establish a connection to a Windows Server computer. The user adds a dial-up connection object, sets the proper network configuration, and the modem is functioning properly. The user submits the user name and password correctly. Unfortunately, the user is unable to authenticate properly. What might be causing this problem?

   a. The user did not configure the gateway properly.

   b. The user was not granted the appropriate dial-in permissions.

   c. The user was not added to the dial-in users group.

   d. Internet Connection Firewall was blocking the authentication

2. DHCP is the option for automatically assigning IP configuration to TCP/IP dial-up clients. True or False?

3. Windows XP Professional supports PPP logon scripts. True or False?

4. Which of the following remote access-related logs are enabled by default?

   a. PPP.LOG

   b. Modemlog_<modem name>.txt

   c. System log

5. Which of the following encrypted authentication options does Windows XP Professional support through remote access? (Choose all that apply.)

   a. PAP

   b. SPAP

   c. DES-3

   d. MS-CHAP

   e. PGP

6. The special protocol _____ allows multiple channels to be aggregated to increase bandwidth.

   a. Multilink PPP

   b. PPTP

   c. PPP

   d. SLIP

7. Where in Windows XP Professional do you specify which users have dial-in permissions to the remote access server?

   a. Network Connections

   b. Control Panel

   c. Remote Access Admin Tool

   d. My Computer

8. Which remote access security option also has an additional option to encrypt data?

   a. Require encrypted authentication

   b. Require C2 encrypted authentication

   c. Require B encrypted authentication

   d. Require Microsoft Encrypted Authentication

9. Which remote access callback option provides the greatest level of security?

   a. Set by Caller

   b. Set by Server

   c. Preset to

   d. Callback and confirm remote access password.

10. Which of the following protocols are supported by both Windows XP remote access clients and servers?

    a. SLIP

    b. PPP

    c. none of the above

    d. all of the above

11. Which of the following are similar technologies used to establish secured WAN links over the Internet?

    a. MPPP

    b. PPTP

    c. SLIP

    d. L2TP

12. Help-U-Sell has just opened a new office in Cedar Park, TX. They have a small workgroup network of eight computers. A cable modem has been installed. Which of the following technologies should be used to provide each system in the office with Internet access and prevent as much unwanted traffic as possible?

    a. IPSec

    b. ICS

    c. ICF

    d. Callback

    e. L2TP

13. Which connection protocol can be used by Windows XP Professional to connect to remote systems over standard telephone lines?

    a. SLIP

    b. PPP

    c. DLC

    d. PPTP

14. By default, Internet Connection Firewall blocks traffic of which service type if it originates from the Internet instead of responding to a request by an internal client?

    a. FTP

    b. L2TP

    c. POP3

    d. IKE

    e. Remote Desktop

    f. Telnet

    g. HTTP

15. The Create a new connection Wizard from Network Connections is used to create both remote access connections and standard LAN connections. True or False?

16. If you want to connect only to servers that offer secured data transmission, which of the following encryption settings should you define for your connection object?

    a. No encryption allowed (server disconnects if it requires encryption)

    b. Optional encryption (connect even if no encryption)

    c. Require encryption (disconnect if sever declines)

17. Windows XP supports Direct Cable Connections under remote access using:

    a. RS-232 Null Modem Cables

    b. APC UPS Cables

    c. LapLink Cables (i.e. parallel pass-through cables)

    d. Printer Cables

18. Remote access is remote control for Windows XP. True or False?

19. Internet Connection Sharing can be used to share which of the following types of connections with a workgroup network?

    a. Internet

    b. LAN dial-up

    c. VPN

    d. Incoming

    e. Bridge connection

20. You can connect to another computer from a remote access client using resources in the same manner as if you were connected on a LAN. True or False?

21. Dialing rules or Dialing locations are used to define the geographic location of a mobile computer so as to prescribe the dialing procedures. True or False?

22. The modem specific log file is enabled through what utility?

    a. Computer Management

    b. Phone and Modem Options

    c. Network Connections

    d. Server applet

23. Which of the following are Internet utilities included with Windows XP Professional?

    a. Internet Explorer

    b. Internet Information Server

    c. Outlook

    d. Telnet

    e. FTP client

24. In which of the following situations would the use of Windows XP Professional as a remote access server be a reasonable option?

    a. A single telecommuter needs to connect into the office network

    b. A domain network needs Internet access

    c. A SOHO network needs Internet access

    d. A high-traffic e-commerce Web site needs hosting

    e. A private network needs internal Web documentation access

25. Offline Files are cached locally at logoff, are accessed in the same way as the original files, and are automatically synchronized by default. True or False?

HANDS-ON PROJECTS

Project 8-1

To create a Dial-up connection object to connect to a private network:

This hands-on project assumes that a modem is installed. You need the phone number of a remote access server to contact. If this lab is to be used as a demonstration only, use 555-1212 as the phone number.

1. Open the Control Panel (**Start** | **Control Panel**).

2. Click **Switch to Classic View** if the Control Panel is currently in Category View.

3. Double-click **Network Connections**.

4. Launch the New Connection Wizard by double-clicking the **Create a new connection** link in the Quick List.

5. The first page of the Wizard is a welcome message. Click **Next**.

6. On the Network Connection Type page, select **Connect to the network at my workplace**. Click **Next**.

7. On the Network Connection page, select **Dial-up connection**. Click **Next**.

8. If you have two or more dial-up devices installed on your system, you will see the Select a Device page. Otherwise, skip to step 9. On the Select a Device page, select the communication device(s) for this connection object. Devices with a marked checkbox are used by this object; devices with an empty checkbox are not. If you select multiple devices, the system attempts to aggregate the links through multilink. Click **Next**.

9. On the Connection Name page, provide a name for this connection object such as **HoP 8-1**. Click **Next**.

10. On the Phone Number to Dial page, provide the dial-up number for your remote access server. Click **Next**.

11. On the Connection Availability page, select whether this connection will be available for Anyone's use or My use only. Click **Next**.

12. Click **Finish**. The Create a new connection Wizard completes the connection object creation (i.e., it now appears in the Network Connections window), but instead of returning you to the Network Connection window, the Wizard launches the new connection object for the first time.

13. On the Connect dialog box, provide the name of the user account to employ when connecting to the remote access system.

14. In the Password field, type the password for that user account. Your keystrokes will be echoed with asterisks instead of the actual character you typed to prevent over-the-shoulder theft of your password.

15. If you want the system to retain your password, select **Save this user name and password for the following users:**, then select Me only or Anyone who uses this computer. If you decide not to check this box, you'll have to provide the password each time this connection object is used to establish the remote access link.

16. Double-check that the listed phone number in the Dial field is correct. If not, change it to the correct number.

17. To initiate the connection, click **Dial**. If this project is being performed as an example rather than a real-life implementation, skip this step.

Project 8-2

To create a dial-up connection object to connect to an ISP:

This hands-on project assumes that a modem is installed. This lab performs a manual ISP configuration, which requires a phone number and valid username and password. If this lab is to be used as a demonstration only, use 555-1212 as the phone number.

1. Open the Control Panel (**Start|Control Panel**). Click **Switch to Classic View** if the Control Panel is currently in Category View.
2. Double-click **Network Connections**.
3. Launch the New connection Wizard by double-clicking the **Create a new connection** link in the Quick List.
4. The first page of the Wizard is a welcome message. Click **Next**.
5. On the Network Connection Type page, select **Connect to the Internet**. Click **Next**.
6. On the Getting Ready page, select **Set up my connection manually**. Click **Next**.
7. On the Internet Connection page, select **Connect using a dial-up modem**. Click **Next**.
8. If you have two or more dial-up devices installed on your system, you will see the Select a Device page. Otherwise, skip to step 9. On the Select a Device page, select the communication device(s) for this connection object. Devices with a marked checkbox will be used by this object; devices with an empty checkbox will not. If you select multiple devices, the system will attempt to aggregate the links through multilink. Click **Next**.
9. On the Connection Name page, provide a name for this connection object, such as **Lab ISP1**. Click **Next**
10. On the Phone Number to Dial page, provide the dial-up number for your ISP. Click **Next**.
11. On the Connection Availability page, select whether this connection will be available for Anyone's use or My use only. Click **Next**.
12. On the Internet Account Information page, provide the username and password for the ISP account.
13. By default, the selections of Use this account name and password when anyone connects to the Internet from this computer, Make this the default Internet connection, and Turn on Internet Connection Firewall for this connection are marked. If this is acceptable, click **Next**.
14. Click **Finish**. The Create a new connection Wizard completes the connection object creation (i.e., it now appears in the Network Connections window), but instead of returning you to the Network Connections window, the Wizard launches the new connection object for the first time.

15. On the Connect dialog box, double-check the name of the user account you need to employ when connecting to the ISP.

16. If you want the system to retain your password, select the **Save this user name and password for the following users:** checkbox, then select Me only or Anyone who uses this computer. If you decide not to check this box, you'll have to provide the password each time this connection object is used to establish the remote access link.

17. Double-check that the listed phone number in the Dial field is correct. If not, change it to the correct number.

18. To initiate the connection, click **Dial**. If this project is being performed as an example rather than a real-life implementation, skip this step.

Project 8-3

To create a VPN connection object:

This hands-on project performs a VPN configuration, which requires a host name or IP address of the remote system to connect to. If this lab is to be used as a demonstration only, use 172.16.1.1 as the IP address of the remote system.

1. Open the Control Panel (**Start | Control Panel**). Click **Switch to Classic View** if the Control Panel is currently in Category View.

2. Double-click **Network Connections**.

3. Launch the New Connection Wizard by double-clicking the **Create a new connection** link in the Quick List.

4. The first page of the Wizard is a welcome message. Click **Next**.

5. On the Network Connection Type page, select **Connect to the network at my workplace**. Click **Next**.

6. On the Network Connection page, select **Virtual Private Network connection**. Click **Next**.

7. On the Connection Name page, provide a name for this connection object, such as **Lab VPN 1**. Click **Next.**

8. On the Public Network page, select **Do not dial the initial connection**. If you want this VPN connection to establish an Internet connection automatically before initiating the VPN link, then select **Automatically dial this initial connection** and make a choice from the pull-down list. Click **Next**.

9. On the VPN Server Selection page, provide the host name or IP address of the remote system to connect to. Click **Next**.

10. On the Connection Availability page, select whether this connection will be available for Anyone's use or My use only. Click **Next**.

11. Click **Finish**. The Create a new connection Wizard completes the connection object creation (i.e., it now appears in the Network Connections window), but instead of returning you to the Network Connections window, the Wizard launches the new connection object for the first time.

12. On the Connect dialog box, provide the username and password needed to authenticate to the remote system.

13. If you want the system to retain your password, select the **Save this user name and password for the following users:** checkbox, then select Me only or Anyone who uses this computer. If you decide not to check this box, you'll have to provide the password each time this connection object is used to establish the remote access link.

14. To initiate the connection, click Dial. If this project is being performed as an example rather than a real-life implementation, skip this step.

Project 8-4

To create an Incoming connection object:

This hands-on project assumes that a modem is installed.

1. Open the Control Panel (**Start | Control Panel**). Click **Switch to Classic View** if the Control Panel is currently in Category View.

2. Double-click **Network Connections**.

3. Launch the New Connection Wizard by double-clicking the **Create a new connection** link in the Quick List.

4. The first page of the Wizard is a welcome message. Click **Next**.

5. On the Network Connection Type page, select **Set up an advanced connection**. Click **Next**.

6. On the Advanced Connection Options page, select **Accept incoming connections**. Click **Next**.

7. On the Devices for Incoming connections page, select the communication device(s) for this connection object. Devices with a marked checkbox will be used by this object; devices with an empty checkbox will not. Click **Next**.

8. On the Incoming VPN Connection page, select whether to allow VPN connections or not. Click **Next**.

9. On the User Permissions page, select users to be allowed to connect over this incoming connection object. Only users marked will be able to use this connection object. Click **Next**.

10. On the Networking Software page, select those components to bind to the incoming connection object. The defaults are usually satisfactory. Click **Next**.

11. Click **Finish**. The new incoming connection object is added to the Network Connections utility awaiting a dial-in attempt.

Project 8-5

To create a direct connect connection object:

 This hands-on project requires two systems in close proximity. One system should be labeled as the host or server; the other system should be labeled as the guest or client. A connecting parallel or serial cable or properly oriented infrared link must be present between the two systems.

1. Go to the system that will act as the host in the direct connection pair. Typically, the host system has the resource that needs to be transferred or accessed by the guest system.

2. Open the **Control Panel** (**Start | Control Panel**). Click **Switch to Classic View** if the Control Panel is currently in Category View.

3. Double-click **Network Connections**.

4. Launch the New Connection Wizard by double-clicking on the **Create a new connection** link in the Quick List.

5. The first page of the Wizard is a welcome message. Click **Next**.

6. On the Network Connection Type page, select **Set up an advanced connection**. Click **Next.**

7. On the Advanced Connection Options page, select **Connect directly to another computer**. Click **Next.**

8. On the Host or Guest? page, select **Host**. Click **Next**.

9. On the Connection Device page, select the link device type (serial, parallel, infrared, etc.) from the pull-down list. Click **Next**.

10. On the User Permissions page, select the user(s) that can connect over this link. Click **Next**.

11. Click **Finish**.

12. Go to the system that will act as the guest in the direct connection pair.

13. Open the Control Panel (**Start | Control Panel**). Click **Switch to Classic View** if the Control Panel is currently in Category View.

14. Double-click **Network Connections**.

15. Launch the New Connection Wizard by double-clicking the **Create a new connection** link in the Quick List.

16. The first page of the Wizard is a welcome message. Click **Next**.

17. On the Network Connection Type page, select **Set up an advanced connection**. Click **Next**.

18. On the Advanced Connection Options page, select **Connect directly to another computer**. Click **Next**.

19. On the Host or Guest? page, select the **Guest** option. Click **Next**.

20. On the Connection Name page, provide a name for this connection object, such as **Lab direct guest 1**. Click **Next**.

21. On the Select a Device page, select the link device type (serial, parallel, infrared, etc.) from the pull-down list. Click **Next**.

22. On the Connection Availability page, select whether this connection will be available for Anyone's use or My use only. Click **Next.**

23. Click **Finish**. The New Connection Wizard completes the connection object creation (i.e., it now appears in the Network Connections window), but instead of returning you to the Network Connection window, the Wizard launches the new connection object for the first time.

24. The Connect dialog box appears. Provide a name and password (for a user account granted access to connect back in step 10). Click **Connect**.

Project 8-6

To Install Internet Information Server on a Windows XP Professional system:

1. Open the **Control Panel** (**Start | Control Panel**). Click **Switch to Classic View** if the Control Panel is currently in Category View.

2. Launch the **Add or Remove Programs** applet by double-clicking on its icon.

3. Select the **Add/Remove Windows Components** item in the left column. This launches the Windows Components Wizard.

4. Select the checkbox beside Internet Information Services (IIS). Click **Next**.

5. When prompted, provide the path to the Windows XP Professional CD. This can involve just inserting the CD into the drive and clicking **OK** or using a Browser dialog box to locate the \i386 directory on the CD.

6. The installation Wizard copies files to your system. This can take several minutes. You might be prompted for the path to the CD a second time. Eventually, click **Finish**.

7. Click **Close** to terminate the Add or Remove Programs applet.

8. Close the Control Panel by selecting **File | Close**.

Project 8-7

To manage resources hosted by a Web server:

1. Open the **Control Panel** (**Start** | **Control Panel**). Click **Switch to Classic View** if the Control Panel is currently in Category View.

2. Double-click **Administrative Tools**.

3. Double-click **Internet Information Services**.

4. Expand the left node items by double-clicking on them until you can see Default Web Site.

5. Select **Default Web Site**.

6. Select **Action** | **Properties**.

7. Select the **Home Directory** tab.

8. In the box labeled **Local Path,** take note of the directory path listed there. It will most likely be "c:\inetpub\wwwroot." This is the top-level root directory for your Web site.

9. Click **OK**.

10. Select **File** | **Exit** to close the IIS tool.

11. Launch Windows Explorer (**Start** | **All Programs** | **Accessories** | **Windows Explorer**).

12. Locate the top-level root directory for your Web site and select it in the left pane of Windows Explorer.

13. In the right pane of Windows Explorer right-click over an empty area, select **New** from the pop-up menu, then select **Text Document** from the fly-open menu.

14. Type in the filename **default.htm**, then press **Enter**. If prompted about whether to change the filename extension, click **Yes**.

15. Open Notepad (**Start** | **All Programs** | **Accessories** | **Notepad**).

16. Select **File** | **Open**.

17. Change the Files of type pull-down list to **All Files**.

18. Locate and select the **default.htm** document.

19. Click **Open**.

20. Type the following into the body of this document: **<HTML><BODY>This is the default document.<P></BODY></HTML>**.

21. Select **File** | **Save**.

22. Select **File** | **Exit**.

23. Launch Internet Explorer from the desktop by double-clicking its icon.

24. Select **File** | **Open**.

25. Type **localhost** and click **OK**.

26. The Web browser should display the default document you created by showing a line stating "This is the default document."

27. Select **File | Close**.

Project 8-8

To configure Internet Connection Sharing:

This hands-on project requires that a network connection already be defined.

1. Open the **Control Panel** (**Start | Control Panel**). Click **Switch to Classic View** if the Control Panel is currently in Category View.

2. Double-click **Network Connections**.

3. Select the predefined dial-up connection item from the Network Connections tool.

4. Select **File | Properties**.

5. Select the **Advanced** tab.

6. Select the **Allow other network users to connect through this computer's Internet connection** checkbox under Internet Connection Sharing.

7. A message dialog box might appear stating that a username and password are not stored for this connection. Click **OK**.

8. Click the **Settings** button.

9. Select the **Services** tab.

10. Select the checkbox beside **Remote Desktop**.

11. Click **OK**.

12. Click **OK**.

Project 8-9

To configure Internet Connection Firewall:

This hands-on project requires that a network connection already be defined.

1. Open the **Control Panel** (**Start | Control Panel**). Click **Switch to Classic View** if the Control Panel is currently in Category View.

2. Double-click **Network Connections**.

3. Select the predefined dial-up connection item from the Network Connections tool.

8

4. Select **File** | **Properties**.

5. Select the **Advanced** tab.

6. Select the **Protect my computer and network by limiting or preventing access to this computer from the Internet** checkbox under Internet Connection Firewall.

7. Click **Settings**.

8. On the Services tab, mark any service that you want ICF to pass without restriction.

9. Select the **Security Logging** tab.

10. Mark the **Log dropped packets** checkbox.

11. Select the **ICMP** tab.

12. Make sure that all checkboxes are cleared.

13. Click **OK**.

14. Click **OK** again.

CASE PROJECTS

1. Your organization has decided to allow several employees to work from home. With Windows XP Professional on the telecommuters' systems, describe your configuration and setup options, including how you can deal with security and non-dedicated connections.

2. After installing a new modem, none of your connection objects will function, even after you've recreated them. Describe the process you would use to troubleshoot this problem.

PRINTING AND FAXING

After reading this chapter and completing the exercises, you will be able to:

♦ Understand Windows XP print terminology and architecture
♦ Understand the special features of the Windows XP print system
♦ Create and manage a printer
♦ Manage printer permissions
♦ Troubleshoot printing
♦ Configure Windows XP fax capabilities

Printing is an integral part of any operating system. Often, people will not understand a concept or layout until they see it on hard copy. In this chapter, you are introduced to some of the concepts associated with Windows XP printing, and then you will learn what is involved in installing and configuring printers for Windows XP. Although this may sound somewhat simplistic, because of the many options that are available when accessing printers in the Windows XP environment, this topic is more complex than it may at first appear. For example, it is important to understand the distinction between printers that are directly attached to a computer and those with built-in network interfaces that are attached directly to a networking medium. You will also learn how to troubleshoot common printing-related problems on Windows XP-based networks and systems. Finally, you will learn how to install and configure Windows XP's fax components.

WINDOWS XP PRINTING TERMINOLOGY

As is the case in other areas of Windows XP system architecture and behavior, Microsoft uses its own unique and specialized terminology to describe and explain how printers interact with the Windows XP system, and how its overall printing capabilities work. For the best results with the Microsoft certification tests, it is important to understand Microsoft's printing subsystem concepts, architecture, and behavior, which is why we begin this chapter with a "vocabulary list" of Microsoft print terminology before we discuss the key components of the Microsoft print architecture and behavior. For convenience, we present these terms in alphabetical order in the following list:

- *Client application*—An application or service that creates print jobs for output, which can be either end-user-originated or created by a print server (*see also* print client).

- *Connecting to a printer*—The negotiation of a connection to a shared printer through the browser service from a client or service across the network to the machine where the shared printer resides.

- *Creating a printer*—Using the Add Printer Wizard in the Printers and Faxes applet (Start|Printers and Faxes) to name and define settings for a print device in a Windows XP-based network.

- *Direct-attached printer*—A print device attached directly to a computer, usually through a parallel port (*see also* network interface printer).

- *Network interface printer*—A print device attached directly to the network medium, usually by means of a built-in network interface integrated within the printer, but sometimes by means of a parallel-attached network printer interface.

- *Print client*—A network client machine that transmits print jobs across the network to a printer for spooling and delivery to a designated print device or printer pool.

- *Print device*—In everyday language, a piece of equipment that provides output service—in other words, a printer; however, in Microsoft terminology, a printer is a logical service that accepts print jobs and delivers them to some print device for output when that device is ready. Therefore, in Microsoft terminology, a print device is any piece of equipment that can produce output, so this term would also describe a plotter, a fax machine, or a slide printer, as well as a text-oriented output device, such as an HP LaserJet.

- *Print job*—The contents of a completely or partially interpreted data file that contains text and control characters that will ultimately be delivered to a print device to be printed or otherwise rendered in some tangible form.

- *Print resolution*—A measurement of the number of dots per inch (dpi) that describes the output capabilities of a print device; most laser printers can produce output at 300 to 600 dpi if not greater. In general, the larger the dpi rating for a device, the better looking its output will be (but high-resolution devices cost more than low-resolution ones).

- *Print server*—A computer that links print devices to the network and shares those devices with client computers on the network. In the Windows XP environment, both Windows XP Professional and Windows .NET Server can function as print servers.

- *Print Server services*—A collection of named software components on a print server that handles incoming print jobs and forwards them to a print spooler for post-processing and delivery to a print device. These components include support for special job handling that can enable a variety of client computers to send print jobs to a print server for processing.

- *Print spooler*—A collection of Windows XP dynamic link libraries (DLLs) used to acquire, process, catalog, and dispense print jobs to print devices. The print spooler, which manages an area called the spool file on a print server, acts like a holding tank: pending print jobs are stored there until they have been successfully output. The term "despooling" refers to the process of reading and interpreting what is in a spool file for delivery to a print device.

- *Printer (logical printer)*—In Microsoft terminology, a printer is not a physical device, but rather a named system object that communicates between the operating system and a print device. The printer handles the printing process for Windows XP from the time a print command is issued until a print job has been successfully output. The settings established for a printer in the Add Printer Wizard in the Printers and Faxes applet (Start | Printers and Faxes) indicate which print device (or devices, in the case of a printer pool) will handle print output, and also provide controls over how print jobs will be handled (banner page, special post-processing, and so forth). Creating a logical printer is detailed in Hands-on Project 9-1. Deleting a printer is covered in Hands-on Project 9-6.

- *Printer driver*—Special-purpose software components that manage communication between the Windows XP I/O Manager and a specific print device. Ultimately, printer drivers make it possible for Windows XP to despool print jobs and send them to a print device for output services. Modern printer drivers also allow the printer to communicate with Windows XP, and to inform it about print job status, error conditions (out of paper, paper jam, and so forth), and print job problems.

- *Printer pool*—A collection of two or more identically configured print devices to which one or more Windows XP printers direct their print jobs. Basically, a printer pool permits two or more printers to act in concert to handle high-volume printing needs.

- *Queue (print queue)*—A series of files stored in sequential order waiting for delivery from a spool file to a print device.

9

- *Rendering*—Windows XP produces output according to the following sequence of steps: (1) A client application or a service sends file information to a software component called the **Graphical Device Interface (GDI)**. (2) The GDI accepts the data, performs any necessary local processing, and sends the data to a designated printer. (3) If this printer is local, the data is directed to the local print driver; if the printer is remote (located elsewhere on the network), the data is shipped to a print server across the network. (4) Either way, the driver then takes the print job and translates it into the mixture of text and control characters needed to produce output on the designated print device. (5) This file is stored in a spooling file until its turn for output comes up, at which point it is shipped to a print device. (6) The target device accepts the input data and turns it into the proper low-level format for rendering on that machine, on a page-by-page basis. (7) As each page image is created, it is sent to the printer's print engine, where it is output on paper (or whatever other medium the print device may use).

- *Spooling*—One of the functions of the print spooler, this is the act of writing the contents of a print job to a file on disk so they will not be lost if the print server is shut down before the job is completed.

Familiarity with these terms is helpful when interpreting questions about Windows XP printing on the certification exam, and in selecting the proper answers to such questions. Testing considerations aside, some familiarity with this lexicon makes it much easier to understand Microsoft Help files and documentation on this subject as well.

WINDOWS XP PRINT SUBSYSTEM ARCHITECTURE

Given all this specialized terminology, it is essential to put it into context within the Windows XP environment, which is why we will describe the architecture of this subsystem next. The Windows XP print subsystem architecture consists of several components that turn print data into a printable file, transfer that file to a printer, and manage the way in which multiple print jobs are handled by a printer. These components are:

- GDI

- Printer driver

- Print spooler

We describe each of these elements in the subsections that follow.

Graphical Device Interface

The Graphical Device Interface (GDI) is the portion of Windows XP that begins the process of producing visual output, whether that output is to the screen or to the printer; it is the part of Windows XP that makes WYSIWYG (what-you-see-is-what-you-get) output possible. In the case of screen output, the GDI calls the video driver; in the case of printed output, it calls a printer driver and provides information about the targeted print device and what type of data must be rendered for output.

Printer Driver

A printer driver is a Windows XP software component that enables an application to communicate with a printer through the IP Manager in the Executive Services module in the Windows XP kernel. A printer driver is composed of three subcomponents that work together as a unit:

- *Printer graphics driver*—Responsible for rendering the GDI commands into **Device Driver Interface (DDI)** commands that can be sent to the printer. Each graphics driver renders a different printer language; for example, Pscript.dll handles PostScript printing requests, Plotter.dll handles the HPGL/2 language used by many plotters, and Rasdd.dll deals with printer languages based on raster images (that is, those based on bitmapped images, which are collections of dots). Rasdd.dll is used by PCL (Printer Control Language) and most dot-matrix printers.

- *Printer interface driver*—You need some means of interacting with the printer, and the role of the printer interface driver is to provide that means; it provides the interface you see when you open the Printers and Faxes applet (Start | Printers and Faxes).

- *Characterization data file*—Provides information to the printer interface driver about the make and model of a specific type of print device, including its features, such as double-sided printing, printing at various resolutions, and accepting certain paper sizes.

Printer drivers are not compatible across hardware platforms, so although several client types (including Windows XP Professional, Windows .NET Server, Windows 2000 Professional and Server, Windows NT 4.0, 3.51, 3.5, and 3.1 Workstation and Server, and Windows 95 and 98) can print to a Windows XP print server without first installing a local printer driver—they'll download the driver from the print server—you must make sure that necessary drivers are available for the proper platforms.

Print Spooler

The print spooler (Spoolsv.exe) is a collection of DLLs and device drivers that receives, processes, schedules, and distributes print jobs. The spooler is implemented as part of the Spooler service, which is required for printing. By default, the Spooler service is installed as part of the base Windows XP installation process (to check its status, look at the Spooler entry in the Services window, or look for Spoolsv.exe in the list on the Processes tab in the Task Manager). The Spooler includes the following components:

- Print router

- Local and remote print providers

- Print processors

- Print monitor

The print spooler can accept data from the print provider in two main **data types**: enhanced metafile (EMF) or RAW. **Enhanced metafile (EMF)** spool files are device-independent files used in Windows XP to reduce the amount of time spent processing a print job—all GDI calls needed to produce the print job are included in the file. **RAW** spool files are device-dependent output files that have been completely processed (usually by their sending application or service) and are ready for output on the targeted print device. After a spool file has been created, control is restored to the application that created the print job, and other processing can resume in the foreground.

 EMF spool files are normally smaller than RAW spool files.

RAW spool files are used for local print jobs, for Encapsulated PostScript (.eps) print jobs, or when specified by the user. Unlike EMF spool files, which still require some rendering once it is determined to which printer they're going, RAW spool files are fully defined when created. The Windows XP print processor also recognizes plain ASCII text files, which may be submitted by other clients (especially UNIX machines); the name of this spool file type is TEXT.

Print Router

The **print router** sends print requests from clients to the print server, so the requests can be routed to the appropriate print provider. When a Windows XP client computer connects to a Windows XP print server, communication takes place in the form of remote procedure calls from the client's print router (Winspool.drv) to the server's print router (Spoolss.dll), at which point the server's print router passes the print request to the appropriate print provider: the local print provider if it's a local job, and either the Windows XP or the NetWare print provider if it is sent over the network.

Print Provider

The **print provider** is server-side software that sends a print job to the proper server in the format required by that server. When a client sends a print job to a remote printer, the print router polls the remote print providers on the client computer and passes control of the print job to the first computer that recognizes the name of the specified printer. Windows XP uses one of the two following print providers:

- *Windows XP print provider (Win32Spl.dll):* Used to transfer print jobs to Windows network print servers

- *NetWare print provider (Nwprovau.dll):* Used to transfer print jobs to NetWare print servers

If the Windows XP print provider recognizes the printer name, it sends the print job along in one of two ways, depending on the operating system on the print server. If the print server is running a compatible network operating system (such as Windows NT 3.x, Windows for Workgroups, or LAN Manager), the print job is routed by NetBIOS to the print server. If the print server is running Windows XP or Windows NT 4.0, the print provider contacts the Spooler service on the print server, which then passes it to the local print provider.

The local print provider writes the contents of the print job to a spool file (which will have the extension .spl) and tracks administration information for that print job. By default, all spool files are stored in the *%systemroot%*\WINDOWS\System32\Spool\Printers directory, although you can change that location if desired (perhaps if you've installed a faster drive) by adjusting the print server settings in the Printers and Faxes utility from the Start menu or the Control Panel. (You can practice changing the location of the spool file in Hands-on Project 9-4 at the end of the chapter.)

Spool files are normally deleted after the print job to which they apply is completed because they only exist to keep the print job from getting lost in case of a power failure that affects the print server. However, you can configure the spooler to retain all print jobs, even after they are printed. This control is accessed on a per-printer basis on the Advanced tab of the printer's Properties dialog box.

If a NetWare print provider recognizes the printer name, it passes the print job along to the NetWare workstation service, which then passes control of the print job to the NetWare redirector for transfer to the NetWare print server.

To send print jobs from a Windows XP client to a NetWare server, you must have Client Service for NetWare (CSNW) installed on the client computer (see Chapter 7, "Network Protocols"). To route print jobs through a Windows Server computer to a NetWare print server, the Windows Server must have the Gateway Services for NetWare (GSNW) installed.

Print Processor

A **print processor** works with the printer driver to despool spool files during playback, making any needed changes to the spool file according to its data type. The print processor itself is a PostScript program that understands the format of a document image's file and how to print the file to a specific PostScript printer or class of printers. Windows .NET Server supports two print processors: one for Windows clients and one for Macintosh clients (Sfmpsprt.dll), which is normally installed only after the Services for Macintosh service is installed. Remember that Services for Macintosh is included only with Windows Server products, which is why this isn't an issue on Windows XP Professional machines.

The built-in Windows print processor in Windows XP Professional understands EMF data files, three kinds of RAW data files, and text files. However, the Macintosh print processor that's installed on a Windows Server when Services for Macintosh is installed understands only Pstscrpt1, which signifies that the spool file contains PostScript code from a Macintosh client, but that the output is not destined for delivery to a PostScript printer. In actuality, this data type lets the print processor know that a post-processing job must be performed to translate the PostScript into the equivalent RAW data for output on the target printer before the print job can be spooled to the targeted print device.

 Windows XP uses a raster image processor to send print jobs from a Macintosh client to a printer. The limitations of this processor mean that print jobs can have a maximum resolution of 300 dpi and must be printed in monochrome, regardless of the capabilities of the targeted printer. However, there are third-party raster image processors available for those who want to use the full capabilities of their printers even when printing through Services for Macintosh.

Print Monitor

The print monitor is the final link in the chain of the printing process. It is actually two monitors: a language monitor and a port monitor. The **language monitor**, created when you install a printer driver if a language monitor is associated with the driver, comes into play only if the print device is bidirectional, meaning that messages about print job status may be sent both to and from the computer. Bidirectional capabilities are necessary to transmit meaningful error messages from the printer to the client. If the language monitor has a role, it sets up the communication with the printer and then passes control to the port monitor. The language monitor supplied with Windows XP uses the Printer Job Language. The **Printer Job Language** provides printer control at the print-job level and enables users to change printer default levels such as number of copies, color, and printer languages. If a manufacturer creates a printer that speaks a different language, it would need to define another language monitor, because the computer and print device must speak the same language for communication to work.

The **port monitor** transmits the print job either to the print device or to another server. It controls the flow of information to the I/O port to which the print device is connected (a serial, parallel, network, or SCSI port). The port monitor supplied with Windows XP controls parallel and serial ports. If you want to connect a print device to a SCSI port or network port, you must use a port monitor supplied by the vendor. Regardless of type, however, port monitors interface with ports, not printers, and are in fact unaware of the type of print devices to which they are connected. The print job is already configured by the print processor before it ever reaches the output port.

Windows XP supports the following port monitors:

- Local port monitor (Localmon.dll)
- Hewlett-Packard network port monitor (Hpmon.dll)
- Line printer (LPR) port monitor (Lprmon.dll)
- AppleTalk port monitor (Sfmmon.dll)
- DEC network port monitor (Decpsmon.dll)

- Lexmark Mark Vision port monitor (Lexmon.dll)

- NetWare port monitor (Nwmon.dll)

- Standard TCP/IP port monitor (SFM)

- Hypertext Transfer Protocol (HTTP) port monitor

- PJL monitor (Pjlmon.dll)

 By default, only the local print monitor is installed. To use another monitor, you have to create a new port when configuring a printer from the Printers icon.

At this point, you've now been exposed to the unique Microsoft printing terminology and to the architecture of the Windows XP print subsystem. Now, you can learn how to work with printers and to define and configure them.

 In the Windows XP world, the focus is on printers, not print devices. As you've seen, in Windows XP parlance, printers are logical constructs—named combinations of output ports, a print driver, and configuration settings that can involve one or more print devices, the physical output devices—such as laser, ink-jet, or dot-matrix printers, plotters, fax modems, or slide makers. All the configuring and manipulation you do in Windows XP is done to printers, not to the print devices.

PRINTER DRIVER SOFTWARE

The function of a printer driver is to provide an interface between the client and the printer, whether that printer is connected to a print server or directly to the client. In other words, the job of printing software is to insulate applications from having to incorporate the logic and understanding necessary to communicate with a large collection of printers. That's why the functions that take application-specific file data and translate them into formats suitable for printing are included in the printer drivers themselves.

Because selecting a particular printer for output is part of the Windows printing process, it makes perfect sense to put this intelligence into the driver. That's because you must indicate what kind of device to which you want to send a print job as a part of instructing an application to print to a specific printer. Because print devices differ so much from manufacturer to manufacturer, and even from model to model, the right place to bury the details is in the printer driver itself. Not only does this shield application developers from having to write code to drive every kind of print device imaginable, it also puts the task of building the file translation routines on the print device manufacturers because they're the usual source of driver software.

PRINTING ACROSS THE NETWORK

Few organizations can afford to give each user his or her own printer, which explains why printing to a remote printer across the network is by far the most common print scenario on Microsoft networks. (In fact, many experts argue that sharing printers was one of the original primary justifications for networking.) Two typical options for printing across the network exist for Microsoft network clients, including Windows XP Professional clients:

- You can print to a printer connected to a print server through a parallel or serial port.

- You can print to a printer connected directly to the network.

The main reason to connect a printer directly to the network is for convenience, because the printer doesn't have to be located near the print server. A print server must still provide drivers and print job management.

THE PRINTING PROCESS

Now that you're familiar with the components of the printing process, here is how they fit together when printing from a Windows XP Professional client:

1. The user chooses to print from an application, causing the application to call the GDI. The GDI, in turn, calls the printer driver associated with the target print device. Using the document information from the application and the printer information from the printer driver, the GDI renders the print job.

2. The print job is passed to the spooler. The client side of the spooler makes a remote procedure call to the server side, which then calls the print router component of the server.

3. The print router passes the job to the local print provider, which spools the job to disk.

4. The local print provider polls the print processors, passing the job to the processor that recognizes the selected printer. Based on the data type (EMF or RAW) used in the spool file, any necessary changes are made to the spool file to make it printable on the selected print device.

5. If desired, the separator page processor adds a separator page to the print job.

6. The print job is despooled to the print monitor. If the printer device is bidirectional, the language monitor sets up communication. If not, or after the language monitor is done, the job is passed to the port monitor, which handles the job of getting the print job to the port to which the print device is connected.

7. The print job arrives at the print device and is printed.

INSTALLING AND MANAGING PRINTERS

The Printers and Faxes window is the starting point for all printer installation and management. To reach it, select Start|Printers and Faxes. If there are no printers installed, double-click the Add a printer command in the Quick List to create a printer (add a local printer definition) or connect to one across the network. After you have created or connected to a printer, it appears in this window with its own icon, as the example in Figure 9-1 shows. To set its properties, right-click the printer and choose Properties from the menu that appears.

Figure 9-1   The Printers and Faxes window

Managing Print Jobs

The Printers and Faxes window comes into play not only when installing and managing printers, but also when managing print queues (see Hands-on Project 9-3). To manage print jobs, open the Printers and Faxes window and double-click the icon for the printer in question. When you do so, you see a window (similar to the one shown in Figure 9-2) that displays all current print jobs for the selected print device.

To manage a print job, select it and then choose the appropriate menu option. For example, to delete a print job, choose Cancel from the Document menu, and the print job is deleted, allowing the next job in the queue to begin. Alternately, you can right-click the print job's list entry, and select Pause or Cancel. If the job has already been partially or completely spooled to the printer, it continues printing until the print device has finished with the spooled data. But no more data will be sent to the printer after you cancel the job.

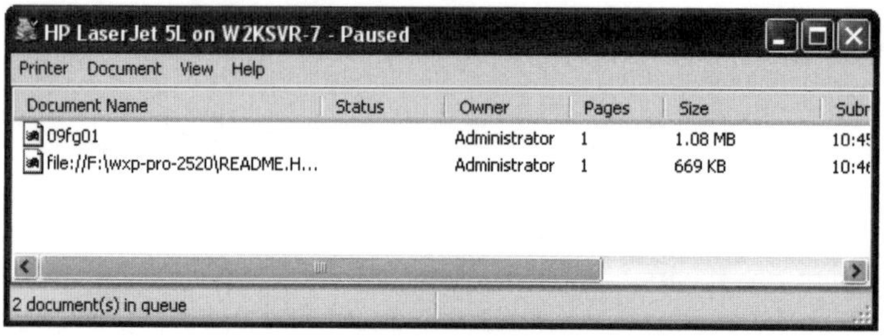

Figure 9-2   A printer's queue window

> To delete print jobs, you need Manage Documents or Manage Printers permissions or ownership of the print job. Administrators and Power Users have Print, Manage Printers, and Manage Document permissions over printers by default.

The functions or commands available through the Printer menu of the print queue window are:

- *Connect*—Used to connect to shared printers when the printer share has been dragged and dropped into the Printers and Faxes applet instead of configured using the Add Printer Wizard.

- *Set As Default Printer*—Sets the system to use this printer as the primary printer choice.

- *Printing Preferences*—Opens the Printing Preferences dialog box for this printer. This is the same dialog box reached by clicking the Printing Preferences button on the General tab of the printer's Properties dialog box.

- *Pause Printing*—Halts the printing of all print jobs through this logical printer. When deselected, printing continues from the same point, even mid-print job, where it was paused.

- *Cancel All Documents*—Deletes all print jobs in the queue.

- *Sharing*—Opens the printer's Properties dialog box with the Sharing tab selected.

- *Use Printer Offline*—Turns a local printer queue "off" in much the same way as the offline status of a physical print device.

- *Properties*—Opens the Properties dialog box for the printer.

- *Close*—Closes the printer window.

The options available from the Documents menu are as follows:

- *Pause*—Pauses the print job. If the print job is already in the process of being sent to the printer, no other print jobs can be sent to the printer until it is resumed or canceled. If the print job is still in the queue, other print jobs will bypass it on their way to be printed.

- *Resume*—Resumes printing of a paused print job.

- *Restart*—Prints jobs again from the beginning.

- *Cancel*—Removes a print job from the print queue.

- *Properties*—Opens the Properties dialog box for the selected print job.

The Properties dialog box of a print job displays details such as size, pages, data format type, owner, time submitted, layout, and paper tray selection. It also allows you to change the printing priority of the print job and to redefine the schedule. The schedule is the same type of control as a printer's activity time period, meaning that you can set it to either no restriction or define a time within which the print job can be sent to the printer.

Creating a Local Printer

In Windows XP jargon, creating a printer means that you're setting up a printer for local use. To do so, double-click the Add a printer command in the Printers and Faxes window and answer the questions as prompted, including the following:

- Is the attached printer plug and play compatible?

- Is the printer local or on the network?

- To which port will the printer be connected?

- What is the make and model of the printer?

- What do you want the printer to be named?

- Do you want the printer to be the default for all print jobs?

- Should the printer be shared with the network?

If you're not sure whether your printer requires some fine-tuning (such as port configuration), you can create the printer and adjust its properties later.

After you have answered all the questions and supplied the needed files for the installation, you can choose to print a test page to make sure you have set up the printer properly. You can practice creating a printer for local use and sharing it with the network in Hands-on Projects 9-1 and 9-2 at the end of this chapter.

Connecting to a Remote Printer

Connecting to a remote printer is even simpler than creating a printer. Once again, double-click the Add a printer link in the Printers and Faxes window, but this time choose to connect to a network printer instead of creating one locally. You are presented with a list of shared printers to which to connect, and have the option of making that printer the default. Select to connect to it, and your work is done. Because Windows XP clients download printer drivers from the print server, you don't have to install drivers locally.

 Windows XP print servers, by default, automatically host and install drivers for Windows XP and Windows 2000. They can also host and install drivers for Windows 95/98/Me, Windows NT 4.0 Intel or Alpha, or Windows XP IA64 if an administrator adds the appropriate drivers.

CONFIGURING A PRINTER

After the printer is created or connected to, configuring it is easy. In the following sections, we explain the options on each tab of the printer Properties dialog box that appears when you right-click a printer in the Printers and Faxes window and choose Properties.

 You can create more than one logical printer for a single print device, so you can set up different configurations for the same print device. Different configurations might include setting up one printer to print high-priority jobs immediately, whereas another might be configured to print low-priority jobs during nonbusiness hours. Just be sure to tell your users to which printer they should connect, so they get the configurations they need.

General Tab

The General tab (see Figure 9-3) in a printer's Properties window contains a variety of controls that you can use to create a text comment that will show up in the Browse list entry for that printer, and to create a separate entry to identify its location. This tab also displays the features and paper sizes currently available for this printer. The Printing Preferences button brings up a window (see Figure 9-4) in which orientation, duplexing, page order, pages per sheet, color, and paper source tray (Paper/Quality tab) are defined. The Print Test Page button sends a default test page to the printer. Note that color printers have an additional tab: Color Management.

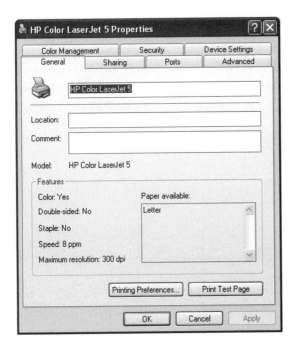

Figure 9-3   A printer's Properties dialog box, General tab

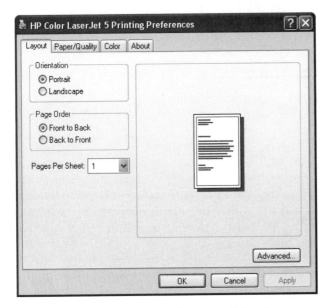

Figure 9-4   The Printing Preferences dialog box

Sharing Tab

The Sharing tab (shown in Figure 9-5) works much like the Sharing tab used when creating a shared directory. Simply select the Share this printer radio button and provide a Share name for the printer. To install additional drivers for several client types that will be connecting to the printer, click the Additional Drivers button.

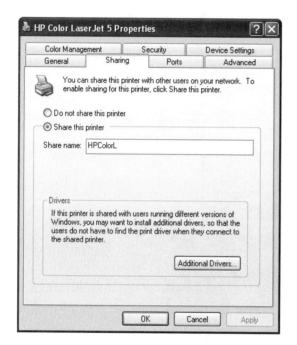

Figure 9-5   A printer's Properties dialog box, Sharing tab

Ports Tab

On the Ports tab (shown in Figure 9-6), you can adjust settings (including interrupts and base I/O addresses) for the ports selected for use with a particular print device. You can also add port monitors by clicking the Add Port button. The bidirectional printing option should be checked for printers that are able to send status information back to the print monitor, where it can provide the basis for user notifications (print job complete, out of paper, paper jam, and so forth).

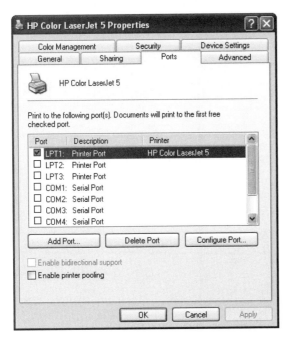

Figure 9-6   A printer's Properties dialog box, Ports tab

This tab is also used to set up a printer pool, in which more than one print device (the physical printer) is assigned to a single printer (the logical printer construct). This option, which works best with identical print devices, even to the amount of memory installed in each, can reduce waiting time on heavily used printers by sending jobs to whichever print device is least busy.

Select print devices that are in close physical proximity to each other for pooling. Users will not be able to tell to which pooled print device a print job went, and they're not going to like running all over to find their print jobs. Also, if there's any difference in speed among the pooled printers, pool the fastest printer first because the pooling software will check the first-pooled printer first.

Advanced Tab

Use the Advanced tab (shown in Figure 9-7) to set the hours during which the printer is available, set printer priority, and define spooling options. The availability hours are used to enable a printer only within a specified time frame. All print jobs sent to the printer outside this time frame are spooled and printed when the start time is reached. The **printer priority** setting determines which logical printer will be given first access to a printer. This setting is used to grant privileged, faster access to a busy printer for an individual or small group. The higher the number, the higher the priority, ranging from 1 to 99. The default is 1. From this tab, you can also select the printer driver to use or install an updated or alternate driver by clicking the New Driver button.

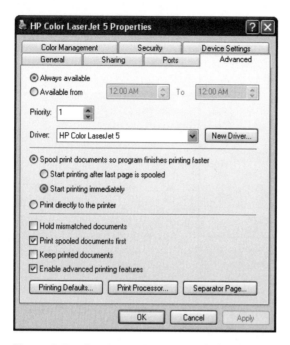

Figure 9-7   A printer's Properties dialog box, Advanced tab

The spooling options define how print jobs are managed. In most cases, the default options will work well for you, because they'll start the printing process quickly and restore control to the application as rapidly as possible. However, here's what the options mean:

- If you choose to print directly to the printer instead of spooling documents, your application won't regain control until the print job is fully sent to the printer, but it will complete the print job faster.

- Waiting to print until the document has completely spooled to the printer does not hold up the application the way printing to the printer does, but it will delay the printing process commensurately with the size of the print job.

- **Mismatched documents** are those for which the page setup and printer setup are incompatible. Holding mismatched documents prevents only those documents from printing, without affecting any others. This setting is useful because it prevents wasted resources, such as printing one character per page, when such documents are sent.

- If you choose to print spooled documents first, the order in which documents spool to the print device overrides any print priorities that you have in place. By default, this option is disabled, so printer priority controls the order in which jobs print.

- If you want to be able to print a document again without resubmitting it from the application, choose to keep documents in the spooler after they've printed.

- Enabling advanced printing features activates functions, such as page order, booklet printing, and pages per sheet, that are only available on specific printers (and enabled on the Device Settings tab and the Printing Preferences button on the General tab).

At the bottom of the Advanced tab are three buttons: Printing Defaults, Print Processor, and Separator Page. The Printing Default button accesses the same dialog box as the Printing Preferences button on the General tab. The Print Processor button is used to select an alternate printing processor and data type format (RAW, EMF, or TEXT). The selections offered are based on the installed printer drivers and associated printer services. In most cases, you will not change these settings unless specified by a proprietary application or printing procedure.

Separator pages can be handy when several people are using the same printer, and you want to be sure that documents from different users don't get mixed up. Windows XP comes with several separator page files: Pcl.sep, Pscript.sep, Sysprint.sep, and Sysprtj.sep, but you can create custom pages in Notepad. Start off the document by putting a character on a line of its own, then use the codes in Table 9-1 to create separator files with the information that you need.

You can define any character as the lead character for the codes, but in our example, we use the exclamation point (!).

Save the separator page file with a .sep extension in the *%systemroot%*\WINDOWS\System32 directory, and it will be among the options available when you configure the separator page through the Advanced tab.

Table 9-1   Separator Page Code

Code	Function
!B!M	Prints all characters as double-width block characters until the !U code is encountered
!B!S	Prints all characters as single-width block characters until the !U code is encountered
!D	Prints the date the job was printed, using the format in the Regional and Language Options settings in the Control Panel
!E	Ejects a page from the printer
!F*pathname*	Prints the contents of the file specified in *pathname*, without any formatting
!H*nn*	Prints a printer-specific control sequence, indicated by the hexadecimal number *nn*. Check your printer manual to get the numbers.
!I	Prints the job number (every print job is assigned a number)

Table 9-1 Separator Page Code (continued)

Code	Function
!L	Prints all the characters following it until reaching another escape code (!)
!N	Prints the username of the person submitting the job
!n	Skips a certain number of lines, where *n* is a number between 0 and 9
!T	Prints the time the job was printed, using the format specified in the Regional and Language Options settings in the Control Panel
!U	Turns off block character printing
!Wnn	Specifies a certain width for the page (counted in characters). The default is 80; the maximum is 256

Color Management Tab

The Color Management tab is used to associate a color profile with a color printer. A color profile is used to control how color is produced by the printer. A color profile takes into account the printer's configuration and the type of media (i.e., paper, film, etc.) being used. This tab is only used by printers supporting color. In most cases, the Automatic selection determines the best color profile to use. However, you can manually install and choose alternate color profiles. Consult your color printer's manual for more information on managing color.

Security Tab

The Security tab (shown in Figure 9-8) contains options quite similar to those used to set up secure files and directories. Here you can set permissions for printers. The Add and Remove buttons are used to alter the list of users and groups with defined permissions for this printer. The Permissions frame lists the permission types (Print, Manage Printers, Manage Documents, and Special Permissions) and offers checkboxes to Allow or Deny individual permissions for the selected user or group.

The three main permissions for printers—Print, Manage Documents, and Manage Printers—encompass the following capabilities:

- *Print documents*—Print, Manage Documents, Manage Printers
- *Pause, resume, restart, and cancel owned document*—Print, Manage Documents, Manage Printers
- *Connect to a printer*—Print, Manage Documents, Manage Printers
- *Control settings for any print job*—Manage Documents, Manage Printers
- *Pause, resume, restart, and cancel all documents*—Manage Documents, Manage Printers
- *Cancel all documents*—Manage Printers

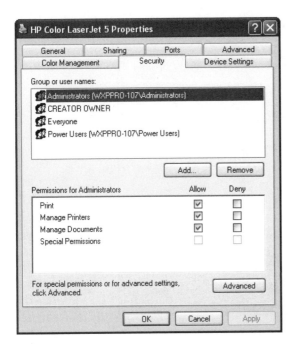

Figure 9-8   A printer's Properties dialog box, Security tab

- *Share a printer*—Manage Printers
- *Delete a printer*—Manage Printers
- *Change permissions*—Manage Printers

The Advanced button reveals another dialog box where more detailed permissions, auditing, and ownership are controlled. On this dialog box (see Figure 9-9), permissions are added on a user or group basis for the detailed permissions of Print, Manage Printers, Manage Documents, Read Permissions, Change Permissions, and Take Ownership. These permission settings can be defined for each user to apply to This printer only, Documents only, or both. The Auditing tab is a control interface similar to the permissions interface where the same types of actions granted through permissions can be set so you can audit them. The audit events created through this object are recorded in the Security log and viewed through the Event Viewer. The Owner tab is used to take ownership for your user account or one of your groups (of which you are a member). Remember that ownership can only be taken, it cannot be given. Try managing printer permissions in Hands-on Project 9-5.

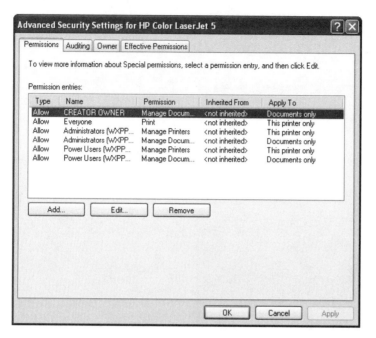

Figure 9-9   The Advanced Security dialog box, Permissions tab

Device Settings Tab

The final tab in the Properties dialog box (shown in Figure 9-10), the Device Settings tab, is used to make sure that the print device itself is configured properly. Most of these settings shouldn't need to be adjusted if you chose the proper printer driver during setup, but these items may be subject to change as you upgrade your printer:

- *Memory*—Be sure that the amount of memory listed on this tab is equal to that installed in the printer. Too little, and you will not get the performance that your printer is capable of. Too much, and the printer may try to take on more than it can handle.

- *Paper trays and other accessories*—Some printers may be upgraded with particular paper trays. If you install one, or rearrange existing ones, you'll need to update the settings here.

There may be other options and functions listed on this tab that are printer model-specific. When these appear, consult the printer's user manual for information on modifying those settings.

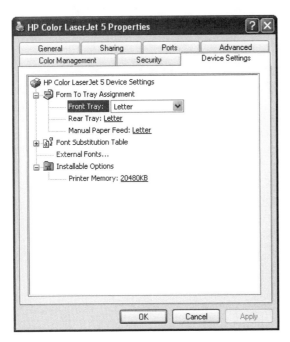

Figure 9-10   A printer's Properties dialog box, Device Settings tab

PRINTERS AND THE WEB

Windows XP includes Web support in its print subsystem, which allows remote users to submit print jobs for printing, view printer queues, and download print drivers. See Hands-on Project 9-8 to configure Windows XP Professional to connect to an Internet printer. These features are afforded through the **Internet Printing Protocol (IPP)**. The Web-based features are accessible only when the print server is running Internet Information Services (IIS).

IPP offers two main benefits. First, it enables Web-based distribution of printer drivers. Second, it offers Web-based print queue management.

To download a printer driver, simply use a URL as the network path when connecting to a network printer. The URL should be formatted as: http://<printservername>/printers/ <printersharename>/.printer.

To access a print queue through the Web, open a URL with the following formatting: http://<*printservername*>/printers/. Select a printer from the list, then use the Web-based menu to perform print queue management. The operations and commands are the same as those accessed through a normal printer queue window.

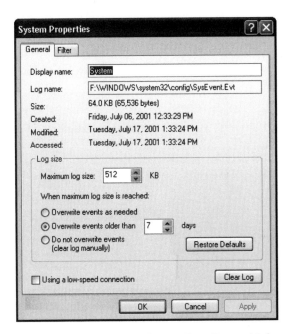

Figure 10-14   System Properties, General tab

Performance Options

You use the Performance Options dialog box (see Figure 10-15) to adjust system performance based on applications and virtual memory. Access this dialog box by clicking the Settings button in the Performance pane on the Advanced tab of the System applet found inside the Control Panel. From there, click the Advanced tab in the Performance Options window. Here you'll find three controls.

First, you can optimize processor scheduling by indicating whether the computer is used primarily for user or interactive programs or background services (the default is programs, as you'd expect for a desktop operating system). The radio button selection of Programs boosts the priority of foreground processes, whereas Background services balances the use of processor resources for foreground and background processes.

Second, you can optimize memory usage in much the same way by indicating whether memory should favor programs or the system cache. The radio button selection of Programs grants more memory to foreground programs; choosing system cache gives the operating system more latitude in managing memory allocations (here again, the default is Programs, as you'd expect for a desktop operating system).

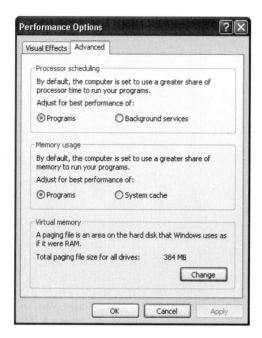

Figure 10-15 The Performance Options dialog box (Advanced tab) offers controls for Processor scheduling, Memory usage, and Virtual memory

Third, you can manage the size of the paging file—that portion of disk space where the operating system stores memory pages not in active use to extend the capacity of memory beyond what physical RAM in the system allows—in the virtual memory pane. In most cases, Windows XP's automatic paging file selection should be adequate, but if System Monitor shows excessive hard page faults, increasing the size of this file (if hard disk space allows) can improve system performance. By default, the paging file size is set between 1.5 and 3.0 times the amount of RAM in the system or 192-384 MB, whichever number is greater.

Use the Change button on the Performance Options dialog box to access the Virtual Memory dialog box, where the size and location(s) of the paging file may be defined. See Chapter 3, "Using the System Utilities" for more details on optimizing paging file sizes.

Setting Application Priority

Windows XP Professional uses 32 levels of application priority, numbered 0 (zero) to 31, to determine which process should gain access to the CPU at any given moment. Users have only minimal control over the initial startup priority level for any launched task. The following list indicates important ranges and specific priority levels:

- 0–15—User-accessible process priorities
- 16–31—System-accessible process priorities

- 0–6—Low user range

- 4—Low value (as set in Task Manager, or with /low parameter to Start command)

- 5—BelowNormal value (as set in Task Manager)

- 7—Normal (default setting for user processes)

- 8–15—High user range

- 10—AboveNormal value (as set in Task Manager)

- 13—High value (as set in Task Manager, or with /high parameter to Start command)

- 16–24—Realtime values accessible to Administrator-level accounts

- 24—Realtime value (as set in Task Manager, or with /realtime parameter to Start command)

- 25–31—Realtime values accessible to operating system only

There are two techniques available to users and administrators to manipulate process priorities: manage already running processes using Task Manager or use the Start command to launch processes with specific priority settings. One reason you may want to manipulate the priority of a process is to give a time-sensitive application priority over another application.

To use Task Manager, right-click any unoccupied region of the taskbar and select Task Manager from the menu. On the Processes tab of Task Manager, select the name of the desired process (usually this is the name of an .exe file that corresponds to the process), then right-click that process to produce another menu. From this menu, select the Set Priority item. This is where you can pick one of the predefined priority settings—Low, BelowNormal, Normal, AboveNormal, High, or Realtime. The current setting is the entry marked with a bullet symbol to the left. You must be logged on with Administrator privileges to use the Realtime setting.

You can use the Start command from a command prompt to launch a new application at some priority level other than the default. You can enter this command from either a command prompt or the Run command. The Start command follows this general syntax:

```
Start /<priority-level> <program>
```

where /*<priority-level>* must be one of /low, /belownormal, /normal, /abovenormal, /high, or /realtime, and *<program>* is a valid path plus filename for the program you want to launch at the specified priority level. For more details on the Start command, enter *start /?* from a command prompt.

10

PERFORMANCE TUNING IN THE SYSTEM APPLET

The System Applet in Control Panel includes an Advanced tab that addresses several Performance entries. To access this utility, follow this menu sequence if you're using the Category View: Start | Control Panel | Performance and Maintenance, then click the System icon in the Control Panel section. The Windows Classic view is simpler: Start | Control Panel | System. Next, select the Advanced tab, then click the Settings button in the Performance pane. You should see a display like the one shown in Figure 10-16, where the Visual Effects tab is selected by default and an Advanced tab is also available, as shown in Figure 10-17.

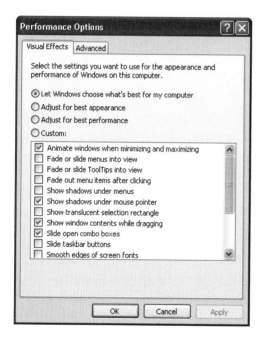
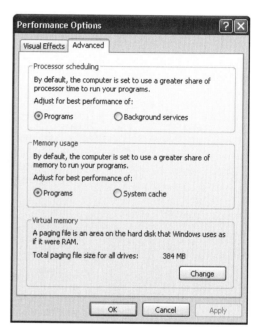

Figures 10-16 and 10-17   The System Applet's performance controls include Visual Effects and Advanced tabs, respectively

The Visual Effects Tab

The Visual Effects tab permits you to control how Windows XP will handle your computer display when managing screen output. By default, the "Let Windows choose what's best for my computer" setting is selected, which permits the computer to trade performance against appearance as the system load increases. You can instruct Windows XP to always "Adjust for best appearance" or to always "Adjust for best performance" if you prefer to lock the system into a completely consistent mode of graphics operation. Finally, for those who love to tweak and tune their systems, the Custom setting permits

16 different visual effects to be manipulated separately. This listing is intended primarily to show the custom settings that Windows enables by default:

- *Animate windows when minimizing and maximizing*—Shows visual effects when minimization and maximization controls are used.

- *Show shadows under mouse pointer*—Produces a drop shadow beneath the mouse cursor as it moves across the desktop (most noticeable with a dark cursor on a white background).

- *Show window contents while dragging*—As windows are dragged on the desktop, the window outline and some or all of its contents will follow the cursor, where the level of detail displayed depends on the speed of motion and the overall processing load.

- *Slide open combo boxes*—When selecting a menu choice involves picking an item from a list of choices or opening a secondary menu (as is the case with some Start menu elements), the resulting text box is sometimes called a combo box. Enabling this control causes the boxes to slide open from left to right.

- *Smooth-scroll list boxes*—When text boxes contain too many items to fit in the display, you must scroll up or down to view additional elements. Smooth-scrolling means that elements move up or down smoothly, rather than popping one or more list elements up or down at a time. When this control is turned off, lists jump up and down in a more jerky fashion.

- *Use a background image for each folder type*—Associates a more specific image with folders based on their type and contents, rather than using a simpler, more generic icon.

- *Use common tasks in folders*—Drives the task-oriented displays in the left-hand pane of most Windows XP windows and creates the linkage between task data and the window itself to permit that data to be displayed. Disabling this control eliminates display of task information.

- *Use visual styles on windows and buttons*—Instructs Windows XP to use shading, 3-D effects, and edge shading on windows and buttons to give them a more realistic appearance. Disabling this control gives such elements a flat, 2-D appearance.

Although these controls may not seem terribly performance-oriented, keep in mind that drawing the desktop and managing how windows, buttons, and icons appear is a big part of what Windows XP does. By deselecting elements that require more computation or lookup (tasks, visual styles, background images, and so forth) you reduce the burden on the CPU. It won't double the speed of a computer, but it will speed things up somewhat. Notice, for example, that selecting "Adjust for best performance" turns off all settings in the Custom combo box, thereby disabling all visual effects.

10

The Advanced Tab

The Advanced tab consists of the following three panes:

- *Processor scheduling*—Permits wholesale manipulation of the priority granted to applications versus services. Because Windows XP Professional is a desktop operating system, it should come as no surprise that the default option here is to select "Programs" (applications running on the desktop, presumably at your command) over "Background services" (system and other services usually intended to respond to requests for services from other remote users). This means that the assumption is that most Windows XP machines should prioritize applications over services. Change this setting only on machines where services are not just installed but used regularly by others. This setting routinely boosts the default thread priority for the item chosen by two.

- *Memory usage*—Prioritizes allocating memory to applications rather than to the system cache, again in keeping with Windows XP Professional's primary role as a desktop operating system (where its normal task is to run applications for users). Normally, the System Cache radio button would be selected only on a server or on a desktop machine, where applications themselves require large amounts of system cache (as they would indicate in their documentation or help files).

- *Virtual memory*—By default Windows XP sets its paging file at 1.5 times the amount of RAM installed, with an upper limit of three times that amount. Figure 10-18 shows a default setup on a system with 256 MB of RAM installed (which explains the paging file size of 384-768 MB). The Virtual Memory window can be used to situate and distribute a Windows XP paging file across multiple drives. To achieve maximum performance from a Windows XP paging file, follow as many of these three rules as you can when altering the default setup:
  - Avoid placing the bulk of the paging file on the system and boot partitions whenever possible. If other partitions share a controller with the boot partition, performance benefits will be diminished, because system disk calls and paging calls must use the same disk controller. To enable crash dumps, it remains necessary to create a minimal paging file on the boot partition, the size of which matches the configuration information on the Advanced tab of the System applet (click the Settings button in the Startup and Recovery pane).
  - Spread the paging file across as many drives as possible. If such drives share a controller, performance benefits will be less than if they have separate controllers.
  - There's no performance benefit to spreading paging files across multiple RAID arrays; if you have more than one on your system, you can safely situate the paging file on any single RAID array.

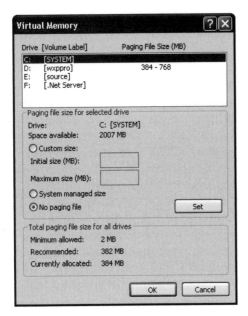

Figure 10-18   A Windows XP Professional default setup

10

Under most circumstances, the defaults for these three settings work nicely on Windows XP machines. Only when the machine acts primarily as a server should the Processor Scheduling and Memory Usage settings be changed. Similarly, only on systems where applications make unusually heavy demands on memory or the operating system should it be necessary to change page file locations and sizes.

RECOGNIZING AND HANDLING BOTTLENECKS

A **bottleneck** occurs when a limitation in a single component slows down an entire system. The first thing to remember about bottlenecks is that they always exist in any computer. Applications, hard drives, operating systems, and network interfaces might all act as bottlenecks from time to time, but for any given configuration, it is always possible to identify one component that slows the others down the most.

There is no single bottleneck monitor that can easily identify all possible problems. However, by using the monitoring tools included with Windows XP Professional, you can identify possible bottlenecks and make necessary adjustments. The goal when tuning a workstation for performance is to make bottlenecks unnoticeable for everyday functions. A computer used for CAD requires much greater throughput than a computer used primarily for word processing. Ideally, a computer should be waiting for user input rather than making users wait for the computer's response; the user becomes the bottleneck.

Although the details will vary from situation to situation, the process of finding and fixing computer system bottlenecks follows a reasonably consistent course, as shown in the following:

1. Create a baseline for a computer. For Windows XP Professional, this includes observations of memory usage, disk usage, CPU usage, operating system resource usage and activity, and network utilization, at the barest minimum. (See Hands-on Project 10-7 for explicit instructions on creating a sample baseline; you can use the same technique to gather current performance data to compare against an existing baseline.)

2. The first step in identifying potential bottlenecks is to compare baseline observations to current system behavior. In most cases, one or more of the baseline values will have changed for the worse. These changes indicate further areas for investigation.

3. Investigate the more common causes of system problems (some of these for Windows XP Professional are documented later in this chapter) to see if any match the symptoms your computer is exhibiting. If you have a match, the causes of bottlenecks are easy to identify and fixes are easy to apply.

4. If the list of "usual suspects" does not produce an obvious culprit, further analysis is required. You can obtain more details of system behavior from System Monitor and other performance tools, analyze their reports and statistics, and pinpoint potential bottlenecks. Use the general analytical techniques and combinations of objects and counters described in this chapter to help in isolating and identifying bottlenecks.

5. Once a potential bottleneck is identified, you make changes to the system configuration to correct the situation. Sometimes this involves software configuration changes; other times it can involve adding or replacing specific hardware components or subsystems.

6. Always test the impact of any fix you try. Compile a new set of statistics and compare them to the same system measurements before the fix was applied. Sometimes, the fix does the trick and values return to normal, or at least come closer to acceptable levels. If the fix doesn't make a difference, further analysis, other fixes, and more testing are required. It's important to keep at the job until something improves the bottleneck.

It's important to understand that though bottlenecks can always be fixed, some fixes are more expensive than others. Remember, you can always replace an overloaded server or workstation with another bigger, faster system, or you can spread the load from a single overloaded system across multiple systems to reduce the impact on any single machine. These kinds of fixes are a great deal more expensive than tweaking system settings or adding more memory or disk space to a machine. However, in some cases, such drastic solutions are necessary. If you monitor performance correctly, such radical changes needn't take anyone by surprise.

Common Bottlenecks

In this section, we explain how to use the counters you have chosen to watch, either alone or in combination, to determine what kinds of bottlenecks might be present on a system. We also discuss steps you might consider taking to correct such bottlenecks.

Disk Bottlenecks

Disk bottlenecks are the most likely problem when disk-related counters increase more dramatically than other counters (or when compared to your baseline) or when disk queue lengths become unacceptably long. Windows XP Professional collects information about the performance of physical disks (the actual devices) by default.

If Disk Queue Length and % Disk time values remain consistently high (1.5 or higher and more than 80%, respectively), it's probably time to think about adding more disk controllers or drives, or possibly switching existing drives and controllers for newer, faster equivalents (such as UltraWide SCSI or a storage area network, or SAN). This costs money, but can provide dramatic performance improvements on systems with disk bottlenecks. Adding a controller for each drive can substantially improve performance, and switching from individual drives to disk (RAID) arrays can also improve performance on such systems. Because high-end disk controllers often include onboard memory that functions as yet another level of system cache, they can confer measurable performance benefits. But unless users need extremely fast disks for 3D ray tracing, CAD applications, modeling, or other data-intensive applications, this is probably overkill for most conventional desktops.

Software can also contribute to disk bottlenecks through poor design, configuration settings that affect disk performance, or outdated drivers. Because tweaking an application's source code is beyond the reach of most system administrators, inspect the application to see if you can increase the size of the files it manipulates directly or the size of data transfers it requests. Larger and fewer data transfers are faster and more efficient than smaller, more frequent transfers. You should also defragment your hard drives regularly to optimize their performance.

Memory Bottlenecks

Windows XP Professional is subject to various kinds of **memory bottlenecks**. To begin with, it's important to make sure that the paging file is working as efficiently as possible; that is, its size is 1.5 to 3 times the amount of physical RAM on a machine (see Chapter 3). On machines with more than one drive, Microsoft recommends situating the paging file somewhere other than the boot partition (where the Windows system files reside) or the system partition (where the boot loader and other startup files reside). If multiple drives are available, it's a good idea to spread the paging file evenly across all such drives (except a drive with the system or boot partition). Better yet is for each drive to have its own disk controller, which allows Windows XP Professional to access all drives in parallel.

You can detect excessive paging activity by watching the page-related counters mentioned earlier and by observing the lowest number of Available Bytes over time. (Microsoft recommends that this number never dip below 4 MB or 4096 KB.) Excessive disk time and disk queue lengths can often mask paging problems, so be sure to check paging-related statistics when disk utilization zooms. Adding more memory can fix such problems and improve overall system performance.

Processor Bottlenecks

Processor bottlenecks are indicated when the Processor object's % Processor time counter stays consistently above 80% or when the System object's Processor Queue Length counter remains fixed near a value of 2 or more. In both cases, the CPU is being overworked. However, occasional peaks of 100% for processor time are not unusual (especially when processes are being launched or terminated). The combination of consistently high utilization and overlong queues is a more common indication of trouble than an occasional high utilization spike.

Even on machines that support multiple CPUs, it's important to recognize that performance doesn't scale arithmetically as additional CPUs are added. A second CPU gives a more dramatic incremental improvement in performance than a third or fourth; however, two CPUs do not double performance. You're often better off responding to CPU bottlenecks by redistributing a machine's processing load, upgrading its CPU, memory, and motherboard, or replacing the machine altogether. Simply upgrading or adding another CPU neither increases the amount of cache memory on a system nor improves the system's underlying CPU-to-memory data transfer capabilities, both of which often play a crucial role in system performance.

When there is more than one CPU on a system, you can choose to monitor their activity on an individual basis or as a group. To monitor a single CPU, select the individual instance of the CPU. The first CPU is instance 0; the second CPU is instance 1. To monitor the activity of all CPUs as a whole, select the _Total instance.

Network Bottlenecks

Network bottlenecks are not typical on most Windows XP Professional machines, because end users seldom load the network sufficiently to experience performance problems. However, it is worth comparing how much traffic is passing through a workstation's network adapter with the traffic through networking medium to which it is attached. Excessive activity can indicate a failing adapter (sometimes called a "jabbering transceiver") or an ill-behaved application. In both cases, the fix is relatively straightforward—replace the NIC or the application, respectively.

Occasionally, however, the network itself may be overloaded. This situation is indicated by utilization rates that exceed the recommended maximum for the medium in use. (For example, Ethernet should not be loaded more heavily than 56% utilization, but token ring can function adequately at loads as high as 97%.) When this happens, as a network administrator you have two options: divide the network into segments and balance traffic so that no segment is overloaded, or replace the existing network with a faster alternative. Neither of these options is especially fast, cheap, or easy, but the former is cheaper than the latter, and may give your network—and your budget—some breathing room before a wholesale upgrade is warranted.

EIGHT WAYS TO BOOST WINDOWS XP PROFESSIONAL PERFORMANCE

Although there are many things you can do to deal with specific system bottlenecks, there are eight particularly useful changes in system components, elements, approaches, or configuration that are likely to result in improved performance by Windows XP Professional. Though these are listed in approximate order of their potential value, all elements on this list are worth considering when performance improvements are needed.

- *Buy a faster machine*—It takes only a year or so for a top-of-the-line, heavily loaded PC to become obsolete these days. When you find yourself considering a hardware upgrade to boost performance, compare the price of your planned upgrade to the cost of a new machine. If you're planning on spending more than half the cost of a newer computer (and can afford to double your expenditure), buy the newer, faster machine. Otherwise, you may be facing the same situation again in a few months. The extra cost buys you at least another year before you must go through this exercise again.

- *Upgrade an existing machine*—You might decide to keep a PC's case, power supply, and some of the adapter cards it contains. As long as the price stays below half the cost of a new machine, replacing a PC's motherboard not only gets you a faster CPU and more memory capacity (both cache and main memory), but it can also get you more and faster bus slots for adapter cards. While you're at it, be sure to evaluate the costs of upgrading the disk controller and hard drives, especially if they're more than twice as slow as prevailing access times. (As we write, garden-variety drives offer average access times of around 8 milliseconds, and fast drives offer average access rates of 2 to 3 milliseconds.)

- *Install a faster CPU*—As long as you can at least double the clock speed of your current CPU with a replacement, such an upgrade can improve performance for only a modest outlay. Be sure to review your memory configuration (cache and main memory) and your disk drives at the same time. A faster CPU on an otherwise unchanged system can't deliver the same performance boost as a faster CPU with more memory and faster drives.

- *Add more L2 cache*—Many experts believe that the single most dramatic improvement for an existing Windows XP PC comes from adding more L2 cache to a machine (or to buy only machines with the maximum amount of L2 cache installed). The CPU can access L2 cache in two CPU cycles, whereas access to main RAM usually takes 8 to 10 CPU cycles. This explains why adding L2 cache to a machine can produce dramatic performance improvements. Although cache chips are quite expensive, they provide the

10

biggest potential boost to a system's performance, short of the more drastic—and expensive—suggestions detailed earlier in this list.

- *Add more RAM*—Windows XP Professional is smart about how it uses main memory on a PC; it can handle large amounts of RAM effectively. It has been widely observed that the more processes that are active on a machine, the more positive the impact of a RAM increase. For moderately loaded workstations (six or fewer applications active at once), 128 MB of RAM is recommended. For heavily loaded workstations, 256 MB or more may improve performance significantly.

When you add RAM to a Windows XP Professional machine, be sure to resize the paging file to accommodate the change properly.

- *Replace the disk subsystem*—Because memory access occurs at nanosecond speeds, and disk access occurs at millisecond speeds, disk subsystem speeds can make a major impact on Windows XP performance. This is particularly true in cases where applications or services frequently access the disk, when manipulating large files, or when large amounts of paging activity occur. Because the controller and the drives both influence disk subsystem speeds, we recommend using only Fast Wide SCSI drives and controllers (or the latest of the EIDE drives and controllers) on Windows XP Professional machines. However, it's important to recognize that a slow disk controller can limit a fast drive and vice versa. That's why upgrading the entire subsystem is often necessary to realize any measurable performance gains.

- *Increase paging file size*—Whenever System Monitor indicates that more than 10% of disk subsystem activity is related to paging, check the relationship between the Limit and Peak values in the Commit Charge pane in Task Manager. (Right-click on any empty portion of the taskbar, select Task Manager, then select the Performance tab and check the lower-left corner of the display.) If the Peak is coming any closer than 4096 KB to the limit, it's time to increase the size of this file. We recommend using a figure somewhere between twice and three times the amount of RAM installed in the machine.

- *Increase application priority*—On machines where a lot of background tasks must be active, you can use the Task Manager's Processes tab to increase the priority of any already running process. Highlight the process entry, then right-click to produce a menu that includes a Set Priority entry. This entry permits you to set the priority to High or Realtime, either of which can improve a foreground application's performance. We recommend that you set only critical applications to Realtime, because they can interfere with the functioning of the operating system. To launch an application with an altered priority level, refer to the section "Setting Application Priority" earlier in this chapter.

Only users with administrator level access to Windows XP Professional can run processes at a Realtime priority level. Be aware that raising the priority of a single process causes other background processes to run more slowly. The other performance improvements in this list should improve system performance across the board; this improvement affects only those processes whose priorities are increased.

OPTIMIZING PERFORMANCE FOR MOBILE WINDOWS XP USERS

Basically, managing performance for mobile Windows XP machines is substantially the same as managing performance for network-connected Windows XP machines. The same observations about optimizing key system resources—particularly RAM, disk, CPU, and communications—still apply, even though the circumstances will sometimes differ.

Key differences are related to how mobile users access shared resources such as redirected files and IntelliMirror and how they use and synchronize Offline Files. Here, common sense goes a long way. If you follow these simple rules, you'll be able to avoid most potential performance problems that offline or remote use can cause, and you should be able to get the best possible results for your mobile users when they're disconnected from the network:

- Make sure the network interface appears higher in the binding order than a modem or other slower link device. Although users will incur an extra time-out when they fire up a remote link for the first time, once that link is active the delay will disappear. Because network interfaces are much faster than modems, this binding order insures the best overall performance.

- Make sure that file synchronization settings for folder redirection and Offline Files do not require machines to synchronize when running on battery. File synchronization can take a while and can consume significant power. Though some risk may be involved—along with a need for user education about those risks—users working on battery power will generally be happier if shutting down a system or exiting some application does not automatically perform file synchronization.

- Make sure your mobile users understand how to use hibernate and standby modes on their battery-powered machines. It's both faster and significantly less power-consumptive to "wake up" from hibernate or standby mode than it is to reboot from a machine that has been shut down.

- Make sure that all Offline Files a user might need are copied to his or her machine before they leave the network environment. The default is to make local copies only for recently accessed files; under some circumstances, this may not be acceptable—particularly when a slow link is the only way to grab missing items while a mobile users operates off the local network.

10

- Refresh rates also apply to Group Policy, which defaults to 90 minutes on Windows XP. For machines operating off-network (particularly using modems), refresh rates should be extended to avoid unnecessary network access.

- To prevent file synchronization over slow links, configure group policy's Configure Slow link speed Properties (located in Computer Configuration, Administrative Templates, Network, Offline Files) to define the threshold at which a link is considered slow as opposed to fast. File synchronization will not occur over slow links.

By reviewing how networked machines normally work on a Windows network, and taking the special needs (and slower speeds) associated with remote access or off-network operation into account, you should be able to formulate a series of policies and settings that will help your mobile users obtain the best possible performance when they're not directly attached to their home networks.

CHAPTER SUMMARY

- ❐ Windows XP Professional provides a number of tools to monitor system performance. By using these tools, it is easy to examine the effects of bottlenecks and to improve system response time.

- ❐ You can use Task Manager to view applications, processes, and overall system performance, or to stop applications and processes (an efficient way to regain control from an application that is experiencing problems). The default configuration of the Processes tab displays imagename (i.e. processname), user name, CPU, and memory usage. Other columns, such as Virtual Memory Size and Thread count, can be added to the Processes tab.

- ❐ The Performance console is an exceptionally useful collection of tools that includes System Monitor, log files, and alerts. System Monitor is used to watch real-time performance or review data collected in log files. Log files record performance data for one or more counters over a specified period of time. Alerts inform administrators when specific counters cross defined threshold levels.

- ❐ The Event Viewer is a less dynamic but equally important tool that tracks logs generated by the system. Event Viewer monitors three different logs: System, Application, and Security. The System log records system information and errors, such as the failure of a device driver to load. The Application log maintains similar information for programs, such as database applications. The Security log monitors system security events and audit activities.

- ❐ Finally, you should keep an eye on logs and performance counters to isolate any bottlenecks that occur in the system. Once you identify the bottleneck, take the steps necessary to remove it and get the system running more smoothly. In addition, try the recommendations listed in this chapter for improving overall system performance.

KEY TERMS

alert — A watchdog that informs you when a counter crosses a defined threshold. An alert is an automated attendant looking for high or low values, and can consist of one or more counter/instance-based alert definitions.

baseline — A definition of what a normal load looks like on a computer system; it provides a point of comparison against which you can measure future system behavior.

bottleneck — A system resource or device that limits a system's performance. Ideally, the user should be the bottleneck on a system, not any hardware or software component.

counter — A named aspect or activity that the Performance tool uses to measure or monitor some aspect of a registered system or application object.

Counter log — A log that records measurements on selected counters at regular, defined intervals. Counter logs allow you to define exactly which counters are recorded (based on computer, object, counter, and instance).

disk bottleneck — A system bottleneck caused by a limitation in a computer's disk subsystem, such as a slow drive or controller, or a heavier load than the system can handle.

event — A system occurrence that is logged to a file.

Event Viewer — A system utility that displays one of three event logs: System, Security, and Application, wherein logged or audited events appear. The Event Viewer is often the first stop when monitoring a system's performance or seeking evidence of problems, because it is where all unusual or extraordinary system activities and events are recorded.

handle — A programming term that indicates an internal identifier for some kind of system resource, object, or other component that must be accessed by name (or through a pointer). In Task Manager, the number of handles appears on the Performance tab in the Totals pane. A sudden increase in the number of handles, threads, or processes can indicate that an ill-behaved application is running on a system.

instance — A selection of a specific object when more than one is present on the monitored system; for example, multiple CPUs or hard drives.

memory bottleneck — A system bottleneck caused by a lack of available physical or virtual memory that results in system slowdown or (in extreme cases) an outright system crash.

network bottleneck — A system bottleneck caused by excessive traffic on the network medium to which a computer is attached, or when the computer itself generates excessive amounts of such traffic.

performance object — A component of the Windows XP Professional system environment; objects range from devices to services to processes.

object — See performance object.

process — An environment that defines the resources available to threads; the executable parts of an application. Processes define memory available, show where the process page directory is stored in physical memory, and other information that the

10

CPU needs to work with a thread. Each process includes its own complete, private 2 GB address space and related virtual memory allocations.

processor bottleneck — A system bottleneck that occurs when demands for CPU cycles from currently active processes and the operating system cannot be met, usually indicated by high utilization levels or processor queue lengths greater than or equal to two.

System Monitor — The utility that tracks registered system or application objects, where each such object has one or more counters that can be tracked for information about system behavior.

thread — In the Windows XP Professional runtime environment, a thread is the minimum unit of system execution and corresponds roughly to a task within an application, the Windows XP kernel, or within some other major system component. Any task that can execute in the background can be considered a thread (for example, runtime spell checking or grammar checking in newer versions of MS Word), but it's important to recognize that applications must be written to take advantage of threading (just as the operating system itself is).

REVIEW QUESTIONS

1. Monitoring is the act of changing a system's configuration systematically and carefully observing performance before and after such changes. True or False?

2. In a system that is performing optimally, the user should be the bottleneck. True or False?

3. Which of the following can Task Manager monitor?

   a. application CPU percentage

   b. total CPU percentage

   c. process CPU percentage

   d. all of the above

4. The longer a system is in productive use, the more its performance _____.

5. Which of the following are methods to access Task Manager? (Choose all that apply.)

   a. Ctrl+Alt+Delete

   b. executing "taskman" from the command prompt

   c. Ctrl+Shift+Esc

   d. Control Panel

6. In System Monitor, the counters are the same for all objects. True or False?

7. A(n) _____ event is issued when a driver fails to load.

8. The _____ provides a detailed description of a counter.

9. To record log files the Performance tool must be open. True or False?

10. A Counter log can include which of the following?

    a. one or more counters

    b. counters from multiple computers

    c. different intervals for each counter

    d. a stop time defined by a length of time

11. A _____ occurs when a system resource limits performance.

12. Which of the following objects can be disabled to prevent performance measurements from being taken?

    a. Memory

    b. LogicalDisk

    c. RAS port

    d. System

13. In general, a bottleneck might exist if a queue counter is consistently _____ than the total number of instances of that object.

14. Which one of the following counters is the most likely indicator of a high level of disk activity caused by too little RAM?

    a. Memory: Pages/sec

    b. Memory: Page Faults/sec

    c. Memory: Cache Faults

    d. Memory: Available bytes

15. Which of the following tools can monitor another computer's information?

    a. System Monitor

    b. Task Manager

    c. Event Viewer

16. The _____ on the Source tab is used to select a window of data from a Counter log.

17. The _____ is used to generate system performance reports.

10

18. What parameter should be used with diskperf to disable only the PhysicalDisk object?

    a. -yd

    b. -yv

    c. -nd

    d. -nv

19. The System Monitor can display only _____ data points.

20. The _____ and _____ event types are available only in the Security log.

21. Of the following commands, which gives the Test.exe application the highest priority level available to ordinary users (not administrators)?

    a. start /abovenormal test.exe

    b. start /normal test.exe

    c. start /high test.exe

    d. start /realtime test.exe

22. Which of the following activities can occur when an alert is triggered?(Choose all that apply.)

    a. an alert to a NetBIOS name

    b. shutdown of the system

    c. start the recording of a Counter log

    d. write an event to the Application log

23. The _____ feature of Event Viewer can be used to quickly locate all audit details for a specific user.

24. The Start command can be used to alter the priority of active processes. True or False?

25. What change to a system is most effective in producing a performance improvement?

    a. adding RAM

    b. replacing network cables

    c. adding more processors

    d. updating drivers

HANDS-ON PROJECTS

Project 10-1

To use System Monitor to monitor performance of memory, processor, disks, network, and applications:

1. Open the Control Panel by selecting **Start | Control Panel**.

2. Double-click the **Administrative Tools** icon.

3. Double-click the **Performance** icon.

4. Select the **System Monitor** node in the MMC console.

5. Click **Add** on the toolbar (it's the plus sign).

6. Select the **% Processor Time** counter from the **Processor** object, which is selected by default.

7. Use the Performance object pull-down list to select the **Memory** object.

8. Select the **Pages/sec** counter, if necessary.

9. Click **Add**.

10. Click **Explain**. Read the detail about the selected counter.

11. Repeat steps 7 through 10 to add some or all of the following counters (if multiple instances of these objects are present, select one or more instances and/or the _Total instance):

   ❑ PhysicalDisk: Current Disk Queue Length

   ❑ PhysicalDisk: %Disk Time

   ❑ PhysicalDisk: Avg. Disk Bytes/Transfer

   ❑ Memory: Available Bytes

   ❑ Memory: Cache Faults/sec

   ❑ Memory: Page Faults/sec

   ❑ Memory: Pages/sec

   ❑ Network Interface: Bytes Total/sec

   ❑ Network Interface: Current Bandwidth

   ❑ Network Interface: Output Queue Length

   ❑ Network Interface: Packets/sec

   ❑ Processor: Interrupts/sec

   ❑ System: Processor Queue Length

   ❑ Thread: % Processor Time

10

- ❐ Thread: Priority Current
- ❐ Process: % Processor Time
- ❐ Process: Elapsed Time
- ❐ Process: Page Faults/sec
- ❐ Process: Thread Count

12. Click **Close**.

13. Launch and close **Windows Explorer** or any other application several times, read files from disk, access network resources, and so on to cause system activity.

14. Notice how the respective lines of the selected counters change according to system activity.

Project 10-2

To use System Monitor to alter the display parameters:

1. Click the **Properties** button on the toolbar (or press Ctrl+Q).

2. Change Sample automatically from every 1 second to **2** seconds.

3. Select the **Data** tab.

4. Select the **\\Memory\Pages/sec** counter.

5. Change the color, width, and style, using the pull-down lists.

6. Select the **Graph** tab.

7. Select the **Vertical grid** and **Horizontal grid** checkboxes.

8. Click **OK** to close the System Monitor Properties dialog box.

Project 10-3

To create, start, and stop a Counter log:

1. Launch the Performance tool if it is not still open from the previous hands-on project.

2. Click the boxed plus sign next to the Performance Logs and Alerts node to expand its contents.

3. Select the **Counter Logs** item.

4. Select **New Log Settings** from the Action menu.

5. Type a name, such as **Set1**. Click **OK**.

6. Click the **Add Objects** button on the General tab, select the **Processor** object in the Performance Objects pane, then click **Add** to add the object, and **Close** to close the window.

You can use this method to select entire objects for monitoring, or you can add counters one at a time. To prevent seeing an error message in step 7, click the Remove button in the Counters list in the Set1 window before proceeding to step 7.

7. Click the **Add Counters** button, select the **% Processor Time** counter in the Select counters from list pane (this is easy; it's selected by default), click the **Add** button to add this counter to the log. Click the **Close** button.

8. Change the Interval from 15 seconds to **2** seconds in the Sample data every textbox.

9. Click **OK** to save your counter log definition. (If you receive an error message, click Yes to create the log now.)

10. Select the **Log Files** tab. Review its controls, but don't make any changes.

11. Select the **Schedule** tab.

12. If you are prompted that the log file path does not exist but can be created, select **Yes** to create the path.

13. In the Start log area, select the **At** option and change the start time to **3** minutes from the present.

14. In the Stop log area, select the **After** option and change the time to **4** minutes.

15. Click **OK**.

16. Notice the new log appears in the list. Within three minutes, its icon will turn green.

17. After the icon turns green, launch and terminate Windows Explorer several times to cause system activity.

18. After four minutes the icon turns back to red. Do not go on with the next hands-on project until the icon is red again.

Project 10-4

To view data from a Counter log with System Monitor:

1. Launch the Performance tool if it is not still open from the previous hands-on project.

2. Select the **System Monitor** node.

3. Right-click the right pane and select **Properties** from the resulting menu.

4. Select the **Source** tab.

5. Select the **Log files** option.

6. Use the **Add** button to locate and select the Counter log created in Hands-on Project 10-3. Click **Open**.

7. Click **OK** in the System Monitor Properties dialog box.

8. Click the **New Counter Set** button in the toolbar (the blank page with a sparkle on the top-right corner).

9. Click the **Add** button (the plus sign) on the toolbar.

10. Click **Add** to add the % Processor Counter to the System Monitor display. Note the Counter log recorded in the previous hands-on project has only this one counter so it is selected by default.

11. Click **Close**.

12. Because the Counter log recorded measurements every 2 seconds for 4 minutes, there are 120 data points that are compressed and averaged to create the display you see. To prevent compression of data, you must select a time range of 100 data points or fewer.

13. Click the **Properties** button on the toolbar.

14. Select the **Source** tab.

15. Click the **Time Range** button to refresh the Counter log data.

16. Click and drag the right slider so that only 198 seconds separate the start and stop ends of the view range.

17. Click **OK**.

18. Notice that now 99 data points are displayed.

Project 10-5

To create an Alert object:

1. Launch the Performance tool if it is not still open.

2. Select the **Alerts** node.

3. Select **New Alert Settings** from the Action menu.

4. Type a name such as **Set1**. Click **OK**.

5. Click **Add**.

6. Click **Add** to add the % Processor Time counter to the alert. Note that this counter is selected by default.

7. Click **Close**.

8. Select **Over** in the "Alert when the value is" pull-down box.

9. Type in **50** in the Limit box.

10. Change the sample Interval to **1** second.

11. Select the **Action** tab.

12. Select the **Send a network message to** checkbox.

13. Type in the username of the account with which you are currently logged on.

14. Select the **Schedule** tab.

15. Select the **Manually (using the shortcut menu)** option in the Start scan area.

16. Click **OK**.

17. Select the new **Alert object** that appears in the list of alerts.

18. Select the **Start** command from the Action menu. Its icon will be green when active.

19. Launch and terminate Windows Explorer several times to force system activity. When the % Processor Usage crosses the 50 percent threshold, a network message will appear on your screen. Click **OK** to close it.

20. Select the **Delete** command from the Action menu. Click **OK** to confirm the deletion. This deletes the Action object.

Project 10-6

To use Event Viewer to view an event detail:

1. Open the Control Panel by selecting **Start | Control Panel**.

2. Open the **Administrative Tools** by double-clicking its icon in the Control Panel.

3. Open **Event Viewer** by double-clicking its icon in the Administrative Tools window.

4. Select the **Application log**.

5. Locate and select an Information detail with a SysmonLog source.

6. Double-click the item to open the event detail.

7. Notice that the Description includes information about the counter and the measured level that caused the alert.

8. Click **OK**.

9. Close Event Viewer.

Project 10-7

To create and view a baseline:

1. Open the Control Panel by selecting **Start | Control Panel**.

2. Double-click the **Administrative Tools** icon.

3. Double-click the **Performance** icon.

4. Click the boxed plus sign next to the Performance Logs and Alerts node to expand its contents.

5. Select the **Counter Logs** item.

6. Select **New Log Settings** from the Action menu.

7. Type a name, such as **Baseline1**. Click **OK**.

8. Click the **Add Counters** button on the General tab.

9. Click **Explain** to open the Explain Text window.

10

10. Use the **Performance object** pull-down list to select the **Memory** object.

11. Select the **Pages/sec** counter in the list under the **Select counters from list** radio button.

12. Read the details in the Explain Text window about the selected counter.

13. Click **Add**.

14. Repeat steps 10 through 13 to add some or all of the following counters (if multiple instances of these objects are present, select one or more instances and/or the _Total instance):

    - PhysicalDisk: %Disk Time

    - Memory: Available Bytes

    - Network Interface: Bytes Total/sec

    - Processor: % Processor Time

    - System: Processor Queue Length

15. Click **Close**.

16. Change the Interval from 15 seconds to **30** seconds.

17. Select the **Log Files** tab. Review its controls, but don't make any changes.

18. Select the **Schedule** tab.

19. If you are prompted that the log file path does not exist but can be created, select **Yes** to create the path.

20. In the Start log area, select the **At** option and change the start time to 3 minutes from the present.

21. In the Stop log area, select the **After** option and change the time to **2** days.

22. Click **OK**.

23. Notice the new log appears in the list. Within three minutes, its icon will turn green.

24. After the icon turns green, continue performing normal or typical work on this system until two days has passed.

25. After one day the icon turns back to red. Do not go on with the remaining part of this hands-on project until the icon is red again.

26. Select the **System Monitor** node in the Performance tool.

27. Right-click the **right pane** and select **Properties** from the resulting menu.

28. Select the **Source** tab.

29. Select the **Log files** option.

30. Use the **Add** button to locate and select the Counter log created in step 7. Click **Open**.

31. Click **OK** in the System Monitor Properties dialog box.

32. Click the **New Counter Set** button in the toolbar (the blank page with a sparkle on the top-right corner).

33. Click the **Add Counters** button (the plus sign) on the toolbar.

34. Use the Performance object pull-down list to select the **Memory** object.

35. Select the **Pages/sec** counter in the list under the Select counters from list radio button.

36. Read the details in the Explain Text window about the selected counter.

37. Click **Add**.

38. Repeat steps 34 through 38 to add some or all of the following counters (if multiple instances of these objects are present, select one or more instances and/or the _Total instance):

   - PhysicalDisk: %Disk Time

   - Memory: Available Bytes

   - Network Interface: Bytes Total/sec

   - Processor: % Processor Time

   - System: Processor Queue Length

39. Click **Close**.

40. Click the **View Report** button from the toolbar. The values listed are an average of all measurements over the entire time period recorded in the log file.

41. Click the **Properties** button on the toolbar.

42. Select the **Source** tab.

43. Click the **Time Range** button to refresh the Counter log data.

44. Click and drag the right and left sliders so that they encompass a time period of 8 hours, such as 9 AM to 5 PM.

45. Click **OK**.

46. Notice that new averaged data points are displayed.

47. Take note of the values seen here, be sure to indicate the time range used for each measurement.

48. Repeat steps 41-47 for the time ranges of 5 PM to 10 PM, 10 PM to 6 AM, 6 AM to 9 AM, and then hourly for each hour of the typical work day (i.e., 9 AM to 10 AM, then 10 AM to 11 AM, etc.)

49. Click the **File** menu, then select **Save As**.

50. Using the Save As dialog box, select a folder and provide a filename to save the console configuration, such as **baseline view1.msc**. Click **Save**.

51. Close the Performance tool by clicking the **File** menu, then clicking **Exit**.

52. At a later date, re-open the Performance tool (see steps 1 through 3).

10

53. Click the **File** menu, then select **Open**.

54. Using the Open dialog box, locate and select the file saved in step 50. Click **Open**.

55. The view should return to that seen in your final action of step 48.

56. The saved data in the first counter log is your baseline. To use the baseline, you must record a new log file over a similar time period, and compare the new data points with the old data points.

57. Click the boxed plus sign next to the Performance Logs and Alerts node to expand its contents.

58. Select the **Counter Logs** item.

59. Click to select the counter log created in step 7.

60. Right-click over this counter log and select **Properties** from the pop-up menu.

61. Select the **Log Files** tab. Notice the Start numbering at field has been incremented.

62. Repeat steps 18 through 48.

63. Compare the measurements you wrote down from the first baseline Counter log with the most resent Counter log. Any discrepancies may Indicate a change In system activity or may point toward a developing bottleneck.

Case Projects

1. Performance on a Windows XP Professional system used by the accounting department has been slowly degrading. You recently added a 100-Mbps network card, thinking that would correct the problem. To your knowledge, no other hardware has been added to the server, but you suspect someone has been adding software.

   Describe the steps you will use to determine what is causing the system to slow down, including which monitoring applications you will use and on which computer they will be run.

2. You are considering upgrading your Windows XP Professional hardware, including memory, hard drive controller, and video card. The only things you are planning to keep are your hard drive, motherboard, and CPU.

   Outline the tools and utilities you will use to measure the performance increase or decrease, as each new component is added. Include information on expected performance changes and actual changes.

11

WINDOWS XP PROFESSIONAL APPLICATION SUPPORT

> **After reading this chapter and completing the exercises, you'll be able to:**
>
> ♦ Understand the runtime environments and application support in Windows XP Professional
>
> ♦ Deploy DOS, Win16, and Win32 applications
>
> ♦ Fine-tune the application environment for DOS and Win16 executables
>
> ♦ Understand how to assign and publish applications using Group Policy
>
> ♦ Address application compatibility issues

In this chapter, you encounter the pieces of the Windows XP Professional operating system that endow it with its outstanding power and flexibility. Its numerous runtime environments include limited support for DOS and 16-bit Windows applications, as well as more modern 32-bit Windows applications. Here, you'll have a chance to examine the various subsystems that Windows XP Professional provides to support DOS applications, plus 16- and 32-bit Windows applications, and understand how they work. You'll also have a chance to learn about Windows XP's mechanisms to ensure compatible operation of multiple applications on a single machine.

WINDOWS XP PROFESSIONAL SYSTEM ARCHITECTURE

Fundamentally, the Windows XP Professional operating system incorporates three primary components: the environment subsystem, Executive Services, and user applications (see Figure 11-1).

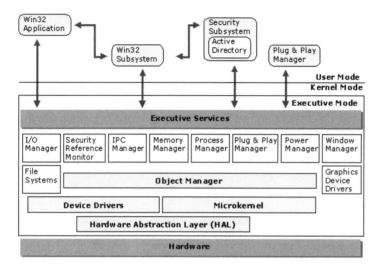

Figure 11-1   Components of the Windows XP Professional architecture

- **Environment subsystems** offer runtime support for a variety of different kinds of applications, under the purview of a single operating system. A **subsystem** is an operating environment that emulates another operating system (such as DOS or 16-bit Windows) to provide support for applications created for that environment, or a set of built-in programming interfaces that support the native Win32 (Windows 32-bit) runtime environment. Just like the applications they support, Windows XP Professional environment subsystems run in user mode, which means that they must access all system resources through the operating system's kernel mode.

- Windows XP Professional **Executive Services** and the underlying Windows XP **kernel** define the kernel mode for this operating system and its runtime environment. **Kernel mode** components are permitted to access system objects and resources directly, and provide the many services and access controls that allow multiple users and applications to coexist and interoperate effectively and efficiently.

- User applications provide the functionality and capabilities that rank Windows XP Professional among the most powerful network operating systems in use today. All such applications run within the context of an environment subsystem in Windows XP user mode. Applications and the subsystems in which they run have a mediated relationship because the client application asks the subsystem to perform activities for it, and the subsystem complies with such requests (or denies them if the requester lacks sufficient privileges).

To understand how these components fit together, we need to revisit the concept of processes and threads, building on concepts introduced in Chapter 1, "Introduction to Windows XP Professional."

Kernel Mode Versus User Mode

Before delving further into the architecture of Windows XP Professional, we'd better make clear the distinction between the Windows XP kernel mode and user mode. The main difference between the two modes lies in how memory is used by kernel-mode components and user-mode components.

In **user mode**, each process perceives the entire 4 GB of virtual memory available to Windows XP as its exclusive property—with the condition that the upper 2 GB of addresses are normally reserved for operating system use. This perception remains unaltered, no matter what kind of hardware Windows XP may run on. Note also that this address space is entirely virtual, and must operate within the confines of whatever RAM is installed on a machine and the amount of space reserved for the paging file's use. Although the upper limit for Windows XP virtual memory addresses may be 2 GB (or 4 GB, for system purposes), the real upper limit for Windows XP physical memory addresses will always be the sum of physical RAM size plus the amount of space in the paging file.

Although processes that operate in user mode may share memory areas with other processes (for fast message passing or sharing information), by default, they don't. This means that one user-mode process cannot crash another, or corrupt its data. This is what creates the appearance that applications run independently, and allows each one to operate as if it had exclusive possession of the operating system and the hardware it controls.

 If a user-mode parent process crashes, it will, of course, take its child processes down with it. (Parent and child processes are discussed later in this chapter.)

Processes running in user mode cannot access hardware or communicate with other processes directly. When code runs in the Windows XP kernel mode, on the other hand, it may access all hardware and memory in the computer (but usually through an associated Executive Services module). Thus, when an application needs to perform tasks that involve hardware, it calls a user-mode function that ultimately calls a kernel-mode function.

Because all kernel-mode operations share the same memory space, one kernel-mode function can corrupt another's data and even cause the operating system to crash. This is the reason that the environment subsystems contain as much of the operating system's capabilities as possible, making the kernel itself less vulnerable. For this reason, some experts voiced concern about the change in the Windows 2000 design that moved graphics handlers to the kernel. But because those graphics components were originally part of the Win32 environment subsystem—which must be available for Windows XP Professional to operate properly—a crash in either implementation could bring down the system. That's why this change has had little effect on the reliability or stability of Windows 2000 or Windows XP Professional.

 For a review of the user mode and kernel-mode architecture of Windows XP Professional, refer to Chapter 1.

Processes and Threads

From a user's point of view, the operating system exists to run programs or applications. But from the view of the Windows XP Professional operating system, the world is made of processes and threads. A **process** defines the operating environment in which an application or any major operating system component runs. Any Windows XP process includes its own private memory space, a set of security descriptors, a priority level for execution, processor-affinity data (that is, on a multiprocessor system, information that instructs a process to use a particular CPU), and a list of threads associated with that process. A list of currently active processes can be seen on the Processes tab of the Task Manager (see Figure 11-2). You access the Task Manager in any of several ways:

- Pressing Ctrl+Alt+Delete and clicking the Task Manager button (in normal Windows logon mode only)

- Pressing Ctrl+Alt+Delete (in Windows Welcome mode only)

- Right-clicking on an unoccupied area of the taskbar on your display, and selecting Task Manager from the resulting pop-up menu

- Pressing Ctrl+Shift+Esc

The basic executable unit in Windows XP is called a **thread**, and every process includes at least one thread. A thread consists of placeholder information associated with a single use of any program that can handle multiple concurrent users or activities. Within a multi-threaded application, each distinct task or any complex operation is likely to be implemented in its own separate thread. This explains how Microsoft Word, for instance, can perform spelling and grammar checks in the background while you're entering text in the input window in the foreground: two threads are running—one manages handling input, the other performs these checks.

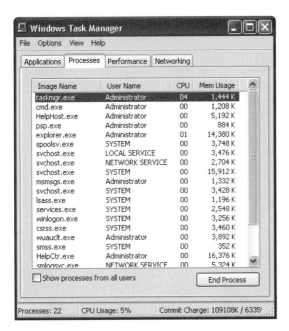

Figure 11-2 The Process tab in Task Manager displays all currently active Windows XP Professional processes

Applications must be explicitly designed to take advantage of threading. Although it's safe to assume that most new 32-bit Windows applications—and the Windows XP operating system itself—are built to use the power and flexibility of threads, older 16-bit Windows and DOS applications are usually single-threaded. Also, it is important to understand that threads are associated with processes and do not exist independently. Processes themselves don't run, they merely describe a shared environment comprised of resources that include allocated memory, variables, and other system objects; threads represent those parts of any program that actually run.

Processes can create other processes, called **child processes**, and those child processes can inherit some of the characteristics and parameters of their **parent process**. (A child process is a replica of the parent process and shares some of its resources, but cannot exist independently if the parent is terminated.) The parent-child relationship between pairs of processes usually works as follows:

- When a user logs on to Windows XP Professional successfully, a shell process is created inside the Win32 subsystem within which the logon session operates. The Win32 subsystem is an operating environment that supports 32-bit Windows applications; this subsystem is required to run Windows XP. This process is endowed with a security token used to determine if subsequent requests for system objects and resources may be permitted to proceed. This shell process defines the Win32 subsystem as the parent process for that user.

11

- Each time a user launches an application or starts a system utility, a child process is created within the environment subsystem where that application or utility must run. This child process inherits its security token and associated information from the parent user account, but is also a child of the environment subsystem within which it runs. This "dual parentage" (security information from the user account and runtime environment from the environment subsystem) explains how Windows XP can run multiple kinds of applications in parallel, yet maintain consistent control over system objects and resources to which any user process is permitted access.

For example, each of the environment subsystems discussed in the following sections is an executable file—a combination of processes and threads running within the context of those processes (a **context** is the current collection of Registry values and runtime environment variables in which a process or thread runs). When an application runs in a Windows XP Professional subsystem, it actually represents a child of the parent process for the environment subsystem, but one that is endowed with the permissions associated with the security token of the account that launches the process. Whenever a parent process halts or is stopped, all child processes stop as well.

Environment Subsystems

Windows XP Professional offers support for various application platforms. Although primarily designed for 32-bit Windows applications, Windows XP Professional includes limited support for backward compatibility for 16-bit Windows and DOS applications.

Windows XP Professional's support for multiple runtime environments, also known as environment subsystems, confers numerous advantages, including:

- It permits users to run more than one type of application concurrently, including 32-bit Windows, 16-bit Windows, and DOS applications.

- It makes maintaining the operating system easier, because the modularity of this design means that changes to environment subsystems require no changes to the kernel itself, as long as interfaces remain unchanged.

- Modularity makes it easy to add or enhance Windows XP—if a new OS is developed in the future, Microsoft could decide to add a subsystem for that OS to Windows XP without affecting other environment subsystems.

The catch to using an architecture that supports multiple environment subsystems is in providing mechanisms that permit those subsystems to communicate with one another when necessary. In the Windows XP environment, each subsystem runs as a separate user-mode process, so that subsystems cannot interfere with or crash one another. The only exception to this insulation effect occurs in the Win32 subsystem: because all user-mode I/O passes through this subsystem, the Win32 subsystem must be running for Windows XP to function properly. If the Win32 subsystem's process ends, the whole operating system goes down with it. This explains why you can shut down processes associated with 16-bit Windows or DOS applications on a Windows XP machine without affecting anything other than those processes (and any related child processes) themselves.

Applications and the subsystems in which they run have a client/server relationship, in that the client application asks the server subsystem to do things for it, and the subsystem complies. For example, if a Win32 client application needs to open a new window (perhaps to create a Save As dialog box), it doesn't create the window itself, but asks the Win32 subsystem to draw the window on its behalf. If the 16-bit Windows on Windows environment is running and another 16-bit Windows application is launched, it will run within the existing 16-bit Windows environment by default.

The client issues the request through a mechanism known as a **local procedure call (LPC)**. The serving subsystem makes its capabilities available to client applications by linking them to a **dynamic link library (DLL)**. You could think of a DLL as a set of buzzers, where each one is labeled with the capabilities it provides. Pushing a specific buzzer tells the server subsystem to do whatever the label tells it to. This form of messaging is transparent to the client application (as far as it knows, it's simply calling a procedure). When a client pushes one of those buzzers (requests a service), it appears as if the act is handled by the DLL; no explicit communication with a server subsystem is needed. If a service isn't listed in the library, an application can't request it; thus, a word processor running in a command-line environment as a DOS application, for example, can't ask that subsystem to draw a window.

Message-passing is a fairly time-consuming operation, because any time the focus changes from one process to another, all the information for the calling process must be unloaded and replaced with the information for the called process. In operating system lingo, this change of operation focus from one process to another is called a **context switch**. To permit the operating system to run more efficiently, Windows XP avoids making context switches whenever possible. To that end, Windows XP includes the following efficiency measures:

11

- It caches attributes in DLLs to provide an interface to subsystem capabilities, so that (for example) the second time Microsoft Word requests a window to be created, this activity may be completed without switching context to the Win32 subsystem.

- It calls Executive Services (the collection of kernel-mode Windows XP operating system components that provides basic system services such as I/O, security, object management, and so forth) directly, to perform tasks without requesting help from an underlying environment subsystem. Because the kernel is always active in another process space in Windows XP, calling for kernel-mode services does *not* require a context switch.

- It batches messages so that when a server process is called, several messages can be passed at once—the number of messages has no impact on performance, but a context switch does. By batching messages, Windows XP allows a single context switch to handle multiple messages in sequence, rather than requiring a context switch for each message.

When LPCs must be used, they're handled as efficiently as possible. Likewise, their code is optimized for speed, and special message-passing functions can be used for different situations, depending (for example) on the size of the messages passed, or the circumstances in which they're sent.

So far, we've covered the broad view of how environment subsystems interact with client applications. Now, let's take a closer look at these subsystems.

The Win32 Subsystem

As the only subsystem required for the functioning of the operating system, the **Win32 subsystem** handles all major interface capabilities. In early versions of Windows NT, the Win32 subsystem included graphics, windowing, and messaging support, but since Windows NT 4.0 was released, these have been moved to the kernel and are now part of Executive Services. This applies equally to Windows 2000 and to Windows XP Professional.

In Windows XP, user-mode components of the Win32 subsystem consist of the console (text window support), shutdown, hard-error handling, and some environmental functions to handle such tasks as process creation and deletion. The Win32 subsystem is also the foundation upon which **virtual DOS machines (VDMs)** rest. These permit Windows XP to deliver both DOS and Win16 subsystems, so that DOS and Win16 applications can run on Windows XP unchanged (we'll talk more about VDMs and the DOS and Win16 subsystems later in this chapter). Try Hands-on Project 11-1 to launch a Win16 application in its own address space.

WIN32 APPLICATIONS

So far, we've examined the components of the Windows XP Professional operating system kernel. Now, it's time to see how applications run under that operating system.

The Environment Subsystem

As we've mentioned, the Win32 subsystem is the main environment subsystem under Windows XP, and the only one required for operation. Strictly speaking, even the other environment subsystems (the scaffolding that supports DOS and 16-bit Windows applications) are Win32 applications that run as child processes to the main Win32 process and support application environments called virtual DOS machines (VDMs) that run under Win32 to support DOS applications. (We explain VDMs and DOS application support in more detail later in this chapter.)

Multithreading

When a program's process contains more than one thread of execution, it's said to be a **multithreaded process**. The main advantage of multithreading is that it provides multiple threads of execution within a single memory space without requiring that messages be passed between processes or that local procedure calls be used, thus simplifying thread communication. Threads are easier to create than processes because they don't require as much context information, nor do they incur the same kind of overhead when switching from one thread to another within a single process.

Some multithreaded applications can even run multiple threads concurrently among multiple processors (assuming a machine has more than one). One more advantage to threading is that it's *much* less complicated to switch operation from thread to thread than to switch from one process to another. That's because every time a new process is scheduled for execution, the system must be updated with all the process's context information. Also, it's often necessary to remove one process to make room for another, which may require writing large amounts of data from RAM to disk for the outgoing process, before copying large amounts of data from disk into RAM to bring in the incoming process.

 As a point of comparison, a thread switch can normally be completed in somewhere between 15 and 25 machine instructions, whereas a process switch can take many thousands of instructions to complete. Because most CPUs are set up to handle one instruction for every clock cycle, this means that switching among threads is hundreds to thousands of times faster than switching among processes.

The big trick with multithreading, of course, is that the chances that one thread could overwrite another are increased with each additional thread, so this introduces the problem of protecting shared areas of memory from intraprocess thread overwrites. Windows XP manages access to memory very carefully, and limits which sections of memory any individual thread can write to by locking them, as you'll see in the next section. This largely avoids the problems associated with shared access to a single set of memory addresses.

Memory Space

Multithreaded programs must be designed so that threads don't get in each other's way, and they do this by using Windows XP **synchronization objects**. A section of code that modifies data structures used by several threads is called a **critical section**. It's very important that a critical section never be overwritten by more than one thread at once. Thus, applications use Windows XP synchronization objects to prevent this from happening, creating such objects for each critical section in each process context. When a thread needs access to a critical section, the following occurs:

1. A thread requests a synchronization object. If it is unlocked (not suspended in a thread queue), the request proceeds. Otherwise, go to step 2.

2. The thread is suspended in a thread queue until the synchronization object is unlocked for its use. As soon as this happens, Windows XP releases the thread and locks up the object.

3. The thread accesses the critical section.

4. When the thread is done, it unlocks the synchronization object so that another thread may access the critical object.

Thus, multithreaded applications avoid accessing a single data structure with more than one thread at a time by locking its critical section when it is in use and unlocking it when it is not.

Input Message Queues

One of the roles of the Win32 subsystem is to organize user input and get it to the thread to which that input belongs. It does this by taking user messages from a general input queue, and distributing them to the **input message queues** for the individual processes.

As we'll discuss later in this chapter, Win16 applications normally run within a single process, so they share a message input queue, unlike Win32 or DOS applications with their individual queues.

Base Priorities

When a program is started under Windows XP Professional, its process is assigned a particular priority class, generally Normal—but there is a range of options (see Figure 11-3). The priority class helps determine the priority at which threads in a process must run, on a scale from 0 (lowest) to 31 (highest). In a process with more than one active thread, each thread may have its own priority, which may be higher or lower than that of the original thread, but that priority is always relative to the priority assigned to the underlying process, which is known as the **base priority**. Managing priorities may be accomplished in one of several ways, and can sometimes provide a useful way to improve application performance. These include Task Manager and the Start command, as discussed in Chapter 10, "Performance Tuning."

Figure 11-3   The Task Manager's Process tab with priority options on display

DOS AND THE VIRTUAL DOS MACHINE

DOS and Win16 applications work somewhat differently from Win32 applications. Rather than each running in the context of its own process, these applications run within a virtual DOS machine (VDM), a special environment process that simulates a DOS environment so that non-Win32 Windows applications can run under Windows XP. In fact, it's reasonable to describe two separate operating environments that can run within a VDM: one supports straightforward DOS emulation and may be called the **DOS operating environment**; the other supports operation of Win16 applications within a VDM, and may be called the **Win16 operating environment**.

Any DOS operating environment under Windows XP occurs within a Win32 process named ntvdm.exe (see Figure 11-4). In fact, if you look at the Processes tab of the Task Manager when a DOS application is active, you'll see this process. The ntvdm process creates the environment wherein DOS applications execute. Each DOS application that is launched executes within a separate emulation environment. Thus, if you launch three DOS applications, three instances of ntvdm appear in the process list. Once a DOS application terminates, Windows XP also shuts down the emulation environment for that application by terminating the associated instance of ntvdm. This frees its system resources for re-use.

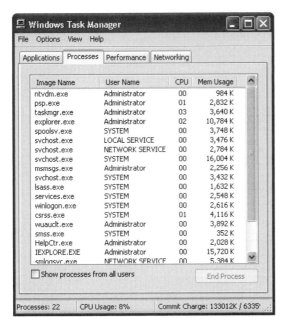

Figure 11-4 The Task Manager's Processes tab shows ntvdm.exe running when a 16-bit DOS application is loaded

The environment created in a VDM is not the same as that available to Win32 applications. Instead, it is equivalent to the environment of Windows 3.x Enhanced mode, in which each DOS application has access to 1 MB of virtual memory, with 1 MB of extended memory and expanded memory if necessary.

By default, all DOS applications run in their own VDMs. By default, all Win16 applications share a single VDM (just as they do in "real Windows 3.x" environments).

VDM Components

The VDM runs using the following files:

- *Ntio.sys*—The equivalent of Io.sys on MS-DOS machines, runs in **real mode** (real mode is a mode of operation for x86 CPUs wherein they can address only 1 MB of memory, broken into 16 64-KB segments). It provides "virtual I/O" services to the DOS or Win16 applications that run in a VDM.

- *Ntdos.sys*—The equivalent of Msdos.sys, runs in real mode. It provides basic DOS operating system services to the DOS or Win16 applications that run in a VDM.

- *Ntvdm.exe*—A Win32 application that runs in kernel mode. This is the execution file that provides the runtime environment within which a VDM runs. If you look at the list on the Processes tab of Task Manager, you'll see one such entry for each separate VDM that's running on your machine.

- *Ntvdm.dll*—A Win32 dynamic link library that runs in kernel mode. Ntvdm.dll provides the set of procedure stubs that fool DOS and Win16 programs into thinking they're talking to a real DOS machine with exclusive access to a PC, when in fact they're communicating through a VDM with Windows XP Professional.

- *Redir.exe*—The virtual device driver (VDD) redirector for the VDM. This software forwards I/O requests from programs within a VDM for I/O services through the Win32 environment subsystem to the Windows XP I/O Manager in Executive Services. Whenever a DOS or Win16 program in a VDM thinks it's communicating with hardware, it's really communicating with Redir.exe.

Virtual Device Drivers

DOS applications do not communicate directly with Windows XP drivers. Instead, a layer of **virtual device drivers (VDDs)** underlies these applications, and they communicate with Windows XP 32-bit drivers. Windows XP supplies VDDs for mice, keyboards, printers, and communication ports, as well as file system drivers (including one or more network drivers, each of which is actually implemented as a file system driver).

AUTOEXEC.BAT and CONFIG.SYS

When a DOS application is started, Windows XP runs the files specified in the application's program information file (PIF) or in AUTOEXEC.NT (see Figure 11-5) and CONFIG.NT (see Figure 11-6), the two files that replace AUTOEXEC.BAT and CONFIG.SYS for VDMs. AUTOEXEC.NT installs CD-ROM extensions and the network redirector. By default, Windows XP provides DOS Protected Mode Interface (DPMI) support, to permit DOS and Win16 applications to access more than 1 MB of memory within a virtual (or real) DOS machine. CONFIG.NT loads into an upper memory area for its VDM, and supports HIMEM.SYS by default to enable extended memory; it also sets the number of files and buffers available to DOS or Win16 programs, and provides necessary details to configure expanded memory.

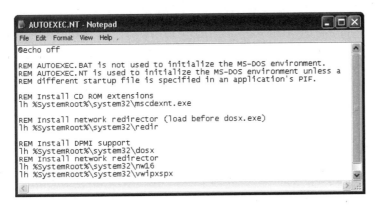

Figure 11-5   AUTOEXEC.NT as it appears in Notepad

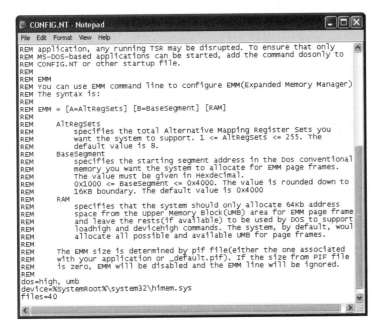

Figure 11-6   CONFIG.NT as it appears in Notepad

Try Hands-on Project 11-4 to explore AUTOEXEC.NT and CONFIG.NT.

CONFIG.SYS isn't used at all by Windows XP, whereas AUTOEXEC.BAT is only used at system startup to set path and environment variables for the Windows XP environment. Neither file is consulted when it comes to running applications or initializing drivers; those settings must exist in the system Registry to work at all.

Once read from AUTOEXEC.BAT, path and environment variables are copied to the Registry, to HKEY_LOCAL_MACHINE\SYSTEM\CurrentControlSet\Control\ Session Manager\Environment (see Figure 11-7).

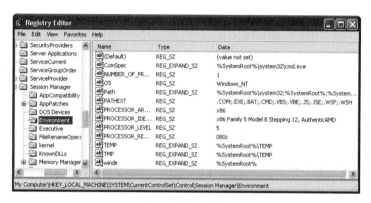

Figure 11-7   The Registry Editor shows the variables defined within the ...\Environment subkey

Custom DOS Environments

Windows XP offers customizable environment controls for its DOS runtime environment. These controls can be used to fine-tune or simply to alter how any DOS application functions. To customize a DOS application's execution parameters, open the Properties dialog box for that executable (.exe or .com) file. This is performed by right-clicking over an executable file and selecting Properties from the resulting menu. Try Hands-on Project 11-2 to explore the properties of DOS applications within Windows XP Professional.

The Properties dialog box for a DOS executable file has nine tabs. The General tab lists the same data items as any other file within the Windows XP Professional environment. The Program tab (see Figure 11-8) offers controls over:

- *Filename*—The name of the file

- *Command line*—Used to add command-line parameter syntax

- *Working*—Used to define the working directory, which is the directory from which the application will load files and where it saves files

- *Batch file*—Used to run a batch file before launching the executable file

- *Shortcut key*—Used to define a keystroke that launches the executable file

- *Run*—Used to define the window size of the DOS environment—normal, maximized, or minimized

- *Close on exit*—Informs the OS to close the DOS window when the application terminates

- *Advanced button*—Allows you to define the path to alternate AUTOEXEC.NT and CONFIG.NT files

- *Change icon button*—Changes the icon displayed for the executable file

Figure 11-8   MASTMIND.EXE Properties, Program tab

The Font tab is used to define the font used by the DOS application. The Memory tab is used to define the memory parameters for the DOS environment that the corresponding ntvdm creates. These controls include settings for conventional memory, expanded memory (EMS), extended memory (XMS), and DOS protected-mode (DPMI) memory.

The Screen tab is used to define whether the DOS application loads full-screen or in a window. It also indicates if the ntvdm should emulate fast ROM, and whether or not it should allocate dynamic memory.

The Misc tab (see Figure 11-9) is used to define the following:

- Allow a screen saver over the DOS window

- Whether or not the mouse is used by the DOS application

- If the DOS application is suspended when in the background

- Whether or not to warn if the DOS application is active when you attempt to close the DOS window

- How long the application waits for I/O before releasing CPU control

- Whether or not to use fast pasting (a quick method for pasting information into the application; this doesn't work with some programs, so disable this checkbox if information does not paste properly)

- Which Windows shortcut keys are reserved for use by Windows XP Professional instead of the DOS application.

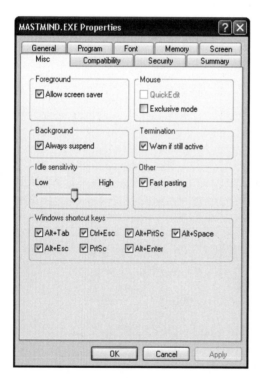

Figure 11-9   MASTMIND.EXE Properties Misc tab

A discrete body of Registry keys, subkeys, and values stored in a file is also known as a **hive**. Such files reside in the *%systemroot%*\system32\ WINDOWS\system32\config directory and normally correspond to some of the root keys shown in Figure 12-1 (e.g., the file named "system" corresponds to the HKEY_LOCAL_MACHINE\SYSTEM root key). For a complete listing of all hives on your system, use Regedit.exe to inspect the contents of the HKLM\SYSTEM\CurrentControlSet\Control\hivelist subkey.

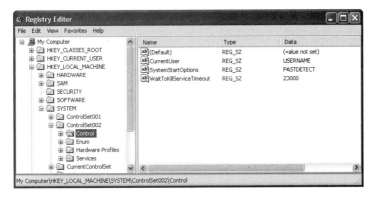

Figure 12-1   View of the hierarchical Registry structure, including five primary keys

Value entries within the Registry are composed of three parts: name, type, and data (value). A Registry value entry's name is typically a multiword phrase, without spaces, with title capitalization, such as AutoAdminLogon in Figure 12-2. The data type of a value entry informs the Registry how to store the value. The **data type** defines whether the piece of data is a text string or a number and gives the numerical base (radix) of that number. Radix types supported by Windows 2000 are decimal (base 10), hexadecimal (base 16), and binary (base 2). All hexadecimal values are listed with the prefix "0x" to identify them clearly (as in 0xF for 15).

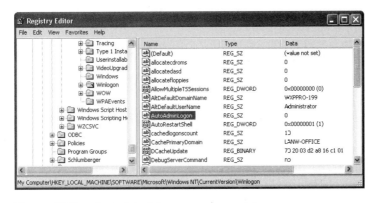

Figure 12-2   AutoAdminLogon value entries

12

The data types supported by Windows 2000 are:

- *Binary*—Binary format
- *DWORD*—Binary, hex, or decimal format
- *String*—Text-string format
- *Multi-String*—Text-string format that contains multiple human-readable values separated by NULL characters
- *Expandable String*—Expandable text-string format containing a variable that is replaced by an application when used (*%systemroot%\File.exe*)

 Once a value entry is created and its data type defined, that data type cannot be changed. To alter a value's data type, you must delete the value entry and re-create it with a new data type.

Important concepts to keep in mind about the Registry are:

- Keys are the top-level, or root, divisions of the Registry
- Keys contain one or more subkeys
- Any subkey can contain one or more subkeys
- Any subkey can contain one or more value entries

Also note that the Registry is not a complete collection of configuration settings. Instead, it holds only the exceptions to the defaults. Processes within Windows XP will operate with their own internal defaults unless a value in the Registry specifically alters that default behavior. This makes working with the Registry difficult: very often the control you need is not present in the Registry because internal defaults are in use. To alter such a setting, you'll need to add a new value entry to the Registry. To accomplish this, you must know the exact syntax, spelling, location, and valid values; otherwise, you will be unable to alter the default behavior. Keep in mind that failing to use the exact syntax, spelling, location, or valid values can result in malfunctions, possibly resulting in an inoperable system. So always edit with extreme care. The *Microsoft Windows XP Professional Resource Kit* includes a help file named Regentry.chm, which lists all possible Registry entries and valid values. This is an invaluable tool when attempting to modify existing Registry entries or when adding new ones.

Each time Windows XP boots, the Registry is loaded into memory from files (see "Registry Storage Files" later this chapter) stored on the hard drive. Each time Windows XP shuts down, the Registry is written from memory back to the files. While Windows XP is operating, the Registry remains in memory. This makes the Registry easy to access and quick to respond to control queries, and it is the reason why changes to the Registry take effect immediately. Only in extreme cases will Windows XP require a reboot to enforce changes in the Registry.

IMPORTANT REGISTRY STRUCTURES AND KEYS

In the following sections, we look at various keys and subkeys in the Registry and explain their functions.

HKEY_LOCAL_MACHINE

The **HKEY_LOCAL_MACHINE** key contains the value entries that control the local computer. These configuration items include information about hardware devices, applications, device drivers, kernel services, and physical settings. These data are used to establish the configuration of the hardware and operating system environment. The content of this key is not dependent on the logged-on user, or the applications or processes in use; it is dependent only on the physical composition of the hardware and software present on the local computer.

This key has five subkeys (see Figure 12-3): HARDWARE, SAM, SECURITY, SOFTWARE, and SYSTEM, which are described in the following sections.

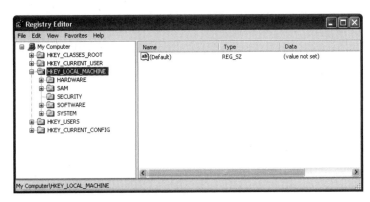

Figure 12-3   The HKEY_LOCAL_MACHINE key

HKEY_LOCAL_MACHINE\HARDWARE

The HKEY_LOCAL_MACHINE\HARDWARE subkey is the container for data related directly to physical devices installed on a computer. This subkey stores configuration data, device driver settings, mappings, linkages, relationships between kernel-mode and user-mode hardware calls, and IRQ hooks. This subkey is re-created each time the system boots and is not saved when the system shuts down. That explains why this subkey does not map to a specific hive file in the *%systemroot%*\WINDOWS\system32\config directory.

The HKEY_LOCAL_MACHINE\HARDWARE subkey contains three subkeys: DESCRIPTION, DEVICEMAP, and RESOURCEMAP. The DESCRIPTION subkey stores data extracted from a device's own firmware or onboard BIOS. The DEVICEMAP subkey stores information about device driver paths, locations, and filenames. The

RESOURCEMAP subkey stores information about the mappings between system resources (I/O ports, I/O memory addresses, interrupts, and direct memory access [DMA] channels) and device drivers. When certain bus types are present in the computer, a fourth subkey named OWNERMAP stores association information about the bus type and device drivers.

The HKEY_LOCAL_MACHINE\Hardware subkey will contain a fourth subkey if your system contains software that supports the Advanced Configuration and Power Interface (ACPI). The ACPI subkey contains all of the operational parameters for that feature.

The contents of the HARDWARE subkey should not be manipulated. This key contains data read from the state of the physical devices and associated device drivers. There should be no need or reason to alter the data because they should always present a proper reflection of the state of the system. Second, these data are most often in binary format; so deciphering the data will be difficult, if not impossible, for most users. If you want to view the data contained in this key, you can do so using the System Information tool. To launch this tool go to Start, Help and Support, then click Support, then choose Advanced System Information from the See Also task items. Alternately, you can go to Start, Run, then type *msinfo32.exe* in the Open textbox or launch it from the Start menu (Start | All Programs | Accessories | System Tools | System Information).

HKEY_LOCAL_MACHINE\SAM

The subkey HKEY_LOCAL_MACHINE\SAM is a hive that contains data related to security. The **Security Accounts Manager (SAM)** database is stored in this key and is where local user accounts and group memberships are defined. The entire security structure of your Windows XP system is stored in this key. In most cases, these data are not accessible from a Registry editor, but instead reside in a file named SAM in the *%systemroot%*\WINDOWS\system32\config directory.

This is another area of the Registry that you should not normally attempt to modify. Most of the data contained in this subkey are in binary or encrypted format. You should employ the user manager tools (that is, the Local Users and Groups section of the Computer Management tool) to manipulate the data stored in this subkey. Additionally, to prevent you from editing it, this subkey has a security setting such that only the System (or the System utility) has rights to read and alter its contents.

HKEY_LOCAL_MACHINE\SECURITY

The subkey HKEY_LOCAL_MACHINE\SECURITY is the container for the local security policy, which defines control parameters, such as password policy, user rights, account lockout, audit policy, and general security options for the local machine. This subkey maps to a hive file named SECURITY in the *%systemroot%*\WINDOWS\ system32\config directory.

 This is yet another area of the Registry that you should not attempt to modify. Most of the data contained in this subkey are in binary format or are encrypted. You should employ the Local Security Policy tool to manipulate the data stored in this subkey (see Chapter 5, "Users, Groups, Profiles, and Policies" and 6, "Windows XP Security and Access Controls"). Additionally, to prevent you from editing this subkey, it has a security setting such that only the System has rights to read and alter its contents.

HKEY_LOCAL_MACHINE\SOFTWARE

The subkey HKEY_LOCAL_MACHINE\SOFTWARE is the container for data about installed software and mapped file extensions. These settings apply to all local users. The \Software\Classes subkey contains the same information as the HKEY_CLASSES_ROOT key; in fact the HKEY_CLASSES_ROOT key is created by copying the data from the \Software\Classes subkey. This subkey maps to a hive file named SECURITY in the *%systemroot%*\WINDOWS\system32\config directory.

HKEY_LOCAL_MACHINE\SYSTEM

The subkey HKEY_LOCAL_MACHINE\SYSTEM is the container for the information required to boot Windows XP. This subkey stores data about startup parameters, loading order for device drivers, service startup credentials (settings and parameters), and basic operating system behavior. This key is essential to the boot process of Windows XP. It contains subkeys called control sets that include complete information about the boot process for the system. This subkey resides in a hive file named "system" in the *%systemroot%*\WINDOWS\system32\config directory.

This subkey also contains additional subkeys with settings for storage devices (such as MountedDevices) and control set boot status (Select), and possibly subkeys left over from upgrading from Windows NT 4.0 (Disk and Setup). The control set keys are named and numbered; for example, ControlSet001 and ControlSet003. In most cases, there will be only two control sets numbered 001 and 003. These two sets represent the original (001) system configuration set and a backup (003) of the last functioning system configuration set. Thus, there will always be a functioning configuration to allow the operating system to boot (see Chapter 13, "Booting Windows XP").

Each control set has four subkeys (refer to Figure 12-1):

- *Control*—This is the container for data related to controlling system startup, boot parameters, computer name, and necessary subsystems to initiate.

- *Enum*—This is the container for data regarding required device drivers and their configuration.

12

- *Hardware Profiles*—This is the container for data specific to the hardware profile currently in use.

- *Services*—This is the container for data about drivers, services, file systems, applications, and other required hardware components necessary to load all installed and active services during bootup. This subkey also defines the order in which services are called and the way that one service can call or query other services.

The value entries under the HKEY_LOCAL_MACHINE\SYSTEM\Select subkey are used to define how Windows XP uses its control. The four value entries are:

- *Default*—Defines which control set will be used during the next bootup

- *Current*—Lists the control set that was used to boot the current session

- *LastKnownGood*—Indicates the control set last used to boot and successfully log on a user (see later in this chapter for details and use)

- *Failed*—Lists the control set that was replaced by the control set from the LastKnownGood control set because of a failure to boot

The HKEY_LOCAL_MACHINE\SYSTEM\CurrentControlSet subkey is a redirector to the actual ControlSet### currently in use rather than a truly distinct subkey. This symbolic link is used to simplify the programming interface for applications and device drivers that need information from the active control set. Because of this redirection, when you need to make modifications to the control set, you should use the CurrentControlSet "subkey" to direct your changes to the active control set properly.

HKEY_CLASSES_ROOT

The **HKEY_CLASSES_ROOT** key (see Figure 12-4) is the container for information pertaining to application associations based on file extensions and COM object data. The contents of this key are copied from the HKEY_LOCAL_MACHINE\SOFTWARE\ Classes subkey. This key is maintained for backward compatibility with legacy applications and device drivers and is not strictly required by Windows XP.

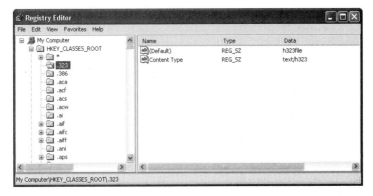

Figure 12-4   HKEY_CLASSES_ROOT contains file extension and com object settings and associations

As with other binary or protected keys, do not edit the contents of this key, or the HKEY_LOCAL_MACHINE\SOFTWARE\Classes subkey, directly. Instead, use the File Types tab of the Folder Options dialog box. To access this dialog box, select the Folder Options command from the Tools menu in Windows Explorer or My Computer or by launching the Folder Options applet from the Control Panel.

HKEY_CURRENT_CONFIG

The **HKEY_CURRENT_CONFIG** key (see Figure 12-5) is the container for data that pertain to whatever hardware profile is currently in use. This key is just a link to the HKEY_LOCAL_MACHINE\SYSTEM\CurrentControlSet\HardwareProfiles\Current subkey. This key is maintained for backward compatibility with legacy applications and device drivers and is not strictly required by Windows XP.

12

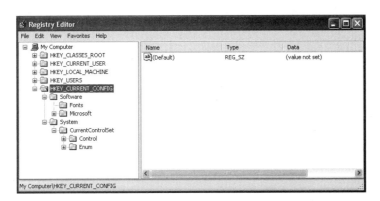

Figure 12-5   The HKEY_CURRENT_CONFIG/ key is maintained in Windows XP for backward compatibility

The contents of this key, and the HKEY_LOCAL_MACHINE\SYSTEM \CurrentControlSet\Hardware Profiles\Current subkey, should not be edited directly. Instead, the Hardware Profiles interface or Device Manager should be used. The Hardware Profiles interface is accessed by pressing the Hardware Profiles button on the Hardware tab of the System applet from the Control Panel. The Device Manager is accessed by pressing the Device Manager button on the Hardware tab of the System applet from the Control Panel or by selecting the Device Manager node from the Computer Management utility in Administrative Tools.

HKEY_CURRENT_USER

The **HKEY_CURRENT_USER** key (see Figure 12-6) is the container for the profile for whichever user is currently logged on. The contents of this key are built each time a user logs on by copying the appropriate subkey from the HKEY_USERS key. The contents of this key should not be edited directly; instead, you should modify a user's profile through conventional profile management techniques (see Chapter 5 for more information on profile management).

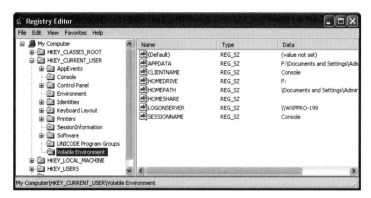

Figure 12-6   HKEY_CURRENT_USER contains data for whichever user is currently logged onto the system

HKEY_USERS

The **HKEY_USERS** key (see Figure 12-7) contains profiles for all users who have ever logged onto this system and the default user profile. The contents of this key are built each time the system boots by loading the default file and the locally stored copies of Ntuser.dat or Ntuser.man from user profiles (see Chapter 5). These locally stored copies are found in the \Documents and Settings\<*username*> directory on a Windows XP Professional system. To remove a user profile from this key, use the User Profiles tab of the System applet from the Control Panel. To alter the contents of a profile, use conventional profile management techniques (see Chapter 5 for more information on profile management) instead of attempting to edit this key directly. Note also that subkeys in this key use Windows Security IDs (SIDs) to identify users, rather than account names, which explains their cryptic alphanumeric names.

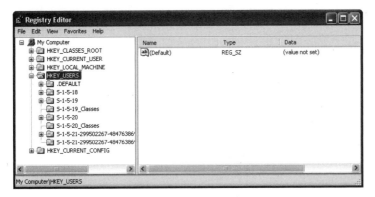

Figure 12-7   HKEY_USERS contains data for any user who's ever logged onto the system, plus a default user profile

HKEY_DYN_DATA

In some Registries, you may occasionally run across another main key named HKEY_DYN_DATA. This root or main key appears only on machines with Windows 95 or Windows 98 applications that use older versions of Plug and Play to detect and track hardware devices as they enter or leave a system. Because Windows XP Professional's Plug and Play implementation is vastly superior to these older versions, this entry exists solely to help the operating system maintain backward compatibility with older versions of Windows.

REGISTRY EDITORS

Because the structure of the Registry is so complex, special tools are required to operate on it directly. The primary Registry editor for Windows XP is launched by executing either Regedit.exe or Reg.exe. **Regedit** (see Figure 12-8) offers global searching, security manipulation, and combines all of the keys into a single display. **Reg** (see Figure 12-9) is the Console Registry Tool for Windows, a command-line utility that permits users, batch files, or programs to operate on the Registry, but that supports no attractive graphical user interface like that for Regedit.

Figure 12-8   Regedit is the older Registry editor that suffices for most uses

12

```
 ⌐ Command Prompt                                          - □ ×
F:\>reg

Console Registry Tool for Windows - version 3.0
Copyright (C) Microsoft Corp. 1981-2001.  All rights reserved

REG Operation [Parameter List]

  Operation  [ QUERY   | ADD    | DELETE  | COPY    |
               SAVE    | LOAD   | UNLOAD  | RESTORE |
               COMPARE | EXPORT | IMPORT ]

Return Code: (Except of REG COMPARE)

  0 - Successful
  1 - Failed

For help on a specific operation type:

  REG Operation /?

Examples:

  REG QUERY /?
  REG ADD /?
  REG DELETE /?
  REG COPY /?
  REG SAVE /?
  REG RESTORE /?
  REG LOAD /?
  REG UNLOAD /?
  REG COMPARE /?
  REG EXPORT /?
  REG IMPORT /?

F:\>
```

Figure 12-9   Reg.exe is a command-line utility that permits users, batch files, or
programs to operate on the Registry

Because it is a command-line utility and does not display the Registry's hierarchical organization in an easy-to-grasp form, Reg.exe is not as convenient or friendly as
Regedit.exe. However, both editors can be used to view keys and values (see Hands-on
Project 12-1), perform searches (see Hands-on Project 12-2), add new subkeys and value
entries, alter the data in value entries, and import and export keys and subkeys. For most
purposes, however, Regedit should be your primary Registry inspection and editing tool.

As already noted many times in this chapter, editing the Registry directly
should not be undertaken without forethought and planning. It is possible to
alter the Registry, whether on purpose or accidentally, in such a way as to ren-
der a system completely unrecoverable. If you don't know exactly what you
are doing, *don't do it!* Please also note that although earlier versions of
Windows included another GUI Registry editor called Regedt32.exe, that program is no longer available as part of Windows XP Professional. However,
executing Regedit32 launches the existing Registry editor tool.

Even when you do think you know exactly what you want to change in the Registry,
it is always a good idea to take precautions, such as the following:

- Back up all important data on the computer before editing the Registry.

- Make a distinct backup of all or part of the Registry. Saving each key or subkey individually is recommended (see Hands-on Project 12-3). Saving parts
  of the Registry to files enables you to restore parts of the Registry instead of
  the entire Registry. Store the backup files on local drives, network drives, and
  floppies or other removable media to ensure access.

- Reboot the machine before editing the Registry.

- Perform only a single Registry modification at a time. Test the results before proceeding.

- Reboot immediately after each change to force full system compliance with new settings in the Registry. This is not strictly necessary, but has often proved to be prudent.

- Always test changes on a nonproduction system hosting noncritical services before deploying on production systems.

REGISTRY STORAGE FILES

The files in which a static image of the Registry are stored reside in the *%systemroot%*\WINDOWS\system32\config and *%systemroot%*\WINDOWS\repair directories of the boot partition (see Figure 12-10). The Registry is not stored in files that match one-to-one with the top-level keys, as we explain shortly, but there are plenty of Registry data mapped into files for safekeeping (and to maintain backup or rollback versions of these data).

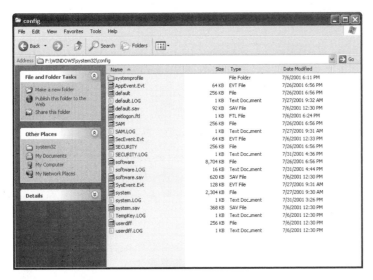

Figure 12-10   Explorer listing of the ...\system32\config folder shows various Registry file types and instances

The Registry is stored in various subkey, logging, and backup files, as indicated in Table 12-1.

Table 12-1 Registry Storage Files

Registry Key/Subkey	Storage Files
HKEY_LOCAL_MACHINE\SAM	Sam, Sam.log, Sam.sav
HKEY_LOCAL_MACHINE\SECURITY	Security, Security.log, Security.sav
HKEY_LOCAL_MACHINE\SOFTWARE	Software, Software.log, Software.sav
HKEY_LOCAL_MACHINE\SYSTEM	System, System.alt, System.log, System.sav
HKEY_USERS\.DEFAULT	Default, Default.log, Default.sav
(Not directly associated with a Registry key)	Userdiff, Userdiff.log
HKEY_CURRENT_USER	Ntuser.dat, Ntuser.dat.log

Note that only four of the HKEY_LOCAL_MACHINE subkeys, the Default subkey of the HKEY_USERS key, and the HKEY_CURRENT_USER key are stored in files. All of the other keys and subkeys are either built "on the fly" at bootup or are copies of a subsection of HKEY_LOCAL_MACHINE.

The HKEY_USERS key is built from the default file (which represents the default user profile's NTUSER.DAT file) and copies of profiles for all users who have ever logged onto the computer. These profiles are cached locally in the \Documents and Settings\<*username*> directory. A copy of the NTUSER.DAT or Ntuser.man file is copied into the repair directory for the currently logged-on user.

Notice that four extensions are used by the Registry storage files to identify the purpose or function of the file:

- *No extension*—The storage file for the subkey itself, also known as a hive file.

- *.alt*—The backup file for the subkey. Note that only the HKEY_LOCAL_MACHINE\SYSTEM subkey has a backup file.

- *.log*—A file containing all changes made to a key. This file is used to verify that all modifications to the Registry are properly applied.

- *.sav*—Copies of keys in their original state as created at the end of the text portion of Windows XP installation.

TechNet now includes a wonderful *Windows NT Magazine* article entitled "Inside the Registry" from Mark Russinovitch, a leading Windows expert. Online, you can find this article at www.microsoft.com/technet/treeview /default.asp?url=/TechNet/prodtechnol/winntas/tips/winntmag/ inreg.asp. Note that even though the article is somewhat outdated, it's still a worthwhile read.

Under Windows NT 4.0, the Registry files stored in the \Config directory were used to build the emergency repair disk (ERD). Under Windows 2000 and XP, these files are no longer copied onto the ERD when it is created. However, you can create your own custom ERD by manually copying the files in the \Config directory to a formatted floppy. You may find having a complete copy of the Registry quite handy when you need to perform a system repair or restore any portion of the Registry because of corruption or human error. If you need to use those files, you can always use the Import command in Regedit to restore that data to a damaged Registry.

REGISTRY FAULT TOLERANCE

If the Registry becomes corrupted or destroyed, Windows XP cannot function or even boot. Several mechanisms have been established to prevent the Registry from becoming damaged or to repair minor problems automatically. The fault tolerance of the Registry is sustained by its structure, memory residence, and transaction logs. These mechanisms ensure that all changes or operations performed on the Registry either succeed or fail. This prevents any partially applied alterations that would result in an invalid value entry or entries. Thus an "all or nothing" guarantee is supported no matter what method of alteration is used, including using a Registry editor or an administrative tool or alterations by an application. If the change action is interrupted (by power failure, too little CPU time, hardware failure, etc.), the Registry remains intact, even if the desired change was not implemented.

As previously mentioned, when a value entry is altered in the Registry, that change applies to the copy of the Registry stored in active memory. This means that the change affects the system immediately in most cases. A change to the Registry is only made permanent when key files are copied back to the hard drive. This activity occurs during a **flush**, a copy procedure to update the files on the hard drive with the new settings stored in the memory-resident version of the Registry. A flush occurs at shutdown, when forced by an application, or just after a Registry alteration.

Transaction logs are files wherein the system records edits, changes, and alterations to the Registry, similar to a list of orders or commands. When a flush occurs, the transaction log is updated to record all changes currently in memory, which will be written to the Registry storage files. This log is used by the system to verify automatically that all Registry changes are correct as the flush concludes.

A flush includes the following sequence of steps:

1. All alterations to a key are appended to that key's transaction log file (.log).

2. The key file is marked as being in transition.

3. The key file is updated with the new data from memory.

4. The key file is marked as complete.

If a system failure occurs between the time that the key file is marked as in transition and when it is marked complete, the original state of the key is recovered using the data from the transaction log. If the flush finishes uninterrupted, the system continues to perform normally.

12

The flush operation is performed on all keys except the SYSTEM subkey. This subkey contains system-critical data and is a major ingredient in a successful boot-up of Windows XP. For this reason, recovery cannot rely upon transaction logs. Instead, Windows XP updates the SYSTEM subkey using a different method:

1. The system file is marked as being in transition.

2. The system file is brought up to date with the state of the Registry from memory.

3. The system file is marked as being complete.

4. The System.alt file is marked as being in transition.

5. The System.alt file is brought up to date with the state of the Registry from memory.

6. The System.alt file is marked as being complete.

This dual-file process, with its primary and backup copies of the SYSTEM subkey file, ensures that no matter at which stage the update process might be interrupted, a complete and functional copy of the SYSTEM subkey file is available. If the failure occurs within the first three steps, the nonupdated System.alt file is used to boot. If the failure occurs within the last three steps, the updated system file is used to boot. Once booting is complete after a failure, Windows XP performs the update again to ensure that both copies of the SYSTEM subkey are exactly the same. However, if the failure occurs during the first three steps, any changes made to the system will have been lost.

Though Windows XP automatically manages the safety of the Registry through its fault-tolerance mechanisms (.log and .alt files), it is still important for you to take proactive measures to back up the Registry. There are several ways to create reliable Registry backups:

- Most Windows XP backup applications (for example, the built-in Backup tool and third-party products such as Veritas Backup Exec and Stac Replica) include support for full Registry backups. With these products, you can back up the Registry as part of your daily automated backup or as a distinct Registry-only procedure. Backing up the Registry with most of these products consists of selecting a "Back up the Registry" or "System State" check box when you make file/folder selections before initializing a backup.

- Regedit can be used to save all or part of the Registry to distinct files. This tool offers an Export command, which may be used to save the entire Registry, a single key, or any subportion of a key to a file (try Hands-on Project 12-3).

- Make a copy of the *%systemroot%*\WINDOWS\system32\config and *%systemroot%*\WINDOWS\repair directories manually. Just copy the contents to another location on your local computer, on a drive elsewhere on your network, or to a floppy disk (if size allows) or recordable CD.

■ Employ the *Microsoft Windows XP Professional Resource Kit* tools, such as Regback.exe. This tool offers command-line scripting capabilities. Explore the *Microsoft Windows XP Professional Resource Kit* for ideas on how to best employ these tools. You can see a syntax parameter listing for these and most command-line tools by issuing a "/?" parameter after the command from a Command Prompt (that is, *reg /?*, or *reg /? | more* if more than one screen's worth of data is displayed).

 No matter which backup method you employ, take the time to make two copies or perform the backup twice. This provides additional insurance in case your first backup fails.

RESTORING THE REGISTRY

Obviously, if you are going to take the time to create backups of the Registry, you must understand how to restore it. You have several options for restoring the Registry, depending on the method used to make a backup. Windows XP itself attempts to maintain a functional Registry, using its own internal automatic fault-tolerance mechanisms. If the automatic restoration process fails, you can first attempt to restore the Last Known Good Configuration. The **Last Known Good Configuration (LKGC)** is the state of the Registry stored in one of the control sets (covered earlier this chapter) when the last successful user logon occurred. If the Registry is damaged in such a way that it cannot fully boot or won't allow a user to log on, the LKGC option can restore the system to its prior working state.

This boot option is accessed by pressing F8 during the initial bootup of Windows XP when the boot menu is displayed. Don't worry; the basic boot menu even prompts you to press F8 if you need an alternate boot method. Pressing F8 reveals a new selection menu similar to the following:

Windows Advanced Options Menu

Please select an option:

Safe Mode

Safe Mode with Networking

Safe Mode with Command Prompt

Enable Boot logging

Enable VGA Mode

Last Known Good Configuration (your most recent settings that worked)

Directory Services Restore Mode (Windows domain controllers only)

12

Debugging Mode

Start Windows Normally

Reboot

Return to OS Choices Menu

Use the up and down arrow keys to move the highlight to your choice.

Use the arrow keys to highlight the Last Known Good Configuration selection, then press Enter. Keep in mind that any changes made to the system between the time the LKGC was stored and its use to restore the system will be lost. If the LKGC fails to restore normal system functions, you have only two options:

1. Use your backup software to restore the Registry files. This is only possible if your backup application offers a DOS-based restore mechanism that can bypass NTFS write restrictions. In other words, the backup software must operate without a functional Windows XP environment when launched from a bootable floppy. This type of software lets you restore files to the boot and system partitions (such as the Registry) so you can return to a functional OS. Unfortunately, these applications are few and far between. One such product is Replica from Stac (*www.stac.com*).

2. Reinstall Windows XP, either fully or as an upgrade. An upgrade may replace the section of the Registry that is causing the problems, allowing you to retain most of your configuration, but this is not guaranteed. A full, new installation of Windows XP will return the system to a preconfigured state and require you to repeat all post-installation changes you may have made.

If you are able to boot into the system, but things are not functioning the way they should; or if services, drivers, or applications are not loading or operating properly, you may need to restore the Registry in part or whole from backup. Simply use the same tool employed to create the backup to restore the Registry. Keep in mind that some tools allow you to restore portions of the Registry instead of the whole thing (see Hands-on Project 12-4).

No matter what method you employ to restore the Registry, it's always a good idea to reboot the system to ensure that the restore operation completed successfully and that the system is using only working (or more correctly, reverted-to) settings. It's also a good idea to retain the copies of the old Registry until you are confident that the system is functioning normally and have had the opportunity to create new backups. In other words, don't throw away the disks, erase the drives, or format the tapes containing the Registry backup; keep a few generations of Registry backups on hand, just in case.

WINDOWS XP PROFESSIONAL RESOURCE KIT REGISTRY TOOLS

The *Microsoft Windows XP Professional Resource Kit* includes several tools that can be used to manipulate the Registry. The *Microsoft Windows XP Professional Resource Kit* is a Microsoft product separate from the Windows XP Professional operating system. The *Microsoft Windows XP Professional Resource Kit* has additional documentation on Windows XP Professional, its operations, and its use, as well as a host of useful tools and utilities not included with the standard operating system software. You can purchase the *Microsoft Windows XP Professional Resource Kit* from Microsoft or from most software or book vendors.

Because many of these tools are command-line tools or require perusal of significant ancillary materials, we recommend that you read over the *Microsoft Windows XP Professional Resource Kit* documentation yourself before actually using these tools. Some of the key utilities include:

- *Regdump.exe*—A command-line tool used to dump all or part of the Registry to Stdout (this is an abbreviation for the standard output file, where the system creates output by default; normally this sends the output to a file whose name you specify when you run the command). The output of this tool is suitable for the Regini.exe tool. This tool is useful when you need to create scripts based on Registry content by creating a dump of existing settings.

- *Regfind.exe*—A command-line tool used to search the Registry for a key, value name, or value data based on keywords.

- *Compreg.exe*—A GUI tool used to compare two local or remote Registry keys and highlight all differences.

- *Regini.exe*—A command-line scripting tool used to add keys into the Registry.

- *Regback.exe*—A command-line scripting tool used to back up keys from the Registry.

- *Regrest.exe*—Another command-line scripting tool used to restore keys to the Registry.

- *Scanreg.exe*—A GUI tool used to search the Registry for a key, value name, or value data based on keywords.

12

CHAPTER SUMMARY

- ❏ The Windows XP Registry is a complex structure consisting of keys, subkeys, values, and value entries.

- ❏ The Registry should be manipulated with extreme caution. Unless absolutely necessary, the Registry should not be edited directly; instead, employ the Control Panel applets and Administration Tools to modify system settings.

- Windows XP maintains a functional Registry through several fault-tolerant measures, including transaction logs and backup of key files.

- The Registry is divided into five main keys. The primary and most important key is HKEY_LOCAL_MACHINE, because it hosts data ranging from system startup information to driver settings to the security database. For some, but not all, of these main keys, Windows XP Professional writes them to files in the *%systemroot%*\ WINDOWS\system32\config directory that are called hives or hive files.

- Windows XP includes two Registry editors, the graphical Regedit.exe and the command-line Reg.exe utility. The former is useful for global searches and general inspection or quick edits, the latter for performing systematic or comprehensive user- or program-driven Registry edits.

- As part of your normal system maintenance and administration, you should create copies of the Registry. Backing up the Registry often is the only way to ensure you have a functional Registry to restore in the event of a failure.

KEY TERMS

Binary — A Registry value entry data type that stores data in binary format.

DWORD — A Registry value entry data type that stores data in binary, hex, or decimal format.

data type — The setting on a Registry value entry that defines the data format of the stored information.

Expandable String — A Registry value entry data type that stores data in expandable text-string format containing a variable that is replaced by an application when used (for example, *%systemroot%*\FILE.EXE).

flush — Forcing the memory-resident copy of the Registry to be written to files stored on the hard drive. A flush occurs at shutdown, when forced by an application, or just after a Registry alteration.

hive — A discrete body of Registry keys, subkeys, and values stored in a file.

HKEY_CLASSES_ROOT — This Registry key contains the value entries that control the relationships between file extensions (and therefore file format types) and applications. This key also supports the data used in object linking and embedding (OLE), COM object data, and file-class association data. This key actually points to another Registry subkey named HKEY_LOCAL_MACHINE\SOFTWARE\Classes and provides multiple points of access to make itself easily accessible to the operating system itself and to applications that need access to the compatibility information already mentioned.

HKEY_CURRENT_CONFIG — This Registry key contains the value entries that control the currently active hardware profile; its contents are built each time the system is booted. This key is derived from data stored in the HKEY_LOCAL_MACHINE\SYSTEM\CurrentControlSet\HardwareProfiles\Current subkey. HKEY_CURRENT_CONFIG exists to provide backward-compatibility with Windows 95/98 applications.

HKEY_CURRENT_USER — This Registry key contains the value entries that define the user environment for the currently logged-on user. This key is built each time a user logs on to the system. The data in this key are derived from the HKEY_USERS key and the NTUSER.DAT and NTUSER.MAN files of a user's profile.

HKEY_LOCAL_MACHINE — This Registry key contains the value entries that control the local computer. This includes hardware devices, device drivers, and various operating system components. The data stored in this key are not dependent on a logged-on user or the applications or processes in use.

HKEY_USERS — This Registry key contains the value entries that define the user environments for all users who have ever logged on to this computer. As a new user logs on to this system, a new subkey is added for that user that is built either from the default profile stored in this key or from the roaming user profile associated with the domain user account.

key — A top-level division of the Registry. There are five keys in a Windows XP Registry. A key can contain subkeys.

Last Known Good Configuration (LKGC) — The state of the Registry stored in one of the control sets when the last successful user logon was performed. If the Registry is damaged in such a way that it will not fully boot or will not allow a user to log on, the LKGC option can restore the system to a previous state. Keep in mind that any changes made to the system between the time the LKGC was stored and its use to restore the system will be lost.

Multiple String — A Registry value entry data type that stores data in text-string format containing multiple human-readable values separated by null characters.

Reg — A special command-line utility that users, programs, or the operating system can use to access, inspect, create, or modify Registry keys.

Regedit — The 16-bit Registry editor. Regedit offers global searching and combines all of the keys into a single display. It can be used to perform searches, add new subkeys and value entries, alter the data in value entries, and import and export keys and subkeys.

Registry — The hierarchical database of system configuration data essential to the health and operation of a Windows XP system.

Security Accounts Manager (SAM) — The database of user accounts, group memberships, and security-related settings.

String — A Registry value entry data type that stores data in text-string format.

subkey — A division of a Registry key, such as HKEY_LOCAL_MACHINE. A subkey can contain other subkeys and value entries.

transaction log — A file created by Windows XP to record Registry changes. These files, with a .log extension, are used to verify that changes to the Registry are made successfully.

value — The actual data stored by a value entry.

12

value entry — A named Registry variable that stores a specific value or data string. A Registry value entry's name is typically a multiword phrase without spaces and with title capitalization.

REVIEW QUESTIONS

1. The Registry is the primary mechanism for storing data about Windows XP. Which of the following are configuration files used by other Microsoft operating systems and may still exist on Windows XP for backward compatibility? (Choose all that apply.)

   a. Win.ini

   b. Autoexec.bat

   c. System.ini

   d. Config.sys

2. The Registry is only used to store configuration data for native Windows 2000 applications, services, and drivers. True or False?

3. Which of the following tools is most highly recommended by Microsoft for editing the Registry? (Chose all that apply.)

   a. Control Panel applets

   b. Regedit

   c. Reg.exe

   d. Administrative Tools

4. The Registry is an exhaustive collection of system control parameters. True or False?

5. When editing the Registry, especially when attempting to alter the unseen defaults, which of the following pieces of information are important? (Choose all that apply.)

   a. syntax

   b. spelling

   c. subkey location

   d. valid values

   e. time zone

6. Changes made to the Registry never go into effect until the system is rebooted. True or False?

7. The Windows XP Professional Registry has how many default keys?

   a. 2

   b. 4

   c. 5

   d. 6

8. Which of the following can host subkeys or values?

   a. data type

   b. key

   c. subkey

   d. value data

9. Each of the highest-level keys of the Registry are stored in a distinct file on the hard drive. True or False?

10. Which Registry key contains the value entries that control the local computer?

    a. HKEY_LOCAL_MACHINE

    b. HKEY_CLASSES_ROOT

    c. HKEY_CURRENT_CONFIG

    d. HKEY_USERS

11. Which Registry key contains the value entries that define the user environment for the currently logged-on user?

    a. HKEY_LOCAL_MACHINE

    b. HKEY_CLASSES_ROOT

    c. HKEY_CURRENT_CONFIG

    d. HKEY_CURRENT_USER

12. Which Registry key contains the value entries that control the relationships between file extensions (and therefore file format types) and applications?

    a. HKEY_LOCAL_MACHINE

    b. HKEY_CLASSES_ROOT

    c. HKEY_CURRENT_CONFIG

    d. HKEY_USERS

13. Which Registry key contains the value entries that control the currently active hardware profile?

    a. HKEY_LOCAL_MACHINE

    b. HKEY_CLASSES_ROOT

    c. HKEY_CURRENT_CONFIG

    d. HKEY_CURRENT_USER

14. From which key can you delete subkeys, using the System applet?

    a. HKEY_LOCAL_MACHINE

    b. HKEY_CLASSES_ROOT

    c. HKEY_CURRENT_CONFIG

    d. HKEY_USERS

12

15. Some Windows 95 or 98 applications require a sixth Registry key. Windows XP adds the _____ key, which is actually a redirector rather than an actual key, to maintain backward compatibility.

16. After you've created a value entry, you can easily change its data type by using the Edit dialog box. True or False?

17. The value entry data type that can store binary, hex, or decimal formatted data is:

    a. String

    b. DWORD

    c. Multi-String

    d. Expandable String

18. Where are the files used to load the Registry at bootup stored on a Windows XP system?

    a. *%systemroot%*\config

    b. *%systemroot%*\system32\config

    c. *%systemroot%*\system\config

    d. *%systemroot%*\system32\repair

19. Which subkey of HKEY_LOCAL_MACHINE is the only subkey to have a backup file?

    a. SAM

    b. SOFTWARE

    c. SYSTEM

    d. SECURITY

20. The process of pushing Registry changes from memory to a hard drive file is known as _____ .

21. Which type of file (specified by file extension) does Windows XP use to record the changes to the Registry for verification purposes?

    a. .alt

    b. .sav

    c. .dat

    d. .log

22. Assume that your system is performing an update to the SYSTEM subkey. While altering the system file, before working on the System.alt file, a system crash occurs. When the system reboots, which of the following will occur?

    a. You'll be prompted whether to use the system or System.alt set of configuration parameters.

    b. The state of the Registry before changes to the SYSTEM subkey will be restored.

    c. The state of the Registry after changes to the SYSTEM subkey will be restored.

    d. The system will fail to boot because of a corrupt SYSTEM subkey.

23. Which subkey usually cannot be edited with a Registry editor?

    a. HARDWARE

    b. SOFTWARE

    c. SAM

    d. CurrentControlSet

24. Which control set subkey is the container for data related to controlling system startup, boot parameters, computer name, and necessary subsystems to initiate?

    a. Control

    b. Enum

    c. Hardware Profiles

    d. Services

25. Which subkey of HKEY_LOCAL_MACHINE\SYSTEM\Select indicates the control set that was last used to boot and successfully log on a user?

    a. Default

    b. Current

    c. LastKnownGood

    d. Failed

HANDS-ON PROJECTS

Project 12-1

 This hands-on project presents the necessary steps in viewing the current value of a value entry or determining if a value entry is even present in the Registry.

To view Registry value entries with Regedit:

1. Select **Start | Run**.

2. Type **regedit**, then click **OK**. The Registry Editor opens.

3. Double-click **HKEY_LOCAL_MACHINE**.

4. Locate and double-click **SOFTWARE** under HKEY_LOCAL_MACHINE.

5. Locate and double-click **Microsoft** under SOFTWARE.

6. Locate and double-click **Windows NT** under Microsoft.

7. Locate and double-click **CurrentVersion** under Windows NT.

8. Locate and select **Winlogon** under CurrentVersion.

9. In the right pane, locate and select **DefaultUserName**.

10. From the Edit menu, select **Modify**.

11. Notice that the value of this value entry is the name of your current user account.

12. Click **Cancel**.

13. In the left pane, scroll up until you see HKEY_LOCAL_MACHINE.

14. Double-click **HKEY_LOCAL_MACHINE**. Leave the system as is for the next hands-on project.

Project 12-2

To search for a value entry with Regedit:

This hands-on project requires that Hands-on Project 12-1 be completed. In this project, you use Regedit to locate a key or value without knowing its path within the Registry. You will begin at the system status point where the previous hands-on project ended.

1. From the **Edit** menu, select **Find**.

2. In the Find what field, type **DefaultUserName**.

3. Click **Find Next**. Regedit locates the first key, value, or data containing that string.

4. Notice that the first found match is AltDefaultUserName (be patient; this first search may take as long as a minute to complete).

5. From the Edit menu, select **Find Next** (or click the hotkey equivalent, F3). This is the actual DefaultUserName value entry that you viewed in Hands-on Project 12-1.

6. In the left pane, scroll up until you see HKEY_LOCAL_MACHINE.

7. Double-click **HKEY_LOCAL_MACHINE**. Leave the system as is for the next hands-on project.

Project 12-3

The ability to make backups of the Registry offers you an additional level of support in the event of a system problem or a human error in regard to the Registry. Plus, backing up the Registry is always a good idea before beginning any modifications to the Registry, either through the manual tool in Regedit or through any of the Control Panel or Administrative Tools utilities.

To back up a Registry key:

This hands-on project begins at the system status point where the previous hands-on project ended.

1. Make sure that the HKEY_USERS key is selected.

2. From the **File** menu, select **Export**.

3. Select a destination folder (such as c:\temp) of your choice in the **Save in:** pull-down menu.

4. Provide a file name, such as **HKUsave.reg**.

5. Make sure the **Selected branch** radio button at the bottom of the Export Registry File dialog box is selected and that HKEY_USERS is listed in the text field.

6. Click **Save**.

7. The Regedit tool will create a backup file of the selected key. Leave the system as is for the next hands-on project.

This procedure can be used to back up the entire Registry or just a small subset of subkeys, simply by selecting different keys or subkeys.

Project 12-4

If you have made any changes to the system or Registry since Hands-on Project 12-3 was performed, you may not want to perform this project, because it will discard those changes by restoring the state of the Registry from the saved file.

To restore a Registry key:

This hands-on project requires that Hands-on Project 12-3 be completed. It begins at the system status point where Hands-on Project 12-3 ended.

1. From the **File** menu, select **Import**.

2. Locate and select your **HKUsave.reg** file.

3. Click **Open**.

4. After a few moments of importing, a message stating whether the import succeeded is displayed; click **OK**.

5. From the **File** menu, select **Exit**.

As with backing up a Registry key, this procedure can be used to restore the entire Registry or just a small subset of subkeys simply by selecting different keys or subkeys. However, it does require that the same amount or even more data be backed up for the material to be restored.

Project 12-5

To use Reg.exe, the Windows Console Registry Tool:

1. Select **Start | All Programs | Accessories | Command Prompt**.

12

2. Type **reg** to produce the basic documentation for the utility.

3. Notice that each major key may be abbreviated for compactness.

4. Type **reg query "HKLM\SOFTWARE\Microsoft\Windows NT\CurrentVersion\Winlogon" /v DefaultUserName** to display the contents of that value entry (it should match your current logon name). Press **Enter**.

Project 12-6

To view security permissions with Regedit:

1. Launch Regedit (**Start**, **Run**, then type **Regedit** into the Open: textbox).

2. From the Window menu, select **HKEY_USERS**.

3. From the **Edit** menu, select **Permissions**.

4. Notice the Permissions dialog box for the Registry is identical to that used elsewhere in Windows XP.

5. Click **Cancel**.

6. From the **File** menu, select **Exit**.

CASE PROJECTS

1. Describe the actions that you can perform manually or that are performed automatically to provide protection or fault-tolerance mechanisms for the Windows XP Registry.

2. You have been asked to perform several Registry modifications to fine-tune an application. You'll be following detailed instructions from the vendor. What steps can you take to ensure that even if the vendor's instructions fail, you'll be able to return to a functioning Windows XP system?

13

BOOTING WINDOWS XP

After reading this chapter and completing the exercises, you will be able to:

♦ Understand the Windows XP boot process

♦ Troubleshoot system restoration by using Safe Mode

♦ Explain the operation of the key Windows XP startup files

♦ Understand the boot options offered through the Windows Advanced Options Menu

♦ Edit the Boot.ini file to manipulate the boot process

♦ Understand how multiboot configurations are created and how they function

On the surface, booting a computer might seem simple. But in reality, booting is a complex process. In fact, it is important to understand each step of the process by which an inert hunk of metal becomes a computer running Windows XP. This understanding is essential for the Microsoft certification exam, and for troubleshooting a system that won't boot properly.

In this chapter, you learn the steps that Windows XP takes to successfully complete a boot process. The process begins with the initial operation of the hardware, as it finds pointers to the software that ultimately leads to the choice of which operating system to run (and as it goes through the process of loading and starting Windows XP). The process culminates when the logon dialog box appears. It is only at this point that the Windows XP boot process is considered to be complete. At logon, the system makes a backup of the Registry and stores it as the Last Known Good Configuration. However, prior to logging on, the kernel, all subsystems, and services are started. This means scheduled tasks will execute at their appointed time and other network users can access shared resources from this system. But to complete the boot process, you must perform a successful logon.

THE BOOT PROCESS

All computers, whether hosting Windows XP or another operating system, go through a similar **boot process** when they are turned on. In Windows XP, this process is broken down into two major phases: the **boot phase** and the **load phase**.

The Windows XP boot process is actually a two-part process that includes both the boot phase and the load phase. The boot process takes place when the computer is first powered on, and when you choose Restart from the Shut Down Windows dialog box. This dialog box appears when you select Shut Down from the Start menu.

WINDOWS XP BOOT PHASE

The six steps of the Windows XP boot phase are as follows:

1. Power-on self test (POST)

2. Initial startup

3. Boot loader

4. Selecting the operating system

5. Detecting hardware

6. Selecting a configuration

Power-On Self Test

The **power-on self test (POST)** is the first step in the boot sequence for any computer with an operating system. The POST determines the amount of real memory, and whether or not all necessary hardware components, such as a keyboard, are present. The actual tests can differ, depending on how the **BIOS (Basic Input/Output System)** is configured. If the tests are successful, the computer boots itself. If the tests are unsuccessful, the computer reports the error by emitting a series of beeps and possibly displaying an error message and code on the screen. The number of beeps indicates the error, but differs from one BIOS to another. The software for the POST resides in a special, battery-powered chip called the **CMOS (complementary metal-oxide semiconductor)**. This chip can store not only the software necessary to conduct the POST, but also basic configuration information that the POST uses to check the amount of RAM installed in a system, along with other key information. Figure 13-1 shows a typical screen that results from the successful completion of the POST on an Intel PC.

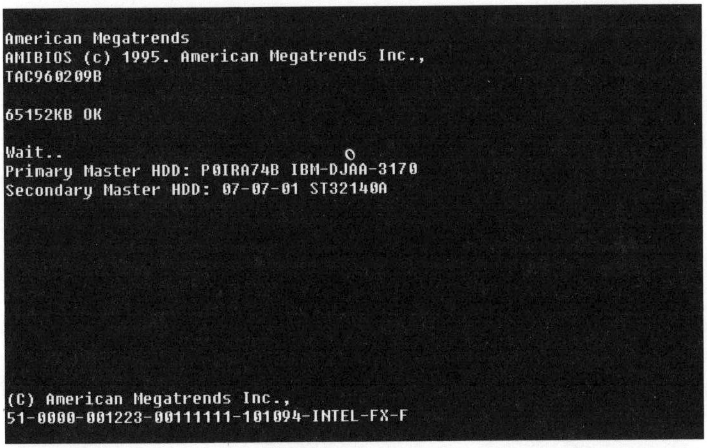

```
American Megatrends
AMIBIOS (c) 1995. American Megatrends Inc.,
TAC960209B

65152KB OK

Wait..                                        o
Primary Master HDD: P0IRA74B IBM-DJAA-3170
Secondary Master HDD: 07-07-01 ST32140A




(C) American Megatrends Inc.,
51-0000-001223-00111111-101094-INTEL-FX-F
```

Figure 13-1   The POST display on a PC

After the system POST is completed, each adapter card in the system performs its own self-test. For example, if a computer has a SCSI card installed in addition to its own built-in adapter cards, it checks its internal configuration and any related devices it sees when it runs its own POST. At the same time, a report on what it finds during this process appears on the computer monitor in text-only form (because there is no real operating system running at this point, screen output at this stage of the boot process is kept as simple and direct as possible). The screen shown in Figure 13-2 adds the report from an Adaptec 2940 SCSI controller to the information already supplied by the POST routine.

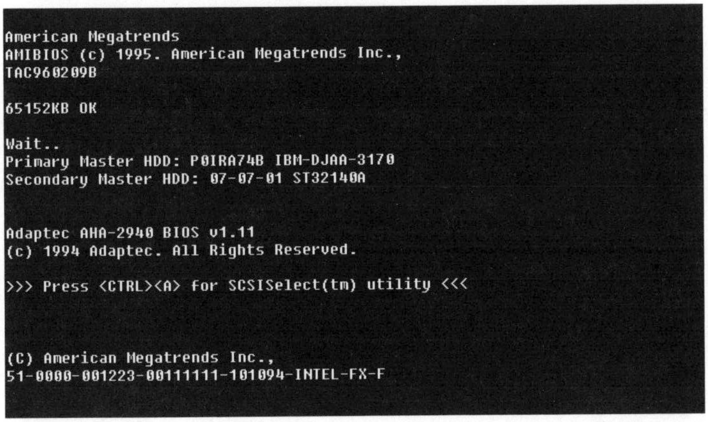

13

```
American Megatrends
AMIBIOS (c) 1995. American Megatrends Inc.,
TAC960209B

65152KB OK

Wait..
Primary Master HDD: P0IRA74B IBM-DJAA-3170
Secondary Master HDD: 07-07-01 ST32140A

Adaptec AHA-2940 BIOS v1.11
(c) 1994 Adaptec. All Rights Reserved.

>>> Press <CTRL><A> for SCSISelect(tm) utility <<<



(C) American Megatrends Inc.,
51-0000-001223-00111111-101094-INTEL-FX-F
```

Figure 13-2   Output from the BIOS on an Adaptec 2940 SCSI controller

Initial Startup

The initial startup sequence involves numerous files and initialization procedures. The first sector of the hard disk contains the Master Boot Record (MBR) and the partition table. The **Master Boot Record (MBR)** begins the boot process by looking up the partition table to determine which partition to use for booting. If you are booting from a floppy disk, the first sector contains the **partition boot sector**.

Table 13-1 outlines the startup files for Windows XP on x86 computers.

Table 13-1 Windows XP Startup Files

Filename	Location	Explanation
Ntldr	Root of startup disk	Windows XP boot loader for PC machines
Boot.ini	Root of startup disk	Windows XP PC boot menu information
Bootsect.dos	Root of startup disk	Provides DOS boot information for dual-boot PCs
Ntdetect.com	Root of startup disk	Windows XP hardware detection program
Ntbootdd.sys	Root of startup disk	Lets Windows XP access SCSI drives on PCs with SCSI controller with onboard BIOS disabled
Ntoskrnl.exe	%systemroot%\system32	Windows XP operating system kernel
Hal.dll	%systemroot%\system32	Hardware abstraction layer code (CPU driver for x86 chips)
SYSTEM key	%systemroot%\system32	Key Windows XP Registry data
Device drivers	%systemroot%\system32	PC-specific device drivers for Windows XP use

When the POST has successfully concluded, the BIOS tries to locate the startup disk. The BIOS represents a chip-based set of routines that DOS and Windows 95/98 use to drive all system input and output, including access to peripheral devices. Windows XP, on the other hand, uses its own built-in input/output logic and drivers, and ignores whatever BIOS is installed in a computer. By doing this, Windows XP is able to manage I/O more carefully than earlier Windows and DOS operating systems. It also helps to explain why applications that attempt to access drivers or the computer's BIOS or hardware directly are treated as ill behaved in the Windows XP environment.

If a floppy disk is in drive A when the BIOS checks that drive, it might use that drive as the startup disk (this decision depends on how the boot sequence has been configured in the PC's CMOS). If there is no floppy disk in that drive, or if the CMOS has been configured to boot from a hard disk, it uses the first hard disk it finds as the boot disk. Of course, if drive A is enabled for booting, and the floppy disk you have inserted in that drive does not have a partition boot sector, you get a "Non-system disk or disk error: Replace and press any key when ready" message, and the system won't start. This is one of the most common causes of boot failure in the Windows XP environment.

If you get the "Non-system disk or disk error" message because the system attempted to boot from a non-system floppy, remove the floppy and cycle the power off and on again. It is important to do this (rather than restarting with Ctrl+Alt+Delete) to avoid transferring boot-sector viruses to the computer.

When the BIOS uses the hard disk as its startup disk, it reads the MBR and loads that into memory. The BIOS then transfers system control to the MBR. The MBR scans the partition table to locate the system partition. When the MBR locates the system partition, it loads sector 0 of the partition into memory, and executes it. Sector 0 (zero) can contain a diagnostic program, a utility such as a virus scanner, or a partition boot sector that contains the startup code for the operating system. Should the computer boot from a floppy, only the partition boot sector is used.

In general, the MBR is independent of the operating system. For example, the same MBR is used in x86 systems to boot to Windows 95, 98, MS-DOS, Windows 2000, Windows NT, Windows XP, and Windows 3.x.

The partition boot sector is completely dependent on the operating system and file system in use. For example, the partition boot sector in a Windows XP computer is responsible for a number of operating-system-specific functions. It must understand enough of the file system in use to find **Ntldr** (the program that locates and loads the Windows XP operating system files in the root folder). On a hard drive with a FAT partition, the partition boot sector is generally one sector long, and points to another location on disk that ultimately permits the computer to find and launch Ntldr. On an NTFS partition, because the partition boot sector can be as many as 16 sectors long, it can contain all the necessary file system code needed to locate and launch Ntldr, without requiring transfer of control to another area on disk. Thus, the partition boot sector is responsible for loading a boot loader (Ntldr) into memory and initiating boot loader execution.

At this point, the **system partition**, the partition that contains the MBR and partition boot sector, must be on the first physical hard drive in the system. However, the **boot partition**—the partition that contains the Windows XP files—can be on the same partition, a different partition on the same drive, or on another drive entirely within the local computer. In other words, you boot Windows XP from the system partition, and run the operating system from the boot partition.

Because this terminology is counterintuitive and because it appears on numerous Windows XP-related Microsoft exams, it's important to remember this reversal of terminology.

Boot Loader

Boot loader processing and files select an operating system to boot, and load the related operating system files from the boot partition. On PCs, once the boot OS is selected from the Boot.ini menu, Ntldr controls the operating system selection and hardware detection processes before the Windows XP kernel is initialized.

Ntldr, Boot.ini, Bootsect.dos, Ntdetect.com, and Ntbootdd.sys may all be present in the root directory of the startup disk (also known as the system partition; see Figure 13-3). Some files might be dimmed because they have the read-only attribute. The partition hosting the boot loader can be formatted with FAT, FAT32, or NTFS. Of this collection of files, Ntldr, Ntdetect.com, and Boot.ini must always be present for Windows XP to boot (the other two are optional, and depend on the configuration of the particular machine in use).

 The Folder Options applet must be configured to show all hidden and system files; otherwise, most of these boot files will not be shown.

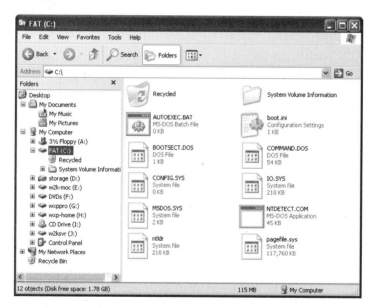

Figure 13-3   The system partition on a typical Windows XP system

 Bootsect.dos appears only if the machine has been configured to dual-boot between Windows XP/2000/NT and DOS, Windows 3.x, or Windows 9x. Ntbootdd.sys appears only when a SCSI controller has its built-in BIOS controller disabled; this file supplies the necessary controller driver that the hardware would otherwise provide.

At this point, Ntldr switches the processor into 32-bit flat memory mode. When an x86 computer starts, it is running in real mode, which means it is functioning as an old-fashioned 8088 or 8086 computer. Because Ntldr is a 32-bit program, it must

change the processing mode to support the 32-bit flat memory model it uses before it can perform any further processing.

Next, Ntldr starts the appropriate file system. The code to access both FAT and NTFS file systems is programmed into Ntldr so that it can read, access, and copy files on either type of file system.

Next, Ntldr reads the Boot.ini file and displays the operating system selections it contains. The screen that appears at this point is usually called the boot loader screen or the **boot selection menu**, and represents the point at which users can select which operating system they would like to load (or which form of Windows XP graphics operation they would like to use).

A typical boot selection menu appears in Figure 13-4. Notice the prompt to access troubleshooting and advanced startup options by pressing F8. These options are discussed in a later section of this chapter.

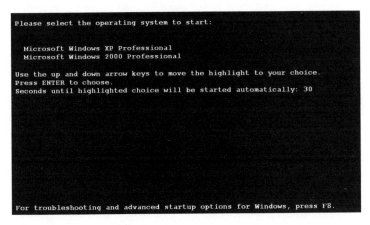

Figure 13-4   A typical Windows XP boot selection menu

Notice on this particular system, Windows XP Professional is present with Windows 2000 Professional. In fact, Windows XP coexists with numerous other operating systems, including those that depend on DOS for their underpinnings.

When you do not manually alter the highlighted selection of the boot menu, a line below the menu displays a counter: "Seconds until highlighted choice will be started automatically: 30." If a selection is not made before the counter reaches zero, the highlighted operating system starts automatically. To change the default operating system to load or the amount of time to wait before automatically loading the highlighted operating system, change the settings in the Boot.ini file, which is discussed in greater detail later in this chapter. In addition, pressing the up arrow or down arrow key halts the timer.

If the user selects an operating system other than Windows XP or Windows NT, the boot loader loads Bootsect.dos and hands over control of the system. The other operating system then starts normally because Bootsect.dos contains the partition boot sector

13

for that operating system. However, if the user selects a version of Windows XP, the boot loader executes Ntdetect.com to gather hardware information.

The remaining functions of Ntldr (operating system selection, hardware detection, and configuration selection) are discussed later in this section. For now, note that Ntldr maintains control of the computer until it loads Ntoskrnl.exe and passes the hardware information and system control to that program.

Detecting Hardware

Ntdetect.com is executed by the boot loader and is used to collect a list of hardware currently installed in the computer. Ntdetect checks the computer ID, bus/adapter type, video, keyboard, communication ports, parallel ports, floppy disks, and mouse or pointing devices. It creates a system profile to be compared to Windows XP Registry entries that describe the system later during the boot process, at which point the operating system looks for discrepancies or potential problems.

Once hardware is detected, the system needs to select a system configuration, otherwise known as a hardware profile. If a single hardware profile is defined, this is the one that is used. If two or more hardware profiles are present, the system attempts to select a profile based on detected hardware. If the system cannot make an automatic selection, you'll be prompted to manually select a hardware profile.

TROUBLESHOOTING AND ADVANCED STARTUP OPTIONS

Windows XP has combined the boot and recovery options of Windows NT and Windows 95/98. The result is a more robust operating system and additional options to restore a malfunctioning system to a functional state. To access the additional startup options, when the boot menu appears, press F8 before the timer expires. Once F8 is pressed, the Windows Advanced Options Menu appears (see Figure 13-5).

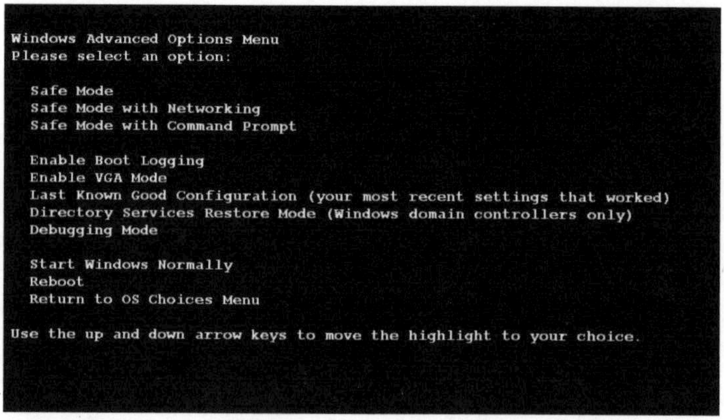

```
Windows Advanced Options Menu
Please select an option:

  Safe Mode
  Safe Mode with Networking
  Safe Mode with Command Prompt

  Enable Boot Logging
  Enable VGA Mode
  Last Known Good Configuration (your most recent settings that worked)
  Directory Services Restore Mode (Windows domain controllers only)
  Debugging Mode

  Start Windows Normally
  Reboot
  Return to OS Choices Menu

Use the up and down arrow keys to move the highlight to your choice.
```

Figure 13-5   The Windows Advanced Options Menu

The contents of this menu are somewhat dependent on installed components, such as the Remote Installation Service, but it typically contains the following items:

- *Safe Mode*—Boots Windows XP with only the minimum required system files and device drivers. Safe Mode does not load networking components (see Hands-on Project 13-3)

- *Safe Mode with Networking*—Boots Windows XP in the same manner as Safe Mode, but adds networking components (see Hands-on Project 13-6)

- *Safe Mode with Command Prompt*—Boots Windows XP in the same manner as Safe Mode, but boots to a command prompt instead of to the GUI environment

- *Enable Boot Logging*—A toggle that enables or disables the boot process and writes details to a log file regarding drivers and services. The log file is located at %systemroot%\Ntbtlog.txt

- *Enable VGA Mode*—Boots Windows XP normally, but uses only the basic VGA video driver (see Hands-on Project 13-5)

- *Last Known Good Configuration*—Boots Windows XP with the **Last Known Good Configuration (LKGC)**, the state of the Registry as it was recorded during the last successful user logon (see Hands-on Project 13-4)

- *Directory Services Restore Mode*—Valid only on Windows XP domain controllers; used to boot Windows XP and restore Active Directory

- *Debugging Mode*—Boots Windows XP normally, but sends debugging information to another system over a serial cable. Details about using this option are included in the *Microsoft Windows XP Professional Resource Kit*.

Advanced Options for booting can be used to recover from a wide variety of system problems or failures. Safe Mode offers the ability to boot into a functioning system even when specific drivers are corrupted or failing. This includes bypassing bad video drivers, network drivers, and GUI controls by booting into Enable VGA Mode, Safe Mode (without networking support), and/or Safe Mode with Command Prompt, respectively. In most cases, this allows you to replace or remove the problematic driver before rebooting back into normal mode.

If a problem is occurring and you are unable to discern its exact cause or nature, you might want to choose Enable Boot Logging from the Advanced Options menu to record the process of steps performed between the boot menu and the logon prompt. The resultant file, *%systemroot%*\Ntbtlog.txt, can provide clues as to the driver, system, or procedure that is causing the system malfunction.

If you've recently installed a driver or entire software product, or just modified the Registry, and the result is a system that does not fully boot, the Last Known Good Configuration is a great first step in returning the system to a functional state. The LKGC returns the system to the state of the Registry at the time of the last successful logon.

13

If none of these options provides you with a method to restore your system, you do have one final option from the Windows Advanced Options Menu, namely Debugging Mode. This mode is used in conjunction with a second computer connected by a serial cable. Debugging Mode causes the boot process to send detailed information on activities to the companion system. This information can be used to determine at what point in the boot process problems are occurring. The information created by Debugging Mode is rather complex and is typically used only by high-end programmers. If you want more details on the Debugging Mode process and how to interpret the extracted data, consult the *Microsoft Windows XP Professional Resource Kit*.

BOOT CONFIGURATION AND SELECTING AN OPERATING SYSTEM

The Windows XP boot configuration can be controlled through its configuration file, Boot.ini. As previously mentioned, Boot.ini is located in the root directory of the system partition, and is used by the boot loader to display the list of available operating systems. This file consists of two sections: [boot loader] and [operating systems]. A typical Boot.ini file is shown in Figure 13-6.

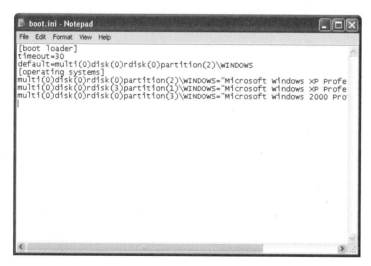

Figure 13-6 Boot.ini viewed through Notepad

[boot loader]

The [boot loader] section of the Boot.ini file contains two items: timeout and default. The *timeout* setting defines the number of seconds the system waits for the user to select an operating system before loading the default operating system. If timeout is set to zero, Ntldr immediately loads the default operating system without displaying the boot loader screen. To cause the system to wait indefinitely for a selection, set the timeout to –1. This setting, however, can only be altered by using a text editor, because it is an illegal value for the setting from the System icon in the Control Panel. (See the section later in this chapter on editing Boot.ini, which explains how to edit this file, and what kind of text editor to use.) The *default* setting in Boot.ini lists the path to the default operating system.

[operating systems]

The [operating systems] section of Boot.ini lists the available operating systems. Each listing contains the path to the boot partition for the operating system, the text displayed in the boot loader screen, and optional parameters. The text is clipped in the screen capture in Figure 13-6, but here's what it looks like in its entirety:

```
multi(0)disk(0)rdisk(0)partition(2)\WINDOWS="Microsoft
Windows XP Professional" /fastdetect

multi(0)disk(0)rdisk(3)partition(1)\WINDOWS="Microsoft
Windows XP Professional" /fastdetect

multi(0)disk(0)rdisk(0)partition(3)\WINDOWS="Windows 2000
Professional"
```

The following list details some of the switches that can be added to the end of entries in the [operating systems] section of Boot.ini. In most cases, you'll want to employ the F8 Windows Advanced Options Menu (see earlier this chapter) to access troubleshooting boot methods. However, you can employ the following switches and switch combinations to mimic the Windows Advanced Options Menu selections in your Boot.ini file:

- /BASEVIDEO—Starts Windows XP in standard VGA mode (640 x 480) with 16 colors
- /BAUDRATE=n—Sets the baud rate for the serial connection used in kernel debugging. The default is 9600, a setting up to 115,200 can be used.
- /BOOTLOG—Enables boot logging
- /CRASHDEBUG—Loads the kernel debugger but remains inactive until a STOP error occurs
- /DEBUG—Loads the debugger and allows access by a host debugger connected to the computer
- /DEBUGPORT={com1|com2|1394}—Sets the port for debugging
- /FASTDETECT={com1|com2|...}—Specifies a serial port to skip during bootup hardware scanning. If no com port is specified, all ports are skipped.
- /MAXMEM=n—Sets the maximum amount of RAM the OS can consume
- /NOGUIBOOT—Boots without showing the splash screen. Does not determine whether Windows XP GUI environment or command prompt is booted.

13

- */NODEBUG*—Disables the debugger

- */NUMPROC=n*—Sets the number of processors on a multi-CPU system the OS is allowed to use

- */SAFEBOOT:MINIMAL*—Boots into Safe Mode

- */SAFEBOOT:NETWORK*—Boots into Safe Mode with Networking

- */SAFEBOOT:MINIMAL(ALTERNATESHELL)*—Boots into Safe Mode with Command Prompt

- */SOS*—Displays the device driver names when they are loaded

 The switches used in the Boot.ini file are not case sensitive.

Advanced RISC Computing Pathnames

In the Boot.ini file, the path pointing to the \WINDOWS directory is written using the **Advanced RISC Computing (ARC) pathname** naming conventions. These pathnames are described as follows:

- *scsi(n) or multi(n)*—This portion of the path indicates the type of the device on which the operating system resides. *scsi* is used if the operating system is on a SCSI hard disk that is connected to a SCSI adapter that has a disabled built-in BIOS. *multi* is used for other hard disks including IDE, EIDE, and SCSI with a built-in BIOS. The *(n)* indicates the hardware adapter from which to boot. It is replaced with a number corresponding to the correct hardware adapter, numbered ordinally (starting with zero).

- *disk(n)*—This portion of the path indicates which SCSI bus number should be used. The *(n)* always equals zero when the adapter is a multiadapter (that is, the ARC494 path starts with multi); otherwise, it is numbered ordinally.

- *rdisk(n)*—This portion of the path indicates the SCSI LUN number or selects which of the hard disks attached to the adapter contains the operating system. *(n)* always equals zero when the adapter is SCSI; otherwise, it is numbered ordinally.

- *partition(n)*—This portion of the path selects the disk partition that contains the operating system files. Partition is numbered cardinally (starting with 1).

- *\path*—The final portion of the path indicates the directory on the partition in which the operating system files are found. The default path for Windows XP is \WINDOWS.

- *fixmbr*—Repairs the Master Boot Record

- *format*—Formats a disk

- *help*—Displays a list of commands available in the Recovery Console

- *listsvc*—Lists the services available

- *logon*—Logs onto Windows XP

- *map*—Displays the drive letter mappings

- *mkdir (md)*—Creates a new folder

- *more*—Displays a text file

- *rmdir (rd)*—Deletes a folder

- *rename (ren)*—Renames a file

- *set*—Displays and sets console environment variables

- *systemroot*—Sets the current folder to the Systemroot folder

Emergency Repair Process

If your problem is caused by corrupt or missing system files, your startup environment, or your partition boot sector, you might want to use the emergency repair process. You must reboot your machine with the Windows XP Setup disks or the Windows XP Professional CD. Setup asks if you would like to install Windows XP. Press Enter to start the installation process. Then you are prompted whether you want to reinstall Windows XP or repair an existing version of Windows XP. Press R to repair Windows XP. Press R again to repair your system using the emergency repair process. You'll then have two options for repairing Windows XP:

- *Fast repair*—Requires no user interaction; automatically attempts to repair problems related to the Registry, system files, the boot volume, and your startup environment

- *Manual repair*—Enables the user to choose to repair the Registry, system files, the boot volume, or startup environment

If the emergency repair process is successful, the PC reboots automatically, and everything should be in working order again. As a last resort, if the emergency repair process cannot repair the system, you might consider reinstalling Windows XP. However, this method is time-consuming, and you might need to reinstall many of your applications and upgrades.

Remote OS Installation

Administrators can also enable **remote OS installation**, which can be used along with the Microsoft IntelliMirror technologies to recover an entire PC, including a user's data, individual configurations, and applications. Remote OS installation is a component of the optional Windows Server **Remote Installation Services (RIS)** (see Chapter 2, "Installing Windows XP Professional"), which allows a user to rebuild the computer's entire image remotely across the network. No on-site technical support is necessary, minimizing both administrative costs and user downtime.

Client computers that can participate in a remote OS installation must have a **PXE (Pre-boot Execution)** environment. Network PCs and computers that comply with an industry-standard hardware guide called PC98 have this ROM. If a computer does not have the PXE remote-boot ROM, an RIS remote-boot disk can be used with a supported PCI-based network interface card (NIC). These client machines must also use a DHCP (Dynamic Host Configuration Protocol) server on the network.

When a user starts a client with either the PXE remote-boot ROM or an RIS remote-boot disk, the client can request an installation of Windows XP Professional from a remote RIS server. The server, in turn, provides one of the following types of installations:

- *CD-based*—Similar to installing the OS with a CD, but the source files are on another machine (the RIS server) on the network

- *Remote Installation Preparation (RIPrep) desktop image*—After installing Windows XP Professional, installing applications, and making configuration changes on one workstation, an administrator clones the image of that machine and replicates it on an RIS server. The entire **Remote Installation Preparation (RIPrep)** image can then be deployed to other workstations with remote OS installation.

Once the images are on the RIS server, the server can be used to install those images to any client that is remote-boot enabled. A user can initiate a network service boot by pressing the F12 key when booting up, at which time the RIS server installs the Client Installation Wizard. This Wizard uses Group Policies to give the user a list of available installation options from Active Directory. If there is only one installation option, the user is simply prompted with a confirmation screen, and the installation begins. Otherwise, the four installation options are:

- *Automatic Setup*—Prompts the user with a list of OS options if there is more than one OS installed, then an unattended installation begins

- *Custom Setup*—Allows the user to specify the computer name and the location where the computer account should reside in Active Directory

- *Restart a Previous Setup Attempt*—Restarts the remote OS installation process if a previous installation attempt failed

- *Maintenance and Troubleshooting*—Provides the user with access to third-party maintenance, pre-OS installation maintenance, and troubleshooting tools

CHAPTER SUMMARY

- ❐ IntelliMirror consists of a set of features within Windows XP utilizing user and group policies, folder redirection, and the Windows Installer Service (WIS) for backing up and restoring users' data, personalized settings, and applications.

- ❐ Windows XP includes built-in backup features. You should thoroughly understand the Backup utility and how it can be used to back up and restore a PC.

- ❐ You can use the emergency repair process or ASR to repair a system that has failed.

- ❐ You can use the System Restore feature to return the system to a previously saved state.

- ❐ You can use driver rollback to remove a bad driver and return to a previously functioning driver.

- ❐ You can rely upon WFP to keep your system files in working order.

- ❐ You can use Automatic Updates to keep your system in line with the latest patches from Microsoft.

- ❐ You can install and use the Recovery Console to recover user settings in the event of a system failure.

- ❐ You can use the Remote Installation Services (RIS) for a complete remote system restoration.

KEY TERMS

backup type — A backup configuration that determines how often data is backed up and how old and new files are handled. The types of backups are copy, daily, differential, incremental, and normal.

Backup utility — Windows XP's built-in tool that enables users to back up and restore their data and system configurations in case of a hardware or software failure.

copy backup — A method of backing up all selected files without marking them as being backed up.

daily backup — A method of backing up only the selected files that have been created or modified on the day that the backup is being performed. They are not marked as being backed up.

differential backup — A method of backing up selected files that have been created or modified since the last full backup. They are not marked as being backed up.

folder redirection — A component of IntelliMirror technologies that uses group policies to place specified user folders on a share on the network.

incremental backup — A method of backing up selected files that have been created or modified since the last normal or incremental backup. These files are marked as being backed up.

IntelliMirror — A set of features within Windows XP that utilizes policies, folder redirection, and the Windows Installer Service (WIS) for backing up and restoring users' data, personalized settings, and applications.

14

normal (or full) backup — A method of backing up all selected files and marking them as being backed up.

PXE (Pre-boot Execution) — A standard environment in PC98-compliant computers and network computers that can be used for a remote OS installation.

Recovery Console — A command-line interface that provides administrative tools useful for recovering a system that is not booting correctly.

remote OS installation — A component of Remote Installation Services (RIS) that can install Windows XP Professional on remote-boot-enabled PCs across a network.

Remote Installation Services (RIS) — An optional service in Windows Server that works with various other services to enable remote installations, including a remote operating system installation.

Remote Installation Preparation (RIPrep) — A type of installation used with remote OS installation whereby an administrator can take an entire image of one Windows XP Professional machine and install it onto other workstations. That image can include the OS as well as installed applications and configuration settings.

System State data — A collection of system-specific data that can be backed up and restored using the Windows XP Backup utility.

Windows Installer Service (WIS) — A Windows XP component that manages the installation and removal of applications by applying a set of centrally defined setup rules during the installation process.

REVIEW QUESTIONS

1. Which of the following types of media can be used to back up a user's data? (Choose all that apply.)

   a. tape drives

   b. external hard drives

   c. logical drives

   d. network shares

2. The Recovery Console can be used to stop and start services. True or False?

3. Which of the following could *not* participate in remote OS installation?

   a. a network computer with no RIS remote boot disk

   b. a PC with a PXE-based remote boot ROM, but with no RIS remote boot disk

   c. a PC with an RIS remote boot disk, but with no PXE-based remote boot ROM

   d. an undocked laptop with an RIS remote boot disk

4. Which of the following backup types backs up only the selected files that have been created or modified since the last normal or incremental backup? (Choose all that apply.)

   a. normal

   b. daily

   c. differential

   d. incremental

5. Windows XP automatically records new restoration points at which of the following events?

   a. 24 hours of computer uptime

   b. every logon

   c. application installation through Install Shield

   d. unsigned driver installation

6. Which of the following boot options is used to send debugging information from one computer to another on the network?

   a. Last Known Good Configuration

   b. Safe Mode with networking

   c. Enable boot logging

   d. Debugging Mode

7. The WFP automatically protects core system files, which includes some font files. True or False?

8. Which of the following IntelliMirror technologies is associated with recovering a user's personal desktop settings?

   a. user data management

   b. software installation

   c. user setting management

   d. user desktop management

9. Which of the following items are backed up when backing up the System State data, using the Backup utility? (Choose all that apply.)

   a. COM+ Class Registration database

   b. Registry files

   c. system boot files

   d. the \system32 directory

10. Folder redirection is set up using the Synchronization Manager. True or False?

14

11. When the _____ repair option is run, the system automatically attempts to repair problems related to the Registry, system files, the boot volume, and the startup environment.

12. Which of the following backup types marks backed up files as being backed up? (Choose all that apply.)

    a. copy

    b. daily

    c. differential

    d. incremental

    e. normal

13. Which of the following users can use the Backup utility to back up secured files on a Windows XP Professional computer? (Choose all that apply.)

    a. a member of the Administrators group

    b. a member of the Backup Operators group

    c. any user that has Log On Locally rights

    d. a member of the Backup utility group

14. Windows XP's Automatic Update is configured to install new updates automatically by default. True or False?

15. ASR is used to perform what action?

    a. restore the entire system from backup initiated with a floppy

    b. recover lost administrator passwords

    c. restore system files required for booting

    d. repair a damaged Registry

16. You can install the Recovery Console by using the WINNT32.exe program on the Windows XP CD with the _____ switch.

17. Driver Rollback is part of which Windows XP tool?

    a. ASR

    b. Device Manager

    c. System Restore

    d. Recovery Console

18. The Desktop Cleanup Wizard automatically launches every 30 days. True or False?

19. _____ can be used along with IntelliMirror technologies to recover an entire PC's image.

20. In order to use the Remote Installation Services (RIS), a machine must be a DHCP client. True or False?

21. Which of the following are types of installations that an RIS server can offer a client?

    a. client-based

    b. RIPrep desktop image

    c. CD-based

    d. network-based

22. A user can initiate a network service boot by pressing the _____ key when booting up.

23. When a client PC requests a remote OS installation, which of the following tools does an RIS server install first on the client?

    a. Recovery Console

    b. Client Installation Wizard

    c. Windows XP Professional

    d. PXE Remote Boot ROM

24. Which of the following setup options can an RIS server provide for a remote OS installation through the Client Installation Wizard? (Choose all that apply.)

    a. Automatic Setup

    b. Custom Setup

    c. Restart a Previous Setup Attempt

    d. Maintenance and Troubleshooting

HANDS-ON PROJECTS

Project 14-1

To enable your files to be synchronized with the network's copy of your files when you log off:

1. Open Synchronization Manager (**Start | All Programs | Accessories | Synchronize**).

2. Click **Setup**, then click the **Logon/Logoff** tab (see Figure 14-6).

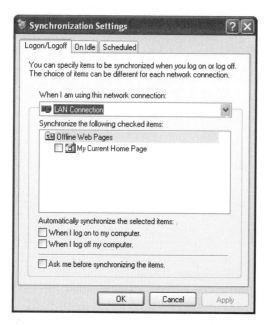

Figure 14-6 Synchronization Settings dialog box, Logon/Logoff tab

3. In the When I am using this network connection list, select the network connection you want to use.

4. In the Synchronize the following checked items list, select the files or folders you want to synchronize when you log onto and log off the network.

5. Under Automatically synchronize the selected items, select both **When I log on to my computer** and **When I log off my computer**.

6. Click **OK** to close the Synchronization Settings dialog box.

7. You can verify file synchronization by creating a document on your system, then logging off. Go to the server system or another client and check to see that the document was automatically stored on the network server.

Project 14-2

This hands-on project assumes the Control Panel is in Classic View.

To remove applications and repair applications:

1. Open the Control Panel (**Start | Control Panel**).

2. Double-click **Add or Remove Programs**.

3. Click the **Change or Remove Programs** button.

4. Follow the prompts to make the necessary changes.

5. Close any open dialog boxes or windows and the Add/Remove Programs applet. Restart your computer if prompted.

Project 14-3

To back up and restore the contents of your My Documents folder using the Windows Backup utility:

1. Select **Start | All Programs | Accessories | System Tools | Backup**.

2. If the tool launched in Wizard mode, click the **Advanced Mode** link to switch to the utility interface.

3. Click the **Backup** tab.

4. Check the box next to **My Documents**. Notice that a gray check mark automatically appears next to the drive containing My Documents and that the checkboxes next to each of the subdirectories under My Documents are automatically checked.

5. In the bottom-left corner, change path in the Backup media or file name field to **c:\backup.bkf**.

6. Look over your options, then click **Start Backup**.

7. When the backup is complete, click **Close** to exit the Backup Progress dialog box.

8. The Backup Job Information dialog box appears. Click **Start Backup**.

To restore your files, perform the following steps:

9. Click the **Restore and Manage Media** tab.

10. Expand the left pane listing of File to view the drive-level contents of the backup you just performed.

11. Mark one or more checkboxes beside folders or files within the backup.

12. Click **Start Restore**.

13. Click **OK** to initiate restore without viewing Advanced options.

14. Once the Restore is complete, close all dialog boxes and close the Backup utility.

14

Project 14-4

To schedule a backup of your My Documents folder, using the Windows Backup utility:

1. Select **Start | All Programs | Accessories | System Tools | Backup**.

2. If the Backup or Restore Wizard does not load, click **Tools**, then **Switch to Wizard Mode**.

3. The Backup Wizard Welcome screen is displayed. Click **Next**.

4. At the next screen, select the **Back up files and settings** radio button. Click **Next**.

5. Select the **My documents and settings** radio button. Click **Next**.

6. Click the **Browse** button to locate the drive and/or folder to store your backup. Type a name for this backup in the File name field, such as **backup.bkf**. Click **Save**, then click **Next**.

7. On the Completing the Backup or Restore Wizard page, click the **Advanced** button and select **Incremental** from the pull-down list. Click **Next**.

8. Read through your verification and compression options. Click **Next**.

9. Select **Replace the existing backups**. Notice that the option at the bottom is no longer dimmed. Check the checkbox so that only the owner and Administrator can access the backups. Click **Next**.

10. In the When to Back Up dialog box, choose **Later**.

11. In the Job name field, type **Daily Backup of My Documents**. Then click **Set Schedule**.

12. Under Schedule Task, choose **Daily** from the drop-down list and set the start time.

13. Click the **Settings** tab to review your options, but accept the defaults. Click **OK** to continue. Click **Next**.

14. When prompted for your account information, enter a user name and password of an Administrator or Backup Operator. Click **OK**.

15. Review your settings, and click **Finish** to schedule the backup.

16. Close the Backup utility.

Project 14-5

To install the Recovery Console:

1. From a Command Prompt (**Start | All Programs | Accessories | Command Prompt**), browse to the i386 folder of a Windows XP Professional CD.

2. Run **winnt32 /cmdcons**.

3. You are prompted by a Windows XP Setup dialog box explaining how to use the Recovery Console. Click **Yes** to install it.

4. The necessary files are copied to your system. When finished, click **OK**.

5. Choose **Start | Shutdown**. Choose **Restart** from the menu, and click **OK**.

6. When prompted, choose **Microsoft Windows Recovery Console** from the list of available operating systems and press **Enter**.

7. You are prompted for which operating system you'd like to log onto. Type the number for your operating system and press **Enter**.

8. You are then prompted for the local administrator password. Type that in. Press **Enter**.

9. Type **help** at the command prompt for a list of commands that you can use in the Recovery Console and press **Enter**.

10. Type **exit** and press **Enter** at the command prompt to exit and restart Windows. This time, choose your Windows XP operating system to boot up.

Project 14-6

To uninstall the Recovery Console:

Before continuing, copy your Boot.ini file and rename the copy Boot.bak. You can use this file later should the Boot.ini file become damaged. Be extra careful with the next step to make sure that you delete only the line for the Recovery Console. An incorrect Boot.ini file could keep your computer from restarting.

1. Double-click **My Computer**. Choose **Tools | Folder Options**. Click the **View** tab.

2. Click **Show hidden files and folders** and clear the **Hide protected operating system files** checkbox. Click **OK**.

3. Browse to the root directory and delete the **\cmdcons** folder and the file called **cmldr**.

4. Using Notepad (**Start | All Programs | Accessories | Notepad**), open the **boot.ini** file in the root directory. Remove the entry for the Recovery Console. For example, you would need to delete the last line in the following sample boot.ini file:

```
[boot loader]
timeout=10
default=multi(0)disk(0)rdisk(0)partition(1)\WINDOWS
[operating systems]
multi(0)disk(0)rdisk(0)partition(1)\WINDOWS="Microsoft
Windows XP Professional" /fastdetect
C:\CMDCONS\BOOTSECT.DAT="Microsoft Windows Recovery
Console" /cmdcons
```

5. Save the file and close it.

6. Close any open windows.

14

CASE PROJECTS

1. You're in charge of backing up all of your organization's data stored on Windows XP Professional machines. Your organization consists of 2500 users, 500 of whom usually dial in from home. All of your users use Windows XP Professional. Which of the following backup methods will you use across your organization? Choose all that apply, and justify your choice(s).

   a. tape backups

   b. Zip drives

   c. folder redirection

   d. remote OS installation

2. Describe the three key features of IntelliMirror and a scenario for each feature that explains how that feature reduces the total cost of ownership (TCO).

3. Describe a situation in which it would make more sense to use the Recovery Console than the emergency repair process.

15

TROUBLESHOOTING WINDOWS XP

After reading this chapter and completing the exercises, you will be able to:

♦ Collect documentation about your systems to aid in troubleshooting and preventing problems

♦ Review common-sense approaches to troubleshooting

♦ Troubleshoot general problems with Windows XP Professional

♦ Use some of the troubleshooting tools found in Windows XP Professional

Troubleshooting Windows XP Professional, as with any operating system, is an important and vast subject area. In this chapter, you learn how to detect, isolate, and eliminate problems with installation, printing, remote access, networking, disks, and other aspects of a Windows XP Professional system.

In addition to the techniques discussed in this chapter, important troubleshooting options and features of Windows XP Professional have already been covered in previous chapters. The Registry is a common location for problems as well as a source for implementing solutions. The Registry is discussed in Chapter 12 "Working with the Windows XP Registry." The Windows boot process can sometimes be prey to problems. These problems and related solutions are covered in Chapter 13, "Booting Windows XP." Catastrophic events, virus infections, or simple hardware failure can leave you without a functioning system. Fault tolerance, system recovery, and working with backups are discussed in Chapter 14, "Windows XP Professional Fault Tolerance." Keep in mind the troubleshooting advice provided in previous chapters as you attempt to prevent and resolve problems involving Windows XP Professional.

GENERAL PRINCIPLES OF TROUBLESHOOTING

When troubles arise in Windows XP Professional, you must take action to resolve the issues at hand as quickly as possible. Troubleshooting is the art and science of systematically diagnosing and eliminating problems in a computer system. Although troubleshooting may sound exciting, in reality it is usually a fairly tedious process. In the following sections, we present some procedures and common-sense guidelines that should improve your troubleshooting skills and help you keep downtime to a minimum.

Collect Information

The first rule of troubleshooting is: You can never have too much information. In fact, information is your best weapon not just for resolving problems, but also for preventing them in the first place. Useful, detailed information typically falls into three areas: your system (hardware and software), previous troubleshooting, maintenance, and configuration activities, and the current problem.

Collecting information about your system's hardware and software is preventive maintenance. All pertinent information, kept in an accessible form and location, is called a **Computer Information File (CIF)**. A good CIF provides detailed information about the hardware and software products that comprise your computer (and even your entire network). A CIF is not just a single file, but an ever-expanding accumulation of data sheets sorted into related groupings. Your CIF should be stored in a protected area (such as a safe or fireproof vault) that can be accessed in the event of an emergency (a bank's safety deposit box won't allow you to get at the information at 3:00 in the morning). Obviously, constructing a CIF from scratch is a lengthy process, but one that will be rewarded with problems solved, easy reconfigurations, or simplified replacement of failed components.

Here are some of the important elements you'll want to include in your CIF:

- Platform, type, brand, and model number of each component
- Complete manufacturer specifications
- Configuration settings, including jumpers and dip switches, as well as what each setting means, including IRQs, DMA addresses, memory base addresses, port assignments, and so forth
- The manual, user's guide, or configuration sheets
- Version of BIOS, driver software, patches, fixes, etc., with floppy copies
- Printed and floppy copies of all parameter and initialization files
- Detailed directory structure printout
- Names and versions for all installed software
- Network-assigned names, locations, and addresses

- Status of empty ports or slots, upgrade options, or expansion capabilities

- System requirements, such as the manufacturer's listed minimum system requirements for its operating system, driver, application, hardware, etc.

- Warranty information, such as service phone numbers and e-mail addresses, and support Web sites

- Complete technical support contact information

- Error log with detailed and dated entries of problems and solutions

- Date and location of the last complete backup

- Location of backup items and original software

- Network layout and cabling map

- Copies of all software, operating system, and driver installation or source CDs and/or floppies

Each of these items should be dated and initialed. However, your CIF is not complete if it contains only hardware and software details. You should also include the nonphysical characteristics of your system, such as:

- Information services present, such as Web, FTP, e-mail, newsgroups, message boards, etc.

- Important applications, such as productivity suites (Microsoft Office), collaboration utilities, white board applications, video conferencing, etc.

- Plans for future service deployments

- A mapping or listing of related hardware and software with each service or application present on the system

- Structure of authorized access and security measures

- Training schedule

- Maintenance schedule

- Backup schedule

- Contact information for all system administrators

- Personnel organization or management hierarchy

- Workgroup arrangements

- Online data storage locations

- In-house content and delivery conventions

- Authorship rights and restrictions

- Troubleshooting procedures

15

Neither of these lists is exhaustive. As you operate and maintain your systems, you'll discover numerous other important items to add to the CIF. Don't be bashful about customizing these lists to meet your particular needs and circumstances—if it doesn't work for you, it doesn't work at all. Period.

 Remember, if you don't document it, then you won't be able to find it when you really need it. A good way to keep any CIF current is to add to, remove, or modify its contents each time you make a system modification. Performing a quarterly or semi-annual audit of each CIF is not a bad idea, either.

It is essential that the contents of the CIF be complete and up-to-date. Without thorough, specific, and accurate information about the products, configuration, setup, and problems associated with your network, the CIF will be all but useless. Keep in mind that the time you spend organizing your CIF will reduce the time required to locate information when you really need it. It is wise to create a correlation system so you can easily associate items in the CIF with the actual component, such as an alphanumeric labeling system. For instructions on how to create a CIF, see Hands-on Project 15-2.

We recommend maintaining both a printed/written version and an electronic version of this material. Every time a change, update, or correction occurs, it should be documented in the electronic version, and a printout made and stored. Murphy's Law guarantees that the moment you need your electronic data most, your system will not function.

Use Common-Sense Troubleshooting Guidelines

When problems occur, you would like to be at your sharpest. However, as a corollary to Murphy's Law, you'll probably find that problems tend to occur when you are stressed, short on time, or when it is just generally inconvenient. If you take the time now to keep your CIF up-to-date and heed the following common-sense guidelines, you'll take some of the headache out of troubleshooting, and you'll be better prepared to resolve problems quickly. Although common sense is sometimes in short supply, it is a key ingredient for successful troubleshooting.

- *Be patient*—Anger, frustration, hostility, and frantic impatience usually cause problems to intensify rather than dissipate.

- *Be familiar with your system's hardware and software*—If you don't know what the normal baselines for your system are, you may not know when a problem is solved or when new problems surface. (See Chapter 10, "Performance Tuning" for information on creating baselines.)

- *Attempt to isolate the problem*—When possible, eliminate segments or components that are functioning properly, thus narrowing the range of suspected sources for a problem or failure.

- *Divide and conquer*—Disconnect, one at a time, as many nonessential devices as possible to narrow the scope of your investigation.

- *Eliminate suspects*—Move suspect components, such as printers, monitors, mice, or keyboards, to a known working computer to see if they work in their new location. If they work, they're not at fault; if they don't, they may very well be involved in the problem you're trying to solve.

- *Undo the most recent change*—If you have recently made a change to your system, the simplest fix may be to back out of the most recent alteration, upgrade, or change made to your system.

- *Investigate common points of failure first*—The most active or sensitive components also represent the most common points of failure—including hard drives, cables, and connectors.

- *Recheck items that have caused problems before*—As the old axiom goes, history does repeat itself (and usually right in your own backyard).

- *Try the easy and quick fix first*—Try the easy fixes before moving on to the more time-consuming, difficult, or even possibly destructive measures.

- *Let the fault guide you*—The adage "Where there is smoke, there is fire" applies not only to the outside world, but to computer problems as well. Investigate components and system areas associated with the suspected fault.

- *Makes changes one at a time*—A long flight of stairs is best traversed one step at a time; attempting to leap several or all of the steps may result in injury or death. When troubleshooting, a step-by-step process enables you to identify the solution clearly when you stumble upon it.

- *Repeat the failure*—Often repeating an error is the only way to identify it. Transient and inconsistent faults are difficult to diagnose until you see a pattern in their occurrence.

- *Keep a detailed log of errors and attempted solutions*—Keep track of everything you do (both successful and failed attempts). This will prove an invaluable resource when an error recurs on the same or a different system, or when the same system experiences a related problem.

- *Learn from mistakes (your own and others')*—Studying the mistakes of others can save you from repeating them; a wise person uses failures to find a better solution.

- *Experiment*—If your diagnosis is inconclusive, try similar tasks to the ones that provoke the problem to see if a pattern develops.

There is probably not much in this list of common sense items that you don't already know. The hardest part is remembering these in the heat of a crisis.

15

TROUBLESHOOTING TOOLS

Becoming familiar with the repair and troubleshooting tools native to Windows XP Professional can save you countless hours when troubleshooting. In the next sections, we detail the use of the Event Viewer and the Computer Management tools.

Event Viewer

The **Event Viewer** is used to view system messages regarding the failure and/or success of various key occurrences within the Windows XP Professional environment (see Figure 15-1). The items recorded in the Event Viewer's logs inform you of system drivers or service failures as well as security problems or misbehaving applications (see Hands-on Project 15-1).

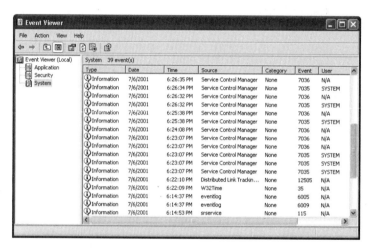

Figure 15-1   Event Viewer with System log selected

Located in the Administrative Tools section of the Control Panel, the Event Viewer is used to view the logs that Windows XP Professional creates automatically:

- **System log**—Records information and alerts about Windows XP Professional's internal processes, including hardware and operating system errors, warnings, and general information messages.

- **Security log**—Records security-related events, including audit events for failed logons, user rights alterations, and attempted object accesses without sufficient permissions.

- **Application log**—Records application events, alerts, and some system messages.

- *Directory Service*—Records events related to the Directory Service.

- *DNS Service*—Records events related to the DNS Service.

- *File Replication Service*—Records events related to the File Replication Service.

Each log records a different type of event, but all the logs collect the same meta-information about each event: date, time, source, category, event, user ID, and computer. Each logged event includes some level of detail about the error, from an error code number to a detailed description with a memory HEX buffer capture. For example, Figure 15-2 shows the properties of a logged event related to the workstation's attempt to register a DNS address, or an A record, with an unreachable directory server. Most system errors, including stop errors that result in the blue screen, are recorded in the System log, allowing you to review the time and circumstances of a system failure. The details in the Event Viewer can often be used as clues in your search for the actual cause of a problem. However, most event log details offer little information on resolving the problems they document.

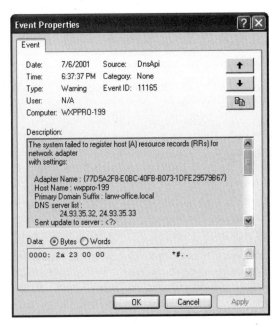

Figure 15-2   Event Viewer's Event Properties windows displays logged event details

Computer Management Tool

Windows XP Professional builds on the robustness of Windows 2000, and on the convenience of its Plug and Play assisted configuration capabilities. In Windows XP, these same capabilities provide easy access to troubleshooting tools for nearly every aspect of the operating system. A large number of these tools are collected into a single interface called the Computer Management tool (see Figure 15-3), found in the Performance and Maintenance Tools display in the Administrative Tools application within the Control Panel.

15

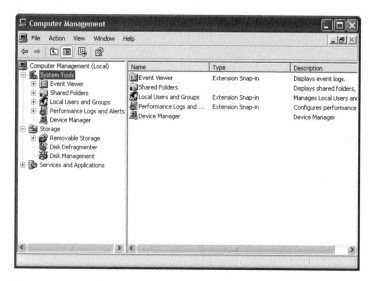

Figure 15-3 The Computer Management tool makes most management tools available through a single management console

The Computer Management tool includes many tools identical to those in Windows 2000; there are some new entries, but some entries have been dropped (system information and logical drives are the most noteworthy in this group). Grouping these utilities in a single interface makes locating and resolving problems on key system components easier than ever before (see Hands-on Project 15-3). The Computer Management console is divided into three sections: System Tools, Storage, and Services and Applications. The System Tools section contains five individual tools:

- *Event Viewer*—Used to view system messages regarding the failure and/or success of various key occurrences within the Windows XP Professional environment. Details of system errors, security issues, and application activities are recorded in the logs viewed through the Event Viewer. See the description of the Event Viewer earlier in this chapter. Hands-on Project 15-1 shows you how to use the Event Viewer.

- *Shared Folders*—Used to view shared folders defined on the local system. This interface shows hidden and public shares, current sessions, and open files, and also allows you to view and alter the share configuration settings for user limits, caching, and permissions.

- *Local Users and Groups*—Used to create and manage local user accounts and groups. (This tool is disabled when the Active Directory is present.) Details on use, examples, and hands-on projects for this tool are included in Chapter 5, "Users, Groups, Profiles, and Policies."

- *Performance Logs and Alerts*—Another means to access the Performance monitoring tool of Windows 2000 (the use of this tool in troubleshooting is rather tedious and complex; see Chapter 11, "Windows XP Professional Application Support," for examples and hands-on projects involving this tool).

- *Device Manager*—Used to view and alter current hardware configurations of all existing devices. Details on how to use, examples, and hands-on projects for this tool appear in Chapter 3, "Using the System Utilities."

The Storage section of Computer Management presents three tools for administering storage devices. Details on use, examples, and hands-on projects appear in Chapter 4, "Managing Windows XP File Systems and Storage."

- *Removable Storage*—Manages removable media such as floppy disks, tapes, and Zip drives.

- *Disk Defragmenter*—Improves the layout of stored data on drives by reassembling fragmented files and aggregating unused space.

- *Disk Management*—Views and alters the partitioning and volume configuration of hard drives.

The Services and Applications section contains management controls for various installed and active services and applications. Though the actual contents of this section depend on what is installed on your system, some common controls include:

- *Services*—Stops and starts services and configures the startup parameters for services (such as whether to launch when the system starts and whether to employ a user account security context to launch the service). Hands-on Project 15-8 shows you one way to use this tool.

- *WMI Control*—Configures and controls the Windows Management Instrumentation service, a service designed for Web-based or network access. This tool allows network management systems (or related software) to interact with agent software on a Windows XP Professional machine to install, set up, or update system or application software and related configuration data.

- *Indexing Service*—Defines the corpus (collection of documents indexed for searching) for the Indexing Service. For information on using this tool, consult the *Microsoft Windows 2000 Server Resource Kit*.

15

Troubleshooting Wizards and Widgets

Continuing the trend established in Windows 2000, Windows XP Professional includes a great many troubleshooting Wizards associated with specific system components or services. For example, the Settings tab in the Display Properties applet (most easily accessed by right-clicking any unoccupied spot on the desktop, then selecting the Properties entry in the resulting pop-up menu) includes a Troubleshoot button, as shown in Figure 15-4. Clicking that button brings up the Video Display Troubleshooter depicted in Figure 15-5; selecting any of its entries leads you through a series of questions with answers and explanations that deal very effectively with common sources of trouble. Similar buttons for other system controls, including Phone and Modem Options (which also has a troubleshooting button), or the Local Area Connection Properties, might be labeled "Repair" instead, but they offer similar kinds of guided troubleshooting support.

Figure 15-4   Settings tab in the Display Properties applet

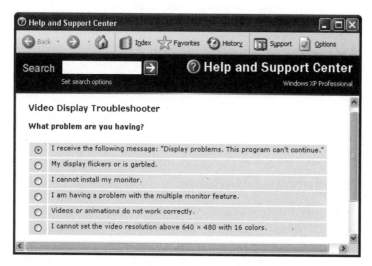

Figure 15-5   The Video Display Troubleshooter

As you investigate the management utilities or Control Panel applets for the system aspects or components you're troubleshooting, don't overlook the kinds of help that the system itself can provide. One of the biggest changes from Windows 2000 to Windows XP Professional is the adoption of a task-oriented metaphor to provide help and guidance, where troubleshooting tasks figure prominently in the lists of tasks for which help and support are available.

TROUBLESHOOTING INSTALLATION PROBLEMS

Unfortunately, the installation process for Windows XP Professional is susceptible to several types of errors: media errors, domain controller communication difficulties, Stop message errors or being hung up on a blue screen, hardware problems, and dependency failures. The following list contains a short synopsis of each error type and possible solutions:

- *Media errors*—Media errors are problems with the distribution CD-ROM itself, the copy of the distribution files on a network drive, or the communication link between the installation and the distribution files. The only regularly successful solution to media errors is to switch media: copying the files to a network drive, linking to a server's CD-ROM, or installing a CD-ROM on the workstation. If media errors are encountered, always restart the installation process from the beginning.

- *Domain controller communication difficulties*—Communication with the domain controller is crucial to some installations, especially when attempting to join a domain. Most often this problem is related to mistyping a name, password, domain name, etc., but network failures and offline domain controllers also can be involved. Verify the availability of the domain controller directly and from other workstations (if warranted), and then check that no entries were mistyped during the installation process.

- *Stop message errors or halting on the blue screen*—Using an incompatible or damaged driver is the most common cause of Stop messages and halting on the blue screen during installation. If any error information is presented to you, try to verify that the proper driver is in use. Otherwise, double-check that your hardware has the drivers necessary to operate under Windows XP Professional.

- *Hardware problems*—If you failed to verify your hardware with the HCL (hardware compatibility list), or a physical defect has occurred in a previously operational device, strange errors can surface. In such cases, replacing the device in question is often the only solution. Before you go to that expense, however, double-check the installation and configuration of all devices within the computer. Sometimes, manual resolution of conflicts that Plug and Play is unable to resolve automatically can cure hardware problems.

- *Dependency failures*—The failure of a service or driver owing to the failure of a foundation class, or of some other related service or driver, is called a dependency failure. An example is the failure of Server and Workstation services because the NIC fails to initialize properly (see Hands-on Project 15-8). Often Windows XP Professional will boot despite such errors, so check the Event Viewer (see Hands-on Project 15-1) for more details (see Figure 15-6 for an example of a warning reported because a common service proves to be unavailable). Most dependency errors usually appear immediately after OS or new software installation, or alteration in system configuration.

15

Figure 15-6   Event Properties dialog box

Just knowing about these installation problems can help you avoid them. However, successfully installing Windows XP Professional does not eliminate the possibility of further complications. Fortunately, Microsoft has included several troubleshooting tools that can help locate and eliminate most system failures (see the "Troubleshooting Tools" section earlier in this chapter).

TROUBLESHOOTING PRINTER PROBLEMS

Problems with network printers can often bring normal activity to a halt. They can occur anywhere between the printer's power cable and the application that's attempting to print. Systematic elimination of possible points of failure is the only reliable method for eliminating such errors. Here are some useful tips for troubleshooting common printer problems:

- Always check that the physical components of the printer—cable, power, paper, toner, and so on—are present, properly loaded, or connected, as appropriate.

- Make sure the printer is online. There is typically a light or an LCD message to indicate this. You may need to press the Reset button or an Online button to set or cycle the printer into online mode.

- Make sure the printer server for the printer is booted.

- Verify that the logical printer on both the client and server sides exist, and check their configuration parameters and settings. For details on logical printers and their multitudes of controls, see Chapter 9, "Printing and Faxing."

- Check the print queue for stalled jobs (see Figure 15-7, which shows a printing print job). Note: if a print job does not show an explicit status (such as waiting, paused, printing, etc.) you can assume it is stalled. The print queue is accessed by clicking the Start menu, selecting Printers and Faxes, selecting the printer whose queue you wish to examine, then clicking the "See what's printing" entry in the Printer Tasks list.

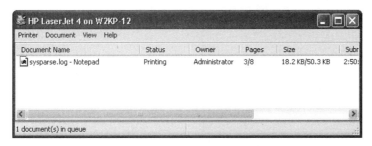

Figure 15-7   The default window for any printer shows the contents of its print queue

- Reinstall or update the printer driver in case it's corrupt or incorrect.

- Attempt to print from a different application or a different client.

- Attempt to print using Administrator access.

- Stop and restart the spooler using the Services tool found through Computer Management (try Hands-on Project 15-4).

- Check the status and CPU usage of the spoolsv.exe process using the Task Manager (see Figure 15-8). If the spooler seems to be stalled—it will either be obtaining no CPU time at all or consuming most of the CPU—you should stop and restart the spooler service.

- Check the free space on the drive where the print spool file resides, and change its destination if less than 100 MB of free space is available. The amount of free space that a spooler file needs is a function of the size and number of print jobs and the logical printer's settings, but in most cases, 100 MB is sufficient. You should change the spool file host drive if there is insufficient space or you suspect the drive is not fast enough. Make this change on the Advanced tab of the Server Properties dialog box accessed from the File menu in the Printer Folder. See Chapter 9 for more information.

15

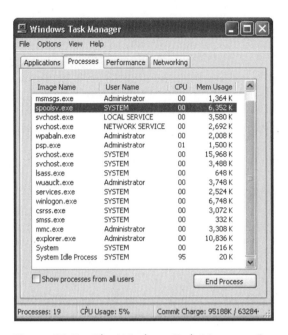

Figure 15-8   The Windows Task Manager, Processes tab

Table 15-1   Printer Troubleshooting

Network Printing Problem	Solutions
Pages print, but only a single character appears on each page. --or-- Pages print but they include control codes. --or-- Pages print, but they show random characters instead of the desired document.	1. If the job has not completed printing, delete it from the print queue to prevent wasting more paper. 2. Remove and reinstall the logical printer and/or the printer driver on the client (if only a single workstation experiences the problem) or on the server (if all workstations experience the problem). 3. Verify that the data type set in the logical printer is correct for the application used, printer driver installed, and capabilities of the physical print device. 4. Stop and restart the spooler service.
An access denied or no access available message is displayed when a print job is submitted.	This is typically caused by improper permissions defined on the printer share. Double-check the permission settings. You may also need to review the group memberships of the affected users if you are employing any Deny permissions on the printer share.
A network attached printer shows an error light on the network interface.	A network communication or identification error has occurred. Cycling the power on the printer may resolve the problem. If not, try disconnecting then reconnecting the network media while the printer is powered off.

Table 15-1b Printer Troubleshooting (continued)

Network Printing Problem	Solutions
No documents are being created by the physical print device, but the print queue shows that the job is printing.	1. View the print queue to see if a print job is stalled or paused. If so, delete or resume the print job. 2. If no other print job is present, delete the current print job and resubmit it from the original application. 3. Stop and restart the spooler service.
The printer share is not visible from a client (i.e., does not appear in Network Neighborhood or My Network Places).	1. The client system may not be properly connected to the network. Shut down the client, check all physical network connections, reboot. Test whether you can access any other network resources. 2. Check the installed protocol and its settings, especially if TCP/IP is being used. 3. Check the domain/workgroup membership of the client.
On larger print jobs, pages from the end of the print job are missing from the printed document.	This can occur when insufficient space is available on the drive hosting the spooler file. Either free up space on the host drive or move the spooler file to a drive with more available space.

For a starter step-by-step on printer troubleshooting, try Hands-on Project 15-4. This list covers most common print-related problems. For more tips on troubleshooting, consult the *Microsoft Windows XP Professional Resource Kit*.

TROUBLESHOOTING RAS PROBLEMS

Remote Access Service (RAS) is another area with numerous points of possible failure—from the configuration of the computers on both ends, to the modem settings, to the condition of the communications line. Unfortunately, there is no ultimate RAS troubleshooting guide, but here are some solid steps in the right direction:

- Check all physical connections.

- Check the communication line itself, with a phone if appropriate.

- Verify the RAS configuration and the modem setup by attempting to establish a connection to another server or by deleting and recreating the connection object. For detailed examples and hands-on projects, see Chapter 8, "Internetworking with Remote Access."

- Check that both the client and the server dialup configurations match, including speed, protocol, and security. See Figure 15-9 for an example of the security settings for a dialup connection. You'll need to view the other tabs to compare and confirm speed, protocol, and other connection settings.

15

Figure 15-9   Setting Security options

- Verify that the user account has RAS privileges.

- Inspect the RAS-related logs: Device.log and Modemlog.txt. Look for errors involving failure to connect, failure to dial, failure to authenticate, failure to negotiate encryption, failure to establish a common protocol, and link termination.

- Remember that Multilink and callback do not work together; you must select one or the other. Because nobody has developed technology to perform multi-line callbacks, only single-line callbacks are possible. Figure 15-10 shows a configuration setting on a connection object that allows the caller to define a specific callback number to complete a dial-up connection (to access the window shown, select Start | Control Panel | Network Connections, then select the connection, then select the Dial-up Preferences entry in the Advanced menu at the top of the Network Connections window).

- Autodial and persistent connections may cause a computer to attempt RAS connection with each logon; in some cases, you may need to disable such settings to permit easier troubleshooting of connection problems.

Most RAS problems are related to misconfiguration. For more details on RAS, refer to Chapter 8 or the *Microsoft Windows XP Professional Resource Kit*.

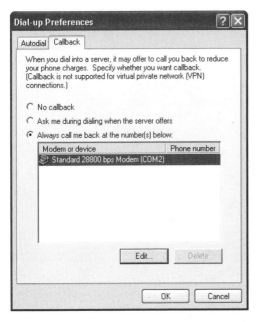

Figure 15-10   Dial-up Preferences, Callback tab

Table 15-2   RAS Troubleshooting

Network Printing Problem	Solutions
The connection object fails to establish a network link with the remote server.	1. Check the username, password, and phone number. 2. Verify that the modem device is powered on and properly connected to the computer and the phone line. You should also check the installed driver and update it if necessary. 3. Verify that the security settings match those required by the remote server. 4. Verify that the protocol settings match those required by the remote server.
The client has multilink enabled and has three identical modems for the connection, but only one modem establishes a network link with the remote server.	1. Verify that the remote server supports multilink and that it has multilink connections enabled. 2. Verify that you need to dial the same or different phone numbers when establishing a multilink connection. 3. Cycle the power on the modems. Verify that they are properly attached to the computer and the telephone line.

15

Table 15-2 RAS Troubleshooting (continued)

Network Printing Problem	Solutions
A network link is broken during a remote session after a successful link is established.	1. Your phone line probably has call waiting and another call came in. Disable call waiting through the connection object. 2. If your telephone line quality is poor (old wiring, phone lines pass by electrical interference, or the weather is bad), connection interruptions are common. You may need to upgrade your internal wiring, request a service upgrade from the telephone company, reroute wiring to avoid interference, or wait until the weather clears. 3. Remote systems can disconnect you for a variety of reasons, most beyond your control and knowledge. In most cases, simply try to re-establish the connection.

TROUBLESHOOTING NETWORK PROBLEMS

Network problems range from faults in the network cables or hardware, to misconfigured protocols, to workstation or server errors. As with all troubleshooting, attempt to eliminate the obvious and easy (such as physical connections and permissions) before moving on to more drastic, complex, or unreliable measures (such as IP configuration, routing, and domain structure). Cabling, connections, and hardware devices are just as suspect as the software components of networking. Verifying hardware functionality involves more than just looking at it; you may need to perform some electrical tests, change physical settings, or even update drivers or ROM BIOS settings.

Common-sense first steps include the following:

- Check to see if other clients or servers or subnets are experiencing the same problem.

- Check physical network connections, including the NIC, media cables, terminators, and logically proximate network devices (such as hubs, repeaters, routers, etc.).

- Check protocol settings.

- Reboot the system.

- Verify that the NIC drivers are properly installed. Use the self-test or diagnostic tools or software for the NIC if available.

- Verify the domain/workgroup membership of the client.

Table 15-3 Network Connection Troubleshooting

Connectivity Problem	Solutions
The client does not seem to connect to the network (i.e., no objects are visible in the Network Neighborhood). --or-- The client is unable to authenticate with the domain.	1. Use the Event Viewer to look for errors in the System log. Resolve any issues discovered. 2. Check the physical network connections, including the NIC, media, and local network devices. 3. Check the NIC driver; update or replace if necessary. 4. Check the installed protocol and its configuration settings. 5. Check the domain/workgroup membership. 6. Reboot the client.
A system disconnects from the network randomly or when other computers boot onto the network.	1. Check to see that you are not violating the length, segments, or nodes-per-segment limitations on the network media in use. 2. Verify that all systems have unique address assignments and system computer names. 3. Check for breaks in the network media or the proximity of electrical or magnetic interference.
Shared network resources, such as folders and printers, cannot be accessed from a client.	1. Check the assigned permissions on the share itself and on the object (if applicable). 2. Check group memberships for Deny permissions. 3. Attempt to access the resources using a different user account or client. 4. Check that the computer is connecting to the network.

TROUBLESHOOTING DISK PROBLEMS

The hard drive is the component on your computer that experiences the most activity, even more than your keyboard or mouse. It should not be surprising that drive failures are common. Windows XP Professional maintains and tunes its file system automatically (see Chapter 4), but even a well-tuned system is subject to hardware glitches. Most partition, boot sector, and drive configuration faults can be corrected or recovered using the Disk Management tool in the Computer Management utility in Administrative Tools (for detailed information on using this tool and on troubleshooting disk problems, see Chapter 4). However, the only reliable means of protecting data on storage devices is to maintain an accurate and timely backup, as discussed in Chapter 14, "Windows XP Fault Tolerance."

MISCELLANEOUS TROUBLESHOOTING ISSUES

The following is a "grab bag" of troubleshooting tips that don't fit into the other categories described in this chapter.

Permissions Problems

Permissions problems (problems with accessing or managing system resources like folders, files, or printers) usually occur when a user is a member of groups with conflicting permissions or when permissions are managed on a per-account basis. To test for faulty permission settings, attempt the same actions and activities with Administrator privileges (try Hands-on Project 15-5). Double-check a user's group memberships to verify that Deny access settings are not causing the problem. This means examining the access control lists (ACLs) of the objects and the share, if applicable (see Figure 15-11).

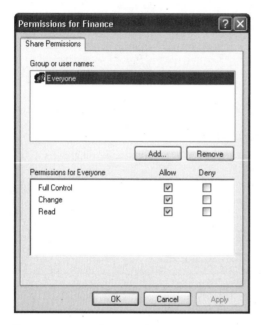

Figure 15-11   Setting share permissions

 It is important to remember that any changes to the access permissions for individual users or groups will not affect those users until the next time they log on. The access token used by the security system is created each time a user logs on, but is not altered as long as they stay logged on. This means that any time you need to make sweeping changes to file system or share permissions, it's a good idea to do so when few users are logged on, and to disconnect those users to force them to log back in under the new permissions regime!

Master Boot Record Problems

As you learned in Chapter 13, the Master Boot Record (MBR) is the area of a hard drive that contains the data structure for initiating the boot process. However, if the

MBR fails, the Emergency Repair Disk (ERD) cannot be used to repair it. Instead, you must use a recovery tool of some kind, for which there are several approaches:

- Boot from the Windows XP Professional boot floppies (all 6 of them), use F8 to select the alternate boot menu, then select the Recovery Console from that menu.

- Reconfigure your system BIOS to boot from your CD player, then boot from the Windows XP Professional installation CD. Here you can select Repair damaged installation as an option, and also access the Recovery Console.

- If neither of the preceding methods works, you'll need to use a DOS 6.0 (or later) bootable floppy to boot into DOS.

If you can access the Recovery Console, use the FIXMBR command to repair the MBR. If you are forced to boot into DOS, then use the FDISK/MBR command. At that point, execute the command *fdisk/mbr*, which will re-create the drive's MBR and restore the system correctly. If you don't have access to the FDISK, you'll have to perform a complete install/upgrade of Windows XP Professional to allow the setup routine to re-create the MBR.

Using the Dr. Watson Debugger

Windows XP Professional has an application error debugger called **Dr. Watson**. This diagnostic tool detects application failures and logs diagnostic details. Data captured by Dr. Watson are stored in the Drwtsn32.log file. Dr. Watson can also be configured to save a memory dump of the application's address space for further investigation. However, the information extracted and stored by Dr. Watson is really only useful to a technical professional well versed in the debugger's cryptic logging syntax.

Windows XP Professional automatically launches Dr. Watson when an application error occurs. To configure Dr. Watson, however, you'll need to launch it from the Start, Run command with *drwtsn32.exe*. Figure 15-12 shows the configuration dialog box for Dr. Watson. As you can see, this dialog box lists the configuration items for the following:

15

- Log File Path—Where the Dr. Watson log file is stored

- Crash Dump—Provides the dump location for an application's virtual machine's address space

- Number of Instructions

- Number of Errors To Save

- Options of what to include in log file and how to notify the user of an application fault

- A list of previous Application Errors, with access to the log file details

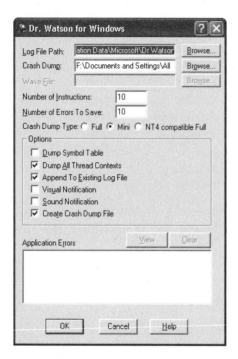

Figure 15-12   Dr. Watson configuration dialog box

APPLYING SERVICE PACKS AND HOT FIXES

A **service pack** is a collection of code replacements, patches, error corrections, new applications, version improvements, or service-specific configuration settings from Microsoft that corrects, replaces, or hides the deficiencies of the original product, preceding service packs, or hot fixes. A **hot fix** is similar to a service pack, except that it addresses only a single problem, or a small number of problems, and may not be fully tested (and is not normally supported, unless you have a special service agreement with Microsoft).

You should apply a hot fix only if you are experiencing the problem it was created to solve; otherwise, the hot fix may cause other problems. Most production environments avoid using hot fixes whenever possible in favor of waiting until the next service pack rolls them up in a form that is fully tested and better supported. The exception to this rule is security-related hot fixes, in which case the affected machine might remain vulnerable to a documented threat or attack if the hotfix is not applied.

Service packs are cumulative. For example, Service Pack 3 (SP3) for Windows 2000 Professional contains SP2 plus all post-SP2 hot fixes. Thus, the latest service pack is all you need to install. For instructions on installing and removing service packs, try Hands-on Projects 15-6 and 15-7.

At this writing, Microsoft has not yet announced a release date for the first service pack for Windows XP Professional. Thus, this section of the chapter is based on pre-release documentation and our experience with Windows 2000 service packs. Take the time to review the documentation included with a real Windows XP Professional service pack once it is available.

It is also common practice among production networks to wait one to three months after the release of a new service pack before deploying it. This gives the installed community time to test and provide feedback about the patch. The track record of service packs from Microsoft is not perfect, so it's better to wait for verification of a service pack's reliability than to deploy it immediately after its release and live to regret it.

Important points to remember about patches such as service packs and hot fixes include:

- Always make a backup of your system before applying any type of patch; this will give you a way to restore your system if the fix damages the OS.

- Be sure you've retrieved a patch for the correct CPU type and language version.

- Always read the *readme* and *Knowledge Base Q* documents for each patch before installing it.

- Update your Emergency Repair Disk (ERD) both before and after applying a patch.

- Make a complete backup of the Registry using the Registry Editor or the REGBACK utility on the *Microsoft Windows XP Professional Resource Kit.*

- Export the disk configuration data from Disk Administrator.

- Because service packs rewrite many system-level files, you must disconnect all current users, exit all applications, and temporarily stop all unneeded services before installing any service pack or patch.

To locate Microsoft Knowledge Base documents, visit or use one of these resources:

- Web site: *http://support.microsoft.com/*

- TechNet CD

- Microsoft Network

- Resource Kit documentation (online help file)

Service packs and hot fixes can be retrieved from:

- Microsoft FTP site: *ftp://ftp.microsoft.com/bussys/winnt/winnt-public/fixes/usa/*

- The Download section of the Microsoft Windows Web site: *http://www.microsoft.com/downloads/*

15

To determine what service packs have been applied to your system, you can use one of the following techniques:

- Enter *WINVER* from a command prompt to view an About Windows dialog box.

- Select Help, About Windows from the menu bar of any native tool such as My Computer or Explorer.

- Use the Registry Editor to view the CSDVersion value in the HKEY_LOCAL_MACHINE\SOFTWARE\Microsoft\WindowsNT\CurrentVersion.

MICROSOFT TROUBLESHOOTING REFERENCES

Several Microsoft resources can aid you in troubleshooting and working with Windows XP Professional:

- *The Microsoft Windows Web site*—*http://www.microsoft.com/windowsxp/*

- *The Knowledge Base*—The predecessor to and a resource for the TechNet CD is the online Knowledge Base. This resource can be accessed by several means, as detailed earlier in this chapter.

- *TechNet*—The best periodic publication from Microsoft is TechNet. This multi-CD collection is an invaluable resource for white papers, FAQs, troubleshooting documents, book excerpts, articles, and other written materials, plus utilities, patches, fixes, upgrades, drivers, and demonstration software. At only $300 per year (as of this writing), it is well worth the cost. It is also available online in a limited form at *http://technet.microsoft.com/*.

- *Resource Kits*—The Resource Kits are useful information sources. These are available in electronic form through the CD-based version of TechNet in their entirety, and through the online version of TechNet in portions. Resource Kits document material above and beyond what's contained in the manuals and on-line help files, and often include additional software utilities to enhance product use. These Resource Kit Utilities (as they're called) often provide valuable administrative functionality not available from built-in consoles and utilities. They are also available in book form through Microsoft Press.

CHAPTER SUMMARY

- ❏ No matter what problems or errors are discovered on your computer system, there are several common-sense principles of troubleshooting you should always follow. These include performing one task at a time, remaining calm, isolating the problem, and performing the simplest fixes first.

❐ Information is the most valuable troubleshooting tool. Making sure you have the best information includes maintaining a Computer Information File and a detailed log or history of troubleshooting activities.

❐ The Windows XP Professional tools most often used for troubleshooting are Event Viewer and the Computer Management tool.

❐ There are five common installation problems: media errors, domain controller communication difficulties, stop message errors or halt on blue screen, hardware problems, and dependency failures.

❐ Printer problems are most often associated with physical configuration or spooling problems.

❐ RAS and network problems may be caused by several types of problems, but the most common type arises from misconfiguration.

❐ Service packs and hot fixes are used to repair portions of Windows XP Professional after its release.

❐ Microsoft has provided several avenues to access information about the operation and management of Windows 2000, including a substantial collection of troubleshooting documentation. Much of this is available at no charge from the Microsoft Web site.

KEY TERMS

Application log — Records application events, alerts, and system messages.

Computer Information File (CIF) — A detailed collection of all information related to the hardware and software products that comprise your computer (and even your entire intranet).

Dr. Watson — An application error debugger. This diagnostic tool detects application failures and logs diagnostic details.

Event Viewer — The utility used to view the three logs automatically created by Windows 2000: the System log, Application log, and Security log.

hot fix — Similar to a service pack, except that a hot fix addresses only one problem, or a small number of problems, and may not be fully tested.

master boot record (MBR) — The area of a hard drive that contains the data structure that initiates the boot process.

Security log — Records security-related events.

service pack — A collection of code replacements, patches, error corrections, new applications, version improvements, or service-specific configuration settings from Microsoft that corrects, replaces, or hides the deficiencies of the original product, preceding service packs, or hot fixes.

System log — Records information and alerts about Windows XP Professional's internal processes.

15

REVIEW QUESTIONS

1. When approaching a computer problem, which of the following should you keep in mind? (Choose all that apply.)

   a. How the problem was last solved.

   b. What changes were recently made to the system.

   c. Information about the configuration state of the system.

   d. Ability to repeat the failure.

2. If a media error occurs during installation, which of the following steps should you take to eliminate the problem? (Choose all that apply.)

   a. Attempt to re-copy or re-access the file that caused the failure.

   b. Switch media sources or types.

   c. Open the Control Panel and reinstall the appropriate drivers.

   d. Restart the installation from the beginning.

3. Which of the following Windows repair tools can be used to gain information about drivers or services that failed to load?

   a. Event Viewer

   b. Registry

   c. System applet

   d. Dr. Watson

4. In addition to the Event Viewer and System Information, which of the following are useful tools in general troubleshooting? (Choose all that apply.)

   a. Advanced Options Boot Menu

   b. Registry Editors

   c. Backup software

   d. Time/Date applet

5. Your best tool in troubleshooting is:

   a. A protocol analyzer

   b. Information

   c. Administrative access

   d. Redundant devices

6. Which of the following are possible troubleshooting techniques for eliminating printer problems? (Choose all that apply.)

   a. Check the physical aspects of the printer: cable, power, paper, toner, and so on.

   b. Check the print queue for stalled jobs.

   c. Attempt to print from a different application or a different client.

   d. Stop and restart the spooler using the Services tool.

   e. Disconnect from the network.

7. Which of the following are common RAS problems?

   a. Telco service failures

   b. Misconfiguration

   c. User error

   d. Communication device failure

8. A user's ability to access a resource is controlled by access permissions. If you suspect a problem with a user's permission settings, what actions can you take? (Choose all that apply.)

   a. Attempt the same actions and activities with the Administrator account.

   b. Delete the user's account and create a new one from scratch.

   c. Double-check group memberships to verify that Deny access settings are not causing the problem.

   d. Grant the user Full Access to the object directly.

9. What application automatically loads to handle application failures?

   a. Event Viewer

   b. System applet

   c. Computer Management

   d. Dr. Watson

10. If you are going to create a CIF, which of the following is the most important?

    a. Include the vendor's mailing address

    b. Keep everything in electronic form

    c. Update the contents often

    d. Use non-removable labels on all components

11. Which of the following are important actions to perform before installing a service pack or a hot fix? (Choose all that apply.)

    a. Make a backup of your system.

    b. Read the readme and Knowledge Base Q documents.

    c. Make a complete backup of the Registry.

    d. Enable virus protection.

12. What are some common-sense approaches to troubleshooting?

    a. Understand TCP/IP routing table configuration

    b. Know your system

    c. Undo the last alteration to the system

    d. Replace all server hardware when one device fails

    e. Let the fault guide you

15

13. You can often resolve problems or avoid them altogether if you take the time to write out a history or log of problems and both failed and successful solution attempts. True or False?

14. When installing a new Windows 2000 domain controller into an existing domain, you can experience communication problems with the current domain controller. After you've verified that the current domain controller is online and properly connected to the network, what other items should be considered as possible points of failure? (Choose all that apply.)

    a. shorten the computer name from 12 to 10 characters.

    b. subnet mask

    c. password

    d. domain name

15. Blue screen or Stop errors are often caused by a system when one or more devices are not found on the HCL. True or False?

16. If the driver for your network interface card fails, which other components of your system are most likely to fail due to dependency issues? (Choose all that apply.)

    a. network protocol

    b. Client Services for NetWare

    c. video driver

    d. WinLogon

17. Errors involving internal processes such as hardware and operating system errors, warnings, and general information messages are recorded in the Application log of the Event Viewer. True or False?

18. Which of the following are valid methods for resolving hardware problems? (Choose all that apply.)

    a. Restart the installation from scratch without any other modifications

    b. Press and hold the Ctrl key during the installation

    c. Remove or replace the non-HCL hardware

    d. Recopy the distribution files

19. An event detail viewed from the Event Viewer's logs provides specific information on the time, location, user, service, and resolution for all encountered errors. True or False?

20. The Computer Management tool offers links to several important administrative and management utilities including: (Choose all that apply.)

    a. Control Panel

    b. Event Viewer

    c. Performance Monitor

    d. Local Security Policy

    e. Local Users and Groups

21. The Storage section of the Computer Management tool offers utilities to perform what types of operations? (Choose all that apply).

    a. Defragmentation

    b. Partitioning

    c. Managing Removable Storage

    d. Compressing Floppies

22. When a printer fails to print your documents, which of the following is a useful first step in troubleshooting?

    a. Replacing the printer

    b. Restarting the spooler

    c. Re-installing the operating system

    d. Delete and re-create the shared printer

23. Both printers and RAS connections can suffer from the most common problem: physical connection interruptions. True or False?

24. When a user complains about being unable to access a resource that other users of similar job descriptions are able to access, what should you consider when attempting to troubleshoot this issue? (Choose all that apply.)

    a. Group memberships

    b. ACL on the object

    c. Domain membership

    d. Speed of network connection

25. When you alter the group memberships of a user, how do you ensure that the changes take effect?

    a. Reboot the server

    b. Enable auditing on file objects

    c. Restart the messaging and alert services

    d. Log the user account out, then allow them to log back in

15

HANDS-ON PROJECTS

Project 15-1

To use the Event Viewer:

1. Open the Event Viewer from the Start menu (**Start | Control Panel |** double-click **Administrative Tools |** double-click **Computer Management |** **Event Viewer** to display the list of available logs).

2. Select the **System** log from the list of available logs in the left pane.

3. Notice the various types of events that appear in the right pane.

4. Select an event in the right pane.

5. Select **Action** | **Properties** (or more simply, double-click the event entry).

6. Review the information presented in the Event Properties dialog box. Try to determine on your own what types of errors, warnings, or information is presented in the detail and why the detail was created.

7. Click the up and/or down arrows to view other event details.

8. Click **OK** to close the event detail.

9. Select **File** | **Exit** to close Event Viewer.

Project 15-2

To extract information for a CIF:

This hands-on project suggests a method to obtain some information about your system for a CIF; it does not constitute a complete or exhaustive collection of data. This activity is only one part of the task of creating a CIF.

1. Click **Start** | **All Programs** | **Accessories** | **System Tools** | **System Information**.

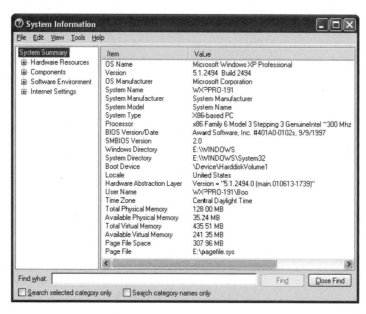

Figure 15-13   The System Information tool

Local Computer Policy

administrative templates, 229

computer configuration

in general, 227

public key policies, 227

in general, 226

IP Security policies, 228–229

Secedit, 231–233

User Configuration, 230–231

local procedure call (LPC), 453

lock out, accounts, 179

logging. *See also* logon; performance monitoring

alerts, 417–419

application log, 572

Event Viewer, 419–420

in general, 415–417

Counter log, 415

Trace log, 415

security log, 572

system log, 572

transaction logs, 501

logon. *See also* logon authentication; Remote Access Service; security; user account

access token, 216

Administrator account, 179

automated, 223

automatic account lockout, 223

customizing

adding security warning message, 221

changing shell, 221–222

disabling default username, 221 disabling Shutdown button, 222

in general, 219–220

in general, 178–179

Guest account, 179

WinLogon process, 219

logon authentication, 178. *See also* security

discussed, 217–218

security ID, 217

shell, 217

long file name (LFN), 121

LPC. *See* local procedure call

M

mask, subnet mask, 273

Master Boot Record (MBR). *See also* booting

booting, 518

troubleshooting, 586–587

MBR. *See* Master Boot Record

MCSE Certification Exam #70–270, 603–609

media folders, Customize tab, 152–153

memory. *See also* storage

bottlenecks, 429–430

support, 7

virtual memory, 18, 86

Virtual Memory Manager, 17, 18

page, 20

memory architecture, 20. *See also* architecture

memory space

Win16–on–Win32

in general, 465

message queue, 466

separate and shared memory, 465–466

threads, 466

Win32, 455–456

Microsoft Management Console (MMC). *See also* Control Panel

in general, 95–96

snap–ins, 95, 96–97

using, 97

Microsoft networking family. *See also* networking

in general, 2

client operating systems, 3

operating systems, 2

Windows XP family, 2–3

Microsoft references, for troubleshooting, 590

Microsoft Speech API (SAPI), 86

MMC. *See* Microsoft Management Console

modem, 313. *See also* Telephony API

options, 334–336

Phone and Modem Options applet, 83

monitor. *See* display

monitoring. *See* performance monitoring

mount point, drive letter and, 117, 132

mouse, Accessibility Options, 76–77

Mouse applet, 82

MPR. *See* Multi–Provider Router

MS–CHAP, 328

MS–DOS, 4, 7. *See also* virtual DOS machine

DOS operating environment, 457

Multi–Provider Router (MPR), 262, 264–265

Multiple Universal Naming Convention Provider (MUP), 262

multiprocessing, 3–4. *See also* process

multitasking, 4

cooperative, 4

preemptive, 4

Win16, 463

multithreading, 4–5. *See also* thread

process, 5

threads, 4

Win32, 454–455

MUP. *See* Multiple Universal Naming Convention Provider

N

named pipes, IPC, 259

NAT. *See* Network Address Translation

NCP. *See* NetWare Core Protocol

NDIS. *See* Network Device Interface Specification

NDS. *See* Novell Directory Services

NetBEUI. *See* NetBIOS Extended User Interface

NetBIOS Extended User Interface (NetBEUI), 258. *See also* user interface

NetBIOS. *See* Network Basic Input/Output System

NetDDE. *See* Network Dynamic Data Exchange

NetWare Core Protocol (NCP), 292

network. *See also* virtual private network

bottlenecks, 430–431

components, 252–253

overview, 252

troubleshooting, 584–585

network access protocols. *See* network protocols; Remote Access Service

network adapter (NIC), booting, 44

Network Address Translation (NAT), 339

network authentication, 224

Network Basic Input/Output System (NetBIOS), 254

IPC and, 260

network bridge, 269–270

Network Connections applet, 83

Network Device Interface Specification (NDIS), 257, 289

Network Dynamic Data Exchange (NetDDE), IPC and, 261–262

Network File System (NFS)

TCP and, 276

TCP/IP and, 255

network protocols. *See also* inter-process communication

connectionless, 254

in general, 253

NetBEUI and DLC, 258

NWLink

advantages, 257

drawbacks, 258

in general, 257

remote access, 314, 317

Point–to–Point Protocol, 318

Point–to–Point Tunneling Protocol, 318–319

PPP multilink protocol, 319

Serial Line Internet Protocol, 319

TAPI, 319–320

TCP/IP

advantages, 254–257

drawbacks, 257

in general, 253–254

Network Setup Wizard, 270

networking. *See also* Microsoft networking family; networking models

bindings management, 271–272

discussed, 265–269

networking models

domain model, 13, 14–15

in general, 13

kernal mode

Executive Services, 17–19

in general, 13, 17

hardware abstraction layer, 19–20

kernal, 19

workgroup model, 13–14

New Technology File System (NTFS), 5, 120. *See also* file system

discussed, 122–123

Encrypted File System, 236–237

file object, 139–140

mounted volume object, 142–143

NTFS folder object, 136–138

NTFS object, copying and moving, 149

permissions

basics, 148–149

file and folder permissions, 144–148

in general, 144

NFS. *See* Network File System

NIC. *See* network adapter

Notepad, Boot.ini file editing, 528

Novell Directory Services (NDS), 289

context, 293

NDS tree, 293

Novell NetWare, 288–289. *See also* Client Service for NetWare

bindery, 289

NDS support, 293–294

NetWare resources, connecting to, 297–298

Novell Directory Services, 289

NWLink and, 289–291

NT LAN Manager (NTLM) authentication, 225

NTFS. *See* New Technology File System

Ntldr, booting, 519

NWLink, 253. *See also* network protocols

advantages, 257

frame type, 257

configuring, Ethernet, 290–292

connectivity, 7

drawbacks, 258

in general, 257

installing, 290

IPX/SPX, 290

NetWare compatibility, in general, 289–290

O

object, 402

performance object, 408, 409

security and, 218

synchronization objects, 455

object linking and embedding (OLE), 261

Object Manager, kernal mode, 19

ODBC. *See* Data Sources

ODI. *See* Open Datalink Interface

offline file, access, 155–157

OLE. *See* object linking and embedding

Open Datalink Interface (ODI), 257, 289

operating system (OS), 2–3

booting multiple operating systems, 35–36, 532

client operating systems, 3

file system and, 36

remote OS installation, 555–556

PXE environment, 556

[operating systems], booting, 525–526

Order Prints Online, 345

OS. *See* operating system

Outlook Express, 342

P

package, 471

Packet Internet Groper (PING)

TCP and, 277–278

TCP/IP and, 255

page, memory, 20

partition. *See* hard drive

password, 216

Password Policy. *See also* security

discussed, 194–195

user account, 177

PCMCIA Cards, 100

peer–to–peer network. *See* work-group model

performance monitoring. *See also* System Monitor; troubleshooting

application priority settings, 422–423

boosting performance, 431–433

bottlenecks

disk bottlenecks, 429

in general, 427–428

memory bottlenecks, 429–430

network bottlenecks, 430–431

processor bottlenecks, 430

in general, 402–403

logging

alerts, 417–419

Event Viewer, 419–420

in general, 415–417

mobile user performance, 433–434

Performance Options, 421–422

System Applet

Advanced tab, 426–427

in general, 424

Visual Effects tab, 424–425

System Monitor

in general, 407

realtime monitoring, 408–415

Task Manager, 403–407

performance object, 408

instance, 409

permissions. *See also* security

NTFS

auditing, 145

basics, 148–149

file and folder permissions, 144–148

in general, 144

troubleshooting, 586

phone. *See also* modem

options, 334–336

Phone and Modem Options applet, 83

photography, Scanners and Cameras applet, 85

PID. *See* Process ID number

PING. *See* Packet Internet Groper

PKZIP, 154

Plug and Play (PnP) capability, 3, 77

Plug and Play (PnP) Manager, kernal mode, 19

PnP. *See* Plug and Play

Point–to–Point Protocol (PPP), remote access, 318

Point–to–Point Tunneling Protocol (PPTP), 316

remote access, 318–319

port, I/O port, 90

POST. *See* power–on self test

power management

Advanced Configuration and Power Interface, 551

Advanced Power Management, 551

hibernate vs. standby, 551–552

Power Manager, kernal mode, 19

Power Options applet, 83–84

Advanced Configuration and Power Interface, 84

Advanced Power Options, 84

power–on self test (POST), booting, 516–517

PPP Multilink, 315, 317

PPP multilink protocol (PPP–MP), remote access, 319

PPP. *See* Point–to–Point Protocol

PPP–MP. *See* PPP multilink protocol

PPTP. *See* Point–to–Point Tunneling Protocol

preventive maintenance. *See also* error; repairs; troubleshooting

Automatic Updates, 551

Desktop Cleanup Wizard, 551

device driver rollback, 549–550

hibernate vs. standby, 551–552

Windows File Protection, 550

print server, 363

managing, 384–385

print spooler

in general, 363, 364, 365–366

data types, 366

print monitor, 368–369

language monitor, 368

port monitor, 368

Printer Job Language, 368

print processor, 367–368

print provider, 366–367

print router, 366

starting and stopping, 386–387

print subsystem architecture. *See also* architecture

in general, 364

Graphical Device Interface, 364

printer driver, 365

Device Driver Interface, 365

printer. *See also* printing

configuring

Advanced tab, 377–380

Color Management tab, 380

Device Settings tab, 382–383

in general, 374

General Tab, 374–375

Ports tab, 376–377

Security tab, 380–382

Sharing tab, 376

installing and managing

in general, 371

local printer creation, 373

managing print jobs, 371–373

remote printer connection, 374

printer priority setting, 377

troubleshooting, 385–386, 578–581

World Wide Web and, 383

printer drivers, 363. *See also* drivers

discussed, 365

software, 369

Printer Job Language, 368

Printers and Faxes applet, 84

printing

across network, 370

mismatched documents, 378

process, 370

rendering, 364

terminology, 362–364

troubleshooting

in general, 385–386

network printing, 386

stopping and starting print spooler, 386–387

process, 404

multithread process, 454

multithreading, 5

system architecture and, 450–452

child process, 451

parent process, 451

Process ID number (PID), 404

Process Manager, kernal mode, 18

processor, bottlenecks, 430

profile

user account, 177

user profile, 177, 191–192

Program Compatibility Wizard, 467–471

publishing, application, 471–472

R

RARP. *See* Reverse Address Resolution Protocol

RAS. *See* Remote Access Service

recovery

PC configuration recovery, 545

Startup and Recovery Options, 93

system recovery, 7–8

Recovery Console, 554–555

redirectors

in general, 262–263

MPR, 262

Multiple Universal Naming
Convention Provider,
262, 264

Multi–Provider Router,
264–265

Server service, 263

Universal Naming Convention
names, 264

Workstation service, 263

Regional and Language Options
applet, 84, 84–85

Registry, 487. *See also* Registry
editors

fault tolerance, 501–503

HKEY_CLASSES_ROOT,
494–495

HKEY_CURRENT_
CONFIG, 495–496

HKEY_CURRENT_
USER, 496

HKEY_DYN_DATA, 497

HKEY_LOCAL_MACHINE

in general, 491

HKEY_LOCAL_MACHINE
\HARDWARE, 491–492

HKEY_LOCAL_MACHINE
\SAM, 492

HKEY_LOCAL_MACHINE
\SOFTWARE, 493

HKEY_LOCAL_MACHINE\
SECURITY, 492–493

HKEY_LOCAL_MACHINE\
SYSTEM, 493–494

HKEY_USERS, 496–497

overview, 488–490

data type, 489

hive, 489

key, 488

subkey, 488

value, 488

value entry, 488

Resource Kit Registry Tools, 505

restoring, 503–504

Last Known Good
Configuration, 503

storage files, 499–501

Registry editors, 497–499

Reg, 497

Regedit, 497

remote access. *See also* Remote
Access Service

advanced connection setup

accepting incoming
connections, 332–333

connecting to another
computer, 333–334

client vs. server–based, 345

configuration, 320–321

connecting to Internet,
321–330

connecting to workplace network, 331–332

hardware installation, 334

phone and modem options,
334–336

security, 336–337

troubleshooting, 346

Remote Access Service (RAS),
83. *See also* logon; network
protocols

discussed, 314–315

features

Autodial and Log–on dial, 316

Callback security, 317

client and server
enhancements, 316

idle disconnect, 316

look and feel, 317

PPP Multilink, 315

restartable file copy, 316

VPN protocols, 316

WAN connectivity, 317

troubleshooting, 581–584

Remote Assistance, 8
  discussed, 287–288
Remote Desktop, 2, 8, 287
  discussed, 288
Remote Installation Preparation
  (RIPrep), 556
Remote Installation Service
  (RIS). *See also* installation
  in general, 44–45, 556
Remote Procedure Call (RPC),
  IPC and, 261
repairs. *See also* preventive
  maintenance
  Emergency Repair Disk, 587
  emergency repair process, 555
  in general, 552
  hot fix, 588–590
  Recovery Console, 554–555
  remote OS installation,
    555–556
  service pack, 588–590
  System Restore, 552–553
Reverse Address Resolution
  Protocol (RARP), TCP/IP
  and, 255
RIPrep. *See* Remote Installation
  Preparation
RIS. *See* Remote Installation
  Service
router, Multi–Provider Router,
  264–265
RPC. *See* Remote Procedure Call

S

SAPI. *See* Microsoft Speech API
ScanDisk. *See* Check Disk utility
Scanners and Cameras applet, 85
Scheduled Tasks applet, 85–86
Secedit, 231–233
sector, 121
Secure Socket Layer/Transport
  Layer Security (SSL/TLS)
  certificate, 225
  Kerberos, 225
security. *See also* logon; Password
  Policy; permissions
  access control, 219
  access control list, 18, 216
  auditing, 233–236
  domain security
    in general, 216, 224
    Kerberos and authentication
      services, 224–225
    NTLM authentication, 225
    Secure Socket
      Layer/Transport Layer
      Security, 225
  in general, 6, 216
    access token, 216
    password, 216
  Internet security, 238
  local security policy
    Account Lockout Policy,
      195–196

  Audit Policy, 196
    in general, 193–194
    Password Policy, 194–195
    Security Options, 198–201
    User Rights Policy, 196–198
  logon, adding security warning
    message, 221
  logon authentication, 217–218
  objects, 218
  offline file access, 155–157
  remote access, 314
    Callback security, 317
    discussed, 336–337
  user account, 177
    Local Security Policy tool, 187
Security Accounts Manager
  (SAM), Registry, 492
security log, 572
security reference monitor
  (SRM), 16, 18
Security tab, printer, 380–382
Sequenced Packet Exchange
  (SPX), 290
Serial Line Internet Protocol
  (SLIP), remote access, 319
server
  print server, 363, 384–385
  remote access component,
    314, 316
  service, 75

service pack, 588–590.
See also repairs

set up. See also booting;
installation

boot disks, 38

in general, 53–54

Administrator, 54

GUI portion, 56–59

option differences, 39–40

text only portion, 54–56

Setup Manager Wizard, 43

settings, Files and Settings
Transfer Wizard, 202

SFC. See System File Checker

Sharing tab

managing shared folders,
149–152

using, 130

shell, 217

changing, 221–222

Shutdown button, disabling, 222

Simple File Sharing, 154

Simple Mail Transfer Protocol
(SMTP)

TCP and, 276

TCP/IP and, 254

Simple Network Management
Protocol (SNMP)

TCP and, 277

TCP/IP and, 255

Simple Object Access Protocol
(SOAP), 3

SLIP. See Serial Line Internet
Protocol

snap–ins, 95

discussed, 96–97

Author Mode, 97

User Mode, 97

SNMP. See Simple Network
Management Protocol

SOAP. See Simple Object Access
Protocol

sound. See also audio

Accessibility Options, 76

Sounds and Audio Devices
applet, 86

Speech applet, 86

spooling. See also printer

printer, 363, 364

SPX. See Sequenced Packet
Exchange

SRM. See security reference
monitor

SSL/TLS. See Secure Socket
Layer/Transport Layer Security

startup. See also booting

advanced options, 522–524

Taskbar and Start Menu, 94

Startup and Recovery
Options, 93

storage. See also memory

basic storage, 114–115

extended partition, 114

primary partition, 114

dynamic storage, 114, 115–119

volumes, 114, 115

Registry storage files, 499–501

removable media, 158

support, 7

string

expandable string, 490

multi–string, 490

support services, 8

SYSPREP. See also installation

installation, 45–47

System Applet. See also Control
Panel; performance monitoring

Device Manager, 88–91

driver signing, 87–88

Environmental Variables, 94

error reporting, 94

in general, 86

hardware profiles, 86

virtual memory, 86

hardware profiles, 91–92

performance tuning

Advanced tab, 426–427

in general, 424

Visual Effects tab, 424–425

Startup and Recovery
Options, 93

system architecture. *See also* architecture

environment subsystem, in general, 448, 452–454

in general, 448–449

context switch, 453

dynamic link library, 453

Executive Services, 448

local procedure call, 453

subsystem, 448

kernal vs. user mode, 449–450

processes and threads, 450–452

Win32 subsystem, 454

System File Checker (SFC), 550

System Monitor. *See also* performance monitoring

in general, 407

events, 407

performance object, 408

realtime monitoring, 408–415

System Restore. *See also* recovery

using, 552–553

System State data, backup, 548

T

TAPI. *See* Telephony API

Task Manager, 403–407

process, 404

TCP. *See* Transmission Control Protocol

TCP/IP. *See* Transmission Control Protocol/Internet Protocol

Telephony API (TAPI), 83. *See also* modem; phone

remote access, 319–320

Telnet, 342

discussed, 343

TCP and, 276

template, administrative templates, 229

Terminal Services, compared to Remote Access Service, 315

text conferencing, 10

TFTP. *See* Trivial File Transfer Protocol

thread, 404. *See also* process

multithreading, 4

system architecture and, 450–452

Win16–on–Win32 memory space, 466

time, applet, 80

Trace log, 415. *See also* logging

transaction logs, 501

transforms, 471

Transmission Control Protocol (TCP). *See also* Transmission Control Protocol/Internet Protocol

Berkeley R utilities, 277

discussed, 255

Domain Name Service, 279

File Transfer Protocol, 276

in general, 275–276

HOSTS file, 278

IPCONFIG, 280–281

LMHOSTS file, 279

Packet Internet Groper, 277–278

Simple Mail Transfer Protocol, 276

Simple Network Management Protocol, 277

Telnet, 276

Trivial File Transfer Protocol, 278

User Datagram Protocol, 276

Windows Internet Naming Service, 279–280

Transmission Control Protocol/Internet Protocol (TCP/IP)

advantages, 254–257

architecture

Address Resolution Protocol, 275

Dynamic Host Configuration Protocol, 275

in general, 272

Internet Control Message Protocol, 275

Internet Protocol, 272–275

configuration, 282–286

connectivity, 7

discussed, 253–254

drawbacks, 257

TCP/IP command line tools, 281–282

Transmitting Subscriber Identification (TSID), 388

Trivial File Transfer Protocol (TFTP)

TCP and, 276, 278

TCP/IP and, 255

troubleshooting. *See also* performance monitoring; preventive maintenance; repairs

access problems, 158–159

booting, 522–524

cached credentials, 201–202

DLL conflicts, 473

in general, 568

collect information, 568–570

use common sense, 570–571

hard drive, 585

installation, 59, 577–578

Microsoft references, 590

miscellaneous issues, 585

Dr. Watson debugger, 587–588

Master Boot Record, 586–587

permissions, 586

network, 584–585

printer

in general, 385–386, 578–581

network printing, 386

remote access, 346, 581–584

tools

Computer Management tool, 573–575

Event Viewer, 572–573

Wizards and Widgets, 575–576

TSID. *See* Transmitting Subscriber Identification

U

UDF. *See* uniqueness database file

UNC. *See* Universal Naming Convention

uniqueness database file (UDF), 41

Universal Naming Convention (UNC), names, 264

UNIX, 15, 260, 261

updates, Automatic Updates, 551

upgrade

compared to installation, 34–35

computer preparation, 13

Dynamic Update, 40

WINNT32, 34

user account, 175. *See also* client; logon

discussed, 176–177

account lockout policy, 177

audit policy, 177

domain user account, 176

groups, 177

local groups, 176

local user account, 176

multiple–user systems, 177

password policy, 177

profile, 177

user profile, 177

Groups node, 187–190

Local Security Policy tool, 187

Local Users and Groups tool, 184

logon

Administrator account, 179

in general, 178–179

Guest account, 179

logon authentication, 217–218

managing

in general, 180

imported user account, 183

User Accounts applet, 181–184

security options, 177

system groups, 190

Users node, 184–187

User Datagram Protocol (UDP), 259

TCP and, 276

TCP/IP and, 254–255

user interface

intelligent user interface, 8–10

NetBIOS Extended User
Interface, 258

user mode. *See also* kernal mode;
networking models

compared to kernal mode,
449–450

in general, 15, 16–17

snap–ins, 97

user name, disabling default
username, 221

user profile, 177

discussed, 191–192

local profiles, 192–193

roaming profiles, 193

User Rights Policy, 196–198.
See also security

V

value, 488

VDD. *See* virtual device driver

VDM. *See* virtual DOS machine

video conferencing, 10

virtual device driver (VDD), 458.
See also drivers

virtual DOS machine (VDM),
16, 454. *See also* MS–DOS

AUTOEXEC.BAT and
CONFIG.SYS, 458–460

components, 458

custom DOS environments,
460–463

in general, 457–458

DOS operating
environment, 457

real mode, 458

Win16 operating
environment, 457

virtual device drivers, 458

virtual memory, 18, 86. *See also*
memory

Virtual Memory Manager
(VMM), 17, 18

virtual private network (VPN).
See also network

remote access, 331

protocols, 316

VMM. *See* Virtual Memory
Manager

VMS, 15

voice conferencing, 10.
See also audio

volume

mirrored volume, 120

spanned volume, 120

storage, 114

simple volume, 115

striped volume, 120

W

WAN. *See* wide area network

WFP. *See* Windows File
Protection

wide area network (WAN),
remote access component,
314, 317

Win16, 7

in general, 463

multitasking, 463

operating environment, 457

well–behaved applications,
466–467

Win16–on–Win32, 463

components, 464–465

memory space, 465–467

Win16–on–Win32 (WOW).
See Win16

Win32, 7

applications

base priority, 456

environment subsystem, 454

input message queues, 456

memory space, 455–456

multithreading, 454–455

critical section, 455

synchronization objects, 455

system architecture, 454

Win32 Win32 Internet API, 262

Windows 95, 2, 3

Windows 98, 2, 3

Windows 2000, 2, 3, 10

Windows File Protection
(WFP), 550

Windows Installer Service
(WIS), 546

Windows Internet Naming Service (WINS)

TCP and, 279–280

TCP/IP and, 256

Windows Manager, kernal mode, 19

Windows Me, 2

Windows Media Player 8, 10

Windows Movie Maker, 10

Windows .NET, 2–3

Windows Network interface (Wnet), 262

Windows NT, 2, 3

Windows Open System Architecture (WOSA), 319

Windows Sockets (WinSock), 260–261

Windows for Workgroups, 2, 3

Windows XP

activation, 52–53

MCSE Certification Exam #70–270, 603–609

removing

destroying partitions, 60

in general, 59–60

Windows XP environment

Active Directory, 6

compatibility, 6–7

connectivity, 7

file systems, 5

FAT, 5

FAT32, 5

NTFS, 5

in general, 3

Plug and Play capability, 3

help and support services, 8

multiprocessing, 3–4

multitasking, 4

cooperative, 4

preemptive, 4

multithreading, 4–5

process, 5

threads, 4

new features overview, 10

remote capabilities, 8

security, 6

storage, 7

system recovery, 7–8

Windows XP family, 2–3

WINNT, 38. *See also* WINNT32

in general, 47–51

WINNT32, 38

in general, 47–51

partitioning hard disk, 51–52

upgrade, 34

WINS. *See* Windows Internet Naming Service

WinZip, 154

WIS. *See* Windows Installer Service

Wnet. *See* Windows Network interface

workgroup model, networking, 13–14

World Wide Web (WWW), 344

printers and, 383

WOSA. *See* Windows Open System Architecture

WOW. *See* Win16

WWW. *See* World Wide Web

X

X.25 standard

Internet connection, 326

TCP/IP and, 256

XML. *See* Extensible Markup Language